D1237848

Effective Management
of
Local Area Networks

Functions, Instruments, and People

Kornel Terplan

McGraw-Hill, Inc.

New York St. Louis San Francisco Auckland Bogotá Caracas
Lisbon London Madrid Mexico City Milan Montreal New Delhi
Paris San Juan São Paulo Singapore Sydney Tokyo Toronto

FIRST EDITION
FIRST PRINTING

© 1992 by **McGraw-Hill, Inc.**

Printed in the United States of America. All rights reserved.

Library of Congress Cataloging-in-Publication Data

Terplan, Kornel.
    Effective management of local area networks : functions,
instruments, and people / by Kornel Terplan.
        p.   cm.
    Includes index.
    ISBN 0-07-063636-2
    1. Local area networks (Computer networks)—Management.
I. Title.
TK5105.7.T47   1992
004.6′8—dc20   92-1181
                                                   CIP

ISBN   0-07-063636-2

For information about other McGraw-Hill materials, call 1-800-2-MCGRAW in the
U.S. In other countries call your nearest McGraw-Hill office.

Acquisitions Editor: Jerry Papke
Book Editor: Sally Anne Glover
Director of Production: Katherine G. Brown
Book Design: Jaclyn J. Boone   TPR4

Contents

Acknowledgments

Three principal sources helped me in writing this book; the Network Management and Network Management Systems services from Datapro, based in Delran (New Jersey), assisted me in determining the right depth for the overall structure of the book; the *EDP Performance Management Handbook*, published by Applied Computer Research in Phoenix (Arizona), helped me evaluate the applicability of the various tools; the "Effective Management of Local Area Networks" course, which I designed and was sponsored by The Technology Transfer Institute, based in Santa Monica (California), enabled me to gather several real-life cases from attendees.

I'm particularly grateful to all the vendors who have supported my work by providing state-of-the-art documentation on tools. In addition, Mark Miller's *LAN Troubleshooting Handbook* helped me by providing easy, understandable tool examples.

I would also like to thank William Ahlstrom from the American University in Washington, D.C., Gail Foster from Northeast Consulting Resources, Vish Narayanan from General Motors, and Charles F. Williams, Telecommunication Director from Walt Disney World for reviewing the whole text. I'm grateful to Bill Gassmann (Digital), Dave Mahler (Remedy), Jeffrey Turner (Novell), and Ray Williams (IBM) for their valuable comments.

I would also like to thank Robin Goodale for copyediting the first version of the text, my daughter Kornelia for typing the manuscript, and Adam Szabo for drawing most of the figures. Without their help I would not have been able to submit my text to my publisher on time.

Hackensack/Groebenzell
February 1992

Introduction

This book stresses three critical factors for successful LAN management: processes, instruments, and human resources. The book itself is structured in eight segments.

Chapter 1 deals with the status of and requirements for LAN management. The status review outlines the differences between LAN and WAN management. The chapter also differentiates LAN management from applications management, and tries to quantify the impact of improperly managed LANs. After identifying the three critical success factors referred to previously, I address the LAN management framework and the most likely managed objects. I end chapter 1 by categorizing end-user requirements for LAN management.

In order to assess potential performance bottlenecks, chapter 2 offers a walk-through of bandwidth selection, media choices, protocols, access techniques, and the most widely used topologies. I also discuss interconnected LANs, including two vital interconnecting devices and how to choose the technology for interconnection. This chapter concludes with a critical assessment of source routing as opposed to spanning tree, and the use of bridges as opposed to routers.

Chapter 3 gives an in-depth discussion of principal LAN management functions, such as configuration, fault, performance, security, and accounting management. When appropriate, I highlight the differences between WAN and MAN management. I also reference cross-function applications. Using principles and priorities established by LAN users, I thoroughly discuss configuration and fault management, giving a number of real-life examples. Each management function has a certain set of typical instruments, which are identified in generic terms.

I also discuss user administration—including interfaces, help menus, advanced tools, and expert systems. This particular function may also be seen as part of operational control, usually supported by fault management. As a summary of LAN management functions and typical instruments, I introduce a matrix that indicates which instruments apply to which LAN management functions.

Chapter 4 discusses LAN management standardization. After outlining the principal directions of LAN management support protocols, I provide a comparison between SNMP (Simple Network Management Protocol) and CMIP (Common Management Information Protocol). Despite growing popularity and support for SNMP managers and agents, CMIP offers a more complete solution with rich functionality, but at a considerably higher price and overhead. Also, migration alternatives and integrated solutions are referenced as part of leading manufacturers' LAN management strategies. In order to support the product selection process for LAN integrators, leading platform solutions are also introduced.

The instrumentation section (chapter 5) deals with various types of tools. Standalone monitors, analyzers, test instruments, platforms, platform-independent applications, and PC-LAN-management solutions are discussed first. Next, I address the LAN management systems of various vendors, addressing in particular the management of Ethernet and token ring segments, wiring hubs, and interconnecting devices. The final part of the chapter evaluates the leading integrator products from IBM, AT&T, and DEC and their role in managing enterprise LANs. In order to facilitate the process of selecting tools, a detailed criteria list is included and explained at length.

In chapter 6, I analyze LAN design and planning. After introducing the principal planning steps, I address planning criteria such as quality, performance, availability, technology and costs. As part of the final design process, the role of modeling instruments is outlined, with selected examples from leading manufacturers. In particular, the cooperation between LAN monitors and modeling packages is analyzed in more detail. But, LAN design and planning are still considered more an art than a science.

Chapter 7 offers a structure for the LAN management support organization. Two groups—planning and operations—are clearly separated. All participating groups and individuals are characterized by their responsibilities, job interfaces, qualifying experiences, training requirements, and typical salary ranges. Examples for building and maintaining the LAN management team are also given. Although still in its infancy, LAN management outsourcing options are also briefly discussed.

Chapter 8 addresses the directions in which LAN management is headed, concentrating on centralization, automation, integration, MIB support, and enhancing the quality of user administration.

This book is intended for users of LANs, network designers, capacity planners who are in charge of planning and administering LANs, and LAN operators who are in charge of operating local area networks. People involved in the selection of components and technology for WANs, MANs, and LANs will also find the book valuable.

The text, which evolved from my research and consulting work, is also easily adaptable for undergraduate college and graduate university courses.

1

LAN management & enterprise network management

The inadequacies of existing LAN-related network management instruments and techniques have made certain LAN-based enterprise networks practically unmanageable, and the following factors have brought this situation to light:

- The rise of hybrid communication architectures.
- Interconnected LANs, MANs, and WANs.
- Implementation of mission-critical applications on departmental processors and on LANs.

Nowadays, effective enterprise-wide communication is expected to address the following concerns:

- Local interconnection between various workstations and servers supporting office automation, shop floor control, and other specific applications.
- Remote interconnection between LAN segments using various interconnecting devices, such as repeaters, bridges, brouters, routers, extenders, and gateways.
- Support for multiple communication forms such as voice, data, image, and video.
- Support for a unified user interface for various applications and for different forms of communication.
- Unified network access in order to ensure interoperability.
- Total connectivity for supporting any-to-any communication.
- Very high availability of applications, servers, and transport facilities.
- Successful integration of the management of voice, data, and image structures in the local area by providing high bandwidth to end users.
- Ability to supervise LAN operations from a central site.

After reviewing trends and present status, this chapter defines the scope and principal driving forces for managing LANs. Emphasis has been placed on LAN management components, and on the critical success factors necessary to meet LAN management user requirements. Object classes are defined, the LAN management framework is introduced, and LAN instrumentation trends are summarized. Also, the challenge of building and maintaining the LAN management team is addressed.

When observing the LAN market, network managers may observe that there has been an over-average growth rate and very high change request ratio. Specifically, they have determined the following:

- The number of vendors selling LAN hardware, LAN software, and interconnecting devices is increasing.
- Users are demanding peer-to-peer communication with as few as possible hubs. The number of LANs, PBXs, and interconnected segments is increasing.
- There are a number of proprietary network management products and solutions that can't yet offer interoperability.
- In addition to special-purpose solutions, SNMP (Simple Network Management Protocol) seems to be arising as the principle upon which LAN management products and concepts are based.
- The need for integrated WAN/MAN/LAN management increases.
- There's a shift towards more centralized LAN and PBX management.
- The role of interconnecting devices and of wiring hubs has changed and is considered more important than before to managing enterprise networks.
- Due to the cross applicability of platforms, many LAN management products vendors will stop designing and implementing proprietary solutions and will migrate to standard platforms.
- These platforms are expected to be offered independently from the hardware on which they run.
- Applications are going to be developed and offered by third parties, addressing high-priority LAN management functions such as fault and performance management.

The following are questions that can't yet be satisfactorily answered by LAN designers and planners:

- How can we optimize LAN performance?
- What's the most economical way to interconnect LANs?
- How can LANs and PBXs be meaningfully combined to manage a local site?
- How could design and planning instruments be used?
- Which routing algorithm is the first choice?
- How can we handle the administration of a large number of physical and logical LAN objects?

- Which LAN management standards will win?
- How will DME (Distributed Management Environment) help to standardize LAN management functions and instrumentation?
- Which and how many human resources are needed to support and manage various user clusters?
- How can LANs be managed from a central—often remote—site?

Scope and driving forces of LAN management

LAN management means deploying and coordinating resources in order to design, plan, administer, analyze, evaluate, operate, and expand local area communication networks to meet service-level objectives at all times, at a reasonable cost, and with optimal combination of resources.

Figure 1-1 shows a typical network of interconnected LANs from the enterprise point of view. Local area networking segments may constitute metropolitan area networks supporting multiple communication forms that are interconnected using wide area networking products and services. Each entity in this WAN/MAN/LAN structure may have independent management functions and instruments. End-to-end management from the enterprise point of view requires that these management entities work together.

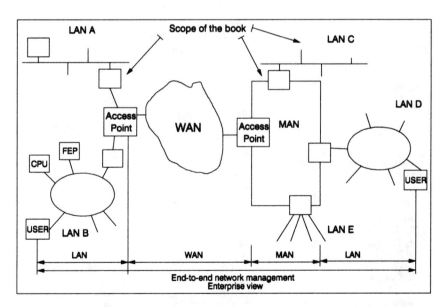

Fig. 1-1. Typical network of interconnected LANs.

The scope of this book is LAN management, consisting of LAN management functions, instruments, and human resources supporting functions and operating instruments. Part of the scope is to define the demarcation line and interfaces between MAN and WAN management. The obvious demarcation line is the WAN-and-MAN access point, represented by interconnecting units such as gateways, routers, brouters, and bridges. Repeaters and extenders are seen within the LAN segments.

In terms of managing networking segments, there are similarities and differences, depending on the geographical reach of the structures. TABLE 1-1 summarizes the major differences between managing WANs and LANs. Managing MANs has special attributes, but due to a number of SNMP-implementation examples, management of MANs seems to be closer to LAN than to WAN management. As a result, this book includes some aspects of MAN management based on FDDI and DQDB.

Most organizations have recognized the strategic importance of their network management. In most cases, better control ensures a higher level of performance, and this performance corresponds with higher productivity. In addition, higher productivity often translates into bottom-line financial im-

Table 1-1. Differences between WAN and LAN Management

| | Type of network | |
Criteria	WAN	LAN
Number of managed objects	Medium; mostly logical components	High; mostly physical components
Status surveillance	Active by eventing	Passive by polling, eventually eventing by traps
Management concept	Centralized and hierarchical	Decentralized and peer-to-peer
Standards	Proprietary and de facto; little OSI-CMIP	SNMP (Simple Network Management Protocol
Number of technological alternatives, protocols and vendors	High	Very high
Systems and network management	Separated becoming integrated	Integrated
Support of network management functions:		
• Configuration management	Weak	Fair
• Fault management	Architecture-specific	Components-specific
• Performance management	Architecture-specific	Components-specific
• Security management	Logical protection	Physical protection
• Accounting management	Host-oriented	Weak
Impacts of outages	Applications-dependent	Depends on the size of LAN segments
Quantification of impacts due to outages	Yes	Yes

provements. This leads us to consider what the principal driving forces are for investing in and spending more on LAN management.

- Controlling corporate strategic assets. LANs are an increasingly essential part of the enterprise's day-to-day business activity. The rapidly declining costs of personal computers, workstations, and departmental computing power is increasing the number of intelligent network elements to be connected and controlled. Completely new networking applications are available to users. But without proper control, the full power and usefulness of these new applications are barely tapped.
- Controlling complexity. The constantly growing number of network components, users, interfaces, protocols, and vendors has left many managers with little or no control over what's connected to the network. In particular, LAN-based servers and stations (clients) are most frequently beyond the scope of central control.
- Improving service. Users are requesting the same and even a better service level, despite growth and changing technology. New users require support and training, and they have high expectations from advanced telecommunication solutions. Expectations are particularly high for standards, availability, and performance.
- Balancing various needs. Those who manage LANs are expected to satisfy certain business needs such as supporting new applications and customers, providing improved connectivity, and ensuring stability and flexibility. At the same time, users' needs, such as availability, reliability, performance, stability, and visibility have to be met in a LAN management environment where there's a lack of procedures and tools. Skills are limited, and there's a serious shortage of personnel.
- Reducing downtime. Ensuring continued availability of networking resources and services is the ultimate goal of enterprise communication. LAN management solutions have to ensure this capability by efficient configuration, fault, and maintenance management.
- Controlling changes. In order to increase integrity between fault, performance, and configuration management, changes have to be planned, scheduled, executed, and documented properly. Due to high flexibility requirements in LAN environments, moves and configuration changes are frequent, but their administration is still very weak.
- Controlling costs. Network management needs to keep an eye on all costs associated with data and voice communications. The network manager is expected to spend only a reasonable amount of money, which still may be considerable. Today, the average enterprise spends approximately 3% to 5% of the total communication budget for network management. This may grow as high as 15% to 20% by the late 1990s. LAN management is expected to receive an increasing portion of this money. If cost management is under control, however, the service level may be improved without increasing costs.

The interpretation of driving forces is different in each operating environment. The recommendations are as follows:

- Use weights when considering each of the criteria defined previously.
- Evaluate corporate LAN management strategies against all criteria.
- Combine the evaluation result with the weights.

TABLE 1-2 displays the driving forces.

Table 1-2. Driving
Forces of LAN Management

Controlling corporate strategic assets
Controlling complexity
Improving service
Balancing various needs
Reducing downtime
Controlling costs
Controlling changes

Components of LAN management

LAN management components are grouped according to the following entities: objects to be managed, technology, management functions, standards, strategies, and costs.

MO (managed object)

Managed objects (MOs) may be further segregated by application, server, PBX, workstation, internet, subnets, and the infrastructure. The number of devices to be monitored, controlled, and managed in a typical LAN is much higher than in a WAN or even in a MAN environment. Successful LAN management requires that all objects be managed equally. In WANs and MANs, it's much easier to partition and segregate managed objects by physical and logical components, by geographical location, and by architecture.

The following gives a sense of how pervasive and how complex a presence LANs have in the market:

- Approximately 40 million personal computers are installed worldwide.
- Approximately 40% of personal computers are interconnected.
- Approximately 3 million local area networks are in use.
- Approximately 25% of the local area networks are interconnected.
- There are multiple architectures and protocols.
- There are multiple topologies.
- There are multiple transport media.
- There are multiple LAN operating systems that don't offer interoperability.
- There is use of proprietary LAN management solutions.

Technology

Today, there are many different technologies, protocols, and suppliers of local area networks. Technology may be meaningfully broken down into: media, typical throughput rates, topology, and access methods. In order to consider how to allocate investments and resources, the following usage breakdown should be considered:

- Media.
  a. Coax—50%.
  b. Twisted pair—33%.
  c. Fiber—17%.
- Data rates.
  a. 1 Mbps—11%.
  b. 4 Mbps—10%.
  c. 10 Mbps—42%.
  d. Others—37%.
- Topology.
  a. Bus—60%.
  b. Ring—11%.
  c. Star—13%.
  d. Tree—16%.
- Access methods.
  a. CSMA/CD—56%.
  b. Other CSMA—13%.
  c. Token—29%.
  d. Other—2%.

But, always remember that LAN technology changes very rapidly. Observations show:

- Clear growth pattern for FDDI.
- Increasing revenue role for Token Ring.
- Ethernet peak revenue role around 1991 to 1992.
- Slow decline in use of other structures.

Network management functions, standards, and strategies

Network management functions are not yet fully supported. LAN management is an afterthought, in many cases following LAN installation by 10 to 15 months. If implemented, fault management functions are seen most frequently. Performance management is mission driven and sporadic. Configuration management shows some progress, but it's not yet the real core function of LAN management. Security is implemented as part of the LAN operating system—usually with very few additions. Accounting management, design, and planning are not yet fully understood, and thus have been rarely implemented.

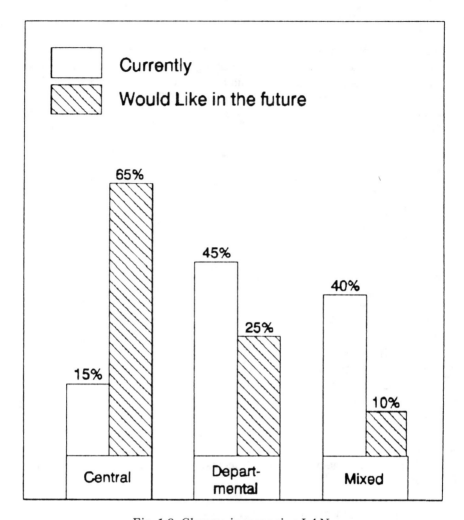

Fig. 1-2. Changes in managing LANs.

Due to the passive nature of LAN connections and some of the objects, there's no information about failing components or inoperative segments available to management. In order to gain such information, active polling of components is necessary. This is the basis for SNMP implementations. But careful consideration is needed to minimize the impact of polling on the LAN bandwidth. This problem may become severe in an interconnected LAN environment, where routers and bridges exchange status information.

Network and systems management are not yet integrated; servers, stations, hubs, and connections are managed separately. In particular, in systems management, menus, front ends, software meters, and local and remote diagnostics are rare or missing.

There are many attempts to standardize LAN management, but the use of proprietary protocols still dominates the market. SNMP has made unexpected progress at the detriment of CMOT and CMOL. But SNMP must not be considered the ultimate solution; it's simply the first step on the way to a fully open local and wide area network management architecture.

Network management strategy shows contradictory trends. At the moment, decentralized (departmental) structures dominate. But indications show a clear trend towards centralized management concepts within the next few years (FIG. 1-2). Plausible reasons for change are:

- Lack of human resources at the departmental level.
- Growing complexity of solutions.
- Growing number of interconnections.
- The high demand of integrated WAN/MAN/LAN management.
- Economies of scale in staffing WAN/MAN/LAN management functions.

There's very little correlation between LAN and PBX management, except for wiring and equipment rooms. This fact adds another dimension to the difficulties of implementing horizontal and vertical management structures.

Costs

LAN downtime causes serious losses because a mission-critical application often runs on LAN segments. A recent large-scale study of Fortune 500 LAN users (Infonetics 1989) reports on lost productivity, revenue, and direct expenses. The principal findings of this study are:

- The average network studied was disabled 23.6 times a year for an average of four hours each time.
- The companies studied lost an average of $3.48 million a year in employee productivity due to LAN downtime.
- Revenue loss among those companies studied averaged $606,000 per year.
- The companies studied spent around $60,000 a year for LAN maintenance.
- The companies studied spent around $650,000 per year in LAN performance upgrades.
- The LANs of those companies studied are growing at a rate of 48% a year, and there's a positive correlation between network size and the number of network breakdowns.
- LAN downtime can be quantified: For each hour of outage, $30,000 to $40,000 may be lost due to a lack of employee productivity.
- There's a quantifiable correlation between the three loss indicators and the use of LAN analyzers and management instruments, proving that the use of such instruments would reduce the duration and frequency of outages.

Personnel costs are increasing exponentially in the LAN management area, alarming MIS and Business Units management. Observation reveals decreasing equipment costs, slightly increasing NOS costs, proportionally increasing communication costs for interconnected LANs, and exponentially increasing costs for the people who manage LANs. TABLE 1-3 shows the principal facts of current LAN management.

Table 1-3. Facts of Current LAN Management

LAN objects
Different technologies, protocols and suppliers
Different LAN operating systems

Network management functions, standards and strategies
Network management functions are not fully supported
No information about failing components
Networks and systems management are not yet integrated
Proprietary protocols dominate the installations
Contradicting trends in network management
Little correlation between LAN and PBX management

Costs
LAN downtime causes serious losses
LAN downtime can be quantified
Human resources costs are increasing

LAN management functions, instruments, and human resources

There are a few factors that determine whether a LAN is managed successfully, or whether its management fails. These factors are: processes/procedures, instrumentation, and human resources.

Processes and procedures

Processes and procedures include applications to the principal functional areas, such as configuration, fault, performance, security, accounting management, and LAN design and capacity planning.

Configuration management is a set of middle- and long-range activities for controlling physical, electrical, logical, and spare-part equipment inventories; maintaining vendor files and trouble tickets; managing cables and wiring; supporting provisioning and order processing; tracking, authorizing, scheduling, and implementing changes; and distributing software. Directory service and help for generating different network configurations are also provided.

Fault management is the collection of activities required to dynamically maintain network service levels. These activities ensure high availability by quickly recognizing problems and performance degradation, and by initiating controlling functions when necessary, which may include diagnosis, repair, test, recovery, workaround, and backup. Log control and information distribution techniques are supported as well.

Performance management is an ongoing evaluation of a LAN. The evaluation's purposes are to verify that service levels are maintained, to identify actual and potential bottlenecks, and to establish and report on trends for management decision making and planning. Building and maintaining a LAN's performance database and automation procedures for LAN fault management are also included.

Security management is a set of functions whose purpose is to ensure a LAN's ongoing protection by analyzing risks, minimizing risks, implementing a LAN security plan, and subsequently monitoring the success of the strategy. Special functions include the surveillance of security indicators, partitioning, password administration, and warning or alarm messages on violations.

Accounting management is the process of collecting, interpreting, processing, and reporting cost- and charge-oriented information on LAN resource usage. In particular, processing of raw accounting data, bill verification, and chargeback procedures are included for data and occasionally for voice.

LAN design and planning represent the process of determining the optimal network, based on data for network performance, traffic flow, resource use, networking requirements, technological trade-offs, and estimated growth of present and future applications.

User administration, including help-desk responsibilities, seems to be viewed as a separate entity by many users. It's actually part of, or at least very close to, LAN fault management. However, for the sake of better visibility, user administration will be separately addressed toward the end of chapter 3. TABLE 1-4 summarizes all relevant LAN management functions. Chapter 3 will address each function individually.

Such processes and procedures are designed and developed by using LAN management platforms that consist of protocols, databases, and user interfaces. Also, applications across these functional groups are expected to be implemented.

Instrumentation

Instrumentation is used for monitoring, testing, and controlling LAN media and devices by implementing remote and centrally located management devices using a network management platform and application programming interfaces. Independent of specific functions and instruments, the typical LAN management framework has three dimensions (Datapro-NM50 1989).

- Console facility with the following principal components:
  a. LAN management applications.
  b. Query languages.

c. Alarm displays and report generators.
d. Expert systems as an option to facilitate diagnostics and problem determination.
- Database facility with:
a. Relational or object-oriented database.
b. Query languages.
c. Database applications for configuration and performance management.
- Monitoring and control facilities with:
a. Application interfaces.
b. Diagnostic programming interfaces.
c. Test programs interfaces.
d. Analyzer device interfaces.
e. Polling mechanisms.

Table 1-4. Overview of LAN Management Functions

Configuration management
- Inventory control
- Configuration control
- Naming and addressing
- Change control
- Cabling control
- Directory services

Fault management
- Status supervision
- Fault detection and alarming
- Diagnosis and testing
- Isolation and correction
- Trouble ticketing
- Help-desk support

Performance management
- Defining performance indicators
- Performance monitoring
- Traffic analysis
- Network modeling
- Network optimization

Security management
- Defining security indicators
- Access authorization
- Password administration
- Ensuring hardware/software integrity
- Ensuring data integrity
- Warnings and alarms about violations

Accounting management
- Collecting resource usage statistics
- Software license compliance
- Billing and chargeback services

Design and planning
- Strategic planning
- Capacity planning
- Analyzing needs
- Logical and physical design
- Contingency planning
- Installation
- Testing

User administration
- Enhancing ease of use
- Maintenance of user data
- Help to users
- Training

The three dimensions are shown in FIG. 1-3.

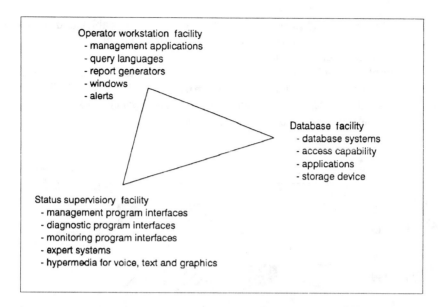

Fig. 1-3. Management frameworks for LANs.

The management framework may be mapped to LAN management functions as defined by standard bodies. The matrix shown in FIG. 1-4 is intended as an aid to investment decisions. Each cell of the matrix has its own priority level. Basically, each dimension of the framework may be supported by multiple functions. Similarly, the same functions may support multiple dimensions of the framework.

The starting point for consolidating processes and instruments is a fragmented structure for managing LANs, characterized by segments for IEEE 802.3 LANs, IEEE 802.5 LANs, bridges, routers, FDDI/DQDB backbones, wiring hubs, and gateways to WANs. Figure 1-5 (Boell 1989) shows an example of this high level of fragmentation.

The database facility may help to increase the visibility of managed objects. Managed objects include:

- Applications (class, users, unattended, self-initiating).
- Servers (central servers for computing or for databases, local file, printer, and communications servers).
- Internets (routers, gateways, brouters, backbone links).
- Subnets (media, adapters, extenders, modems, bridges, repeaters).
- Infrastructure (directory, application interfaces, feeder, environmental control). In particular, the object "infrastructure" requires in-depth investigation. The infrastructure includes active components, such as end-user devices, boards, network interface cards, media access units,

active hubs, and also passive components such as cables and passive hubs. Additional passive components may include electrical and electro-mechanical parts of managed objects, such as fans, clocks, and power supplies. Moving these fault-sensitive components physically out of the main cabinet will significantly improve physical access and increase maintainability. In order to monitor passive components, external moni-tors have to be used (FIG. 1-6) (Boell 1989).

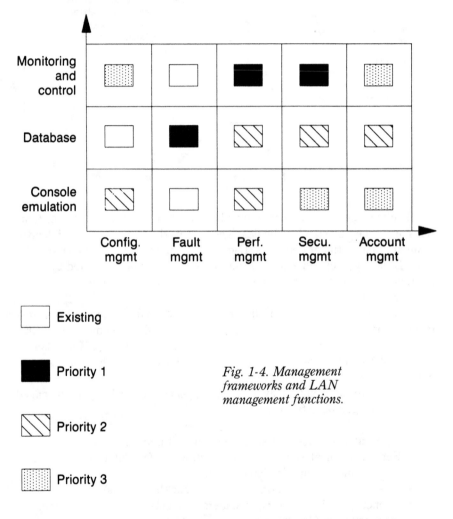

Fig. 1-4. Management frameworks and LAN management functions.

Figure 1-7 shows the two dimensions of managed objects and LAN man-agement functions. Future plans may concentrate on horizontal management (more functions for few objects) or vertical management (more objects, but few functions). Chapter 5 deals with the various types of instruments and offers a number of practical examples.

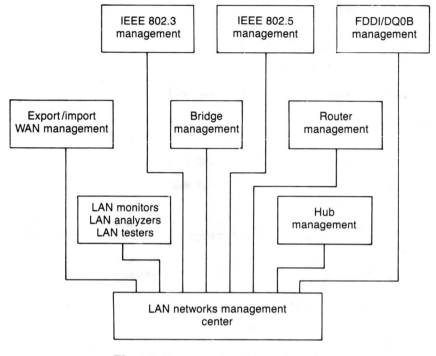

Fig. 1-5. Fragmented LAN management.

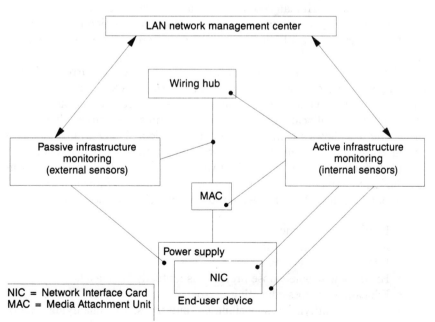

Fig. 1-6. Active and passive infrastructure components.

Managed objects

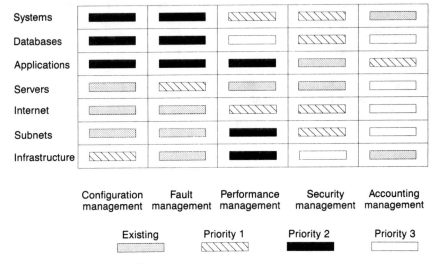

Fig. 1-7. Managed objects and LAN management functions.

Human resources

The third critical success factor is human resources who execute functions using various tools. Human resources should also have a clear understanding of the responsibilities, interfaces to other organizational units, internal/external job contacts, and qualifying experiences that are required to accomplish tasks.

This third critical success factor, human resources, is currently in the evolutionary state of cross-educating users and/or WAN management staff to execute LAN management responsibilities. There are various models showing how to allocate responsibilities to human resources. The most promising one shows a combination of centralized and decentralized human resources, each with some level of distributed duties—particularly for fault and performance management. The two basic phases of building and retaining the LAN-management team are common to all management teams.

In building the LAN management team, emphasis should be on:

- Identifying team members.
- Recruiting the right candidates.
- Interviewing effectively.
- Hiring new people whose presence is mutually beneficial.
- Educating or cross-educating personnel.
- Clearly identifying responsibilities, interfaces, and qualifying experiences.
- Agreeing on a realistic salary range.

In keeping the LAN management team together, emphasis should be placed on:

- Salaries and benefits.
- Job security.
- Recognition of work accomplished.
- Offering dual-path career ladders.
- Effective and continuous training.
- Quality of assignments.
- Adequate tools to support LAN management functions.
- Quality of work environment.
- Realistic service expectations.
- Continuous employee satisfaction.

Chapter 7 addresses human resources, their profiles, and the most likely levels of demands.

Requirements for managing local area networks

As critical applications have been moved to or implemented on LANs, users are increasingly demanding improved LAN management. The following details LAN management criteria:

- Level of service.
  - a. Availability of statistics and historical data that may be stored in a performance or statistical database.
  - b. Realtime supervision of important LAN performance indicators, such as congestion, resource use, number of transmitted and rejected frames, transmit times, and access delay.
  - c. Low monitoring overhead through dynamically adapting polling rates to actual resource use.
- Increased productivity.
  - a. Maintain end-user service level despite growth and technological changes, without staff explosion.
  - b. Heal, bypass, or circumvent failed LAN servers after automatically detecting and interpreting problems.
  - c. Operate fully when interconnecting components have failed; this assumes the existence of powerful backup strategies and components.
  - d. Coordinate remote monitoring, control, and management through centrally located instruments.
- Flexible change management for rapid, continual response to changing LAN applications, subscribers, devices, tariffs, and services.
  - a. Maintain a LAN configuration database containing attributes, connectivity information, and dynamic status indicators.
  - b. Automate operations, alerting, and diagnostics, using powerful filtering and fault management procedures.

- Better platform.
    a. Straightforward human interface using the most advanced technology for the graphics, called a graphical user interface (GUI).
    b. Horizontal and vertical integration using the most advanced solutions from hierarchical network management systems and opportunities provided by network management platforms.
    c. Powerful LAN management platform for offering user-friendly solutions for problem detection, determination, and restoration.
- Migration to standards.
    a. Replacing specific instruments with generic applications that address multiple LAN management areas such as fault, performance, configuration, security, and accounting management; one popular example is trouble ticketing.
    b. Migration to LAN standards that are widely used and well supported by the majority of vendors; included are SNMP, CMIP, and CMOL.

TABLE 1-5 summarizes the requirements, using a table format.

Table 1-5. Classification of Requirements

Service level
- Availability of historical data
- Realtime supervision of indicators
- Low monitoring overhead

Productivity
- High end user service
- Efficient workarounds
- Automated switchover
- Remote monitoring
- Flexible change management
- Configuration database
- Automated operations

Platform
- Graphical user interface
- Horizontal and vertical integration
- Ease of use

Migration to standards
- Applications instead of just instruments
- Use of SNMP, CMIP, and CMOL

Summary

The most important points in chapter 1 may be summarized as follows:

- A trend towards more interconnected LANs indicates that the number of standalone PCs and standalone LAN segments will decrease.
- The bandwidth requirements in LAN segments and in interconnected LANs will grow substantially as the convenience of total connectivity is fully recognized by users.
- The number of managed objects will grow and will accommodate most components of LAN segments and interconnected LANs.
- LAN software vendors are under increasing pressure to incorporate more management tools into the network, rather than forcing users to purchase tools separately. This reflects the general trend toward incorporating more functionality into the NOS, such as bridging and routing capabilities, and network management.
- Users can also expect to see an increasing number of tools that assist in tracking problems across multiple LANs in a multivendor environment. The progress of standards development will influence the effectiveness of these tools, as well as determine how quickly they and other comprehensive LAN integrated network management systems will appear on the market.
- More automation in operating LANs is expected by linking LAN and WAN management systems. This trend will help to distribute management tasks by decreasing the demand for human resources at the distributed sites.
- More cross-functional applications are expected from third parties, allowing LAN-component vendors to concentrate on hardware and software features, and to leave management application design and implementation to experts.
- Future LAN management architectures and products will distribute functions, instruments of systems, and network management; however, the overall control may remain central, for various economic reasons.
- Future implementations will be based on *de facto* management standards, most likely SNMP; middle- and long-range implementations will use more open, more robust network management standards such as OSI and GNMP.

2

Classification of local area networks

In order to develop a better understanding of LAN management functions and instruments, this chapter begins with a discussion of the basic attributes of LAN topologies, protocols, access schemes, transmission media, and interconnecting devices. After addressing transmission schemes, I describe and compare physical transmission media, and I follow with a discussion of the use of hubs. A section on protocols discusses the logical-link layer and connection-oriented and connectionless alternatives. Topologies include bus, ring, star, and tree. Each is compared using a detailed list of comparison criteria.

The next section on access control techniques addresses random, centralized, and decentralized solutions and highlights the most widely used techniques. It's expected that LAN network operating systems will have an important impact on LAN management. The section also includes a brief evaluation of the existing management capabilities of leading operating systems. The section concludes by introducing interconnecting schemes and devices, such as repeaters, extenders, bridges, brouters, routers, and gateways.

The major emphasis in this chapter is on how to predict potential bottlenecks of certain LAN components. It's also important to analyze how LAN components can contribute to effective management by providing information on physical and/or logical status. Such information delivery may support either solicited or unsolicited management techniques. Also, the debate between the use of inband or outband management connections is raised.

LAN transmission schemes

In order to clarify bandwidth requirements, FIG. 2-1 shows typical data rates, distances, and the applicability of networking techniques. This graphic shows that:

- There's a wide range of typical bandwidths.
- WANs have to offer more bandwidth and more flexibility.
- Computers may easily be connected via LANs.
- The appropriateness of MANs is indicated in the high-speed LAN area.
- Using T1/T3, J1 and E1 channels, wide area networking will offer more bandwidth.
- The introduction of Sonet, B-ISDN and SMDS may further increase this bandwidth and offer more standardization.
- PC LANs will remain in the low bandwidth area, and will remain a subset of general-purpose LANs.
- It's not likely that PBX-based LANs will substantially increase the offered bandwidth.

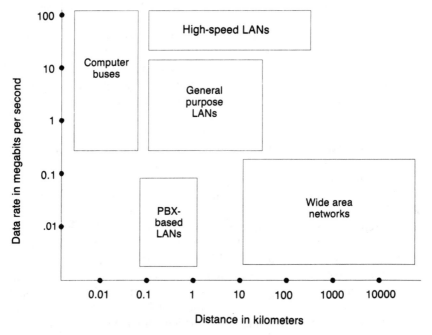

Fig. 2-1. Classification of networking techniques.

Local area networks support two techniques for transmitting information over communication facilities: baseband transmission and broadband transmission. Baseband transmission uses digital signaling to transmit signals over dedicated or shared channels. Whichever channel is used, the entire channel capacity is used to transmit signals between senders and receivers. For regenerating signal forms, repeaters are used. If the channels are shared, the technique of time division multiplexing (TDM) is used to control the access rights for subscribers. Figure 2-2 shows this arrangement, in which the signal flow is bidirectional. Baseband has the following attributes:

- Inexpensive.
- Very flexible for extensions.
- Easy to handle.
- Limited bandwidth.
- Typically, limited distances.

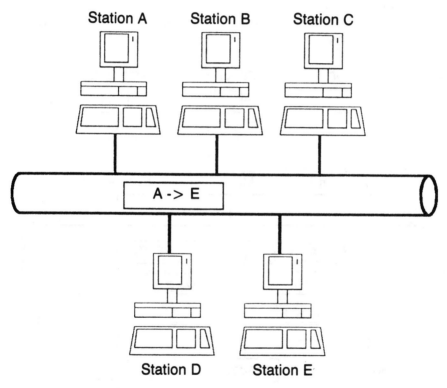

Fig. 2-2. Baseband transmission.

Broadboad transmission typically uses analog transmission with wider frequencies than baseband. In this case, signals are continuous and nondiscrete. For modulation, the amplitude, frequency and phase of the signal may be used. For regenerating signals, amplifiers are used. This technique is more effective against noise and interference. The total bandwidth is usually divided into separate channels. Each channel may support different users and communication forms simultaneously by implementing the technique of frequency division multiplexing (FDM). Figure 2-3 shows this arrangement, in which the signal flow is usually unidirectional unless manufacturers don't provide two independent paths for improving connectivity. Broadband has the following attributes:

- Technology is well proven, thanks to cable television.
- Longer distances than with baseband.
- Integration of multiple communication services due to the simultaneous use of multiple channels.
- Relatively expensive due to modems and active network elements such as headends and amplifiers.
- Limited flexibility. When new stations are connected, the whole network has to be tuned again.
- Relatively difficult access to stations connected to other communication channels. Relatively expensive bridges are required.

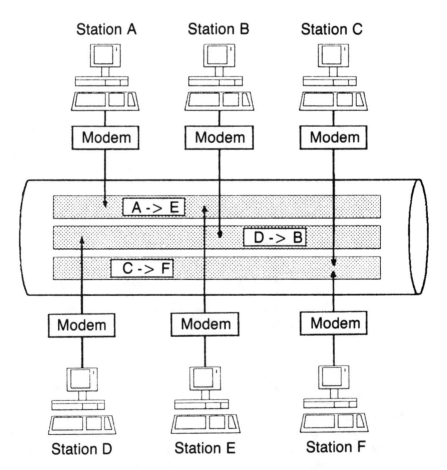

Fig. 2-3. Broadband transmission.

Baseband techniques are used for all bus- and token-based topologies. Broadband is used most frequently with bus topologies. The impact of the two techniques on LAN management may be summarized as follows:

- Fault management and error recovery techniques may be completely different with each transmission technique.
- Broadband allows the dedication of a channel to exchanging and transporting LAN management information.
- Outband management techniques may be applied in both cases.

Transmission media

The telecommunications industry employs a variety of media for the transmission of information in wide, metropolitan, and local area networks. In the LAN area, there are three generic media types that will be described and evaluated in more detail later in this book.

- Twisted pair.
- Coax.
- Fiber.

Figure 2-4 shows a simplified view of the structure of twisted-pair cables.

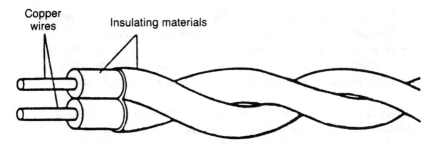

Fig. 2-4. Twisted-pair structure.

Twisted-pair cable is one of the most commonly used wiring materials for supporting low- to medium-speed analog and digital signal transmission. It consists of a pair of insulated copper wires, typically about 1 mm thick, with the wires twisted in a helical form in order to reduce potential electrical interference from adjacent pairs. The transmission capacity of the cable is determined by its dimension and the distance that the signal propagates. For example, for data rates in the 1 Mbps range, a transmission distance of 1 km can be achieved. For voice signals, the distance can be extended as far as 6 km without a repeater.

Most high-performance LAN implementations employ a thicker sheath, called shielded-twisted-wire-pair cabling. Due to its lower electrical interference, higher transmission rates over longer distances may be supported.

Figure 2-5 displays a typical coax cable structure. A *coaxial cable* consists of a stiff copper wire as its core, surrounded by an insulation material, which is

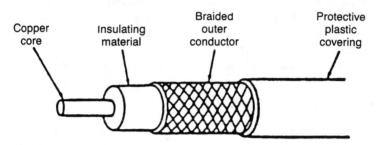

Fig. 2-5. Coax structure.

covered with a cylindrical conductor, usually in a woven braided mesh. The whole cable is then wrapped into protective plastic covering. Because of this construction, coaxial cables have an excellent noise immunity and a larger transmission capacity than twisted-pair cables. The cable length can easily be extended with a variety of cable taps, splitters, couplers, controllers, and repeaters to reach nearly all remote users.

There are two types of coaxial cables:

- Baseband is usually used for digital transmission and is typically less than one-half inch in diameter, with a 50-ohm impedance.
- Broadband is usually used in the television industry; it's normally divided into multiple frequency channels. The standard broadband cable is one-half inch in diameter, with a 75-ohm impedance.

Coax cables are less subject to cross-talk and interference than twisted-pair cables and are able to support much higher throughput rates—up to 100 Mbps. In some cases, the LAN industry uses the same cable and electronic components that are used by cable television applications.

An *optic fiber* is a dielectric waveguide that operates at optical frequencies. The cable consists of: a single solid dielectric cylinder as its core, usually made of glass; a solid dielectric refractive coating, usually made of glass or plastic, to protect the core; and an elastic, abrasion-resistant plastic material for encapsulating the cable to add further protection from environmental contaminants. The most important consideration with fiber cables is how to keep light propagating for a longer distance without suffering a loss.

The transmission capacity of a fiber depends on the light refraction techniques used. There are two modes of light refraction: *monomode* and *multimode*. Monomode fibers require laser diodes as the light source. Multimode fibers require LEDs as the light source and are suited for shorter distances.

Figure 2-6 shows a simplified method of operating monomode and multimode fiber cables.

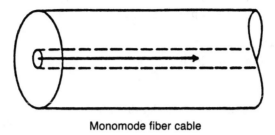

Monomode fiber cable

Multimode fiber cable

Fig. 2-6. Monomode and multimode fiber cables.

There are several reasons to consider wireless technology. It's predictable; wireless LANs are portable; you don't have to use cabling (a particular advantage in old buildings), and it has easy installation and maintenance. There are four choices when considering this technique:

- Microwave.
- Satellite.
- Infrared beams.
- Radio.

Infrared beams can carry traffic in the tens of megabits per second range over short distances—normally less than two kilometers. Dust, snow, rain, haze, and fog can lessen the ability of this transmission media to carry traffic.

Radio may be used for both short and long distances. However, this transmission technique is also subject to various types of interference. Results of recent experiments show that spread-spectrum technology is superior to FM radio due to the lower level of sensitivity to signal bouncing.

Wireless technology requires other types of transceivers for sending and receiving. Additional components, such as antennas, may also be required, increasing the number of passive devices to be managed. Wireless technology presents another alternative communication path to support outband network management. It's too early to say whether this technology will seriously compete with wire technology. But, wireless technology is definitely here to stay as an alternative or as a backup solution. Interesting solutions are:

- InfraLAN from BICC.
- Wavelan from from NCR.
- Altiar from Motorola.

In order to help planners consider different media alternatives, TABLE 2-1 compares the generic alternatives using various criteria, such as the bandwidth supported, number of nodes supported, distance that can be covered without interconnecting devices, implementation and maintenance costs, the maturity of the technology, common applications, noise immunity, ability to change, key advantages, and disadvantages. Relevant to the transmission, there are two basic alternatives:

- Balanced transmission (Miller 1989)
- Unbalanced transmission (Miller 1989)

Table 2-1. Comparison of LAN Media

| Feature | LAN media alternatives | | | | |
	UTP	STP	COAX	Fiber	Wireless
Bandwidth	Low 100 Mbps	Low 500 Mbps	Medium-high 1 Gbps	High 1 Gbps	Low-medium 2 Mbps to 15 Mbps
Number of nodes	Low	Low	Medium-high	Low-medium	Varies
Maximum distance	100 m at 10 Mbps	100 m at 16 Mbps	600 m at 10 Mbps	2 km at 100 Mbps	Varies 50 – 100 feet
Noise immunity	Poor	Good	Good	Excellent	Good
Ability to change	Very good	Good	Fair	Poor	Excellent
Cost	Low	Moderate	Moderate	High	High
Technology	Mature	Mature	Mature	Emerging	Emerging
Common applications	Hub network lobe wiring	Token Ring	Ethernet	Backbone	Temporary networks
Key advantages	Low cost	Reliability	Cost/bandwidth	FDDI support	Ability to reconfigure
Key disadvantages	Noise	Cost/Performance	Cable problems	Cost	Cost and bandwidth

In a balanced design, the currents flowing between the generator and receiver in each of the wires are equal in magnitude, but opposite in direction. Twisted-pair and twinax cables are examples of balanced transmission lines.

In an unbalanced design, the current flowing in the signal conductor returns via a ground connection that may be shared with other circuits. Both the current and the voltage in the signal conductor are measured with respect to this signal-return conductor. Coax cable is an example of unbalanced transmission.

Leading manufacturers typically offer complete cabling systems, including different types of (proprietary) cables and wiring concentrators. The following tables summarize the three packages: TABLE 2-2 for IBM (Martin 1989); TABLE 2-3 for AT&T; and TABLE 2-4 for DECConnect (Martin 1989).

Table 2-2. IBM Cabling Systems

- **Type 1 cable.** Type 1 cable consists of two solid, #22 AWG twisted-wire pairs surrounded by an outer braided shield. Both twisted-pairs are suitable for data use. Several varieties of Type 1 cable are available, including cable for indoor use in conduits, cable suitable for installation in wiring plenums, and cable for outdoor installation.
- **Type 2 cable.** Type 2 cable also contains two solid, #22 AWG twisted-wire pairs surrounded by an outer braided shield. Between the braided shield and the outer protective sheath are four additional solid #22 AWG twisted-wire pairs suitable for use in telephone communication. Several varieties of Type 2 cable are also available for indoor use in conduits or in wiring plenums.
- **Type 5 cable.** Type 5 cable contains two optical fibers within a single outer cover. Type 5 cable can be installed indoors, outdoors, and in dry, waterproof underground conduits.
- **Type 6 cable.** Type 6 cable is similar to Type 1 cable, except that it uses stranded #26 AWG wire. Type 6 cable is typically used for constructing patch cables that interconnect longer lengths of Type 1 and Type 2 cable.

The ultimate purpose of each package is to provide a unique interface at the "wall" (FIG. 2-7), which can offer great flexibility to any of the cable types under consideration. This cabling converter could play an important role in managing the passive objects of a LAN infrastructure.

Each physical layout and logical topology may be completely different. The physical wiring structure is responsible for supporting the targeted logical topology. This support has different levels of sophistication, depending on the intelligence of wiring hubs. Wiring hubs are gradually becoming the focal points of physical LAN management. Not just cables and network interface cards, but also interconnecting devices, may be managed from the same central place. Figure 2-8 shows a generic example of a wiring hub from SynOptics, indicating the management of wires and other devices, and illustrating wiring and device status.

The allocation of media to particular bandwidths is not apparent anymore. The 10BaseT applications have made a breakthrough on replacing coax with twisted-pair cable. Despite distance limitations, this new media allocation opens new considerations for even higher bandwidths. A fundamental problem of LANs is that at higher data rates, even with low electrical power, unshielded wiring turns into a broadcasting antenna. And at the same time, FCC antiradio emission requirements are violated.

Table 2-3. AT&T Cabling System

Product Code	Description		Speed in Mbps	Distance in Meters	# of Workstations
			Performance specifications[1]		
1061	Copper LAN, Non-Plenum[2]		16	100	104
2061	Copper LAN, Plenum		16	100	104
1010	Copper LAN, Non-Plenum		16	38	72
2010	Copper LAN, Plenum		16	38	72
FOBC	Fiber Optic Building Cable (FOBC)[3]		100	100	500
1290	Composite Non-plenum	Type 1010 FOBC	16 100	38 100	72 500
2290	Composite Plenum	Type 2010 FOBC	16 100	38 100	72 500
1090	Composite Non-plenum	Type 1010 Type 1061 FOBC	16 16 100	38 100 100	72 104 500
2090	Composite Plenum	Type 2010 Type 2061 FOBC	16 16 100	38 100 100	72 104 500

[1]Up to but not exceeding the speed, distance, and number of workstations listed

[2]All LAN Cables are 24 gauge unshielded twisted pair

[3]Fiber Optic Building Cable is 62.5/125μm

Table 2-4. DEC Cabling System

- **ThinWire Ethernet cable.** ThinWire Ethernet cable is a flexible coaxial cable, about 1/4-inch thick, that is similar to the type of coaxial cable that is used for closed-circuit television transmission. It is used for relatively short distance communication at 10 Mbps over an Ethernet type of local area network. Ethernet is described in detail in Chapters 6 and 20.
- **Standard Ethernet cable.** Standard Ethernet cable is relatively rigid, 1/2-inch-thick coaxial cable that is typically used to interconnect several smaller networks that use the ThinWire Ethernet cable.
- **Twisted-Wire-Pair Data Communication cable.** This cable is unshielded and contains four twisted-wire pairs. It is used for connecting terminals and other types of computer equipment to a network using slow-speed, non-LAN types of data communication.
- **Telephone cable.** This is standard telephone cable that contains four unshielded twisted-wire pairs. It is used for ordinary voice telephone communication.
- **Video cable.** This is standard closed-circuit television coaxial cable and is used for video applications.

The impact of media on LAN management may be summarized as follows:

- Each type of media has specific limitations on the practical throughput rates.
- Each type of media is sensitive to different types of environmental impacts.
- A wiring hub may be used as the physical focal point for LAN management.
- Media emission rates may limit applicability and may impact security measures.

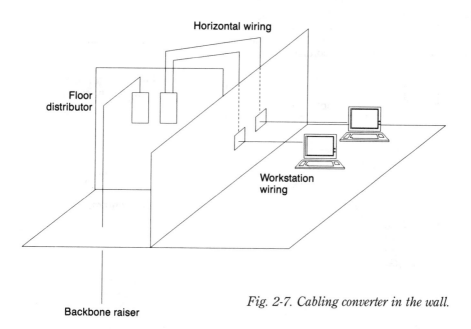

Fig. 2-7. Cabling converter in the wall.

LAN topology alternatives

Network topology is defined as the way network nodes are geographically connected. Similarly, a LAN's type is determined by its topology. Depending on which technical reference you use, the type of LAN topology varies. In general, there are two types of LAN topology: constrained and unconstrained. A *constrained* topology can consist of ring, bus, and star connections. An *unconstrained* topology can consist of everything else (e.g., mesh, fully connected, etc.). Only the constrained topology is discussed here, as it represents the majority of LANs (See chapter 1).

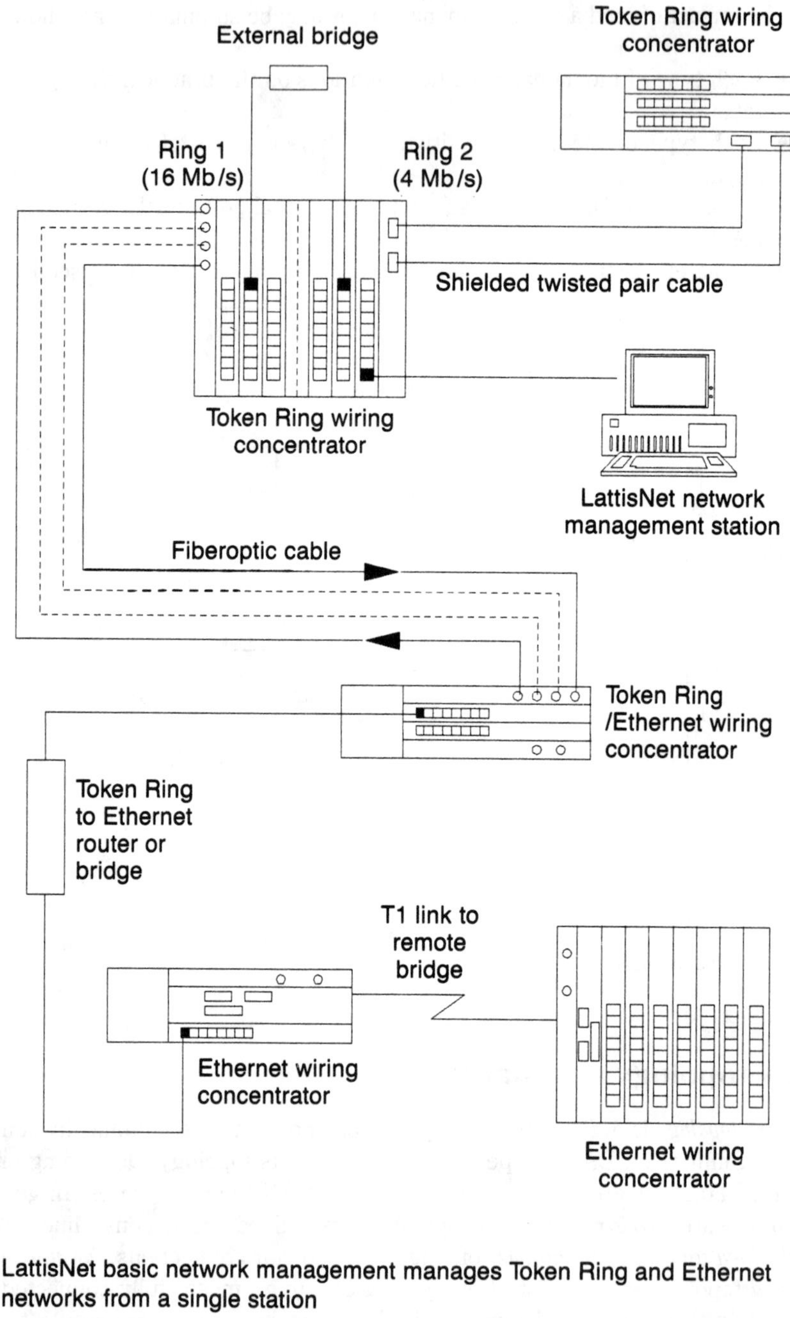

Token Ring wiring concentrator

External bridge

Ring 1 (16 Mb/s)   Ring 2 (4 Mb/s)

Shielded twisted pair cable

Token Ring wiring concentrator

LattisNet network management station

Fiberoptic cable

Token Ring /Ethernet wiring concentrator

Token Ring to Ethernet router or bridge

T1 link to remote bridge

Ethernet wiring concentrator

Ethernet wiring concentrator

LattisNet basic network management manages Token Ring and Ethernet networks from a single station

Fig. 2-8. Wiring hub example.

Star topology

In a *star topology*, all nodes are connected to a focal node, generally referred to as the hub or control node, in a point-to-point (direct) manner. All transmissions go through the control node. Therefore, the main function of the control node is to manage the network. The transmission medium for a star LAN network can be twisted-pair, coaxial, or fiber-optic cable. The star topology can be combined with other topologies, such as a ring topology, to form a hybrid network deriving advantages from both topologies. An example of a star LAN is Xerox's Fibernet II, a point-to-point topology with dual fiber-optic buses, one for transmitting and one for receiving, with a carrier-sensing multiple access/collision detection (CSMA/CD) protocol (see discussion in bus topology). Figure 2-9 shows a general star network structure (LO 1990).

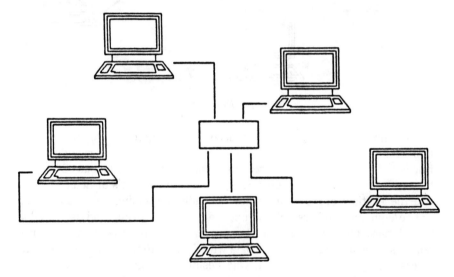

Fig. 2-9. Star topology.

Ring topology

In a *ring topology*, nodes are connected by point-to-point links in a sequential manner to form a closed path. A signal is passed along the path one node at a time before returning to its originating node. Each node requires an interface device to recognize its own address for receiving messages, and also to act as a repeater for forwarding messages to other nodes. The transmission medium for a ring LAN can be either twisted-pair, baseband coaxial, or optic-fiber cable. A ring topology can be combined with star topology to form a star-ring LAN, thus incorporating the advantages of both topologies. Figure 2-10 depicts a general ring topology (LO 1990).

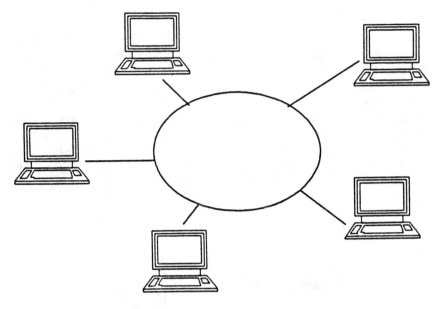

Fig. 2-10. Ring topology.

To implement a ring LAN, you need to be aware of the following conditions. First, prewiring of a ring LAN is difficult. When a node is added to the ring in order to support a new user, transmission lines must be placed between the new node and its two topologically adjacent nodes. It's difficult to anticipate the locations of the future nodes. Secondly, any adding/deleting of a node or line/equipment failure will disrupt the network, causing end-user productivity losses. Thirdly, when and where to remove transmitted data on the ring requires some intelligent design. Data will continue to circulate along the path unless it's specifically removed. One desirable design is to let the sender remove data already received since it allows an automatic acknowledgment and also allows multibroadcasting addressing when one message is simultaneously transmitted to many nodes. Wiring hubs, introduced in the previous sections, may help by offering software techniques for physically reconfiguring rings. Examples of the ring topology are IBM's Token Ring offerings, with 4 and 16 Mbps throughput rates.

Bus topology

In a *bus topology*, all nodes are connected to a common transmission medium in an open manner. (See FIG. 2-11.) Each node has its unique address; when a message is sent, it's sent to all nodes, and the receiving node must be able to recognize its own address to receive. The common transmission medium used for bus LANs is coaxial cable because of its passive nature and easy implementation without disrupting the operation. However, fiber-optic cables can be used for a bus LAN, although they require more skill to implement.

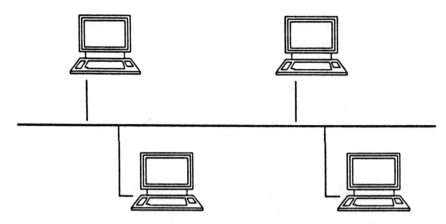

Fig. 2-11. Bus topology.

Because of the bus topology's sharing nature, some type of controlling mechanism must be in place to prevent several nodes from transmitting simultaneously. The two most popular controls are polling and contention. These control techniques will be covered in more detail in the following section. An example of a bus LAN is Ethernet, which employs the CSMA/CD access control with a 10 Mbps transmission capacity. Ethernet has been studied widely, and there are many reports on its performance characteristics (LO 1990).

Tree topology

The bus topology can be extended to a tree topology in which multiple bus branches join at various points to form a tree LAN. Figure 2-12 shows a general tree topology.

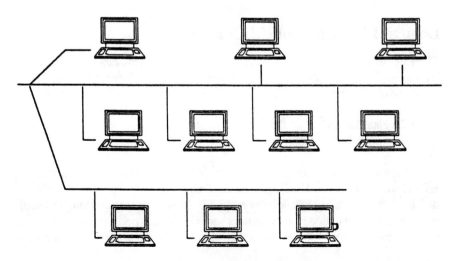

Fig. 2-12. Tree topology.

In order to aid in appropriate topology selection, TABLE 2-5 compares the four generic topologies using such criteria as technical reliability, complexity, flexibility, expandability, cost and capacity.

Table 2-5. Topology Comparison

Feature	Bus	Star	Ring	Tree
Reliability	High	Moderate	Moderate	High
Complexity	Moderate	Low	Low	Moderate
Flexibility	High	Moderate	Moderate	High
Expandability	Moderate	Moderate	Moderate	High
Cost	Moderate	High	Moderate	Moderate
Capacity	Moderate	Low	High	High

The impact of topology choice on LAN management may be summarized as follows:

- Each topology choice:
  a. represents a different fault-management solution.
  b. represents a different built-in management capability.
  c. represents a different single-point-of-failure consequence.
- Each topology is:
  a. associated with a different feasible throughput rate.
  b. associated with a different feasible medium.
  c. strongly associated with an access control technique that may greatly influence performance.

Logical Link Control (LLC) Protocols

The LLC sublayer of the IEEE 802.2 recommendation provides services to the layer above, and controls the sublayer below. Figure 2-13 illustrates the generic structure of the first three LAN layers, dividing layer 2 into two sublayers:

- Logical Link Control (LLC).
- Medium Access Control (MAC).

There are many similarities between OSI layer 2 services, implemented by HDLC (or SDLC or UDLC) and LLC. There are two types of operations defined between the network layer and LLC. Type 1 operation (Martin 1989) provides a facility called connectionless service. With type 1 operation, there's no need for the establishment of a logical connection between the communi-

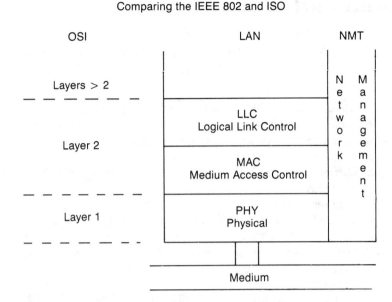

Fig. 2-13. Lower layer of LAN communication structures.

cating partners because each data unit transmitted is processed independently. Type 1 operation is sometimes referred to as a *datagram service*. This service doesn't offer sequence checking, acknowledgment on behalf of the receiver, flow control, or error recovery.

Type 2 operation is a connection-oriented service. Before transmission begins, the logical connection has to be established. The connection is maintained during transmission and will be terminated when the transmission ends. Type 2 operation offers sequence checking, flow control, error recovery, and retransmission of data units that are not correctly received (Martin 1989).

The services between LLC and MAC are well defined for the three leading MAC sublayers that control access to the physical transmission medium. These are CSMA/CD, token bus and token ring. Slightly different rules apply for FDDI (fiber distributed data interface).

Access control techniques and FDDI will be addressed in following sections. The impact of LLC protocols on LAN management may be summarized as follows:

- Transmission efficiency is represented by the ratio of control to data characters.
- Error recovery and retransmission rates are significantly influenced by the selected media.

Access control techniques

Access control techniques can be categorized according to the location of the control entity. Most frequently, they're separated into three groups (Martin 1989).

- Random control. With random control, any station can transmit, and specific permission is not required. A station may check the medium to see if it's free before starting the transmission. The most widely used techniques are:
  a. Carrier sense multiple access with collision detection (CSMA/CD).
  b. Slotted ring.
  c. Register insertion.
- Distributed control. With distributed control, only one station at a time has the right to transmit, and that right is passed— as a token—from station to station. The most widely used techniques are:
  a. Token ring.
  b. Token bus.
  c. Carrier sense multiple access with collision detection (CSMA/CD).
- Centralized control. With centralized control, one station controls the LAN (or interconnected LANs), and other stations must receive permission from the controlling station for starting transmission. Known techniques—not limited to LANs are:
  a. Polling.
  b. Circuit switching.
  c. Time division multiplexing.

The following discussion analyzes these leading access control techniques in greater depth (Infotel Systems 1990).

Figure 2-14 shows a typical example of a transmission with CSMA/CD. Device "A" is transmitting. "B" and "C" have data but refrain from sending because they sense activity on the channel. "A" finishes sending. "B" and "C" sense that the channel is idle, and both begin sending. "B" and "C" sense collision and send a jamming signal for a short period to ensure detection of the collision, then they back off. "B" and "C" start random timers. "B" times out first and starts sending. "C" senses that the channel is busy and refrains from sending. "B" finishes sending. "C" senses that the channel is idle and starts sending. This access technique is the basis of Ethernet.

Figure 2-15 illustrates the principal transmission steps of Token bus. "A" and "C" have data to send, but must wait for the token. "A" receives the token from another device. "A" transmits data. "A" passes the token to "B." "B" has no data, and sends the token to "C." "C" sends data, then passes the token to the next device in the sequence. Token bus is the basis of the MAP/TOP implementation.

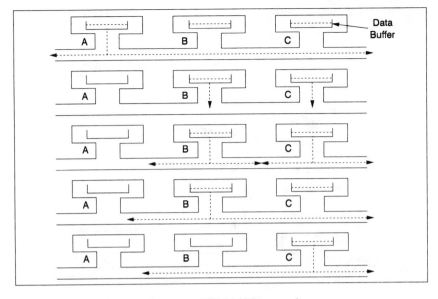

Fig. 2-14. CSMA/CD example.

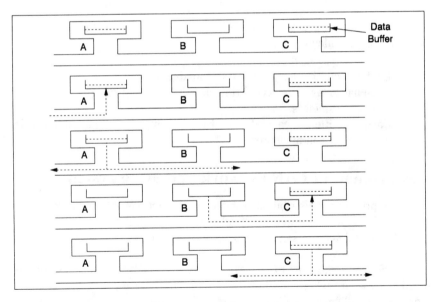

Fig. 2-15. Token-bus example.

Figure 2-16 displays the basic steps involved in using Token Ring. "A" receives the token. "A" sends a message to "C." "C" copies and passes the frame on. "A" sees the returning frame. "A" issues the token to "B." Token Ring is the predominant architecture of IBM. A performance assessment and comparison will be presented in chapter 3.

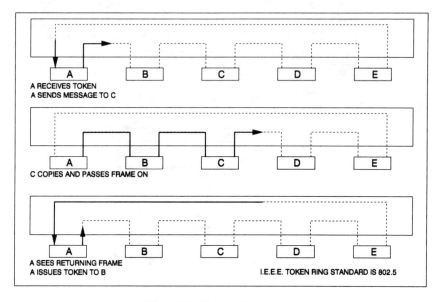

Fig. 2-16. Token-ring example.

The impact of access control techniques on LAN management may be summarized as follows:

- Each affects the use level of the available bandwidth.
- Each has an average access time as a function of principal LAN performance parameters.
- Each has different capabilities for recognizing errors and implementing error correction measures.

Assessment of LAN network operating systems

With the progress of distributed architectures, functions of local operating systems could be implemented practically everywhere in the network. Servers have been updated by segments in a network operating system (NOS), as shown in FIG. 2-17 (Fortier 1989).

NOS allows the user to request services in the LAN, and NOS doesn't need to be aware where and how the servers have been provided. Thus, this application will show a global character. The ultimate step is a global operating system (GOS) with no local autonomous operating system or network, but one homogeneous operating system built on the available hardware (FIG. 2-18) (Fortier 1989). Common operating system functions include:

- Controlling access to servers.
- Controlling access to applications.

- Ensuring fault tolerance.
- Managing files efficiently.
- Partitioning LANs.
- Providing multiprotocol transport interfaces.
- Managing memory.
- Managing input/output.
- Managing devices.
- Managing printing.
- Supporting electronic mail.
- Managing names efficiently.
- Supporting interconnectivity.
- Managing a network.

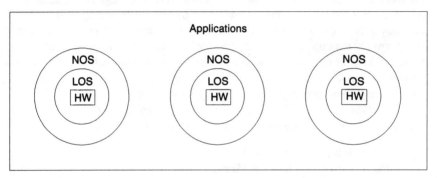

HW   Hardware
LOS   Local Operating System
NOS   Network Operating System

Fig. 2-17. Network operating systems.

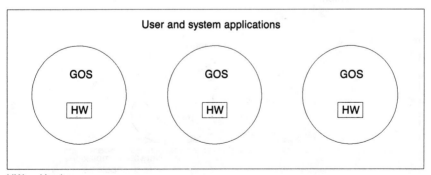

HW   Hardware
GOS   Global Operating System

Fig. 2-18. Global network operating systems.

In terms of network-management related activities, even the leading manufacturers' solutions show gaps and weaknesses. Solutions such as IBM's OS/2 LAN server, 3COM's 3+Open, AT&T's LAN Manager/X, and Ungermann-Bass's Net/One incorporate some of the core services of the LAN Manager from Microsoft. In addition, there are around forty other companies that have OEM agreements with Microsoft. But still, market dominance of Novell's Netware— a rather proprietary solution—prevails.

Figure 2-19 illustrates the relative position of four products in terms of network size and complexity. As can be seen, each product has its strengths and weaknesses. After analyzing built-in network management capabilities, you'll find that none of these products provides an optimal solution. With the exception of Banyan (Vines), all other vendors try to combine external monitoring and fault management, as can be seen with Novell (NetWare + LANtern) and IBM (LAN Network Manager). Segments of configuration management (naming and addressing), accounting, security, and some performance management features are provided by built-in NOS features. These features must operate as part of the network management architecture, which may be completely separated from the NOS or GOS and may be provided by proprietary solutions from LAN vendors or implemented by systems vendors. Proprietary, *de facto*, or open network management protocol standards may be selected for communication.

The IBM solution (Martin 1989) shows the various layers of support. At the lowest layer, there are three choices of media access control:

- Token Ring (4 or 16 Mbps).
- PC Network Baseband (2 Mbps).
- PD Network Broadband (5 Mbps).

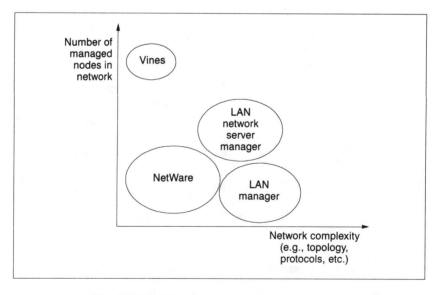

Fig. 2-19. Positioning network operating systems.

The logical link control covers layer 2 of the OSI reference model, and equals the IEEE 802 recommendations. NetBios still plays an important role by interfacing presentations and applications. The NetBios interface offers reliable data transfer and datagram service. On top of NetBios, another program called the IBM PC LAN Program provides a messaging facility and offers print, file, and file sharing services.

Advanced Program-to-Program Communication/PC (APPC/PC) provides an alternative to NetBios as an interface for LAN communication. Any of the three LAN products may use APPC/PC. APPC/PC offers more flexibility, but the migration to this interface will take time due to the investments made in the previous technology.

In addition to these basic offerings, IBM has implemented several connectivity products to interconnect LANs of different types or to connect LANs with host computers and WANs. These products are (Martin 1989):

- IBM Token Ring Bridge Program.
- IBM Token Ring/PC Network Interconnect Program.
- IBM PC 3270 Emulation Program.
- IBM LAN Asynchronous Connection Server Program.
- IBM Series/1 PC Connect Program.

Other companies that offer connectivity products position themselves relative to IBM connectivity products or relative to the interfaces at the transport and session layers.

The impact on LAN management of network operating systems may be summarized as follows:

- Each uses the built-in capabilities of the operating systems of the network and/or servers.
- Each represents different alternatives for connecting NOS to the network management station (protocols and inband/outband).
- Each embeds external monitoring capabilities into network operating systems.

The role of private branch exchanges (PBXs) in LAN management

Considering the wide distribution range of voice communication, the same physical infrastructure may be used for accommodating data, or, in the future, other communication forms. But, such integration is just not happening.

Some considerations used against voice wiring and in favor of cable-oriented LANs are: voice wiring uses low-bandwidths that are sufficient for voice only; voice-wiring line quality is sufficient for voice only; voice wiring has a single point of failure; voice wiring volume is high, due to central control with the star topology.

But, there also are many benefits to PBX-based solutions: availability of circuits to a large community of end users, low-risk technology, good administration, and easy migration to higher bandwidths offered by ISDN basic or primary services.

Basically, the packet-switching technology of LANs is competing against the circuit-switching technology of PBXs. New developments have brought both technologies closer to each other. Some of the facts are:

- More topological alternatives for PBXs.
- The use of wiring hubs for LANs.
- The use of voice-wiring technology for considerably higher bandwidth.
- More centralized management for LANs.

As a result, a number of feasible configurations can be implemented. The PBX may be considered an entry point to the campus or premises (FIG. 2-20); PBXs can be connected by a LAN backbone (FIG. 2-21); PBXs can be used for bridging LANs with low data traffic (FIG. 2-22); data circuit switches (DCS) can be on a twisted pair basis with LANs to economically connect low-speed terminals with each other or with hosts and their applications (FIG. 2-23). In overall LAN-management architectures, PBXs are expected to provide the functionality of an element management system, working independently from or connected to LAN-management integrators.

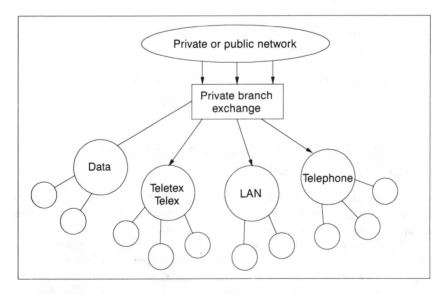

Fig. 2-20. PBX as an entry point.

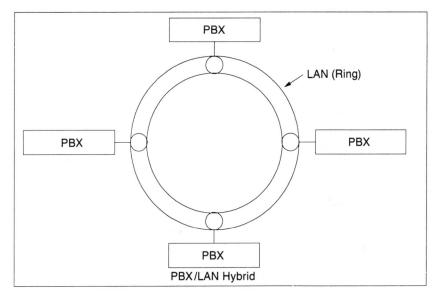

Fig. 2-21. Networked PBXs.

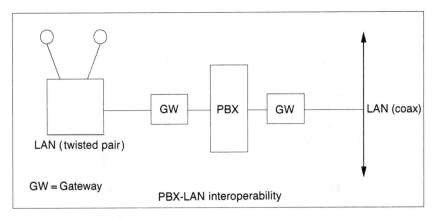

Fig. 2-22. PBX as bridge between LANs.

The impact of PBXs on LAN management can be summarized as follows:

- High applicability of built-in management capabilities.
- Alternatives of connecting PBXs to the network management station (protocols and inband/outband).
- External monitoring features of PBXs.
- Use of PBXs for supervising the physical (wiring) infrastructure of premises.
- Better specification of what network management applications are needed for PBXs.

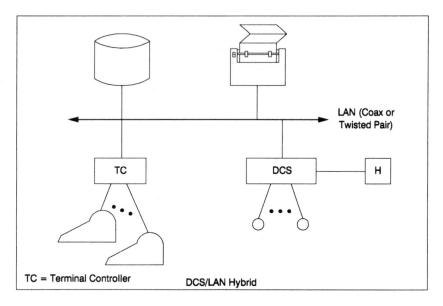

Fig. 2-23. Use of DCS and LAN in combination.

Interconnecting local area networks

When considering the ability to ensure enterprise-wide connectivity for users and local area networks, interconnectivity strategies gain in importance. The following are important topics when considering interconnecting local area networks: evaluating interconnection strategies, optimizing interconnecting topologies, evaluating and selecting interconnecting devices, and evaluating and selecting interconnecting facilities.

Developing interconnection strategies includes making decisions about how and whether existing WANs and interconnected LANs can coexist. In certain circumstances, WANs may be replaced by interconnected LANs. However, this is a long process. Strategy development also includes evaluating the kind of interconnection, in other words, whether low-level or high-level gateways are required. Depending on needs, different levels of intelligence for interconnecting devices may be required. Repeaters, extenders, or bridges may be very suitable for extending the geographical reach of LAN segments; for more flexible connectivity, routers should be considered; finally, for application-level connectivity, gateways are required.

In terms of topology, two alternatives are in competition: peer-to-peer interconnections, and hierarchical interconnections. In a peer-coupled architecture, the primary issue is what connections should exist. If "mesh" and "tree" topologies are allowed, a large number of possibilities exist for even a small number of interconnected LANs. Each configuration will result in a different performance level, depending on inter-LAN traffic patterns. Figure 2-24

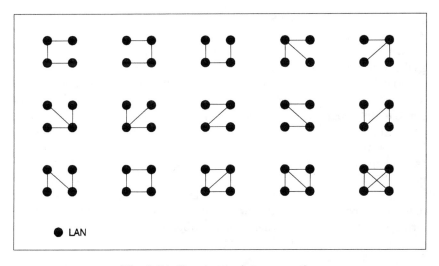

Fig. 2-24. Peer-to-peer interconnection.

shows a few alternative topologies with just four LAN segments. Each configuration results in different performance, depending on traffic, the bandwidth
of the connections, and backup facilities.

The hierarchical topology based on a backbone is shown in FIG. 2-25. Connecting to a backbone requires the construction of a backbone. The backbone
network is not limited by geography; it may be constructed for a wide, metropolitan, or local area. A backbone could use technology that's identical to that

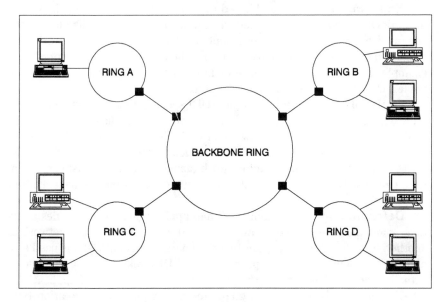

Fig. 2-25. Hierarchical interconnection.

of access LANs, or the backbone technology could be totally different. Besides known WAN and LAN topologies, there are two emerging technologies that compete for use as backbone: FDDI (fiber distributed data interface), and DQDB (dual queue dual bus).

FDDI is a token-passing network based on two rings of fiber-optic cable in its fullest form. The packets on each of the rings rotate around the rings in opposite directions. An FDDI network can achieve burst speeds of 100 Mbps and sustained data transmission speeds of around 80 Mbps. A full-blown FDDI network can stretch 100 km and connect over 500 stations spaced as far as 2 km apart. Even with a high cost factor, FDDI offers benefits that can't be found with any other communication medium.

Speed   First and foremost among FDDI's advantages over first-generation, copper-based LANs is the far greater speeds at which data can be transferred over the network. Ethernet's 10 Mbps and even IBM's Token Ring speed of 16 Mbps offer considerably less throughput in comparison to FDDI's speed of 100 Mbps.

Security   Security issues are always a concern for any network where critical data is readily available on the network. From the standpoint of the physical media's security, a fiber-optic medium is much more effective than a copper-based medium, which emits electromagnetic interference patterns that can be monitored. This problem is completely eliminated with fiber optics. Metal cables are also much easier to tap into than fiber optic cables. Tapping into a coaxial cable is almost as easy as attaching a clamp to the cable. To tap into a fiber optic cable, the cable must be cut and very precisely sliced back together or the transmission is impaired and the brake detected.

Noise immunity   Metal-based (coaxial cables or twisted-pair wiring) networks are subject to EMI (electromagnetic interference), unlike light-wave communications. With the proper installation techniques, FDDI networks can stretch significantly beyond distances reached by previous networks. For example, Ethernet networks are limited to a distance no greater than 2.8 km, while FDDI can cover a distance of 100 km.

Fault tolerance   Built into the FDDI specification are certain levels of fault tolerance—a critical need in high-performance applications. In a fully configured FDDI network with two fiber-optic rings, a break or failure in one of the rings would not disable the network. An FDDI network, because of its built-in station management and network management functions, can reconfigure itself so that all nodes maintain communication at the normal speeds of the network.

Determinism   In certain realtime applications, network designers must know the time needed to transfer data from one node on the network to another, or from a supercomputer to a peripheral device, if FDDI is used as a high-speed connection to peripherals. The FDDI token-passing scheme is actually a timed token protocol that allows for just these types of applications.

The protocol is designed to guarantee a maximum token rotation time decided by a bidding process between the nodes on the network when the network is initialized. The node requiring the fastest transfer time can dictate the token rotation time for the ring. In this way, network developers can know the maximum time between a node's acquiring the token and, consequently, the maximum time needed to communicate with any other node on the network.

Many FDDI networks will actually be hybrid implementations where the type of FDDI station used—whether single or dual attachment—will depend on the application being run and the objectives of the network designer. FDDI node processors are those modules that provide connectivity to FDDI and that handle much of the protocol processing. During the early stages of implementation, it's just as important for the FDDI node processors to offer the network designer a certain degree of flexibility as it is for the node processors to support the high transmission rates of FDDI.

Because they provide that critical connection point to an FDDI network, the capabilities of node processors today and over the next several years should be of extreme importance to network implementors and OEM manufacturers who will be incorporating FDDI into their product lines. Some of the characteristics to carefully consider in a node processor are its design flexibility, internal bandwidth, host bus interface, and its ability to handle FDDI's demanding protocol processing requirements.

"Nodes" are responsible for connecting bridges, routers, computers, and other devices to the FDDI backbone. A special consideration is the use of encapsulation or transparent protocol. Protocol encapsulation limits the use of FDDI backbones to the same protocol. Transparent protocol implementation doesn't have the same restriction, enabling users to construct hybrid FDDI backbone networks.

Figure 2-26 shows the standardized FDDI layers and their mutual interfaces:

- PMD—Physical medium dependent, which describes the electrical/ optical link connection to the FDDI ring.
- PHY—Physical layer protocol, which interfaces to PMD and handles the encoding and decoding of information.
- MAC—Media access control, which connects PHY to higher OSI layers, providing packet framing and token control.
- STM—Station management, which provides managing, monitoring and configuring of the network.

Station management is still a proprietary solution, but in most cases, SNMP Agent Software is implemented. Figure 2-27 displays the loopback capability of FDDI I over a secondary ring; optical bypass is demonstrated in FIG. 2-28.

DQDB uses two optical-fiber buses to connect basically the same types of objects as with FDDI. But DQDB offers a higher bandwidth (140 Mbps). These buses are separated from each other and are undirectional. Both buses use the same frequency for signaling. Multiple slots may constitute a frame,

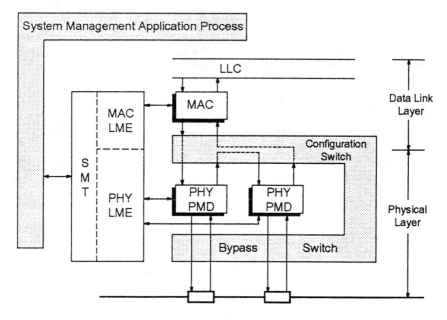

Fig. 2-26. FDDI layers.

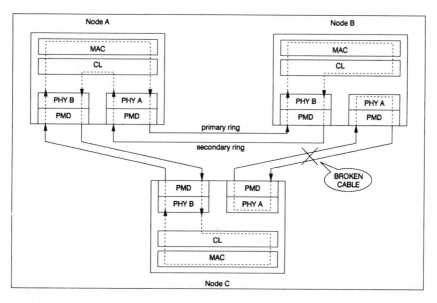

Fig. 2-27. Loopback with FDDI I.

which is generated by the frame generator at the beginning of the bus. Since network nodes are tied to each other as a logical bus, each node is located both upstream and downstream from bus nodes (FIG. 2-29).

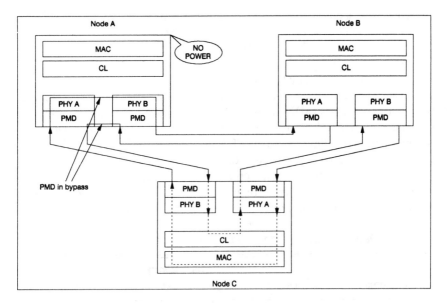

Fig. 2-28. Optical bypass in FDDI I nodes.

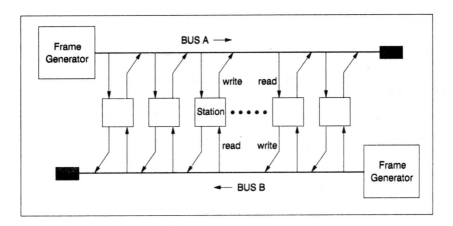

Fig. 2-29. Distributed Queue Dual Bus.

DQDB technology revolves around the fact that all stations have knowledge of the frames queued at all other stations. Under DQDB, the end nodes continuously transmit empty data frames around each ring. Whenever a station on one of the network nodes has something to send, it generates a frame request on the bus that's carrying traffic away from its node. Stations upstream receive the request, then reserve and empty the frame for the requesting station's data; when the packet stream circles around again, the frame is sent for transmission to its destination.

If fallback security is required, a DQDB network can be configured as a looped bus in which the two ends of the buses are colocated. If a fault occurs in one of the buses, the nodes at either end of the fault become the beginning and the end.

Each of the buses may be used by selected stations, enabling them to use synchronous communication-transmission protocols. Providers offer compatibility with broadband ISDN. Many telecoms and private enterprises offer comparisons between both alternatives. During the usual comparison, FDDI II (at this moment in pending status) and T/E facilities are included as well. TABLE 2-6 presents a comparison of these three technologies, using various criteria such as access technique, architecture, transport medium, throughput rate, standardization, applicability of required connections, use of isochronous or synchronous transmission protocols, and suitability for public networks.

Table 2-6. Comparison of FDDI, DQDB, and T/E Services

| Features | Technology | | |
	DQDB	FDDI	E/T Multiplexers
Media access	Distributed queue	Token	Time division multiplexing
Architecture	Dual bus	Single or dual ring	Point-to-point dedicated lines
Transport medium	Independent	Fiber optics	Manufacturer dependent
Throughput rate	Up to 140 Mbps	100 Mbps	34 – 45 Mbps
Connectionless	Yes	Yes	Frame relaying
Isochronous/ Synchronous	Yes	FDDI II planned	Yes
Standardization	IEEE 802.6 ETSI	ANSI	Manufacturer proprietary
Driving forces	AT&T, BOCs, PTTs	FDDI manufacturers	Private industry
Suitability for public networks	Yes	No	Not likely
Product status	Trial	FDDI I available FDDI II concept	Available

There are multiple alternatives for interconnecting LANs. The most important ones are:

- Private or public packet switching.
- ISDN.
- Point-to-point or multipoint leased lines (copper).

- Point-to-point leased lines (fiber).
- Microwave.
- Satellite.
- Fast packet switching (frame and cell relay).
- B-ISDN.
- SMDS (Switched Multimegabit Data Service).
- Sonet or SDH.

In particular, SMDS seems to be getting a lot of attention as the interconnecting technology of the future. As a MAN alternative, Switched Multimegabit Data Service (SMDS) seems to be very useful for transmitting large data files and graphics that low-speed services such as X.25 can't easily handle. And SMDS may offer an alternative to installing more expensive private-line facilities covering the speed range from 1.544 Mbps to 45 Mbps. This service will run on circuits provided by the RBOCs and connect the physical interface between a bridge or router and the SMDS network. In terms of management, the providers are expected to make network management raw data available (e.g., in MIBs). Polling the MIBs for SMDS operational and statistical data, data may be transmitted and further processed by the management station. Basically, SMDS is using short, fixed-length packet sizes for transmitting voice, data and video.

LAN-to-LAN connections may require very broad bandwidth over the next few years. Sonet and ATM are interesting choices in this respect. *Sonet* is a set of international standards for transmission over fiber, with speeds ranging from 51.84 Mbps to over 13 gigabits per second. Synchronous Digital Hierarchy (SDH) is a subset of Sonet standards, and is used in European and Asian networks.

Asynchronous transfer mode (ATM) is a cell-based switching technology for fast packets that uses 53-byte cells, without regard to the communication form. ATM is critical to the deployment of multimedia networks.

Frame relay is also receiving attention. *Frame relay* is a network access technique that transmits data packets of variable lengths with a minimum of error checking. In interconnecting LANs, frame relay has the benefit of not force-fitting LAN applications into a specific frame size. The variable lengths of packages require minimal data conversion between frame relay and devices attached to local area networks.

Broadband ISDN offers even higher bandwidth for interconnecting LANs. But this technique is not expected to be in service before the second half of the 1990s.

The technical differences may be significant, but most experts believe pricing and availability will be the major factors affecting the choice between these three leading technologies. Figure 2-30 displays these alternatives by showing various throughput rates constrained by the technologies to the bandwidth demand of the interconnection (Boell 1989).

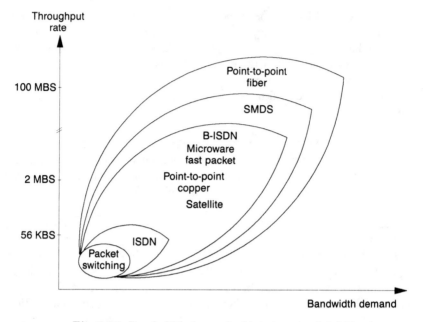

Fig. 2-30. Bandwidth demand of interconnected LANs.

The following is the impact of interconnecting strategies on LAN management, topologies, and facilities:

- Performance bottlenecks due to WAN-facility bandwidth.
- Low processing efficiency of FDDI nodes.
- Too many hierarchical steps in LAN interconnection topology.

Interconnecting devices

Depending on the interconnecting goals, different interconnecting devices can be implemented. Decisions should be based on consideration of flexibility, protocol support and transparency, processing delays, scope of functionality, and cost.

Repeaters   Repeaters are devices with amplification, signal reshaping, and retiming functions whose purpose is to extend the cabling distance. Their attributes are:

- Amplification, reshaping, and retiming to extend the cabling distance.
- Connections at layer 1.
- No modifications on access protocols.
- No path optimization.

- The possibility of media change.
- Weak security features.
- Number limited by higher level protocols.
- Special solutions:
  a. Buffered repeater.
  b. Remote repeater.
  c. Fiber repeater.

Figure 2-31 shows the location of repeaters in relation to standards.

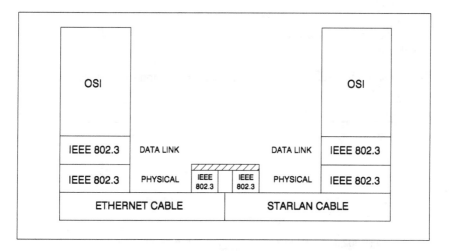

Fig. 2-31. Repeater structure.

Extenders   Extenders are devices that offer connection to local area networks for standalone user devices, which may be terminals or workstations. The principal attributes of extenders are:

- Connections at layer 1 for both local and remote users supporting various serial interfaces (V.24, RS-232, V.35, X.21.)
- Use of internal or external clocking.
- Use of private or public communication services.
- Support of rates between 1.2 Kbps to 128 Kbps.
- Minimal support of higher layers—usually just support of SDLC or HDLC.
- Transparency to higher-level protocols such as TCP/IP, XNS, OSI, Dec-Net, etc.
- Minimal network management capabilities.

MAC bridges   MAC bridges are devices for offering connectivity at the layer 2 MAC level between various access protocols and media. The attributes of MAC bridges are:

- Connectivity function.
- Connection at layer 2A.
- No change on LLC protocol.
- Address analysis and filtering.
- Significant reduction of collisions.
- Rule-of-thumb saturation limit is: 20% of packets have to be bridged.
- Isolation of troubles.
- Media change is possible.
- Weak security features.
- Buffering is usually supported.

Figure 2-32 shows the level of MAC bridges in relation to the standards.

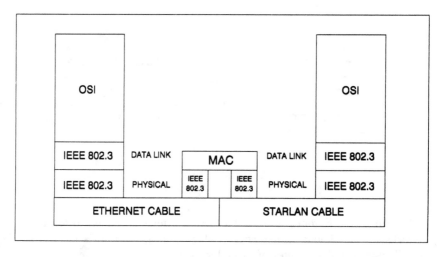

Fig. 2-32. MAC-level bridge.

Bridges   Bridges are devices for offering connectivity at layer 2 between various access protocols and media. The attributes of bridges are:

- Connection between various access protocols.
- Connection at layer 2.
- Packet deassembly and reassembly.
- No path optimization.
- Weak security features.
- Significant "software" work for bridging Ethernet and Token Ring (TABLE 2-7).
- Routing bridges may be the future solution, with router functions using the spanning tree algorithm.

Table 2-7. Software Work Required
to Connect Ethernet and Token Ring

	CSMA/CD		Token Ring	
CSMA/CD	− PAD		− PRE	+ SD
	− FCS		− SD	+ AC
			− LEN	+ FC
			− FCS	+ FCS
		+ PAD		+ ED
		+ FCS		+ FS
Token Ring	− SD		− FS	
	− AC	+ PRE		
	− FC	+ SD		
	− ED	+ LEN		
	− FS	+ PAD		
		+ FCS		− FS

Figure 2-33 shows the scope of bridges in relation to the standards.

There are two principal alternatives for bringing LAN segments in terms of selecting the communication path. In source routing, the originating device locates the target device by sending out broadcast messages. The originator first sends a broadcast message around its own ring. If the target is on the ring, it responds to the message, a copy of which reaches every ring in the bridged token ring network. The target sends back a message containing routing information. If no messages are returned, the target is not on the network.

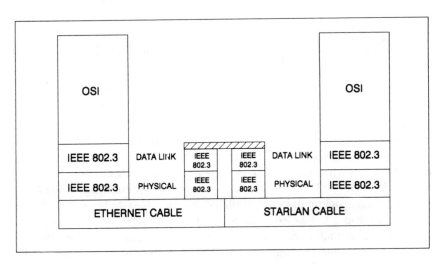

Fig. 2-33. Bridge structure.

There are two types of source-routing broadcast messages: all routes, and single routes. Figure 2-34 illustrates this process. An all-routes broadcast message takes every possible route to reach its target. In a mesh network, the target address receives several copies of the broadcast message, and it responds to each one. But the message will not be sent to the same ring twice. Thus, looping may be avoided. Single-route broadcast messages use a spanning-tree structure to guarantee that only one copy of the originated message may receive the target. In any case, the originating station may receive multiple copies of the response. On the basis of this information, the originator decides which route to choose; IBM products select the route of the first returned message. The number of source-routing messages is small, but even that number can significantly affect remote bridges. With source routing, the routing tables are maintained in the user workstation, offloading some of the bridges.

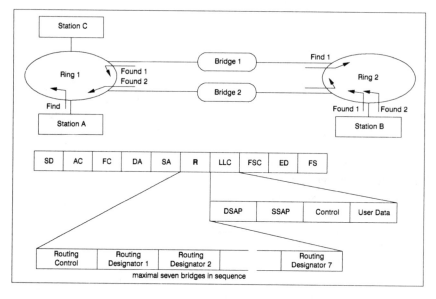

Fig. 2-34. Source-routing bridges.

Spanning-tree bridges offer a loopless network topology with only one single logical path between the originator and target. In most cases, this topology works fine. But when there's link or node congestion, performance might be severely impacted. The use of alternate routes could prevent this when alternate routes and backup links are available, but they have to be activated after the primary route has failed. The available bandwidth is usually not used effectively. The limitations are particularly severe when WANs are used to connect LAN segments using bridges. Manufacturers of bridges with spanning-tree algorithms try nevertheless to improve performance by offering three special functions:

- Parallel line support that allows the use of multiple wide-area links.
- Load-balancing algorithms that distribute the load between the physical links.
- Preserve-packet-sequence service that reassembles the packet at the receiver into the original sequence, which might have been lost due to parallel transmission.

It's very likely that future bridges will support a combination of both techniques. More thoughts from the designers' perspective will be addressed in chapter 6.

Routers   Routers are devices for offering connectivity at layer 3 for networks with the same protocol at layer 3 and higher. The attributes of routers are:

- Connectivity for networks that operate the same protocol at layer 3 and higher.
- Determining the optimal path for routing.
- Addressing conversion into Internet.
- Applicability for a wide variety of LANs, MANs, and WANs.
- Use of a unique network protocol that's absolutely necessary.
- Traffic management services such as routing, flow control, message fragmentation, and error-checking.
- Brouters (bridges and routers in the same hardware) supporting multiple protocols.

Figure 2-35 shows the place of routers or bridges in the connection reference model. Due to the common debates on whether routers or bridges are the right choice for certain internetworking environments, some of the manufacturers offer both on the same hardware platform, which then supports multiple protocols.

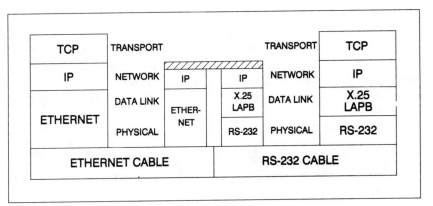

Fig. 2-35. Router structure.

Gateways   Gateways are devices offering connectivity for completely different networks and architectures. Their most significant attributes are:

- Connectivity between completely different networks.
- Support for practically all seven layers.
- Considerable development expense.
- Questionable life cycle.
- Possibility that performance could become a problem.
- In certain cases, the use of gateways is unavoidable.

Figure 2-36 displays communicating partners and the gateways between them. This figure emphasizes that gateways offer conversion services to all communication layers.

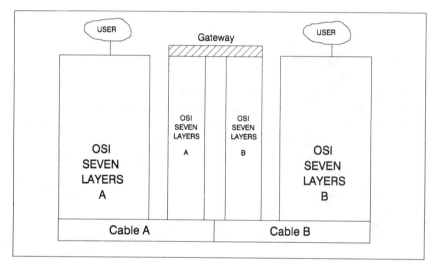

Fig. 2-36. Gateway structure.

There are two principal conclusions concerning interconnecting devices: with an increase in the intelligence level of the interconnecting devices, the expected design, development, and maintenance costs increase, and the expected processing time required in the interconnecting components increases.

The following is the impact of interconnecting devices on LAN management:

- Spanning-tree or source-routing algorithms used for locating the communicating partners.
- Choosing the right interconnecting devices for the LAN segments.
- Applicability of interconnecting devices for managing LANs.

- Support of proprietary, *de facto*, or open network management protocols.
- Peer-to-peer network management relationships to other managed objects, such as wiring concentrators.
- The feasibility of using interconnecting devices with WAN techniques, such as frame relay, SMDS, and Broadband ISDN.

Summary

This section has walked through the most important managed objects in the world of standalone and interconnected local area networks. In addition to giving an overview of how those components operate, emphasis has also been placed on what their impact is on LAN management. Details of their impact are discussed further in chapter 3, covering LAN management functions, and chapter 5, discussing LAN management instruments. RISC technology may dramatically change the role of interconnecting components in handling large applications, merging traffic onto high-speed pipes, and concentrating network management.

3

LAN management functions

Successful LAN management stems in part from the ability to manage several functions, each of which is supported by a large number of processes and procedures. These functions are categorized according to definitions of standard bodies. When considering broad definitions, those for LAN management have many similarities with the definitions that apply to managing wide area networks. LAN management functions are categorized as follows (also see TABLE 3-1).

Configuration management is a set of midrange and long-range activities for: controlling physical, electrical, logical, and spare-part equipment inventories; maintaining vendor files and trouble tickets; managing cables and wiring; supporting provisioning and order processing; tracking, authorizing, scheduling, and implementing changes; and distributing software. Directory service and help for generating different network configurations are also provided.

Fault management is the collection of activities required to dynamically maintain network service levels. These activities ensure high availability by quickly recognizing problems and performance degradation, and by initiating controlling functions when necessary; these controlling functions may include diagnosis, repair, testing, recovery, workaround, and backup. Log control and information distribution techniques are supported as well.

Performance management involves an ongoing evaluation of the LAN; the purposes of performance management are to verify that service levels are maintained, to identify actual and potential bottlenecks, and to establish and report on trends for management decision making and planning. Building and maintaining a LAN's performance database, and automation procedures for LAN fault management are also included.

Security management is a set of functions whose purpose is to ensure a LAN's ongoing protection by analyzing risks, minimizing risks, implementing

Table 3-1. LAN
Management Functions

Configuration management
Fault management
Performance management
Security management
Accounting management
User administration

a LAN security plan, and subsequently monitoring success of the strategy. Special functions include the surveillance of security indicators, partitioning, password administration, and warning or alarm messages for violations.

Accounting management is the process of collecting, interpreting, processing, and reporting cost-oriented and charge-oriented information on LAN resource usage. In particular, processing of raw accounting data, bill verification, and chargeback procedures are included for data, and occasionally for voice.

LAN design and planning involve the process of determining the optimal network, based on data for network performance, traffic flow, resource use, networking requirements, technological trade-offs, and estimated growth of present and future applications. LAN design and planning are addressed separately in chapter 6.

User administration, including help-desk responsibilities, seems to be viewed as a separate entity by many users. It's actually part of or at least very close to LAN fault management. However, for the sake of better visibility, user administration will be separately addressed toward the end of the chapter.

The principal goals of this chapter are to:

- Address LAN management functions.
- Assess the present status of implementation.
- Define information demand.
- Determine the appropriate instruments for each function.
- Recommend how instruments should be allocated to functions.
- Define appropriate human-resource profiles for supporting LAN management functions.

LAN configuration management

Figure 3-1 shows the relevant configuration management functions as they relate to a simplified topology of interconnected LANs. LAN configuration management is the focal point of all other LAN management functions, providing actual configuration details and receiving change requests. Figure 3-2 illustrates how information is exchanged with the other functions.

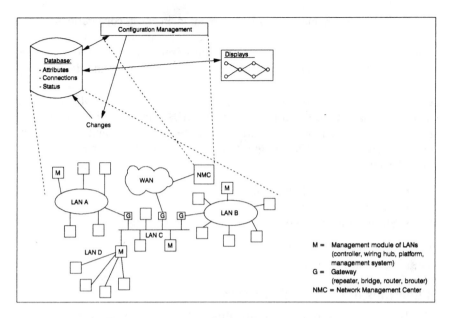

Fig. 3-1. Configuration management functions.

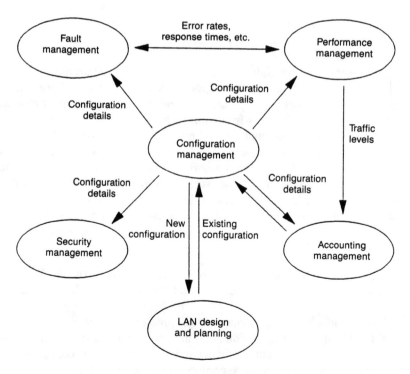

Fig. 3-2. Central role of configuration management.

Configuration management is fragmented in most corporations at this time. There are different files or databases that maintain attributes of object groups such as modems, applications, multiplexers, hubs, repeaters, bridges, routers, switches, servers, workstations, and so on. The standards may help, assuming they don't give contradictory recommendations. The closest help is expected from SMI (Structured Management Information) and MIB (Management Information Base). In particular, the MIB I and MIB II recommendations are gaining support as SNMP penetrates the LAN fault management area. For successful LAN configuration management, three information areas are relevant:

- Attributes of each managed object.
- Up-to-date connectivity data.
- Status of managed objects.

In the following sections, the main functional areas of LAN configuration management are outlined in some depth.

Functions of LAN configuration management

Inventory control and topology service   Inventory and topology service are concerned with maintaining an accurate inventory of hardware, software, and circuits as well as with the ability to change that inventory in a smooth and reliable manner in response to changing service requirements. Configuration management affects LAN designs, performance issues, and even LAN security.

At present, inventory information is segmented, stored usually in flat files, and not organized by WANs, MANs, or LANs. Furthermore, there's no real separation between network management and systems management of LANs. In most cases, the guidelines from standards organizations in terms of managed objects and their attributes could not be taken into consideration.

One of the most basic issues for the LAN administrator is maintaining system configuration maps. *System configuration* is the list of system parameters showing who has access to given network software and given databases. While most LAN operating system software gives the administrator the ability to add, delete, and modify system configuration parameters, it typically provides little functionality in monitoring system configuration. The usual content of the inventory database may include:

- Details of addressable devices of any type on the network. A name is assigned to each device address, and the record includes the type and location of the device, a contact and phone number at the device location, and a history of device service, problems, and repair.
- Details of the configuration of all interconnection devices. The records in the database are automatically updated whenever the configuration is updated. Updates could be done centrally or locally.

- Information about the filtering database in each interconnecting device, such as bridges and routers. If the centrally located network management system is used for the general update, the results may be automatically copied into the configuration files of the interconnecting devices.
- Access control information, defining the destinations to which certain devices can transfer data, is maintained in the configuration database, as well. The network management product may be used to update access group memberships, after which the information is automatically copied to all interconnecting devices.
- Status of all essential managed objects. Status includes: in-service, out-of-service, back-to-service, and undefined.
- Records of the statistics for network and interconnecting devices performance are extracted periodically from the managed objects.
- A record of events is reported to the network management product. The event log can contain a certain number of events, providing an audit trail in case of network problems.
- All trouble tickets, including their subjects, symptoms, originator, and contents.

The recommendations from various standards bodies detail three areas:

1. Attributes of objects with static information including names, addresses, parameters settings, location, electric parameters, and so on. TABLE 3-2 shows an example as recommended by the Network Management Forum.

   At the most detailed level, protocol alternatives are addressed by the OSI layers, individually. Network-layer protocol options may include the following characteristics: complete source routing, partial source routing, record of route, quality of service, padding, segmentation, lifetime, aging, PDU size, congestion notification.
2. Connectivity data indicating the topology; sometimes alternate routes are included as well. These data are extremely important for internetworked LANs using either spanning-tree or source-routing algorithms. Connection parameters are most frequently maintained at the network layer. These connection parameters may include: inactivity timer, retransmission timer, persistence timer, window timer, bound-on-reference timer, time to reassign after failure, time to wait for reassignment, supervisory timer for connection establishment, supervisory timer for connection release, window size, maximum number of retransmission, checksum option setting, etc. The items to be included depend on the specifics of the installation.
3. Dynamic indicators that represent the status and help identify problems; these indicators are the bridges to fault management. Usually, status, service-level, use, and throughput indicators are included.

Table 3-2. Attributes of Objects

Class Name: Equipment

Class Definition: A physical unit. Equipment may be nested within equipment, thereby creating a parent/child relationship. A facility is supported by equipment at each end. Equipment may also connect or terminate circuits.

Equipment includes telecommunication systems that provide a service to an end user, the management systems that are used to manage such systems, and the end-user hosts and terminals. Equipment also includes physical units of functionality within these systems (e.g., CPU).

Data Elements:
Equipment type
Equipment ID
Equipment alias
Equipment status
Equipment release
Parent equipment ID
Child equipment IDs
Location ID
Network IDs
Customer IDs
Provider IDs
Service IDs
Vendor IDs
EMS IDs (= equipment IDs)
Contact IDs
Effective time

Class Name: Facility

Class Definition: A physical connection between equipment in two different equipments without any intervening equipment. A facility is geographically distributed functionality and excludes the equipment within the associated equipments. The function of a facility is to support the transport of circuits (0 or more).

Data Elements:
Facility type
Facility ID
Facility alias
Facility status
Endpoints (= 1 or if known, 2 Equipment IDs)
Network IDs
Vendor ID
Effective time
EMS IDs
Contact IDs

Class Name: Circuit

Class Definition: A logical point-to-point connection between two end equipments that traverses one or more facilities and possibly one or more intermediate pieces of equipment. Circuits may be simple or complex. A simple circuit is supported by two end pieces of equipment and an interconnecting facility. A complex circuit is supported as well by intermediate equipments and additional facilities. In general, a complex circuit consists of an ordered sequence of (1) less complex circuits of the same bandwidth and (2) associated cross-connects within any intermediate equipments.

A parent/child relationship may also exist between circuits in that a circuit may share the bandwidth of another circuit.

Data Elements:
Circuit type
Circuit ID
Circuit status

Table 3-2. Continued

Circuit alias
Circuit bandwidth
Endpoints (= 2 Equipment IDs)
Facility IDs (1 or more)
Parent circuit ID
Child circuit IDs
Component circuit IDs (for complex circuits)
Cross-connect IDs (for complex circuits)
Circuit group ID
Network ID
Customer ID
Provider ID
Service IDs
Effective time
EMS IDs
Contact IDs

The Management Information Base (MIB) of SNMP has received a lot of attention recently. MIB conforms to SMI for TCP/IP-based internets. While the SMI is equivalent for both SNMP and OSI environments, the actual objects defined in the MIB are different. In fact, the internet SMI and the MIB are completely independent of any specific network management protocol, including SNMP.

The current SNMP MIB is divided into four areas: system attributes (MIB I and II), private attributes (proprietary vendor extensions), experimental attributes (tested objects), and directory attributes (future use).

MIB I includes eight functional groups for approximately 160 managed objects: system, interfaces, address translation, Internet protocol, Internet control-message protocol, transmission-control protocol, user-diagram protocol, exterior-gateway protocol. MIB II adds two more functional groups of transmission media and SNMP statistics.

The MIB is a virtual store of information contained within a managed device—also known as the SNMP agent. This information base is made up of objects consisting of name, syntax, and encoding information. The name is called the Object Identifier and is unique for each object. Syntax is the means by which a value, such as the number of packets sent, is displayed. Syntax types include counter, gauge, object string, network address, and integer. MIB II specifies a new type of object string called a display string, which allows a string of information to be displayed to an operator without requiring the management system to execute the string. The encoding mechanism converts machine code into English, allowing a programmer or network administrator to interpret information that the network management station is collecting. The MIB adheres to the American National Standards Institute's ASN.1 Basic Encoding Rules. The encoding specifies whether an object is designated read only, read write, write only, or not accessible. In addition, status information specifies whether an object is mandatory, optional, obsolete, or decremented.

The SNMP group of MIB II contains new object identifiers that provide statistical information about network performance to the network administrator. The objects allow the NMS (network management station) to track the amount of management traffic being responded to by a device. Parameters such as the number of SNMP packets into and out of a device, the number of packets with bad community names, number of packets that didn't conform to ASN.1 encoding specification, and the total number of requests for information are provided by the SNMP group. Having this type of information on hand is becoming increasingly important as the size and complexity of networks increase exponentially.

MIB II helps find the common denominator between SNMP agents of different companies. At least the "system" branch of MIB has to be the same. Vendors augment their MIBs with specific attributes. In this case, there are two important comments: the SNMP manager has to take advantage of these extensions, and vendors have to talk to each other and try to agree on additional standards for the "private" areas. In any case, the configuration data builds the basis for documentation systems. Figure 3-3 shows a simple configuration display on the basis of SNMP MIB, as applied by SNMP Research using the SET command.

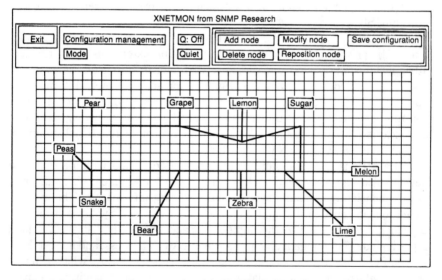

Fig. 3-3. Configuration example with SNMP-MIB using the SET command.

Continuous monitoring in remote LAN segments requires a large number of indicators that are not included in the MIB I and II recommendations. RMON MIB provides the missing gap for this support by enabling monitored and analyzer data to be sent to the SNMP management station.

RMON MIB defines the next generation of network monitoring with more comprehensive network fault diagnosis, planning, and performance tuning features than any current monitoring solution. The RMON MIB is organized into nine groups including segment statistics, history, alarms, hosts, hosts top N, traffic matrix, filters, packet capture, and events. Each agent need only implement any one group to conform with the standard. Thus, customers of RMON MIB agents need to carefully determine the features they desire and seek to verify the existence of those features in actual products. Leading manufacturers of LAN monitors, analyzers, and test equipment are expected to support the new standard.

WizardWare from the Tivoli company allows the user to accurately model the distributed computing and networking environment, namely the managed objects, the operations they support, and the relationships between the resources. WizardWare employs a specific object-oriented model that allows the user to easily and dynamically define various aspects (managed objects and operations) of the distributed computing and networking environment. The product provides a consistent environment that exploits the object-oriented model to transform a highly heterogeneous problem into a homogeneous solution. WizardWare is outstanding in its ability to add Unix users to the distributed computing environment, to reassign Unix mailboxes, to build user domains by pointing and clicking on icons, to drag resources, and to dynamically modify the attributes of a user or a managed object. In particular, inventory control and change management are well supported by this solution.

More examples of documentation alternatives will be given in the section on cable management.

Change management   Changes can't be avoided in present local area networks. Well organized change management procedures guarantee knowledge of the actual status of the configuration database. Thus, long procedures within fault management processes may be completely avoided.

It's recommended that you use a very formal procedure. Part of this procedure is meeting the change coordinator's demand for information. For scheduling and evaluating changes, the following information is needed by network configuration management (Terplan 1991):

1. Change coordinator segment.
   - Identification of the change.
   - Change number.
   - Date of request.
2. Requester segment.
   - Name and affiliation.
   - Location.
   - Change description.
   - Network components involved, by inventory identification.
   - Network components affected by change.
     ~ Minor impacts—change nondisruptive.
     ~ Regular impacts—change may be disruptive.
     ~ Major impacts—change disruptive.

- Due date.
- Priority.
- Reason for change.
- Personnel involved in executing the change.
- Fallback procedure if change fails.

3. Approval segment.
   - Date of approval.
   - Signature.
4. Evaluation segment.
   - Result of change.
   - Downtime due to change.
   - Date of actual implementation.
   - Cancellation or postponement.

Usually, this information is provided and updated by using inventory control products. After evaluating the information provided, approval is issued, unless objections are stated. The approval contains the accurate schedule and responsibilities (e.g., installation or software group). More frequently, single changes may invoke a chain of additional change requests for related LAN components. After execution, the documentation should still be completed, including updates in the inventory and vendor files, or in the configuration database.

Naming and addressing   Naming and addressing are not always considered part of configuration management. Most frequently, they're considered granted by the services of a LAN's operating systems. This is actually true, because LAN operating systems vendors provide utilities for users and administrators. Users usually identify their service needs by names that are translated by the NOS into addresses. This translation is becoming increasingly complex and complicated for interconnected LANs. Vendors are expected to "hide" the internal processes from LAN users. Leading vendors, such as Novell, Banyan, Microsoft, IBM, and 3COM, are currently addressing the need for improvement.

The principal features of advanced name services are:

- Location transparency.
- No need to know the server's name to log in.
- Centralized log in helps access.
- No need for separate log ins to multiple servers.
- Message exchanges at the symbolic level.
- No need to update servers separately to add a user to the network.
- Utilities provide reports on network configuration across server boundaries.
- No need to know what server a resource is on to access it.

TABLE 3-3 (Robertson 1990) offers a comparison between the name services from Novell, Microsoft and Banyan. In addition to these solutions, it's worth mentioning IBM's Single System Image and 3COM's 3+Open Directory. Both companies state their intentions to offer X.500-based directory services in the future.

Table 3-3. Comparison of Naming and Addressing Services

| | Operating system | | |
Features	Novell NNS	Microsoft LAN Manager	Banyan StreetTalk
Name structures	User name *Domain	User name *Domain	Item group *Organization
Auto-replication per server			
• User name	Yes	Yes	No (3)
• Other name levels	Not available	Not available	Group*Org
• Permissions, rights	No	No	No
• Login scripts, profiles	Yes	Yes, but not automatic	No
Reliability orientation			
• Level of duplication	High (1)	High (1)	Low (2)
• Consistency of data	Medium	Medium	High
• Bandwidth, impact of replication	Medium	Medium	Very low
• Bandwidth, impact of search	Low	Low	Medium (Low) (3)

(1) User names located on many servers

(2) User names located on only one server

(3) StreetTalk's Directory Assistance feature in VINES 4.0 allows large-scale searches of user name information on designated replication centers, and does not require querying each server individually.

From a LAN management point of view, it's important to:

- Offer transparency.
- Provide asset management capabilities.
- Access the database where names and addresses are uniformly identified.
- Help network administrators in giving unique names and addresses to components.
- Integrate conversion capabilities into LAN-internetworking devices.
- Learn about the abilities of bridges, brouters, routers, and gateways to interpret names and addresses.

TCP/IP is emerging as the protocol stack of choice for interconnecting

LANs. In such internetworks, the following parameters are used for supporting configuration management:

- IP address that can be hard coded or obtained via one of the three protocols (Huntington-Lee 1991):
    a. BOOTP.
    b. Reverse Address Resolution Protocol (RARP).
    c. Dynamic RARP (DRARP).
- Entry gateway addresses that are usually hard coded.
- Name server location that's usually hard coded.
- Host or processor name that's hard coded or obtained by using a boot procedure; configuration data can be downloaded via BOOTP.

Some of the SNMP-based products can graphically depict the actual LAN configuration. This feature is very helpful for improving integrity between configuration and fault management. In most cases, however, the SNMP manager station can't provide the desired support for inventory and change management.

Cable management   During the last few years, a number of computerized cable management (CMS) products have become available to better manage equipment. Because of overcrowded conduits, lack of standard cabling for data processing equipment, and excessive changes, customers have started to request the routine installation of standard media. Standard media are expected to support both voice and data communications. The use of standard media has to be combined with a powerful documentation and reporting system. Basically, there are three choices for improving the quality of cable management: use a product that fits into the environment without any customization needs, abandon the company's own strategy and outsource cable management to vendors, or design, develop, and implement a system.

When evaluating CMS systems, there are several features that are essential. The ability to track cables and cable pairs end-to-end is the most basic capability of a good CMS. The system should be able to display cable records from their originating PBX or computer ports through several levels of patching, cross-connect hardware, and finally to the end-user's desk. The system should explicitly display information, including individual cable numbers, the location of cable terminations on main and intermediate distribution frames, and cross-connect between lateral and riser cables. The system should also be able to relate this information to user and department names or room and telephone extension numbers.

This capability enables a system administrator to quickly identify available riser pairs, spare station cables, and available equipment ports. Moves, changes, and troubleshooting can be accomplished faster if this information is accurate.

It's also important that a CMS system have the capability to automatically generate information, such as on-screen cable trace, bill of quantity, cableway analysis, cable route, cable usage, cableway accommodation, cable numbers, terminations, and cross-connects. This feature is overlooked in most CMSs, which require the user to manually enter these data for each individual cable run. In a small installation, this is not a major data entry problem. But it's not practical for large organizations with a lot of move and change activity, or when purchasing a CMS in anticipation of managing a new installation.

If the CMS can generate detailed cable information automatically, it can be used to guide installers during the placement of new cables. With this feature, the user can actually begin to manage the cable plant as it's being built.

If purchasing a system to automate an existing plant, however, this feature will be of little use initially. The user will still probably have to go through the exercise of data entry. In the long run, however, it will save time and aggravation when installing new cables.

Scanning existing drawings would accelerate this process. During this process, paper-based documentation is converted into electronic form. Rather than manually digitalizing or recreating an entire drawing, scanners read the raster images into the system. The scanned drawing can be used as is, or parts can be changed, and new information added. Scanned images can be referenced in the nongraphic relational database, since attributes can be assigned to those images. Thus, scanned raster images can be converted into intelligent objects with database attributes. Using CAD capabilities, scanned raster images can be combined with vector images. In order to save storage, use standard output formats, including Run Length Code (RLC), Tagged Image File Format (TIFF) or CCITT recommendations for maximum compression. CADSCAN is a widely used solution for scanning cabling (Isicad 1991).

It's important that the format is compatible with other existing formats in the cable management area. Typically, these systems tie the user into a particular numbering or termination scheme, generally the way the telephone company did it in the past (Nuciforo 1989).

The chosen system should also be able to manage the attached equipment, as well as the cable plant itself. The system should enable the user to have telecom equipment (both in-use and spare), including active and available equipment ports, location and status of end-user equipment such as telephones, terminals, and modems, as well as pending equipment orders.

A CMS system should be able to generate customized management reports. Hard-copy reports should be available from the CMS, detailing particular aspects of the telecom system. These include cable placement schedules showing the location of individual cables, riser cross-connect reports showing pair availability; work orders for adds, moves, and changes, and other management reports. Most CMSs have some report-generating capability, since it's inherent in all database management packages.

Your CMS system should have the ability to manage a wide variety of media. This important CMS feature is too often overlooked during product evaluation. The user should be able to manage different types of media, including associated equipment, termination, and cross-connect hardware.

Almost all users have, and will continue to have, multiple types of media installed in their facilities. It would be counterproductive to buy one CMS for managing unshielded twisted pair and a separate system to manage the other media. The CMS chosen today must be flexible enough to support media that the user may install in the future.

The ability to manage the facility as well as the cable is an essential CMS system feature. The need for this capability is directly attributable to the market movement toward decentralized systems. The distance limitations of LANs and other distributed systems require: up-to-date records of telecommunication closet sizes and locations; the sizes, lengths, and quantity of conduits and cable ties between equipment rooms; and the available riser space.

Most computerized cable management systems don't adequately provide this information, and some vendors have ignored the requirement altogether. There are several vendors who have tried to address this issue by integrating computer-aided design packages with the CMS.

Cable management systems reside on a variety of hardware platforms. For the most part, these are standalone PCs; however, they may be networked so as to enable distribution of the database resources in a client/server environment. A typical standalone hardware configuration includes the following (Rothberg 1991):

- VGA graphics card with 640-by-350 resolution.
- 80386 or 80486 processor (or compatible).
- 2 Mbytes to 4 Mbytes of memory.
- Hard disk with approximately 5 Mbytes of RAM available for software.
- Mouse or pointing device.
- Printer.

Cable management software systems can manage a variety of wiring resources, including data, voice, LAN, and, in some cases, HVAC and control cables. Ideally, the software should perform the following functions (Rothberg 1991):

- Cable and path identification.
- Cable route presentation.
- Assignment of cable facilities and routes.
- Tracking conduit "fill" and usage.
- Identification of unused cable facilities.
- Equipment inventory for attached components.
- Feasibility check during planning.
- Proactive troubleshooting.
- Tracking service order activity.
- Maintenance of trouble report database.
- Mechanisms for management reporting and operation reporting.

Cable management systems use a variety of database resources. These relational database systems provide superior flexibility because they can use structured queries to construct different views of the information. In the case of a server-resident database in a multiuser environment, the system should also facilitate remote procedure calls (RPCs), minimizing the amount of data to be transmitted and the client workstation's processing requirements.

The database software is expected to work with the CAD portion. The LAN designer uses the CAD half to locate equipment and to establish cable routes. The facilities designer responsible for planning office space and infrastructure can use the graphics part to locate walls and furniture. Once the physical design is complete, the designer can work with the LAN administrator to locate workstations and servers, patch panels in racks, put file servers in closets, and map the cable paths between equipment. The LAN designer then uses the database half to connect the equipment in the design. After the design satisfies both parties, work orders are printed by the CMS.

The documentation of the principal layout helps both troubleshooters and LAN designers. (Figure 3-4 shows the physical layout of LANs in various

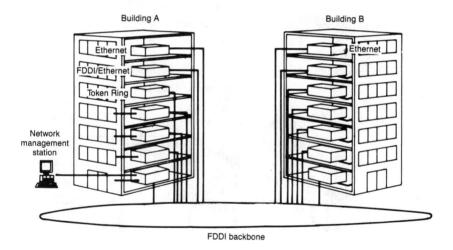

Fig. 3-4. Physical layout of LANs.

buildings. TABLE 3-4 documents a design cable schedule. Figure 3-5 details the wiring sequence of interconnected token rings. Figure 3-6 displays a sample for the wiring closet design of Starlan.)

The physical layout and port allocation of wires help to centralize the status updates via software techniques that are part of LAN management applications. There's a growing trend towards alliances between manufacturers of wiring hubs and other LAN components, such as NICs, bridges, and routers. Figure 3-7 shows an example, with a wiring hub in the middle of managed objects.

Table 3-4. Design Cable Schedule

Cable No.	Cable Type	Length	End	Gland/ Connector	Equipment Number	Equipment Description	Location Drawing No.
OGTX0001	50core	43	A	N	TTTMDF	Telephone—main distribution frame	North section layout M
			Z	N	OGTIDF	Telephone—intermediate distribution frame	North section layout M
Status markers	DTR			Route T910 T902 T901 0902 0901			
ORTX0001	50core	42	A	N	TTTMDF	Telephone—main distribution frame	North section layout M
			Z	N	ORTIDF	Telephone—intermediate distribution frame	North section layout M
Status markers	DTR			Route T910 T903 T904 0904 0903			

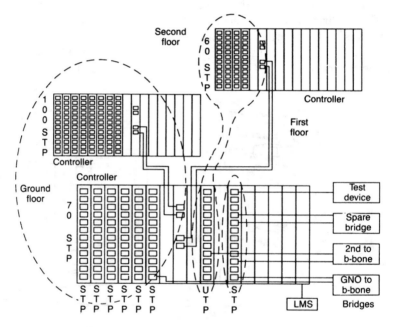

Fig. 3-5. Wiring of an interconnected token ring.

In order to facilitate easy and fast access to cabling documentation, it's recommended to convert textual and graphical data into hypertext and to use powerful storage devices (e.g., jukeboxes) for storing hypertext. It's expected that hypermedia will become an essential part of help-desk instrumentation.

Directory services It's very unlikely that integrated configuration databases will be supported soon. But, users still must administer their local area networks. As mentioned earlier, vendors are working on links between existing data files and databases using X.500 as standardized service.

This function is intended to provide a more or less temporary solution for accessing and updating LAN-configuration, management-related information

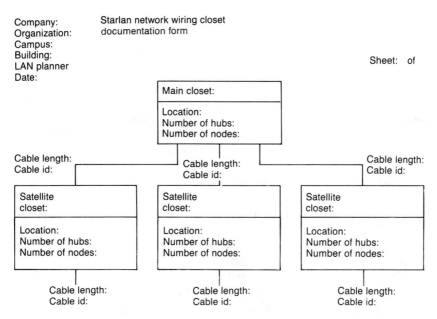

Fig. 3-6. Sample of a wiring closet design from Starlan.

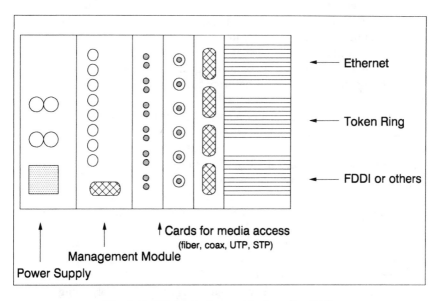

Fig. 3-7. Wiring hub example from SynOptics.

stored in various systems, databases, and files. These systems could be network elements or network element management systems that maintain data about specific objects they control and manage, or applications that run on a variety of processors and operating systems. Although applications don't control or manage network elements directly, they play an integral part in managing information about these elements.

The directory service is needed to maintain a centralized, logical view of the data stored in the attached network management systems. The data would actually physically reside in many of these different systems. Applications could then be written without regard to a specific database management system. Database calls would simply be made to the directory in a standard format. The directory would then forward the data request to the appropriate system for processing. Each remote system participating in the directory would have to translate the data request into the correct database call for its particular database management system and its schema.

Another illustration of a need for this type of architecture is with interfaces to other customer applications, such as inventory and change management. Many large customers have inventory systems that support the administration of the network elements comprising their corporate networks. There are more than 100 different inventory systems on the market that store data in a multitude of relational and proprietary database management systems. These inventory systems are usually mainframe based, since they must support upwards of 100 simultaneous users. The integrated network management system can't support this type of application, nor can customers be expected to recoup their investments in those systems if it did. They would, however, like the integrated network management system to have the ability to pass configuration information obtained from other network element management systems directly to their inventory systems in realtime. This way, configuration changes would only have to be made to one system accessing the directory, and the update could be propagated to all other systems requiring the data.

The directory service should manage updates to multiple systems. If an update requires records stored in several systems to be updated, some type of integrity locking must be performed on those records in each system. These locks should not be released until confirmation of a successful update has been returned from each system or some time limit threshold has been exceeded. If a successful acknowledgment is received from each system participating in the update, the locks should be released. Otherwise, the update should be aborted and backed out from each of the systems participating in the update.

The directory service is expected to incorporate a security scheme. It should be able to let customers define which terminals, user IDs, and applications can have access to different types of data. It should further define what type of access they can have. The directory service is probably going to implement the emerging OSI standards for directory services (X.500). Although these standards are not yet agreed upon, users should be aware of the progress in this area. OSI is currently working to see how the directory services attributes can be used to support distributed database access.

Typical instruments for supporting LAN configuration management

In order to facilitate the work of LAN administrators, several products may be considered for use. Generic groups of products include: databases, document managers, document/file organizers, configuration trailing tools, realtime user tracking products, front ends or platforms, audit trail utilities, and disk usage utilities.

Databases are used for relational or object-oriented storage of LAN configuration data. Usually, these products are well known and widely used for other purposes. Population of the database is the responsibility of the customer and/or of the vendor. These types of databases are more frequently associated with LAN managers than with LAN agents. Such databases will probably be increasingly considered, as MIB implementations proliferate. At the moment, most MIBs use flat files. Databases are expected to work with CAD software in order to provide powerful cable management capabilities.

Document managers help end users locate files and documents by the use of symbolic names. With document managers, users need to know only basic information to locate a file; users can call up a file by author, subject, project name, or creation date. Users can search any field to find a file anywhere in the network.

Several document managers also load the software that created the file, allowing the recipient user to work on the document. Other document managers can work with E-mail systems. Frequently, they're combined with drawing products by allowing mutual information exchange.

Document/file organizers are very useful when many people need to access a document. These systems also act as front ends, since they insulate users from the complexities of the directory structure.

Configuration trailing tools are inserted into a server or workstation, and automatically read the configuration of that unit, printing out an inventory of disk drives, I/O ports, graphics adapter boards, and software, including operating systems and applications.

The first step in collecting network information is to determine who is using the network and when. In instances when all users must log off or be logged off before initiating a backup, a realtime user tracking tool is useful.

Realtime user tracking tools provide value-added functions that go beyond the listing of active users generally available from the LAN network operating system. Some of these value-added features include graphical floor plans, identification beyond bridges and routers, and sorting capabilities.

Front ends are menu creation programs that make the network easier to use by isolating the user from operating system commands. Essentially, front ends allow users to initiate programs and manage files by selecting items from a menu. Some products enhance security management by adding greater password protection.

The best front-end products let the manager design menus from a centralized point and distribute them, rather than having to create menus at each workstation. These products may also include other features such as a screen-blanking utility, software meter, and selected user statistics.

Audit trail systems are a key component of security management, although the function can be considered part of accounting management. Audit trail systems provide information on user activity on the LAN. Additionally, these systems can assist in billing management by providing the data needed to charge back usage.

An audit trail system must provide streamlined, useful information. LAN managers may wish to audit only certain users, operations on files with certain extensions or in certain subdirectories, certain types of operations, or certain servers. All file and directory creations, deletions, and renames may need to be reported. A system error log report, listing all system error messages, may be advantageous in order to alert the LAN manager of potential problems.

Disk usage utilities are unsophisticated instruments that help to analyze the use profiles of the configuration database server. Such an analysis may help to decide whether to share or dedicate the server. In addition to use indicators, service-related metrics such as queuing time in front of resources may be reported.

TABLE 3-5 summarizes the typical instruments for configuration management.

Table 3-5. Typical Instruments of Configuration Management

Databases
Document managers
Document and file organizers
Configuration trailing tools
Realtime user tracking products
Front ends or platforms
Audit trail utilities

Staffing LAN configuration management

LAN administration is a clerical-type activity that requires people who have a combination of clerical and project control skills. The principal responsibilities of LAN administration include the following:

- Administers LAN configuration, including logical, electrical and physical attributes.
- Maintains LAN database.
- Maintains vendor data.
- Coordinates planning and executing changes.

- Administers names and addresses.
- Defines and supervises authorizations.
- Maintains trouble tickets and trouble files.
- Coordinates complex problem solving.
- Helps to establish powerful security policy.
- Organizes data export and import with central database.

LAN administrators interface with all other groups within LAN management. Outside contacts include users and vendors. Besides a general knowledge of LANs, specific knowledge of databases, file management, and data maintenance is required. Continuing education is also required. A person with a business administration degree may be appropriate for the job.

Fault management of local area networks

Figure 3-8 shows the relevant fault management functions related. Basically, four steps form the prerequisites of successful fault management. These are:

1. Understand the particular LANs used. The following information has to be gathered:
   - Topology.
   - Protocols.
   - Media.
   - Bandwidth.
   - Applications.
2. Establish a logical procedure for sectionalizing a problem. Problems can usually be determined by moving, replacing, and testing the cables, servers, and workstations.
3. Apply the proper tools for diagnosing problems that are not immediately obvious.
4. Educate users and troubleshooters on how to use procedures and instruments.

This chapter addresses only steps 2 through 4. It's assumed that users understand the particular LANs used.

Figure 3-9 shows the fault management process in flowchart form. As a result of trouble calls or monitored messages, events, and alarms, problems in network elements and facilities may be detected, recorded, and tagged. The dynamic trouble-ticketing process, using different agents for ticket opening, status review, consolidation, and ticket closing, is in charge of directing the steps of problem determination. Besides trivial responses on behalf of the help desk, temporary fixes are offered in the form of work-arounds and switchovers to spare elements. Problem determination on the second and third level may involve more sophisticated techniques and tools for identifying the nature

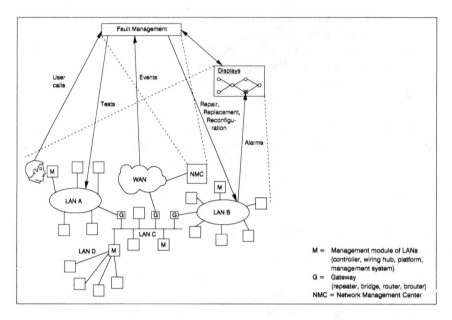

Fig. 3-8. Fault management functions.

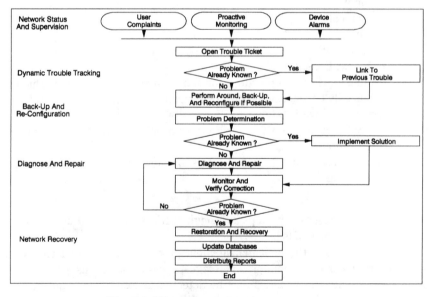

Fig. 3-9. The process of fault management.

of the problem and solving it by repair and/or replacement. Prior to restoration of a normal condition, end-to-end tests are recommended. The same or similar tests may be used for proactive fault management of LANs. In the following section, each main functional area of LAN activity is addressed.

Status supervision

On the electronics level, monitored status can appear in various forms (FIG. 3-10). Monitors and LAN analyzers are able to convert these signals into meaningful metrics. After conversion, status information may be forwarded to a

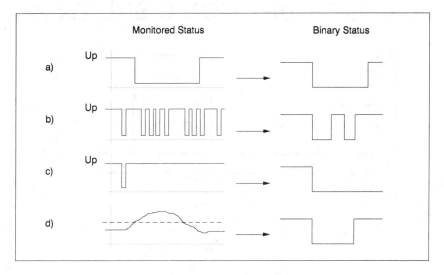

Fig. 3-10. Monitoring status.

central LAN management entity. This procedure can be illustrated by the dialogue between SNMP managers and agents. The manager polls the agent MIB, and reads the status information that's transmitted to the manager's status database. Network status consists of the vector of the element status, as shown in FIG. 3-11. Such vectors may construct the agent MIB of managed

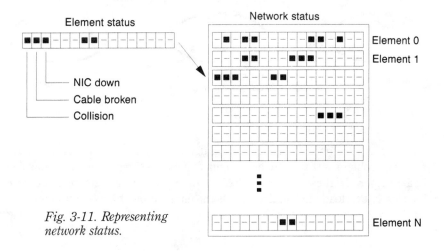

Fig. 3-11. Representing network status.

objects. The information in the vector is periodically polled by the management station. The network status may be actually shown using various display devices. Figure 3-12 shows an example using windowing.

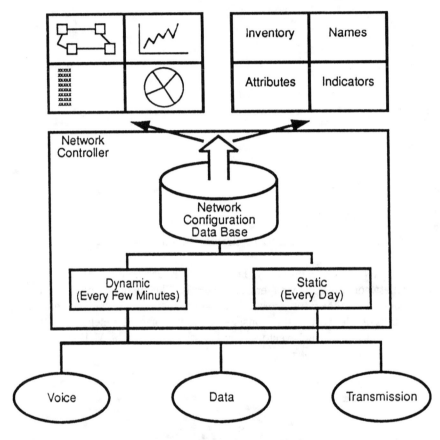

Fig. 3-12. Network status display.

Fault detection and alarms

Solicited and unsolicited events help in detecting abnormal operations. Usually, the problem is that there are too many messages generated in an unsolicited manner. If these are not filtered, LAN operating personnel become hopelessly overloaded. The first step is the elimination of irrelevant messages.

The second step is to put together related messages to define events. Finally, events will be assigned priorities and/or thresholds. Threshold violations and events of certain priorities will trigger alarms. Figure 3-13 illustrates this filtering process. In managing local area networks, logs are initiated by the event level, only; it's very unlikely that messages are logged in addition to events. It would mean a substantial increase in log volumes. One example of log entries is shown in TABLE 3-6. This is a good combination of readable text and trouble identification that can be used for further analysis and problem correlation.

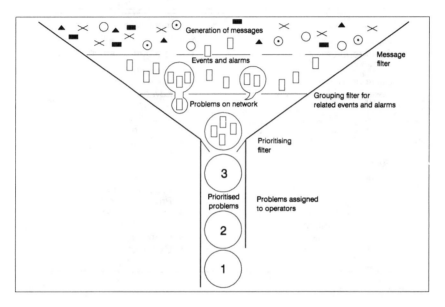

Fig. 3-13. Filtering procedure.

Table 3-6. Event-Log Entry

				Events
12:25:1989	15:37	27	08004e016a81	Local configuration update
12:25:1989	15:23	26	08004e1123f2	Filtering database full
12:25:1989	15:06	25	08004e016d13	Network manager console restarted
12:25:1989	14:43	24	08004e137f04	New root bridge
12:25:1989	14:41	23	08004e4585cb	Bridge port state change
12:25:1989	12:39	22	08004ea46d9e	Device restarted

The alarms generation process is accomplished in most LANs by the local LAN manager (e.g., the network management system at the level of the SNMP manager). Depending on the complexity and size of the LANs, event management can become a very extensive activity. To understand the way to properly arrange for event management, study TABLE 3-7. This table outlines the most important attributes of events.

Table 3-7. Event Management Overview

Determination of event detection	Event priority
Status change detection	Event effects
Event report generation	Event-type dependent information
Global filtering	• Alert time
Distribution filtering	• Received time
Event processor filtering	• Severity
	• Alarm type
• Logging	• Object class
• Sampling	• Object name
• Status posting	• Facility type
	• Equipment type
Event distribution	• Source
Event types	• Location
	• Problem type
• Configuration events	• Problem identification
• Fault events	• Text message
• Performance events	• Alarm identification
• Security events	• Correlation
• Accounting events	• Owner of alarm

Problem determination and isolation

The activities of problem determination and trouble isolation are triggered by alarms from network components. Network components can be any of the managed objects. In LANs, problem determination is usually organized according to five tiers.

Tier one problems are handled by the LAN help desk. Usually, these are of a nontechnical nature and can be resolved by troubleshooting over the phone. If it's simple a matter of educating end users, 80% to 85% of problems can be solved this way. The online trouble ticket database can be queried to determine whether the problem has been reported by any other location among the LAN segments, and whether there's a known fix. Problem diagnosis is rarely necessary.

Tier two problems are handled in part by LAN help desk operators and in part by LAN analysts. These problems comprise about 5% to 10% of all problems reported to the LAN help desk and are of too technical a nature to be resolved by the help desk. An example of such a problem is when some unknown problem causes the server to malfunction. The problem diagnosis effort can be considerable.

Tier three problems are handled by LAN analysts supporting LAN hardware and software. Problems administered by this group are generally of a critical and complex nature and may require the involvement of vendor specialists. Problems of this nature comprise only about 3% to 5% of all problems and are usually recognized immediately by users or are referred on by LAN help desk. Problem diagnosis requires a considerable human resource effort and complex instrumentation.

Tier four problems are handled by LAN application specialists. If the symptoms indicate that application-related problems are the probable source, trouble tickets are dispatched to these persons. Such problems account for 1% to 3% of all problems recorded. Problem diagnosis usually requires a considerable human resource effort and a lot of time.

Certain tier five problems can only be handled by vendors. When the diagnosis points in this direction, trouble records are dispatched to vendors. Electronic data exchange is a viable technique for this purpose. The problem diagnosis effort is considerable, but there's generally a lesser need for human resources. This tier accounts for between 3% and 5% of all problems.

In particular, tiers three and four require very sophisticated troubleshooting and problem isolation procedures. TABLE 3-8 shows the logical troubleshooting sequence for CSMA/CD networks. Development of the logical sequence is based on the principle of the progressive search, starting with the most likely error causes (FIG. 3-14) (Datapro NM50 1989).

The elements of TABLE 3-8A through 3-8D include isolation checklists for network, node, software, hardware, and hidden-component failures. Also, individual checklists may be of great help in isolating problems. TABLE 3-9 shows a generic checklist for Token Ring LANs.

In both cases (TABLES 3-8 and 3-9), a basic level of fault management instrumentation is assumed. It's extremely important to isolate the problem as quickly as possible, and, as soon as possible, get beyond the symptoms to the diagnosis and repair stages. Decision tables and flowcharts may contribute to rapid problem isolation. Following analysis of initial symptoms, specific flowcharts may be involved, as shown in FIG. 3-15 with an entry menu. Even this high-level entry requires the skills and experience of tier 1 and tier 2 problem determination staff. More specific flowcharts address:

- Operational problems (FIG. 3-16).
- Backbone problems (FIG. 3-17).
- Interconnecting device problems (FIG. 3-18).
- Workstation problems (FIG. 3-19).

Table 3-8. Problem Isolation for CSMA/CD Networks

Network Hardware Problems

If network hardware has failed, check that:

1. The network software is correct.
2. The network print and file servers are online.
3. The network is not overloaded with traffic.
4. Terminators are in place.
5. End connectors are correctly installed.
6. Barrel connectors are tightly connecting.
7. No coaxial sections are broken.
8. There are no cable breaks, cuts, abrasions.
9. The "state" of Ethernet is not jammed.
10. The gateways and repeaters are functioning.
11. Fan-out units are not jammed.
12. Individual network segments function.
13. Repeated segments are functioning.
14. Gateway segments are functioning.
15. Individual network cable sections are operational.
16. Transceiver tap components are functioning.
17. Transceivers are not jabbering/chattering.
18. Transceiver electronics are operational.
19. There are no software node incompatibilities.
20. Ethernet versions/variations match.
21. There is no outside electrical or radio frequency interference.

If all checks succeed, then you have a hidden component failure.

Network Software Problems

If network software has failed, check that:

1. The network software is correct.
2. The network is not overloaded with traffic.
3. The "state" of Ethernet is not jammed.
4. Each software node is compatible.
5. Ethernet versions/variations match.
6. The network software is performing tasks.
7. The operating network software is not corrupted.
8. The software is compatible with physical devices.

If all checks succeed, then, you have a network hardware failure or a hidden component failure.

Hardware or Software Problems

First, isolate the location:

1. Apply binary search method or apply sequential search method.
2. Check for failed node/nonoperation.
3. Check the software indicators.
4. Apply the multimeter.
5. Apply the transceiver tester.
6. Attach the time domain reflectometer.
7. Gather statistics and diagnose with the protocol analyzer.

Table 3-8. Continued

On location:

1. Check to confirm that components are plugged in.
2. Jiggle components in case of short circuit.
3. Check for electrical shorts/breaks.
4. Replace failed components or interchange suspect components.

Software Problems

First, isolate the location:

1. Gather statistics and diagnose with the protocol analyzer.
2. Analyze the network software.
3. Locate failed node/nonoperation.
4. Check the software indicators.
5. Root out nonfunctioning nodes.

On location:

1. Reboot system.
2. Restart software.
3. Replace software.
4. Debug/fix software.
5. Power cycle individual hardware components.

Node Problems

If a node has failed, check that:

1. The workstation or node unit is plugged in.
2. The workstation has electrical power.
3. The workstation is functioning.
4. The workstation sees Ethernet and TCP/IP.
5. The transceiver drop cable connections are secure.
6. The transceiver drop cable is correct.
7. The transceiver electronics function.
8. The transceiver tap installation is to specification.
9. The Ethernet controller functions.
10. The Ethernet address is correct.
11. The Internet address is correct.
12. All other nodes are working.
13. Some other nodes are working.
14. The Ethernet versions/variations match.

If all checks succeed, then you have a network software failure, a network hardware failure, or a hidden component failure.

Diagnostics, backup, repair, and recovery

As a result of efforts made during the previous phase, LAN troubleshooters at least know where to go to gather more detailed information on the nature of the problem. Statistics show that many problems are encountered with cabling. In particular, cards and wiring must be checked with care.

Cards Network interface cards, cables, and other low-level hardware all have an impact on the LAN's operation, performance, speed, and throughput.

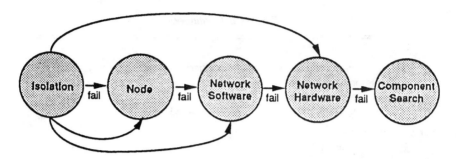

Fig. 3-14. The logical LAN troubleshooting sequence.

Table 3-9. Problem Isolation Checklist for Token Ring

1. Perform network interface card board diagnostics by using the diagnostics disk.
2. Assess impacts and conflicts with other boards. The easiest way is to insert the cards one by one, starting with the network interface card.
3. Inspect the network interface cards for mechanical failures.
4. Check whether the power supply follows power and fuse standards.
5. Check the wiring hubs by following the procedures recommended by the manufacturers.
6. If both the network interface card and cable pass the test, but the trouble still exists, use other wiring hub ports and retest.
7. Verify that the station inserts in the ring properly by observing indicators provided by the wiring hub manufacturers.
8. Replace cables if necessary.
9. Change media if necessary.
10. Verify that no shorts are between pins of wiring hubs and connectors.
11. Validate the names and addresses using diagnostic programs, network management software, or LAN analyzers.
12. Try to control most of the above from the network management service station—LAN network manager from IBM—or by other products.

Fault isolation process

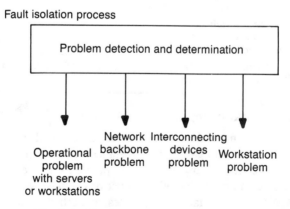

Fig. 3-15. Problem isolation entry menu.

Entry point: Operational difficulty with servers or workstations

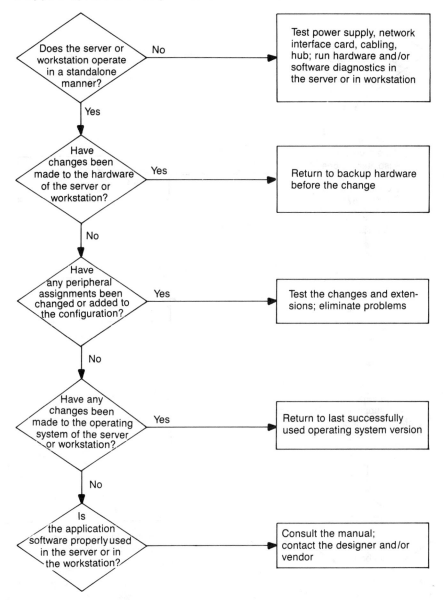

Fig. 3-16. Operational problem with servers or workstations flowchart.

If interface cards and cables are working properly, you can't expect speeds greater than the rated throughput. If an interface card is not working properly or a cable is not correctly terminated, errors may occur. In this case, the LAN will run significantly slower due to retransmissions of mutilated and lost packets. A defective card can significantly slow down a network.

Entry point: Backbone problem

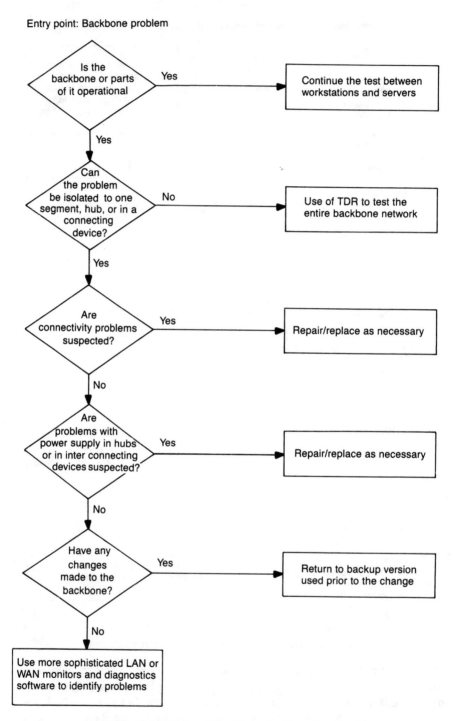

Fig. 3-17. Network backbone problem flowchart.

Entry point: Interconnecting devices problem

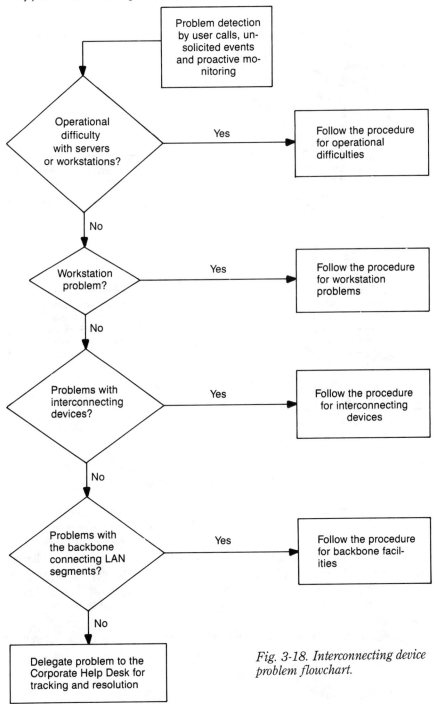

Fig. 3-18. Interconnecting device problem flowchart.

Entry point: Workstation problem

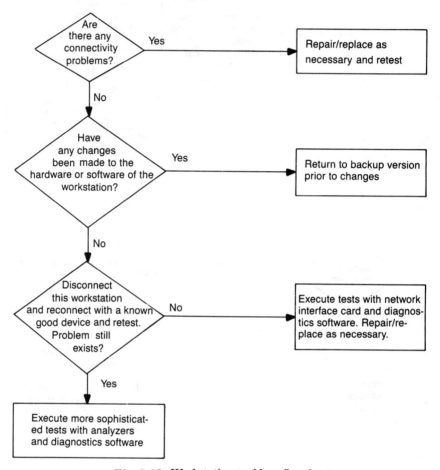

Fig. 3-19. Workstation problem flowchart.

Wiring A network manager can perform continuity, loopback, and reflectometry tests to diagnose cabling problems. These tests help ensure that the cable system is working correctly. The most common problem with LAN cabling is broken cable or improper termination. Most connectors don't handle movement well and, if left lying on the floor, they may be stepped on and broken. A regular inspection of the cable ends and connectors will help identify defective termination. There's a wide range of tools available for diagnosing cable problems.

For identifying problems, the following instruments may be considered for use:

- Ohmmeters.
- Outlet testers for power supply.

- Coax connectors, T-connectors, and terminators.
- Oscilloscope.
- TDR (time domain reflectometer).

Special transmission problems, such as crosstalk and noise, must not be ignored, either.

Crosstalk   Crosstalk is caused by the inductive or magnetic field coupling from one line into another line. It's most pronounced in cables having bidirectional transmission in the same sheath, such as twisted pair.

Noise   Noise is defined as any unwanted signal that enters the transmission line from another source and impairs communication signals. There are two classes of noise:

- Radio frequency interference.
- Electromagnetic interference.

Fiber-optic-based LANs require different equipment. While they provide significant advantages over conventional LANs, the fiber LAN's design necessitates more sophisticated test equipment. Fiber LAN diagnostic tools must provide comprehensive design verification, including the capability to precisely determine bandwidth, sensitivity, and linearity. These measurements can only be performed with fiber-optic test equipment that includes sophisticated parametric capabilities.

The market is experiencing an influx of test equipment that helps technicians diagnose and maintain a fiber-optic-based wiring system. These instruments vary in complexity from pocket-sized power measuring units to console-type testers. Only those instruments that are optical in nature can make performance measurements on the optical parts of any electro-optical system. Fortunately for electronics test engineers, the few optical instruments used outside research laboratories are relatively simple in design.

Special techniques may be applied in the diagnosis of server outages. In client-server environments, server failures may impact a significantly large number of clients, and this must be avoided. The techniques frequently used include detection of bad disks, mirrored disks, data protection, and transaction logging.

The techniques mentioned may fall under the auspices of fault or security management. Reliable software designs that ensure against data loss in the event of hardware failure are becoming more prevalent on the LAN market. Several server fault recovery methods are currently available (Datapro NM50 1989):

- Disk bad-track handling. Very few disks have no flaws; thus, it's important to provide software that can detect flaws and deal with them transparently.
- Mirrored disks. This involves writing data to two separate disk drives so that both drives will contain the same data. In the event that one drive

has an error, the alternate drive will continue operating without interruption to the LAN system. But, this increases hardware cost.

- Transaction commit, concurrency, and recovery. This feature gives an application the capability to protect data files from application failure. By grouping several I/O requests into a single transaction, the operating system will not write the transaction to disk until the application has terminated or issues a commit command.
- Transaction logging. This technique is essentially realtime backup, and is a powerful fault management feature. After data is written to disk, the information is echoed to the server's local tape unit. As each I/O is performed on files, the data is written to the tape drive. If there's a system failure, the file state may be recovered by repeating the I/O requests for that file from data written to the tape.

When selecting a means for distributing LAN connections, LAN wiring hubs are becoming the predominant choice of LAN users. As users realize the advantages of the integrated star topology associated with hubs (central access, network management, and space concentration), they're driving vendors to provide more and more devices that are integrated into such hubs. Devices include Ethernet stars, token ring stars, Appletalk stars, FDDI stars, bridges, routers, terminal servers, gateways, and some connectivity devices.

This high level of integration introduces the serious danger of the hub becoming a critical point of possible failure, which could result in bringing down full enterprise networks. Fault management solutions should concentrate on surviving cable plant failures and surviving hub failures.

Surviving cable plant failures Without sufficient redundancy, a cable that's connecting hubs can disable the entire enterprise network. Prevention of cable failures includes manual or automatic switch-over to a redundant link, correlative loop and continuous idle.

Surviving hub failures Since active electronics are involved, hubs are more likely to experience failures. Two types of solutions should be implemented to survive hub failures: engineering hubs (power supplies, modular construction, automatic switchover, and decentralization of functions); and network design and implementation methods to plan hub topology with fault tolerance (see chapter 6 for more details).

In combination with the methods just mentioned, *continuous backup systems* should be considered, as well. A continuous backup system is a utility that replicates all changes that are written to a disk as they're made. These systems don't necessarily replace the traditional tape-oriented backups that most network managers depend on today. Rather, they supplement tape backup. Most offline products may back up easily and quickly, but if it's necessary to retrieve a file, it often requires help from a skilled LAN operator. An online index of every file backed up may help to quickly locate a file when needed. This solution takes advantage of characteristics that are inherent in Unix networks. In addition, the following features are important when evaluating products: multithreading capability supporting parallel backup to the same tape; automatic backup by setting intervals; status display identifying problems such as pending work, I/O errors, file updates during the backup process, and communication link problems.

However, there are problems with traditional backup methods. Such backups often skip files that are in use when the backup routine attempts to copy them. Since traditional tape backup doesn't capture incremental changes to a file as they occur, an operator can't restore a file to its most up-to-date condition. The file can only be restored to the condition it was in at the time of the backup.

In addition, traditional tape backup doesn't provide system fault tolerance. If the server drive fails, the system fails and can't be used until the server drive is repaired or replaced and the data files are restored.

Continuous backup systems often have built-in fault tolerance, enabling them to remain operational when the primary disk drive or the primary server fails. This is a great benefit to users who depend on their systems for mission-critical applications. Also, continuous backup systems enable the LAN manager to restore files to the exact condition they were in when the system failed. And since continuous backup systems capture every change to a file, retrieving the status of open files should never be a problem.

There are basically three different techniques to support continuous backup:

- Use of ordinary local area network file servers, including the server's primary drive, a control drive, and a backup drive (e.g., RetroChron from Vortex).
- Use of a server dedicated solely to backup. Usually, this solution is NOS dependent (e.g., FullTime from Emerald).
- Software-only implementation working in both single-user and networking environments (e.g., Nonstop from Nonstop Networks).

In certain cases, LAN analyzers have to be used to identify problems of the higher protocol layers. These instruments actually collect everything that flows through the interface. Depending on the required presentation level, LAN analyzers display results that correspond to layer 4 or layer 7, or somewhere in between.

Finally, TABLE 3-10 shows a few examples of symptoms that indicate failure. This table may be considered—in combination with trouble tickets—as a basis for designing and implementing expert systems to support fault management.

Dynamic trouble ticketing

In order to control the processes of problem determination, isolation, diagnostics, backup, repair, and recovery, trouble tickets are very useful. They may be centrally placed, as shown in FIG. 3-20. The trouble ticket database will likely be relational for ensuring flexible information retrieval. This database may be linked to the configuration database.

Table 3-10. Possible Causes of Failure, According to Symptoms

Symptoms	Probable Cause

Performance management

Symptoms	Probable Cause
Slow response	Overloaded segment or network Too many taps on a coax segment Improper grounding
Collisions	Overloaded segments or network Improper grounding Too many taps on a coax segment Improper shielding from noise Drop cable not properly connected Bad transceivers Mismatched hardware Bad tap Defective drop cable
Retransmissions	Overloaded segments and network Tap probe is not in contact with coax No transceiver heartbeat Improper shielding from noise

Fault management

Symptoms	Probable Cause
No network service	Overloaded segments or network Open break on network Open short on network Bad tap Tap probe not in contact with coax File server has broken down File server is overloaded Systems software fault
Workstation jammed	Overloaded segments or networks Drop cable not properly connected Defective drop cable No transceiver heartbeat Bad transceiver Systems software fault Mismatched hardware
Bad packets	Overloaded segments or network Improper shielding from noise Bad transceiver Transceiver edge connector broken Transceiver tap probes broken Drop cable not properly connected Drop cable has defect Bad tap Malfunctioning interconnecting device Mismatched hardware
File problems	Improper shielding from noise Bad transceiver Drop cable not properly connected Drop cable has defect Bad tap Systems software fault Mismatched hardware

Table 3-10. Continued

Symptoms	Probable Cause
Fault management	
Nodes not responding	Open break on segments
	Open short on segments
	Malfunctioning repeater or other
	interconnecting device
	Transceiver edge connector broken
	Transceiver tap probes broken
	Mismatched hardware
	Improper shielding from noise

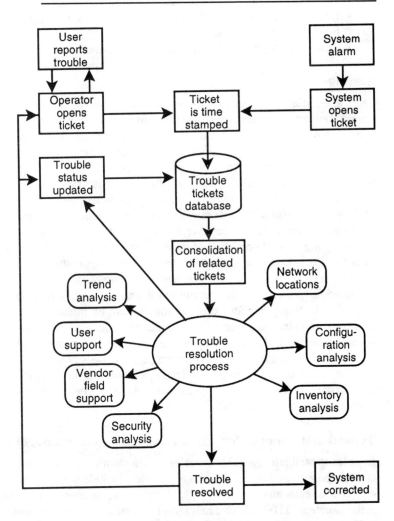

Fig. 3-20. Dynamic trouble tracking.

The trouble ticketing process drives problem resolution by maintaining communication connections to a variety of functions within and outside fault management. In the event the network is unavailable, parts of it are down, or performance is impaired anywhere on the network, trouble ticket activity would be invoked. The word problem means an incident or event that causes a LAN not to function as expected. Problems may be categorized as follows:

- Handling errors that result from users, due to lack of education or training.
- Device or equipment faults detected automatically or semiautomatically.
- Facility faults detected automatically or semiautomatically.
- Intermittent faults of equipment and/or facilities, with discontinuous or fluctuating characteristics.
- Chronic faults whose trend is to cause increasingly severe faults.

Testing

Tests are initiated on demand. The goals are twofold: to get more detailed information on faults, and to ensure that repair and recovery have successfully been accomplished. Tests can basically be categorized as nonintrusive tests, intrusive tests, remedial functions, or analog measurements.

Nonintrusive tests, as the name implies, are tests that don't interfere with main-channel data traffic. A series of these tests can therefore be performed without the need for any coordination with the main application or the associated personnel. *Intrusive tests*, on the other hand, cause some interruption in main-channel data traffic. However, these tests offer more precise information about the high-speed operation of modems and the quality of the whole transmission channel. *Remedial functions* are necessary to restore and reconfigure the network to bypass any fault that has been diagnosed. *Analog measurements* can provide further quantitative information about signal strengths and signal degradation. Some of these measurements may be intrusive, such as those that need to substitute a test tone for the main-channel data signal. Others, such as those that identify changes in phase jitter and signal level, are nonintrusive. These analog measurements are not precise and may only be used to indicate problems on a particular analog circuit. Further intrusive tests are then generally required to pinpoint the source of the problem—the failing modem or the telephone line.

Typical instruments for supporting LAN fault management

In order to facilitate the LAN troubleshooter's work, several products may be considered for use. Generic groups of products include ohmmeters, outlet testers, coax connectors, T-connectors, terminators, oscilloscopes, time domain reflectometers (TDRs), LAN analyzers, LAN monitors, NOS monitors, trouble ticketing systems, and continuous backup systems.

An *ohmmeter* is a simple tool that measures impedance. You can use an ohmmeter to locate open or shorted cable. If the impedance reading matches the rated impedance of the cable, the cable is fine. If the reading doesn't match the rated impedance, then the LAN has a short, a crushed cable, or a cable break somewhere along the cable run. Ohmmeters cannot be used in fiber-optic-based LANs.

Sometimes the problem is not the cable, but rather the electrical outlet, and then you would need an outlet tester. For example, if an outlet is not grounded properly, noise or current may be introduced through the power supply into the workstation, and then through the network interface card onto the copper-based (twisted pair or coaxial) LAN cable.

Coax connectors, T-connectors, and terminators are also important products for a LAN troubleshooter. Extra terminators are a basic requirement, particularly on a bus network. Extra terminators can be used to isolate sections of the cable for testing.

An *oscilloscope* allows the network manager to examine the cable's waveform. An oscilloscope helps detect the existence of noise or other disturbances on the wire, such as continuous voltage spikes. Again, this applies only to LANs that use copper-based wiring.

A *time domain reflectometer* operates by sending an electrical pulse over the LAN cable, monitoring for signal reflections. On a good cable there will be no reflections, indicating that the cable is clean, with no breaks or shorts. If there's a break or short in the cable, however, the time it takes for the pulse reflection to return gives the TDR a very accurate idea of where the fault is located. Many TDRs can locate cable breaks to within a few feet. TDRs have traditionally been relatively expensive instruments. A new, less expensive generation of TDR equipment is now available. These new instruments are more compact than their predecessors, often measuring about the size of a paperback book or smaller. The newer TDRs are also easier to use and still accurate to within a few feet.

Fiber-optic instruments can be divided into three general categories: power meters, optical time domain reflectometers (OTDRs), and optical bandwidth test sets.

Power meters (optical loss test sets) measure the optical power from a length of fiber in much the same way that conventional power meters measure electrical power. These tools are used to perform a one-way loss measurement. The loss may occur in the fiber, connectors, splices, jumper cables, and other system areas. Some power meters also have a built-in transmit source. Two sets, both with transmit and receive capability, are used together to make measurements in both directions without having to relocate personnel or equipment. The individual power meter is a single unit consisting of an optical receiver and an analog or digital readout. A light source, typically at the point of origination, supplies the power that's detected at the end of the fiber link or test access point. The meter displays the power detected in decibels. The wavelength range often given indicates the various wavelengths that the meter can detect. The resolution parameter indicates the smallest step that the meter will display.

Network managers can use *optical time domain reflectometers* (OTDRs) to characterize a fiber wherein an optical pulse is transmitted through the fiber and the resulting light that's scattered and reflected back to the input is measured as a function of time. OTDRs are useful in estimating the attenuation coefficient as a function of distance and in identifying defects and other losses. These devices operate on basically the same principles as copper-based TDRs. The difference is one of cost.

Optical bandwidth test sets consist of two separate parts: the source, whose output data rate varies according to the frequency of input current applied to the source (specified by frequency range parameter); and the detector, which reads the changing signal, determines the frequency response, and then displays a bandwidth instrument. The instrumentation is calibrated using a test fiber; the actual measurement results are compared to the calibrated value to display the bandwidth value.

LAN analyzers are products for in-depth measurement for diagnosing problems. They passively listen to traffic, and may time-stamp events and register dialogues between users and servers. In certain cases, the same instruments may be used as load generators.

LAN monitors are products for supervising the principal status and use indicators on a continuous basis. They're inexpensive and don't introduce too much overhead.

NOS monitors are products that may be seen as extensions of LAN operating systems. They can usually be easily activated or deactivated. The overhead doesn't seem to be critical.

Trouble ticketing systems are vendor-independent products that are usually offered together with configuration management instruments, and run on dedicated servers.

A *continuous backup system* is a utility that replicates all changes that are written to a disk as they're made. These systems don't necessarily replace the traditional tape-oriented backups that most network managers depend on today. Rather, they supplement tape backup. (TABLE 3-11 summarizes the typical instruments for fault management.)

Staffing LAN fault management

LAN fault management is a combination of help desk and analysis activities. The help desk tasks are more human oriented, and analysis is more technology oriented. The principal responsibilities of the help desk include:

1. Supervising LAN operations.
2. Registering troubles identified by monitors and users.
3. Opening trouble tickets.
4. Implementing procedures for "tier one" problem determination.
5. Invoking corrections.

6. Escalating problems, depending on priorities, to central network management center or to peer help desks.
7. Communicating with users.
8. Communicating with vendors.
9. Activating and deactivating local area networks.
10. Generating reports on network problems.
11. Closing trouble tickets.
12. Reviewing documentation of change management.
13. Setting priorities for problem diagnosis.
14. Registering security management problems.

The principal responsibilities of LAN-analysis activities are:

1. Conducting LAN tuning studies.
2. Executing specific LAN measurements.
3. Designing and executing performance and functionality tests.
4. Defining performance indicators.
5. Selecting LAN management instruments.
6. Surveying performance needs of LAN users.
7. Maintaining the LAN performance database.
8. Generating reports.
9. Maintaining the LAN baseline models.
10. Sizing LAN resources.
11. Customizing LAN instruments.
12. Analyzing work load and use trends.
13. Preparing checklists and fault management procedures for the LAN help desk.
14. Helping to install LAN management instruments.
15. Specifying and documenting LAN configurations.

Table 3-11.
Typical Instruments
of Fault Management

Ohmmeters
Outlet testers
Terminator testers
Oscilloscopes
Time domain reflectometers
Power meters
Optical time domain reflectometers
Optical bandwidth testers
LAN analyzers
LAN monitors
NOS monitors
Trouble ticketing systems
Continuous backup systems

Help desk personnel and analysts interface with all other groups within LAN management. Outside contacts include users and vendors. Besides communication skills, basic knowledge of LANs is required for the LAN help desk functions. Analysts require in-depth knowledge of all managed LAN objects. Continuing education is required for both positions; communication-oriented courses should be required of LAN help desk personnel, and a B.S. in Engineering is recommended for LAN analysts.

Performance management of local area networks

Figure 3-21 shows the most important performance management functions. Performance management functions are not yet fully implemented; in most cases, only ad hoc measurements are conducted. In the following section, the main functional areas of LAN performance management are outlined in some depth. LAN performance indicators may be grouped into fixed, variable and performance measurement metrics (LO 1990).

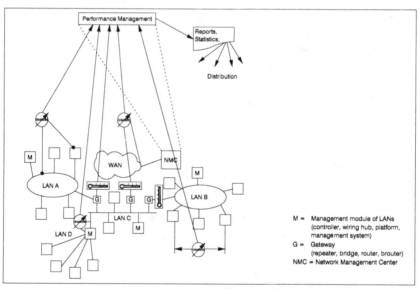

Fig. 3-21. Performance management functions.

Fixed metrics

Transmission capacity The transmission capacity is normally expressed in terms of bits per second. Although the bite rate is fixed, the total capacity can be divided into multiple smaller capacities to support different types of signals. One of the common myths regarding LAN transmission capacity is that Ethernet is saturated at an offered load (the actual data carried on the channel, excluding overhead and retransmitting bits) of 37%. Many studies have shown that Ethernet can offer a 10 Mbps data rate under a distance of one kilometer with the CSMA/CD protocol.

Signal propagation delay   Signals are limited by the speed of light, and the longer they propagate, the longer they delay. *Signal propagation time* is the time required to transmit a signal to its destination and generally is 5 microseconds per kilometer. Therefore, cabling distance is a factor that affects signal propagation delay. In the case of satellite communication, signal propagation delay plays an influential role, as the distance between an earth station and the satellite is about 22,500 miles. Within LANs, the internodal signal propagation delay is negligible. However, the signalling technique used (i.e., baseband or broadband—see details in chapter 2) can produce different levels of delays.

Topology   As described in chapter 2, a LAN can be either a star, tree, ring, bus, or combination of star and ring. The type of LAN topology will affect performance. For example, a bus LAN (e.g., Ethernet) and a token ring LAN (e.g., IBM's Token Ring) have a different built-in slot time—the time of acquiring network access. The topology also limits the number of workstations or hosts that can be attached to it. Ethernet limits the number of nodes per cable segment to 100, and the total number of nodes in a multiple-segment Ethernet is limited to 1,024. A single IBM Token Ring supports 260 nodes. The higher the number, the greater the performance impact, since all network traffic is generated from these nodes.

Frame/packet size   Most LANs are designed to support only a specific, fixed-size frame or packet. If the message is larger than the frame size, it must be broken into smaller sizes occupying multiple frames. The greater the number of frames per message, the longer delay a message can experience. Like every other LAN, Ethernet, for example, has a minimum packet size requirement: it must not be shorter than the slot time (51.2 microseconds) in order to be able to detect a collision. This limit is equivalent to a minimum length of 64 bytes, including headers and other control bytes. Similarly, Ethernet has a maximum of 1,518 bytes as the upper boundary, in order to minimize access time.

Variable metrics

Access protocol   The type of access protocol used by a LAN is probably the most influential metric that affects performance. IBM's Token Ring uses a proprietary token access control scheme, in which a circulating token is passed sequentially from node to node to grant transmissions. A node must release a token after each transmission and is not allowed to transmit continuously on a single ring architecture. Ethernet, on the other hand, employs the I-persistent CSMA/CD access control, in which a node that waits for a free channel can transmit as soon as the channel is free with a probability of I (i.e., 100% chance to transmit).

User traffic profile   A computer system and network is lifeless without users. There are many factors constituting a user's traffic profile:

message/data arrival rate (how many key entries a user makes per minute); message size distribution (how many small, medium, and large messages are generated by a user; type of messages (to a single user, multiple users or all receivers); and the number of simultaneous users (all active, 50% active, or 10% active.)

Buffer size   A buffer is a piece of memory used to receive, store, process, and forward messages. If the number of buffers is too small, data may suffer delays or even be discarded. Some LANs have a fixed number of buffers, and some use a dynamic expansion scheme based on the volume of the messages and the rate of processing. In particular, LAN internetworking devices are likely sources of buffer problems.

Data collision and retransmitting   Data collision is inevitable, especially in a bus LAN, unless the transmission is controlled in an orderly manner. Two factors need to be considered: how long it takes nodes to detect a data collision, and how long it takes to actually transmit the collided messages. Various detection schemes are used by different topologies. For example, Ethernet employs a *"jam"* time, which is the time allowed for transmitting 32 to 48 more bits after a collision is detected by a transmitting station, so that other stations can reliably detect the collision. The more influential factor is the time it takes to actually transmit the data after collision. Many LANs use a binary exponential back-off scheme to avoid a situation in which the same two colliding nodes collide again at the next interval. Both collision detection and retransmitting contribute delays to the overall processing delay. Generally, waiting time is dependent on network load and may become unacceptably long in some extreme cases.

Performance measurement metrics   The performance of a LAN can't be quantified with a single dimension. It's very hard to interpret measured metrics without knowing what applications and what users are involved. The following measurement metrics are generally obtainable.

Resource usage   Processor, memory, transmission medium, and in some cases, peripheral devices all contribute to the processing of a user request (e.g., open a file, send a message, or compile a program). How much of their respective capacities are used and how much reserved capacities are left need to be evaluated in conjunction with processing delay information (in some cases, the user's service-level goals).

Processing delays   A user's request is likely to suffer delays at each processing point. Both host and network can cause processing delays. Host delays can be divided into system processing delays and application processing delays. Network delays can be viewed as a combination of delays that is due to hardware and software. However, at the end-user level, a total processing delay (or response time) is the only meaningful performance metric.

Throughput   Transmission capacity can be measured in terms of throughput, the number of messages or bytes transmitted per unit of time. In LAN measurement, throughput is an indication of the fraction of the nominal network capacity that's actually used for carrying data. In general, packet headers are considered useful in estimating throughput, if no other measurement facilities are available, since the header contains the number of bytes in a frame. A metric related to throughput is channel capacity. Each transmission medium has a given maximum capacity (e.g., bits per second) which is a function of message volume and message size.

Availability From an end user's point of view, service availability is determined by both availability and consistency. A network can be in operation, but if a user suffers long delays, as far as the user is concerned, the network is virtually unavailable, since its availability is unreliable. Therefore, reliability measurement is a permanent measurement metric. However, most LAN measurement tools are only able to measure availability (up and down times), since timing measurement may add several orders of magnitude of complexity to measurement tools.

Fairness of measured data Since network traffic tends to be sporadic, the measured period and the internal data recording rate are quite important. An hourly averaged measured data rate may not be able to reveal any performance bottlenecks; a one-second recording rate can generate an enormous amount of data that requires both processor time and storage. As a general practice, a peak-to-average ratio is used in which data in short intervals with known high activity are collected. The ratio between the high activity periods and the average periods can be established for studying network capacity requirements. (TABLE 3-12 shows all of the metrics in a table format.)

Table 3-12. LAN
Performance Indicators

Fixed metrics
- Transmission capacity
- Signal propagation delay
- Topology
- Frame/packet size

Variable metrics
- Access protocol
- User traffic profile
- Buffer size
- Data collision and retransmission

Performance metrics
- Resource usage
- Processing delays
- Throughput
- Availability
- Fairness of measured data

Performance monitoring

In order to recognize performance bottlenecks, measurements must be performed. LAN analyzers support this activity very well. Both Ethernet and Token Ring types of LANs can be measured. Figure 3-22 shows the measurement results for an Ethernet LAN, reporting on number of frames transmitted, and the number of active stations (Saal 1989).

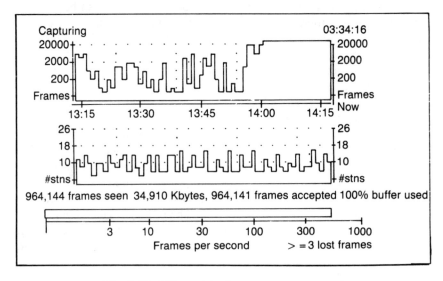

Fig. 3-22. Ethernet performance measurements.

Figure 3-23 shows the relative traffic statistics to and from stations in an Ethernet environment. This input is very useful when evaluating alternatives for bridging/separating stations. Figure 3-24 displays the distribution diagram of frame sizes for Ethernet. This may be used in performance optimization studies when deciding on the optimal number of stations and access time in an Ethernet segment.

As an option, exceptional reporting is supported by setting saturation thresholds for the number of frames and/or number of active stations. If a threshold has been violated, performance alarms are sent to the management entity. Figure 3-22 shows such a case, as the number of frames transmitted hits the 20,000 limit. Prerequisites for using this performance alarm feature are:

- Continuous measurement.
- Low overhead of information collections.
- Reasonable instrumentation price.

In Token Ring networks, the trace and performance tool (TPT) can be used to analyze distribution, use, and overhead (see FIG. 3-25). The result indi-

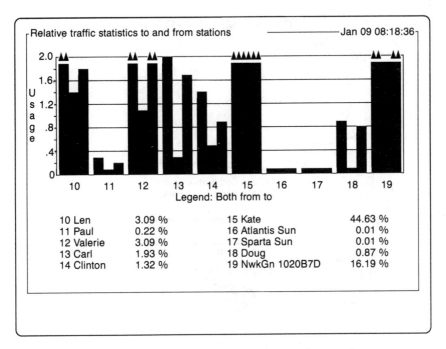

Fig. 3-23. Relative traffic statistics to and from stations.

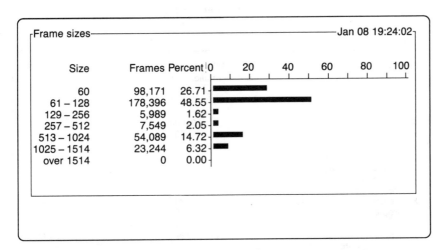

Fig. 3-24. Frame sizes distribution.

cates 23% payload, and 2% overhead, a typical measurement result for this type of LAN. Figure 3-26 shows another example, when two different LAN architectures, such as CSMA/CD and Token Ring, are bridged together. The indicator "Percent Frames Lost" may be used as a trigger for performance alarms when a threshold is violated.

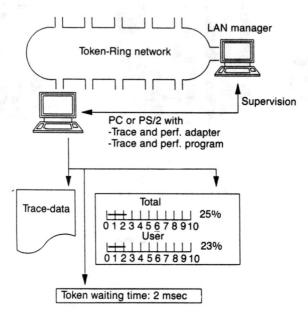

Fig. 3-25. Token ring performance measurement results.

DFIPQB02	IBM LAN manager	Page 1 of 3
Normal	Bridge profile	

Bridge name . . . .:   NS23

A   Bridge version information . . . .:   0100006403831
B   Bridge type . . . .:   0003
C   Bridge number . . . .:   4
D   Largest frame size . . . .:   2052
E   Frame forwarding active . . . .:   Yes
F   Single-route broadcast mode . . . .:   Automatic
G   Performance notification interval . . . .:   00
H   Percent frames lost threshold . . . .:   00.10
I   Routing information . . . .:   063000110030

J   LAN type . . . .:   CSMA/CD LAN 2 Mbps   Token-Ring 4 Mbps
K   LAN segment . . . .:   003   002
L   Adapter address . . . .:   10005A087C8E   10005A001B0A
M   Adapter name . . . .:
N   Single-route broadcast . . . .:   Yes   Yes
O   Hop count . . . .:   7   7

Esc = Cancel   F1 = Help   F3 = Exit   End   PgDn

Fig. 3-26. Bridge profile.

Protocol analysis may be part of performance measurement, as well. Also, complete traces may be generated for in-depth protocol analysis, as shown in TABLE 3-13 for DECNET and in TABLE 3-14 for NetBios.

Table 3-13. DECNET Trace Example

```
┌SUMMARY─DST──────────SRC──────────────────────────────────────────────────────────
│    6  VAX Server  ←VAX Client   NSP DATA Begin-End D=1413 S=0C39  DACK=0
│    7  VAX Client  ←VAX Server   NSP ACK  Data       D=0C39 S=1413  DACK=1
│    8  VAX Client  ←VAX Server   NSP DATA Begin-End D=0C39 S=1413  DACK=1
│    9  VAX Server  ←VAX Client   NSP ACK  Data       D=1413 S=0C39  DACK=1
│   10  VAX Server  ←VAX Client   NSP DATA Begin-End D=1413 S=0C39  DACK=1
│   11  VAX Client  ←VAX Server   NSP ACK  Data       D=0C39 S=1413  DACK=2
│   12  VAX Client  ←VAX Server   NSP DATA Begin-End D=0C39 S=1413  DACK=2
│   13  VAX Server  ←VAX Client   NSP ACK  Data       D=1413 S=0C39  DACK=2
│   14  VAX Server  ←VAX Client   SCP DISC  Reason=0
│   15  VAX Client  ←VAX Server   NSP CTRL Disconn Confirm  D=0C39 S=1413
│   16  VAX Server  ←VAX Client   SCP CONN  D=17 (FAL)  S=CAL
│   17  VAX Client  ←VAX Server   NSP CTRL Connect Confirm  D=0C3A S=2814
│   18  VAX Server  ←VAX Client   NSP DATA Link       D=2814 S=0C3A           L
│   19  VAX Client  ←VAX Server   NSP DATA Link       D=0C3A S=2814           L
│   20  VAX Server  ←VAX Client   NSP ACK  Oth-Data   D=2814 S=0C3A           L
│   21  VAX Server  ←VAX Client   NSP DATA Begin-End D=2814 S=0C3A  DACK=0
│   22  VAX Client  ←VAX Server   NSP ACK  Data       D=0C3A S=2814  DACK=1
│   23  VAX Client  ←VAX Server   NSP DATA Begin-End D=0C3A S=2814  DACK=1
│   24  VAX Server  ←VAX Client   NSP ACK  Data       D=2814 S=0C3A  DACK=1
│   25  VAX Server  ←VAX Client   NSP DATA Begin-End D=2814 S=0C3A  DACK=1
└──────────────────────────────────────────────────────────────────────────────────
```

Table 3-14. NetBios Trace Example

```
┌DETAIL──────────────────────────────────────────────────
│ TCP:  [49 byte(s) of data]
│ TCP:
│ NET:  ----- NetBIOS Session protocol -----
│ NET:
│ NET:  Type = 00 (Session data)
│ NET:  Flags = 00
│ NET:  Total session packet length = 45
│ NET:
│ SMB:  ----- SMB Get Disk Attributes Response -----
│ SMB:
│ SMB:  Function = 80 (Get Disk Attributes)
│ SMB:  Tree id    (TID) = 8F15
│ SMB:  Process id (PID) = 1D3B
│ SMB:  Return code = 0,0 (OK)
│ SMB:  Number of clusters per disk   = 10405
│ SMB:  Number of sectors per cluster = 4
│ SMB:  Sector size              = 512
│ SMB:  Number of free clusters  = 4522
│ SMB:  FAT ID byte              = F8
│ SMB:
└─────────────────────────Frame 38 of 48──────────────────
                          Use TAB to select windows
```

Tuning of local area networks

Figure 3-27 shows the principal steps and functions needed for analyzing and tuning local area networks. Requests for analysis and performance improvement occur when the service-level expectation can't be met, or performance studies are required when proactive performance evaluations are initiated.

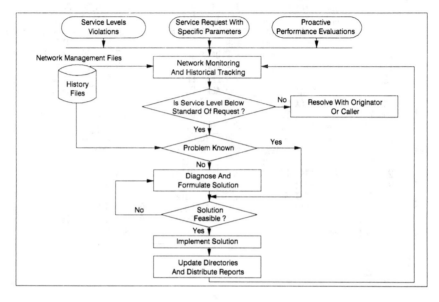

Fig. 3-27. Performance tuning procedure.

The process starts with defining performance metrics, and continues with monitoring in the LAN segment by extracting data from the performance database. In most cases, however, the level of detail doesn't satisfy the information need. The database is considered the basis of thresholding and performance reporting. On rare occasions, the experience file of historic tuning data may help to quickly recognize similarities with past problems. Once the hypothesis has been formulated, cost efficiency and technical feasibility should be tested step-by-step in order to exclude uneconomical and nonfeasible alternatives. Frequently, technical and economic performance evaluations are supported by modeling techniques. After implementation, measurements should check and prove performance improvement. In the case of nonfeasibility or insufficient improvement, an additional hypothesis should be worked out. If the results are still unsatisfactory, capacity planning actions are required.

Regarding tuning, all LAN components may be performance bottlenecks; priorities and weights have to be set after performance measurements have been conducted and evaluated. As a result of evaluating LAN-tuning reports, primary tuning targets are (Axner 1991 and Gilliam 1990):

- LAN operating systems.
- LAN servers, in particular file-servers and communication servers
- LAN drivers.
- Workstations.
- Peripherals.

LAN operating systems

The most prominent factor affecting the performance of a local area network is the network operating system. The function of the operating system is to move the data within the network, to manage the files, and to control the input and output requirements. The more efficiently the operating system is able to perform these tasks, the more efficiently the network will operate.

The ability to manage files will depend on the way the disk drive is organized. Many networks are designed using the MS-DOS method of file organization. Under this method, there's no index method, and there's a 32-megabyte limit on the size of the file. If the file size is larger, it must be broken up into different 32-megabyte files; to the system it looks as if there are two or more disk drives.

Because of these limitations, managing large database files can put extra stress on a network. This stress, in turn, limits the operating system's ability to efficiently manage large files, because if the file is divided into different 32-megabyte files, the operating system has to rely on file allocation table (FAT) to know how the files are to be assembled and that they belong together.

MS-DOS 4.0 and OS/2 have eliminated this restriction. File sizes can be as large as the disk itself. However, MS-DOS and OS/2 still use DOS-like functions of file organization. In order to move around this barrier, vendors are continuing to develop their own operating systems. For example, 3Com's 3+ Open and Novell's NetWare provide a more efficient index-type file organization that overrides the FAT. These more modern capabilities provide the network user with much faster access and file allocation procedures for using and storing large files.

Servers

The network server, like the operating system, has a major impact on the overall performance of the network. A server's performance is based on clock speed, wait states (i.e., the number of cycles the processor goes through to access the memory and power). Obviously, a 80386 25-megahertz server will provide faster performance than a slower 80286 server. A server with zero wait states will be faster than those with one or two wait states, since the zero wait state avoids going through one or two cycles for each access.

A common mistake users make when trying to improve server performance is to add more RAM. There's a break-even point at which additional RAM will not gain any performance improvement. The amount of RAM that should be used on the network is greatly dependent on the applications and the environment. Guidelines for calculating RAM requirements can be found in all vendor's operational manuals, but these are only guidelines—not hard and fast rules.

If a department LAN has five or six users, three megabytes of RAM should be enough. Adding 16 megabytes to a LAN of this size would probably produce some marginally improved performance, but it would be inefficient; much of the extra RAM would not be used. Another important factor in LAN performance is the speed of the server's memory. A good rule to follow is that the speed of the memory should be just enough so as not to add extra wait states to the processor. Adding 100-nanosecond memory chips would not necessarily gain added performance over 60-nanosecond chips, if wait state is created on the processor.

The performance considerations for RAM are not limited to just the number and speed of the chips, but also to the location of the RAM within the processor. Location refers to extended, not expanded, memory, a topic that causes great confusion.

Expanded memory is memory that starts above 1,024 kilobytes. It was developed before the more efficient "protected mode" of the 80286. Expanded memory operates by reserving 64 kilobytes within the base 640 kilobytes of memory. When an application needs to use the expanded memory, it must place the data in this area and then call an expanded memory function to move the data to the upper memory area.

With the development of the 80286 protected mode, extended memory simply changes the processor mode, (from unprotected to protected) and then accesses the memory areas directly. This is accomplished faster then expanded memory, as the extra steps (i.e., calling up the separate memory routines) are eliminated. The operating system is allowed to switch to extended mode (such as through IBM's PC/LAN). Banyan's Vines and Novell's NetWare continuously operate in the protected mode.

The disk server CPU and support hardware (RAM) clearly affect performance. If the file-server runs software for the 8088 CPU, then RAM can't normally exceed 640 bytes. Some network operating systems can take advantage of expanded RAM cards to work above 640 bytes. File servers with 80286 or 80386 processors have more RAM available, which will improve file server performance. These systems make more effective use of RAM with file changing and directory hashing, which allow data normally stored on disk to be loaded into RAM. In addition, the file server can access the RAM data in nanoseconds. This allows faster execution, faster table interrogation, and expeditious data movement. The disk drive subsystem is also important in its own right. Many subsystems (e.g., Novell) use a proprietary disk file structure to achieve higher performance than DOS. This disk format can improve throughput as much as 50%. Also, the larger the disk capacity, the quicker the disk drive can move the file server. The IBM PC AT disk subsystem is relatively slow, primarily due to the method used by the disk controller to talk to the CPU. With advanced SCSI controllers and high performance drives, data can be delivered much more rapidly. A PC AT with an SCSI disk controller may now be able to move 250 kilobytes per second or more. Many vendors now use the SCSI disk drive interface.

One bottleneck in the process, however, occurs when the data comes from the disk too fast for the CPU to keep up. A solution is to use a disk coprocessor that can hold onto the remaining data until the CPU catches up. Another bottleneck occurs when the data or program files on the drive become fragmented. Most new files are laid out on the disk in a contiguous order, but as time goes by, portions of the file may be rewritten to different sections of the disk. This results in the disk drive taking longer to collect all parts of a file. The easiest way to solve this problem is to do a periodic, complete backup; reinitialize the disk drive, and restore the files from the backup tape.

In addition to the file and disk organization, the way in which the disk drive is managed is another area of importance. The management of the disk drive involves considerably more than deleting old files and creating more descriptive directories; disk drive management provides the means to access the data on the disk.

The speed at which the read/write mechanism operates is a function of the controller and the disk drive working together. However, in order to reduce the amount of work involved in read/write, you need to focus on the network operating system. One method to make the read/write process more efficient is through "caching." A cache uses a portion of the server's RAM as a temporary "holding area" for data. Caching is based on the principle that if a particular block of data has been accessed once, either read or written, it will probably be accessed again during the session. Once a file or block of data is accessed, the operating system maintains a copy of the block in cache memory. If the data block is accessed again, it can be read from the cache without having to retrieve it from the disk. Since a cache is reserved space within the RAM, its use greatly reduces the system's response time; RAM access is much faster than access to data on the physical drive.

The size of the cache can be determined by the LAN user when the system parameters are set. When the LAN is started, the cache is established according to the system parameters, and the contents are normally held within the cache until the machine is turned off.

LAN drivers

Another important set of elements affecting local area network performance are the software routines called "drivers." Drivers accept requests from the network and provide the interface between the physical devices (disk drives, printers, network interface cards) and the operating system. The drivers also control the movement of data throughout the network and verify that the data have been received at the appropriate address.

The critical role that drivers play, however, means that driver problems can have a large impact on the performance of the overall network. Drivers have traditionally been supplied by the LAN vendors and have been tailored to their operating systems and varied according to size. Today, it's more likely third-party software developers will provide customized drivers for networks.

These customized drivers, however, can be rather detailed and lengthy. If a driver takes up too much RAM, other applications will have insufficient room in which to operate, causing them to alter their normal operating procedures in order to reduce memory requirements. Also, the larger a driver is, the more code it has to execute, causing the network to delay when responding to additional requests, such as requests for printer services or requests from other users for processing jobs.

Interface cards can also affect performance. Memory management is crucial to speed and performance. Factors such as DMA versus shared memory, and onboard processors and buffers can mean large differences in two cards' actual throughput on the network. The performance difference, for example, between Ethernet cards can be as high as 50%.

Workstations

Another element affecting performance is the network workstation. The performance of a workstation has more impact on both the perceived system performance and the actual system performance than any other component. For example, a high-performance file server on a 10 Mbps LAN will show the inefficiency of an IBM PC workstation with limited RAM; the workstation is now the bottleneck since it can't accept or display data as fast as the file server, and the network hardware can supply it. At times, it's cheaper and more particular to upgrade the workstation, rather than the LAN itself. Adding more RAM or a coprocessor could improve grade of service without a single change to the network. The protocol software can also affect workstation performance. A full seven-layer OSI (Open Systems Interconnection) stack could require considerable resources to run. Even at the network layer, packet sizes, transfer buffers, and other workstation network software settings can have a major effect on the network performance.

The network workstation is just as important to the overall performance of the LAN as the server and operating system. The workstation executes the network's protocols through its driver software; a faster workstation will add to the performance of the LAN. One factor to consider is whether the workstation should contain a disk drive of its own or not. Obviously, a diskless workstation will ease the budget, and improve security somewhat.

But diskless workstations have their own set of costs. For one, these workstations are dependent on shared resources. If the work being performed at the station doesn't involve sharing resources, a workstation with its own disk may be more appropriate. Moreover, diskless workstations add to the traffic load on the LAN. This could be significant, especially if the workstations are for programmers who typically don't need to share files but who often work on files that are extremely large.

Peripherals

Printing requirements also affect LAN performance in a variety of ways. Modern printers provide much more advanced printing capabilities than were available just a few years ago. Complete pages are transmitted at a time, with improved fonts and high-end graphics.

These printing capabilities, however, if not handled properly, can degrade network performance. If you run into such performance problems, and if enough printers are available, redirecting the printing job to a local printer can help. You can also add another server dedicated to handling printer functions.

Another way to avoid bottlenecks caused by heavy printing requirements is to use a network operating system that incorporates a spooler to control these requirements. Spoolers are designed to accept a printing request from the network, logically and in order, and they complete print requests without additional help from workstations.

Effective filtering across bridges ensures that traffic volume is not too high throughout the network, and keeps performance constantly high. If high volumes indicate the need for partitioning, it's recommended to place bridges between departments. The first part of FIG. 3-28 indicates that most informa-

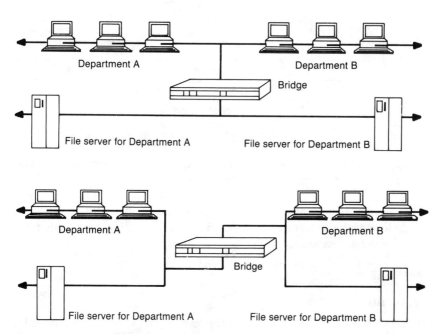

Fig. 3-28. Reconfiguration of LAN bridges.

tion arriving at the bridge is addressed to a file server on the other port, and must be forwarded by the bridge. After partitioning, most information arriving at the bridge is addressed to a file server on the same port, and may be discarded by the bridge. The two segments thus work in much greater harmony, and with improved efficiency.

Modeling and performance optimization

In order to optimize performance, you first need to analyze throughput capabilities and limits. The following three figures (FIGS. 3-29 through 3-31) show the dependence of throughput rate as a function of an access indicator. The access indicator computes the average access time in function of LAN parameters such as number of stations, token size, estimated number of simultaneously active stations, speed of propagation, bandwidth, average message size, bit latency, average collision distance, repeater delay, and so on.

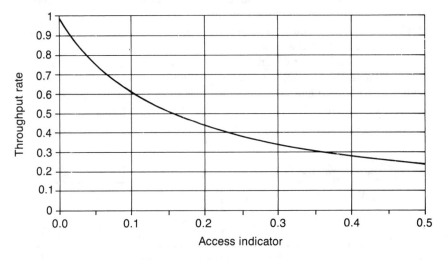

Fig. 3-29. CSMA/CD throughput.

Figure 3-31 (Infotel 1990) compares the throughput performance for both principal access methods. The results are as follows:

1. Relatively constant throughput by the 4 Mbps Token Ring.
2. Reasonable performance of the 16 Mbps Token Ring over a long range of the access indicator "A."
3. A throughput drop on the 10 Mbps Ethernet to a stable 35% to 40% use ceiling.

Reporting of performance

All users' expectations can't be met by the reporting capabilities of LAN analyzers. Most frequently, measurement data are ported from the analyzer to other

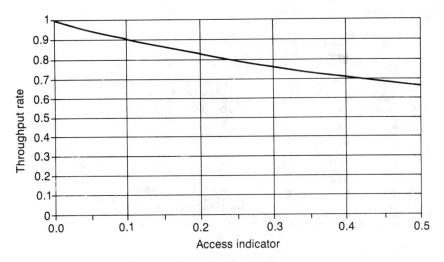

Fig. 3-30. Token ring throughput.

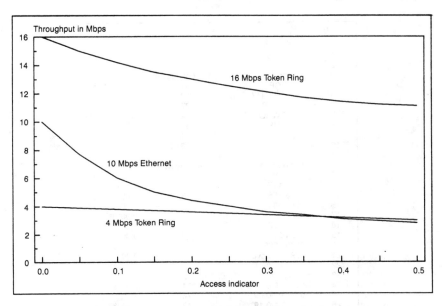

Fig. 3-31. Comparison of CSMA/CD and token ring.

databases, or to spreadsheets for further processing. Figure 3-32 shows an example of raw data (Saal 1989). The measurement files are saved in CSV (Comma Separated Value). These files are accessible by the spreadsheet product.

Using simple computations with the spreadsheet, and inserting labels, the readability can be significantly improved. The results are shown in FIG. 3-33; they include total frames, frames distribution by protocols, distribution of

D Size	E Dest	F Source	G Protocol	H Summary
83	Janus	Backbone	DNS	C ID = 2 OP = QUERY NAME = 41.0.53.36.in-addr.arpa
60	[36.53.0.41]	Backbone	TCP	D = 1023 S = 515 ACK = 101396550 WIN = 4092
60	Backbone	[36.53.0.41]	TCP	D = 515 S = 1023 ACK = 3999834114 WIN = 2048
78	Janus	Backbone	DNS	C ID = 3 OP = QUERY NAME = Janus.southlan.edu
81	Janus	Backbone	DNS	C ID = 4 OP = QUERY NAME = suwani.southlan.edu
79	Janus	Backbone	DNS	C ID = 5 OP = QUERY NAME = navajo.southlan.edu
68	Janus	Backbone	DNS	C ID = 6 OP = QUERY NAME = rt-robot
67	Janus	Backbone	DNS	C ID = 7 OP = QUERY NAME = Mathilda
63	Janus	Backbone	DNS	C ID = 8 OP = QUERY NAME = pda
68	Janus	Backbone	DNS	C ID = 9 OP = QUERY NAME = suwani
81	Janus	Backbone	DNS	C ID = 10 OP = QUERY NAME = rt-robot.southlan.edu
80	Janus	Backbone	DNS	C ID = 11 OP = QUERY NAME = Mathilda.southlan.edu
76	Janus	Backbone	DNS	C ID = 12 OP = QUERY NAME = pda.southlan.edu
81	Janus	Backbone	DNS	C ID = 13 OP = QUERY NAME = suwani.southlan.edu
60	Janus	Backbone	DNS	C ID = 14 OP = QUERY NAME =
60	Opus	Janus	DNS	C ID = 1103 OP = QUERY NAME =
60	Janus	Backbone	TCP	D = 53 S = 1106 ACK = 523912858 WIN = 4096
60	Janus	Opus	DNS	R ID = 1103 STAT = OK NAME =
134	[36.53.0.41]	Backbone	PRINTER	R PORT = 1023 Tango.SOUTHLAN.EDU: /usr/lib/lpd: : Your
60	[36.53.0.41]	Backbone	TCP	D = 1023 S = 515 FIN ACK = 101396550 SEQ = 3999834194 LEN = 0

Fig. 3-32. Formatting output of LAN analyzers.

	A B	C	D	E
1	Frames in DB:	106		
2				
3	Protocol	Number of packets		
4	TCP	37		
5	PRINTER	2		
6	SMTP	27		
7	RWHO	4		
8	DNS	35		
9	Telnet	1		
10		106		
11				
12	Packet size	Packets by size		
13	0-59	0	0.00%	0
14	60-127	86	81.13%	1
15	128-255	6	5.66%	2
16	256-383	0	0.00%	3
17	384-511	0	0.00%	4
18	512-1023	14	13.21%	5
19	1024-2047	0	0.00%	6
20	2048-4095	0	0.00%	7
21	4096 and over	0	0.00%	8
22		0		
23	Interarrival time	Packets by interval		
24	0-0.000009	1	0.94%	0
25	0.00001-0.09	76	71.70%	1
26	0.1-0.19	12	11.32%	2
27	0.2-0.29	4	3.77%	3
28	0.3-0.39	1	0.94%	4
29	0.4-0.49	0	0.00%	5
30	0.5-0.59	2	1.89%	6
31	0.6-0.69	0	0.00%	7
32	0.7-0.79	3	2.83%	8
33	0.8-0.89	1	0.94%	9
34	0.9 and up	6	5.66%	10

Fig. 3-33. Using spreadsheets for reporting.

packet sizes, and interarrival time clusters. The same data may be displayed using graphical features of the spreadsheet product. Similar results may be accomplished with products such as SAS or MICS, or with the reporting capability of a relational database.

Rhodes (1991) recommends concentrating on the following generic report types for supporting performance and configuration management: bandwidth inventory (status, changes, use); circuit status; subscriber's inventory (status, adds, drops); overview of LAN addresses; equipment inventory (status, changes, use); key changes over time interval; LAN/WAN connections overview and use; passwords in use; PBX inventory; incident reports by category; inventory of instruments.

Typical instruments for supporting LAN performance management

In order to facilitate the work of the LAN performance analyst, several products may be considered for implementation. Generic groups of products include:

- LAN analyzers. Products for in-depth measurement for diagnosing problems. They passively listen to traffic, and may time-stamp events and register dialogs between users and servers. In certain cases, the same instruments may be used as load generators.
- LAN monitors. Products for supervising the principal status and use indicators on a continuous basis. They're inexpensive and don't introduce too much overhead.
- NOS monitors. Products that may be seen as extensions of LAN operating systems. They can usually be easily activated or deactivated. The overhead doesn't seem to be critical.
- Disk usage monitoring. Utilities are needed to monitor disk usage for those operating systems not providing detailed information (such as NetWare). This helps the LAN manager assess whether a user is monopolizing the server and facilities configuration management in terms of sizing out file server needs. Additionally, the manager will be able to forecast the need for new facilities at future times. Disk usage statistics include the number of files that are in a given directory or volume, the owner of the file, the size of the file, and access chronology. Exception reporting for users colonizing more than a specified threshold of space is available with some products. Also, some products allow the end user to check disk usage. Other products provide partial NetWare security reports by listing users, access privileges, and group membership.
- Traffic monitoring tools. To undertake performance management, a network manager needs a complete matrix of LAN traffic patterns. With this information the manager can subsequently look at the LAN configuration to determine, for example, if a server is being used too heavily,

or if the network should be partitioned using bridge technology. A protocol analyzer provides detailed information about packets and related Protocol Data Unit (PDU) headers that populate the LAN transmission medium, and the analyzer can compile traffic matrices.

Software-based traffic monitors will collect some of the needed traffic statistics. In addition to traffic collection, some of these systems can send probes to diagnose nodal problems. Some systems log errors and issue an alarm when a user-selected threshold is exceeded. A typical performance tool monitors traffic and records how much data is sent to and received from every network node, documenting the packet size, frequency, and type (data or system packet). For system packets, these monitors typically distinguish between commands and internal operating messages. The data should be collected into sequential ASCII files or a spreadsheet file.

- Modeling devices. These consist of products that help in running experiments without the actual network. As a result, the impact of parameter changes and load increases can be evaluated very rapidly. TABLE 3-15 presents a summary of typical instruments of performance management.

Table 3-15.
Typical Instruments
of Performance
Management

LAN analyzers
LAN monitors
NOS monitors
Disk usage monitors
Traffic monitoring tools
Modeling devices

Staffing LAN performance management

LAN performance management consists of technically oriented analysis activities. Principal responsibilities include: conducting LAN tuning studies, executing specific LAN measurements, designing and executing performance and functionality tests, defining performance indicators, selecting LAN management instruments, surveying performance needs of LAN users, maintaining the LAN performance database, generating reports, maintaining the LAN baseline models, sizing LAN resources, customizing LAN instruments, analyzing workload and use trends, preparing checklists and processes for the LAN help desk, helping install LAN management instruments, and specifying and documenting LAN configurations.

LAN analysts interface within LAN management and with all other groups. Outside contacts include users and vendors. In-depth knowledge of all managed LAN objects is necessary. Continuing education is required. A B.S. in engineering is a prerequisite or target for LAN analysts.

Security management of local area networks

Figure 3-34 shows the most important security management functions. Security management functions are not yet fully implemented in LANs.

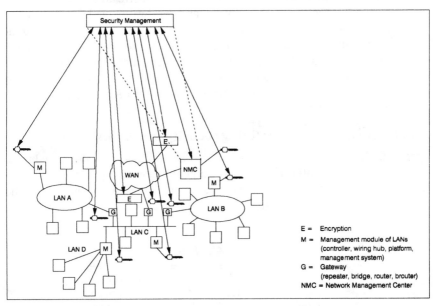

Fig. 3-34. Security management functions.

Security on LANs must be discussed separately because such networks are used more publicly than wide area networks. LAN security risks involve tapping, radiation leakage, file and program protection, and physical security. Authentication, audit trails, and encryption may be handled similarly to WANs and other networking resources. The reasons for different security measures and instrumentation are the following:

- PC LAN users are more sophisticated than terminal users: with more knowledge about the LAN and operating systems, they generally have an increased understanding of internal security structures.
- In the LAN environment, more devices store and maintain data. Protecting these data becomes increasingly difficult.
- There are far too many utilities available to bypass copy protection, expose disk structures, and perform sophisticated file/disk copying. For all practical purposes, data are exposed to security risks.

- Cables are one of the primary and easiest places for security violations to occur. Both copper-based and fiber-optic cables can be tapped, each using different technologies at different costs. Tapping, in combination with monitoring devices, allows the violator to read passwords, analyze traffic patterns, and actually capture sensitive information. In addition, electromagnetic signal leakage causes additional vulnerability for LAN security.

Usually, low-security LANs are less expensive and allow the choice of a wider selection of software and hardware, while high-security requirements may reduce the selection list to only a few options. Additional hardware and more expensive software are generally required for the more secure LAN installations. Implementation of a very secure LAN is considerably more costly than a single work-group LAN. In the following section, the main functional areas of LAN security management are outlined in some depth.

Analyzing threats and defining security indicators

One of LAN management's functions is to decide which indicators need to be supervised. Access authorization, user authentication, and password administration are the most important indicators. In order to find and implement the most efficient ones, it's useful to construct the LAN Threat Matrix (TABLE 3-16).

Table 3-16. LAN Threat Matrix

Threats	Passive Threats	Active Threats	Unintentional Operational Threats
Principal network segments			
End user	H	H	L
Workstation	H	H	L
LAN: Cable	M	M	M
Fiber	L	L	M
MAN: Cable	L	L	L
Fiber	L	L	L
WAN: Cable	H	H	M
Fiber	L	L	L
Microwave	H	H	M
Satellite	M	M	M
Servers (HW, SW)	L	M	M
Databases	L	M	L
Applications	M	H	L

H = High threat
M = Medium threat
L = Low threat

The construction of this matrix occurs in multiple steps: classification of threats, such as natural disasters, hackers, sabotage by hostile employees, user mistakes, viruses, and industrial espionage; identification of principal network elements that may be vulnerable to threats; evaluation of the risks as high, medium or low.

Results may help to better distribute investments in the LAN security area. There's no absolute security, not even with unlimited financial resources. Depending on the industry, the enterprise has to find the right balance between security risk and investment. At least, a strategy for detecting LAN's penetration must be established. Key items for the detection of security violations are: looking for changes in the average number of active users, looking for unusual references to sensitive data stored on servers, monitoring more frequently during periods of hardware and software configuration changes, looking for nonscheduled changes in access control parameters, and looking for unexplained system crashes.

Analyzing and selecting security services

There's no single service that can prevent all types of security violations. But careful selection of combined services may help guarantee an adequate solution for security management. Services are addressed here for all parts of the network previously mentioned (Ruland 1987).

Authentication check on communication partners Using this service, the partners who are going to communicate with each other identify themselves prior to starting the communication establishment phase. It may involve people or applications.

There are two alternatives: single authentication, indicating that one communicating party checks on the identity of the other; mutual authentication, whereby both communicating parties check the identity to the other. The authentication process may be repeated at random even during the active communication phase.

Authentication check of the data sender There must be a guarantee that the data sent is from an authorized source. This check can't avoid duplication of data. The service is recommended only for a connectionless communication establishment. For connection-oriented communication, it's already a part of data security.

Access Control Access control must guarantee that only authorized partners gain access to network partitions, such as LANs, MANs, and WANs, and to selected resources, such as operating systems, files, databases, applications, and processing peripherals.

Ensuring data privacy This service protects data from being read by unauthorized parties. Privacy may relate to the connection, to special files, or even to selected fields of files.

Avoidance of traffic flow analysis This special service helps prevent unauthorized users from making conclusions based on analysis of the pattern of communication traffic between different kinds of users. Traffic analysis protection must be considered for end-to-end encryption (Cooper 1990). The intent of traffic analysis protection is to mask the frequency, length, and origin destination patterns of the message traffic. If encryption were performed in the presentation layer, an analyst could determine which presentation, session, and transport entities could be associated with a particular traffic pattern. Performing encryption at the transport layer would limit the information association by not identifying higher-level entities. Additional protection can be provided by continually or randomly flooding the communication channel with dummy traffic. The price paid is lost channel efficiency.

Ensuring data integrity   Similar to link-level data communication protocols, this service offers protection against the deletion, change, insertion, and repetition of data segments or selected fields. As an option of this service, automated recovery may be invoked whereby people can request retransmission of disrupted messages. Integrity may relate to the connection, to special files, or even to selected fields of files.

Sender and/or receiver acknowledgment   The sender/receiver receives a confirmation or acknowledgment that a certain amount of information has been sent/received. This service helps to avoid occasional debates about information exchanges not properly protocoled by either sender or receiver.

LAN security issues fall into the following three major areas (Datapro NM50 1989): physical access, logical access, and administrative control.

Physical access   Security in any data processing environment starts with controlling access to the equipment. Although intrinsically distributed in topology, LAN security requires installing the file-servers and printers in secured access rooms. Access to the LAN's cabling system is also a concern because of the potential to "tap" into the network, insert new nodes, or monitor network data traffic. Access control to the PC workstation itself must be considered. Even without the network or server available, the local hard disk of the workstation can pose a security risk for loss of data.

Logical access   Physical access techniques are designed to keep unauthorized users off the network. Logical access techniques are designed to keep unauthorized network users away from authorized files. Access to the data is the responsibility of the network operating system. It's via the NOS (Network Operating System) that the logical control for information access is carried out. Password access to servers, and I/O rights to directory or file structures represent typical support features provided by a network operating system. The level of security required by any site will dictate the LAN manager's final choice of LAN software.

Administrative control   An important but often neglected aspect of LAN security is the role of the LAN manager. It's this individual who is responsible for physical and logical access control, in addition to undertaking fault recovery procedures, performing backups, and monitoring for potential security infractions.

Analyzing and selecting investment directions

Investment can be directed towards improving server security, connection security, station security, or a combination of all these types of security. The techniques used are a combination of those addressed in the previous section. In summary, the following components-managed objects—can be protected:

- Server security.
  - a. File servers.
  - b. Print servers.
  - c. Applications.
  - d. Files.
  - e. Network operating systems.
  - f. Passwords and authentication.
- Connection security.
  - a. Shielded twisted pair.
  - b. Unshielded twisted pair.
  - c. Coax.
  - d. Fiber.
  - e. Microwave.
  - f. Encryption devices.
  - g. Radiation.
- Station security.
  - a. Chip key or chip card.
  - b. Public and private keys in connection with servers.
  - c. Biometrics that are using physiological (retina of the eye, palm, fingerprint) or behavioral (voice, signature dynamics, keystroke dynamics) attributes of the user.

Implementing security management services

In order to provide powerful services as addressed in the previous section, adequate solutions—a combination of tools and techniques—are required. The following services may be implemented:

Use of cryptography   Cryptography means the method and process of transforming intelligible text into an unintelligible form and reconverting the unintelligible form into the original through several transformation processes. The information process that transforms intelligible text to unintelligible text is known as enciphering or *encryption*. The reverse is known as deciphering or *decryption*.

Encoding (encryption)   This technique can significantly safeguard the security of the transmission against passive security violations. Usually, this technique is used in combination with others, such as preventing traffic flow analysis. Basically, there are two alternatives:

- Use of private keys, called the *symmetric technique*: one key is used for both sending and receiving parties. Whoever owns this key is able to encrypt and reconstruct. Thus, the key has to be kept private.
- Use of public keys, called the *asymmetric technique*: two keys are used, one for encrypting and the second to reconstruct on the receiver side. One key is of little help to the penetrator; that's why one of the keys is publicly available. Usually, the key on the receiver side is private.

Basically, there are two levels of encryption: link encryption and end-to-end encryption. Link encryption means a separate encryption process for each node-to-node transmission link. Full text, including headers and routing information, can be encrypted on the links. This process involves only the first two OSI layers. At each intermediate node, decryption and reencryption take place, thereby exposing the information to some node processes. With end-to-end encryption, link encryption (including packet and datagram encryption) protects information from source to destination. This may be essential if the source node and/or the destination node require protection within intermediate nodes because of concern over proprietary or sensitive data exposure or because the intermediate nodes may have less robust security features than desired. End-to-end encryption is generally performed at the higher layers (e.g., the transport layer) so that address information necessary at intermediate nodes will not be packaged within the encrypted data. This usually requires software encryption. If misrouting occurs, there will be no information compromise using end-to-end encryption.

Digital signature   In order to send beyond any reasonable doubt to the receiver, the technique of digital signature may be used. This uses the public key method in combination with an additional private key for preventing any unauthorized reads during transmission.

Hash function   In order to reduce the computation needs of public key techniques, the hash function concentrates only on certain segments of the source message. Checksum is computed and added to the critical segment prior to transmission. It's practically impossible to find another message segment with exactly the same checksum. The same hash function will be used at the receiver to reconstruct the source message.

Authentication for identifying authorized or unauthorized users   As indicated earlier, communicating parties usually want to identify each other prior to establishing the communication connection. This technique checks on the validity of authorizations. Authentication may use attributes or behavioral characteristics.

The subjects are: communicating parties, such as users, applications, processes, and entities; communication and processing media corresponding to the parts of the network; messages representing data and information.

Automatic dial-back   Upon password receipt, the receiver disconnects and after table-lookup dials back using a prestored number. In this case, only the sender is authenticated. The advantage is that the availability of specialized audit trails and realtime monitoring may deceive the intruder by playing along with him or her in order to trace the physical location and escalate alarm actions. The disadvantages are the need for an additional network element (hardware or software), the restriction to a specific device location, readability of the called number—if not encrypted—and, probably, higher costs.

User passwords are vulnerable. There are some safeguards against this. The NOS can insist on changing passwords regularly or at random. Minimum and maximum lengths of use may be required, as well. Certain third-party products help in this respect by not allowing escaping (Sabre menu), disabling devices (Sitelock), or offering virus-checking facility (Sitelock) in addition.

Authentication by special equipment Recently, new solutions have been introduced for identifying the user to his or her workstation or terminal. The use of chip cards is based on a personalized set of information hardcoded into the chip. Loss of the card or key may still lead, however, to unauthorized use (Brigth 1990).

Authentication by personal attributes In very sensitive areas, personal attributes, such as keystroke dynamics, signature dynamics, voice, color of eyes, hand scans, fingerprints, and the like, may be used as the basis for identification. The cost of this technique, however, can very rarely be justified.

Improving data integrity Similar to data protection, this technique deals with solutions based on a checksum computation. The results are used to expand the message that will be sent to the destination address. The techniques are expected to be sophisticated enough not to be broken easily. The original message and the checksum are encrypted together. Also, time stamps and message identification have to be added to help reconstruct the message. Those additional flags may be encrypted as well.

Prevention of traffic flow analysis using fillers Fillers may be used to fill time gaps between real data transmissions. If both communications can be encrypted together, the penetrater can't recognize any rationale or trend, or any random, periodic, or other pattern by listening to the traffic. But, on the other hand, the use of fillers is not unlimited. It may become very expensive, and communication facilities may be temporarily overloaded, resulting in serious performance bottlenecks.

Routing control by dynamic bandwidth management State-of-the-art networking services enable users or the security officer to dynamically change or adapt the bandwidth assignment. This reassignment ensures higher security, when, for example, communication forms, applications, or users are temporarily separated in order to avoid security risks due to resource sharing.

Use of an arbiter (judge) function For ensuring the reconstruction of all transactions and messages sent and received, a central administration function may be required. The function is similar to the control entity in a message switching system. The function may be implemented as one of the responsibilities of the security officer.

LAN virus safeguards   A *virus* is a program that destroys data files or application programs or both. They have existed in one form or another since data processing started. With the widespread use of bulletin boards in inter-connected LANs, virus programs are finding their way onto many LAN servers. Recommended actions are:

- Prohibiting downloading of free software to use on LANs or PCs.
- Requiring tests of all new programs on a test server, not connected to LANs and WANs. The tests should check for accuracy of output and potential destructive tendencies. The programs must be pushed to their input and output maximum values to test their accuracy under extreme conditions.
- Through audit trails, identifying the person who has uploaded the program to the LAN.
- Limiting the upload authorization and privileges.
- Routinely scanning for viruses on servers and workstation.

In evaluating products, both detection and removal capabilities must be evaluated. They have to be rated based on their ability to handle a number of virus infection scenarios, including boot-sector virus infections and file infections by common and exotic viruses.

In order to evaluate feasible solutions against potential threats, TABLE 3-17 summarizes the threats and their remedies (Patterson 1991).

Table 3-17. Security Threats and Their Remedies

Threats	Cryptography	Authentication	Check-Sum	Remedies: Traffic Management	Audit Trails	Authorization	Virus Safeguard	Disaster Recovery
Natural disaster								x
Hackers	x	x	x		x	x	x	
Hostile employees	x	x	x		x	x	x	
User mistakes		x	x		x	x	x	
Viruses							x	x
Industrial espionage				x				

LAN security in a broader sense includes power supply, reliability of servers, and the choice of backup media (Theakston 1991). For the highest level of security, online resiliency services are recommended. The size of batteries in the UPS determines the load that can typically be supported. The support times range between 15 and 60 minutes, with power ranging from 500 Va up to 5 kVa.

The resiliency of the file servers is very critical in most environments. Two techniques are widely used, particularly in PC LANs: disk mirroring and disk duplexing. With disk mirroring, data is simultaneously written to two disks. If one disk fails, processing carries on using the second unit. Disk duplexing works like disk mirroring, but security is further enhanced by duplexing the disk controller.

The choice of a backup medium depends in most cases on the cost. Device classes, such as Exabyte (based on video recording products), digital audio tape (from audio recording), and erasable optical storage devices (based on compact disk technology) help to provide sufficient storage at various prices. Besides investment cost, the most significant factor is time to write and read the data. During the write, data has to be locked to other users. The shorter the time, the less impact is on LAN performance. Restoration time depends on searching efficiency, and on reading the data. The first is more significant than the second. The expected performance in this respect depends on the technology chosen.

Figure 3-35 shows an example for implementing LAN security management services. The figure indicates both active and passive actions on behalf of the LAN security officer.

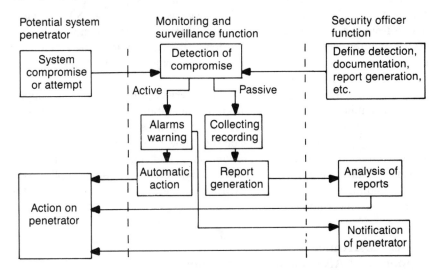

Fig. 3-35. Implementing LAN security services.

Securing the LAN-management system

A protocol analyzer in the hands of the wrong person can be a security threat. If an infiltrator can get access to a LAN port or is able to tap the cable, the analyzer can reveal useful penetration information. An analyzer can capture the entire dialog taking place over the LAN, and can display passwords in an easily readable form. Appropriating passwords is easy with analyzers, but passwords may still be useful in a properly designed LAN. It's possible, for example, to restrict the station(s) a user can log in from; thus, although the infiltrator may have the manager's password, he or she or she can't log in as the supervisor without using the actual manager's terminal. In addition, audit trail utilities can report log-ins and log-outs, with special attention paid to the manager's ID. This is why reliable security measures that go beyond basic password protection are needed.

While protocol analyzers can present problems for LAN security, they can in turn be used to monitor the network for infractions. One simple technique involves looking for stations that are not supposed to be on the network. The manager can set the display to depict unknown stations. This is done by declaring an easily readable name for each LAN station. If a program claims to lock certain files, for example, the analyzer can be used to test that claim. With some analyzers, the network manager can write programs in C for specialized functions, such as monitoring compliance with security procedures. For example, such a program might look through the data to find stations that are logged on to a file server but show no activity for long periods of time. This may indicate a station where the user has walked away without logging off, which is a violation of security policies in most institutions.

Many LAN management systems will use SNMP. Currently, SNMP shows many voids in terms of security. The goals of improving SNMP security derive from the special threats against SNMP. Principal threats are (Galvin 1991): unauthorized access; modification of information (e.g., parameters for the SET command); changed sequence of messages; information disclosure; service denial; traffic analysis.

When SNMP is used, SNMP security services are necessary to support the goals of minimizing risks. Service implementation should, however, remain simple, and overhead should remain low. With these two objectives in mind, security services must concentrate on the following (Galvin 1991): data origin authentication, data integrity, data sequencing, and confidentiality. The mechanisms and algorithms, which are not much different from other applications, use the community string in the SNMP message header to accommodate the information concerning security.

Typical instruments for supporting LAN security management

In order to facilitate the work of LAN security officers, several products may be considered for use. Frequently, products from the fault and performance management areas may be used. Generic groups of products include LAN analyzers, LAN monitors, NOS monitors, continuous backup systems, audit trail utilities, and access surveillance tools.

LAN analyzers Products for in-depth measurement for diagnosing problems. They passively listen to traffic, and may time-stamp events and register dialogs between users and servers. In certain cases, the same instruments may be used as load generators.

LAN monitors Products for supervising the principal status and use indicators on a continuous basis. They're inexpensive and don't introduce too much overhead.

NOS monitors   Products that may be seen as extensions of LAN operating systems. They can usually be easily activated or deactivated. The overhead doesn't seem to be critical.

Continuous backup systems   A continuous backup system is a utility that replicates all changes that are written to a disk as they're made. These systems don't necessarily replace the traditional tape-oriented backups that most network managers depend on today. Rather, they supplement tape backup.

Audit trail utilities   Audit trail systems are a key component of security management, although the function can be considered part of accounting management. Audit trail systems provide information on user activity on the LAN. Additionally, these systems can assist in billing management by providing the data needed to charge back usage.

An audit trail system must provide streamlined and useful information. LAN managers may wish to audit only certain users, operations on files with certain extensions or in certain subdirectories, certain types of operations, or certain servers. All file and directory creations, deletions, and renames may need to be reported. A system error log report, listing all system error messages to alert the LAN manager of potential problems, may be advantageous.

Access surveillance tools   These are logging instruments for analyzing access by authorization. Also, access denies, including reasons, are included. A post processor is one tool that provides statistics on security violations by LAN workstation and/or LAN-user. The result of using such tools may be to tune security services and other instruments.

Virus safeguard tools   Usually, software programs to detect and remove viruses that are usually infecting the boot sector or files. TABLE 3-18 summarizes the typical security management instruments.

Table 3-18. Typical Instruments of Security Management

LAN analyzers
LAN monitors
Continuous backup systems
Audit trail utilities
Access surveillance tools
Virus safeguard tools

Staffing LAN security management

Security management of LANs is not yet considered a separate functional area. This may very likely change as more and more mission-critical applications are moved to LANs and interconnected LANs.

In smaller organizations, the LAN administrator is expected to be responsible for principal security management functions, including the definition and supervision of access authorization, security risk analysis, and determination of feasible security services. In this function, the LAN administrator interfaces to the LAN manager, and to vendors of LAN security management products.

Accounting management

Figure 3-36 shows the most important accounting management functions. Accounting management functions in LANs have not yet been consistently implemented. Many users consider LANs a part of a company's infrastructure, and are more willing to invest in software meters than in accounting procedures. There are two situations to consider: accounting for LAN segments, and accounting for interconnected LANs.

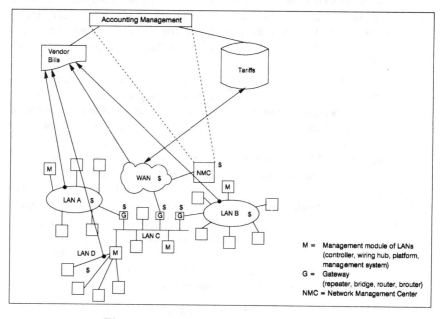

Fig. 3-36. Accounting management functions.

In the first case, simple techniques, such as software meters and audit trails, may be used. In the second case, there are similarities with WANs; LAN segments are considered a traffic source for a wide area network. In such a case, traffic volumes have to be identified by their source. Interconnecting devices are expected to provide for raw accounting data. In the following section, the main LAN accounting management functions are briefly addressed.

LAN accounting management functions

Cost control is a must. LAN management needs to be fully aware of expenses. Cost components for LANs usually include:

- Hardware: servers, peripherals, LAN interconnecting devices, wiring concentrators, workstations, network interface cards, modems, CDU/CSUs, memory.

- Cables: purchase price and maintenance fee for cables, and their connecting devices.
- Software: LAN operating systems, drivers.
- LAN management systems: management systems, monitors, databases, test instruments.
- Facilities: leased lines, packet switching, circuit switching, microwave, satellites, or radio to connect LAN segments to each other.
- People: LAN Manager, LAN Administrator, LAN Analyst, LAN Troubleshooter, LAN Designer and Planner, LAN Installer.
- Other fixed costs: building, preventive maintenance, etc.
- Other fixed operating costs: energy, heating and cooling, LAN management services (when outsourcing agreements are in place).

As a result of cost quantification, the "price" of LAN ownership may be determined, too.

Bill verification

Correctly processing vendor bills is principally a question of establishing well-defined procedures that are than carried out by trained accounting personnel. No significant problems exist in this area, as they may with costing and billing.

What's most important, however, is the procedure to verify the accuracy of vendor bills before these bills are paid. Significant overcharges can often be found through precise written procedures that analyze and verify vendor bills. Additionally, to prevent duplicate charges and/or penalties, clearly defined procedures for tracking and recording all bills are necessary.

Usually, bill processing is part of more complex billing systems. Network billing systems can capture call data directly from voice-switch SMDR ports. Calls can then be grouped for reconciliation and user billing. A central database also permits call pattern studies and exception monitoring of network abuse. Some systems can even help the manager estimate and prepay call charges, and avoid carriers' late payment penalties. Attention needs to be paid to correctly linking the billing system to configuration management—in particular, with inventory control and order processing.

Interconnected LANs may use various transport capabilities; in each case the supplier will bill for the facilities. Additional bills are expected from vendors of LAN hardware and LAN software components.

Determining resource use

Using measurement tools, resource use can be pinpointed for LAN management. Not every resource, but certainly the most important ones, need to be measured. Depending on available instrumentation, resources, such as servers and channels, may be measured continuously or periodically. As basis indicators for accounting, the following ones may be considered: number of transmitted bytes or frames or packets, number of server accesses, and resource use on servers.

Sampling (periodic monitoring) applies when continuous monitoring of each segment can't be cost justified. It's extremely important to collect information on traffic as it leaves the LAN segment. Unfortunately, bridges, routers, brouters, and gateways are usually not equipped with internal traffic monitoring features.

Billing

A chargeback system can be defined as the assignment of communication costs to users. In some organizations, real dollars change hands, in others, bookkeeping entries are made, or statements are issued, but money transfers don't take place.

To be successful, a chargeback system must:

- Be understandable to the user.
- Be predictable so managers can plan effectively.
- Reflect economic reality.

The benefits of a chargeback system are:

- It's a proven way of allocating expensive resources.
- It encourages users to make economical use of services.
- It promotes efficient service by controlling demand.
- It decentralizes control to enable users to make choices.

Potential drawbacks of a chargeback system are:

- It entails overhead costs that reduce profits.
- It makes life difficult for LAN management centers.
- It usually results in complex rates and rules.
- It may result in underused resources.
- It encourages large groups to seek special benefits.
- It may remove an essential source for some users.

LAN management has to decide on the LAN usage indicators that will be used as the basis of the chargeback system. Depending on this decision, usage information has to be collected and processed. Corporate policies differ, and the following three alternatives may be distinguished.

Zero chargeback   Some corporations don't charge users with any LAN-related costs. These are simply considered corporate overhead, similar to the company cafeteria or company newspaper. Other corporations use a variation of this in "showback accounting," whereby user groups are provided with "average cost" information, but no actual chargeback.

Partial chargeback   Most corporations levy partial chargebacks against users. In these situations, some LAN costs are absorbed by the corporation, some by certain groups such as corporate IS, and the remaining costs are charged directly to the user, based on specific rates and usage factors.

Full chargeback   A few companies attempt to charge all LAN costs to the user based on services provided. Very often these charges involve negotiated costs and prices. Profit centers may use this approach.

Typical instruments for supporting LAN accounting management

In order to support LAN accounting management functions, several products may be considered for use. Resource use may be determined by LAN analyzers or monitors. For supporting billback and bill verification, new applications need to be designed and implemented. Costing remains for a period of time a manual process. Generic groups of products include the following.

LAN analyzers   Products for in-depth measurement for diagnosing problems. They passively listen to traffic, and may time-stamp events and register dialogs between users and servers. In certain cases, the same instruments may be used as load generators.

LAN monitors   Products for supervising the principal status and use indicators on a continuous basis. They're inexpensive and don't introduce too much overhead.

NOS monitors   Products that may be seen as extensions of LAN operating systems. They can usually be easily activated or deactivated. The overhead doesn't seem to be critical.

Audit trail utilities   Audit trail systems are a key component of security management, although the function can be considered part of accounting management. Audit trail systems provide information on user activity on the LAN. Additionally, these systems can assist in billing management by providing the data needed to charge back usage.

Software meters   Products helping to control software product licensing, and deterring illegal copying. The frequency of use is recorded for costing and charging. The information collected also helps bill verification. But, the security risk of viruses must not be ignored. Often, vendors bring in dormant modules that may destroy (deactivate, disable) the product, unless bills have been paid properly. (TABLE 3-19 summarizes the typical accounting management instruments.)

Table 3-19. Typical Instruments of Accounting Management

LAN analyzers
LAN monitors
NOS monitors
Software meters
Audit trail utilities

Staffing LAN accounting management

Accounting management is not yet a dedicated organizational entity. In most corporations, the LAN administrator is expected to be responsible for LAN-accounting related functions. This situation will most likely change, as a significant amount of money is going to be spent on transmission facilities for interconnecting LANs.

User administration   LAN management and software cover a wide range of applications and functions. In broad terms, this LAN management function can be divided into two classes: user support and system support.

User support capabilities insulate users from the complexities of the LAN and reduce the amount of training and interaction that must be undertaken by the LAN manager. These tools include front-end, document-organizer, and remote-user support.

System support capabilities give the network manager information about the LAN itself. System support utilities provide data on user activity, disk usage, network traffic, system configuration, and so on. These tools complement local area network operating systems. Some available tools address shortcomings of LAN operating systems.

User administration functions   User administration functions have two major goals: to enhance the end user's working environment and to help detect, diagnose, and correct problems caused by users, applications, or managed objects.

Front ends are menu-driven interfaces that insulate users from the native environment. The menus will convert from the user-friendly commands to the necessary DOS or LAN operating system commands. End users should not be expected to know DOS, the LAN software protocol stack, and other details such as software version numbers.

Many front end systems provide a template that the network manager can customize for different LAN user groups; these menus can typically be produced at the manager's terminal and distributed over the network. A front end may perform additional functions as well. Some front ends provide basic usage tracking. While these reports are not as detailed as those produced by sophisticated audit trail tools, front end systems can report how much time a user spends on a particular application. Others may blank out the screen after a period of inactivity or even log off the user. Other front ends have a software meter, which monitors application usage, to support adherence to the license restrictions.

Maintenance of user data   Remote user support tools allow the network manager to gain access to the remote workstation or PC; access to the keyboard and screen can be acquired remotely so that the manager can determine the possible problem source. In some systems, the manager is automatically informed regarding what hardware the user has. In addition, some of these systems maintain statistics on who was helped, the nature of the assistance, and the duration of the session. This data can be used to bill back support costs and/or to design training programs.

Detecting, diagnosing and correcting problems   This function is implemented with a combination of local and remote help desks. A local help desk may be useful for a large site serving multiple local area networks. The help desk is expected to be equipped with various analyzer instruments, automated call distributors, and with troubleshooting guidelines.

Local help desks are expected to work with the central help desk in troubleshooting serious problems. Trouble tickets are electronically communicated to central help desk.

A centralized help desk may be useful in situations where there are many distributed local area networks that are geographically far from each other, but which may be internetworked using bridges, routers, brouters, or gateways.

The central help desk is equipped with various standalone instruments, LAN management products or platforms, automated call distributors, and troubleshooting guidelines. A central help desk may be shared between WANs and LANs. Management of MANs will most likely be integrated in the future.

The help desk has a special combination of instruments and a varying degree of administration experience. In order to support administration functions, implementation may be borrowed from WAN help desks.

Automated operations are very helpful in accelerating problem recognition and elimination. The problem is that there's always some event that they're not prepared to handle because it has not come up before or it's not considered part of the system's work (Weissmann 1991). In such situations, an automated or semiautomated problem management system must take over. A good system must be rule based, and have a base of knowledge that it applies to the LAN problem. The content of this knowledge includes the following: who should be contacted, when they should be contacted, how they should be contacted, what to do if they can't be contacted, what to do if they don't fix the problem, and how long to wait for a fix before further escalation.

Such a system is basically a realtime update of the available human resources that may be dispatched to solve LAN problems. Many extensions may be considered, which include voice output, use of various priorities of escalation, and use of artificial intelligence for the rule base.

Many problems that end users attribute to LANs are, in fact, problems that stem from the user's lack of familiarity with the various LAN applications he or she wants to employ. Network managers can resolve such problems by using remote access tools to determine the causes of application problems.

Typical instruments for supporting LAN user administration

In order to support administration functions, a variety of instruments may be used. Basically, there are two groups of instruments: user support tools and system support tools. User support tools insulate users from the complexities of the LAN, and reduce the amount of training and interaction that must be undertaken by the LAN manager. Systems support tools give LAN managers information about the LAN itself. These utilities provide data on user activity, disk usage, network traffic, system configuration, and so on. Many tools that were described earlier may also be used for supporting LAN user administration.

Besides monitoring devices, referenced before, special user administration tools include the following.

Front ends These instruments offer better user interfaces through menus and application customization techniques. They're installed as add ons to the operating system in servers, or as support programs in the workstations.

Remote user support tools These instruments offload end users from diagnosing problems at their own workstations or servers. The central or local help desk may gain access and troubleshoot the problem.

Console emulation tools Products to consolidate operations by physically linking LAN management instruments to a management workstation. Dedicated windows may be opened for each individual management system. Alarm correlation, however, is accomplished by the LAN operator.

Help desk instruments New techniques and instruments include:

- Automated call distributors.
- Interactive voice response. Also, integrated interactive voice response (IIVR) may be used to support the help desk of local area networks. IIVR is a dynamic voice mailbox for exchanging experience data on certain troubles. The IVR approach allows receiving the data from the trouble database; the voice mail option allows help desk personnel to expand or even change the information stored.
- Voice mail.
- Jukebox storage for diagnostics and trouble tickets.
- Hypertext for user education, trouble tickets, diagnostics, and tutorials.
- Expert systems for easy problem determination rules.

(TABLE 3-20 summarizes the instruments for user administration.)

*Table 3-20. Typical Instruments
of User Administration*

Front ends
Remote user support tools
Console emulation tools
Help-desk instruments

Summary

After discussing individual LAN management functions and generic instruments, it's useful to summarize the general applicability of instruments to functions. TABLE 3-21 shows the applicability matrix; "X" indicates the most likely use of instruments by a particular LAN management function. The two major conclusions are:

- Most instruments are universal enough to be used by multiple functions.
- Each function requires a combination of instruments.

Instruments will be addressed in greater depth in chapter 5.

Table 3-21. Instruments' Support for LAN Management Functions

Instrument Types	Functions						
	CM	FM	PM	SM	AM	PL	UA
Databases	x		x			x	x
Document managers	x	x			x		x
Configuration trailing products	x						x
Document and file organizers	x						x
Management information base	x	x			x		
User tracking products	x			x	x		
Audit trail utilities	x			x	x		
Virus safeguards				x			
Disk usage utilities	x				x		
Protocol analyzers		x	x	x			
Network monitors		x	x		x		
NOS monitors		x	x				
Time domain reflectometers		x					
Software diagnostic tools		x	x				
Ohmmeters		x					
Outlet testers		x					
Terminator testers		x					
Oscilloscopes		x					
Power meters		x					
Optical bandwidth testers		x					
Network usage meters			x		x	x	
Traffic monitors			x		x	x	
Emulators			x			x	
Simulators			x			x	
Access surveillance tools				x			x
Backup utilities				x			x
Remote end-user support tools							x
Help-desk utilities							x
Front-end utilities							x
Console emulation tools			x	x			x
Trouble ticketing systems		x	x		x		x
Modeling devices			x			x	
LAN management systems	x	x	x	x	x	x	x

CM	Configuration management
FM	Fault management
PM	Performance management
SM	Security management
AM	Accounting management
PL	LAN design and planning
UA	User administration

4

Standardizing
LAN management

LAN management product solutions are greatly affected by emerging standards, which are the topic of this chapter. Standards include *de facto* solutions, such as TCP/IP-based techniques, and open solutions, based on OSI recommendations. After summarizing the driving forces for standards, the five emerging trends will be briefly introduced. The competing and complementary standards, OSI-CMIP and TCP/IP-SNMP will be addressed in greater depth, including principles of work, implementation examples, and comparison of functionality. The final part of this chapter will deal with leading manufacturers' strategies. These strategies include architectures and platform examples. The distributed management environment (DME) decision on how to integrate leading solutions will also be addressed.

The need for standardization

Enterprise-wide networking requires that each client and server be able to communicate with all others. That's not an easy requirement to meet in a multivendor environment with many different products and networking architectures. The origin of the incompatibility problem lies in the fact that manufacturers developed their own solutions to providing interoperability among their own devices. This level of interoperability may involve a tremendous amount of investment by leading manufacturers, such as IBM, Unisys, DEC, Tandem, Novell, Xerox, and so on. These companies will not likely be willing to give up their architectures and investments just to support standards. But communication standards can improve the efficiency and reduce the cost of linking clients and servers.

Both ISO and IEEE were working on defining standards for the communications industry, but neither could be responsible for devising one single

145

standard. What finally emerged from the efforts of these and other standards-creating bodies was not a single standard, but the Open System Interconnection (OSI) Reference Model, a framework that could accommodate many standard protocols and combinations of protocols. At the top of the OSI model are the application, presentation, and session layers. Together, they're responsible for turning conditioned, formatted data into a stream that can travel on a generic network, defined by the bottom layers. These bottom layers—transport, network, data link, and physical—transfer traffic effectively and efficiently to the destinations. The same seven layers operate at the receiving end, in the opposite order, to condition and format the arriving information stream. Network management applications are implemented in layer 7 using CMISEs (common management information service elements). The underlying layers are used as service providers.

In order to serve users' connectivity and standardization needs faster, TCP/IP (Transmission Control Protocol/Internet Protocol) has been introduced. TCP/IP differentiates between three groups of layers, namely application, logical and physical (FIG. 4-1). Migration to OSI is very likely. The most pressing concern with TCP/IP was to manage network layer gateways in the internet. An interim solution called Simple Network Management Protocol

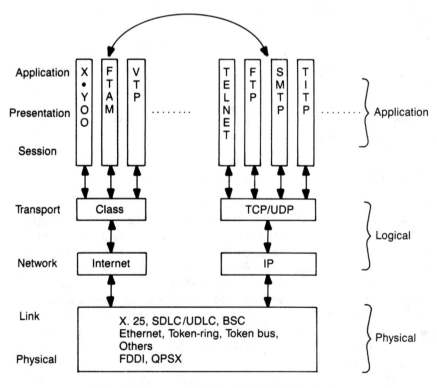

Fig. 4-1. Layers of OSI and TCP/IP standards.

(SNMP) was provided, with the long-term solution of using the OSI management framework and protocols. This approach is referred to as CMIP over TCP (CMOT). Both protocols work with the same core management information base (MIB), defined for the TCP/IP-Internet.

MAP/TOP envisions local area networks with heterogeneous nodes, some of which have implemented the entire seven layers of OSI protocol stacks, and some of which have implemented the lower layers only.

Thus, MAP/TOP had to find unique ways to manage its objects. In managing full stack nodes, OSI network management solutions are called for; in other cases, with a thin protocol stack, very basic management capabilities are in place.

The standardization process altogether shows satisfactory progress at lower layers. Besides working standards at the physical, data link, and network layers of WANs, lower layers have been successfully standardized for MANs and LANs. Figure 4-2 shows the results, including the reference to coexistence with OSI standards. TABLE 4-1 gives short definitions of the standards shown in FIG. 4-2.

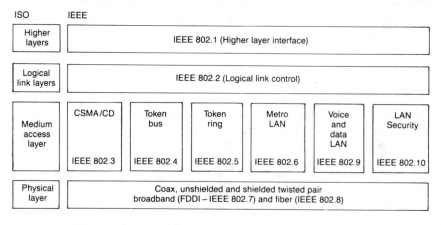

Fig. 4-2. Cooperation of IEEE 802-X and OSI standards.

In summary, there are five emerging network management standards:

- Open System Interconnection (OSI) Management, which employs the Common Management Information Protocol (CMIP). The OSI, ISO/IEC Joint Technical Committee 1 (JTCI) has defined five sets of management facilities within the scope of OSI Management: configuration, performance, fault, accounting, and security. While current ISO standards-development activities may seem to have little impact on LAN management, future LAN management systems will undoubtedly be OSI compliant, to facilitate exchange of management data with other LAN systems and with wide area network (WAN) and integrated network management systems.

- TCP/IP's SNMP (Simple Network Management Protocol). This protocol is viewed as an interim solution for managing multiple Internet networks, linked via gateways. SNMP exploits the capabilities of the User Datagram Protocol (UDP).
- CMOT (CMIP over TCP/IP). The Internet Activities Board (IAB) has adopted CMOT as the long-term solution for managing TCP/IP-based networks and for providing a migration path from TCP/IP to a full OSI stack.
- CMOL (CMIP over LLC). In order to manage Token Ring and Ethernet networks with a homogeneous protocol stack, IBM and 3COM are offering Heterogeneous LAN Management (HLM) specifications. HLM is based on CMIP, but will address low protocol layers. In addition, the LLC (logical link control) layer of the IEEE 802.2 standard is considered the target. The combination of both will give a lot of implementation help to practical environments.
- GNMP (Government Network Management Profile). The GNMP mandates CMIP as the management information exchange protocol. Managed objects are included from international standard publications. Five systems management functions are outlined: object management, state management, attributes for representing relationships, alarm reporting management, and event reporting. GNMP is the management information specification of the networks defined by GOSIP.

Table 4-1. Definition of 802.X Standards

802.1—an overview on LAN architecture, LAN and higher layer (i.e., metropolitan area networks) interface, internetworking, and network management. It is still in the draft stage.

802.2—defines logical link control and was recommended as standards in 1985 and adopted by ISO and OSI standard 8802/2 in 1987.

802.3—defines CSMA/CD access and physical layer specifications and was recommended as a standard in 1985 and adopted by ISO as an OSI standard 8802/3 in 1987.

802.4—defines token-bus access and physical layer specifications and was recommended as a standard in 1985 and adopted by ISO as an OSI standard 8802/4 in 1987.

802.5—defines token-ring access and physical layer specifications and was recommended as a standard in 1985 and adopted by ISO as an OSI standard 8802/5 in 1987.

802.6—defines metropolitan area network (MAN) access and physical layer specifications. It is still in the draft stage.

Open network management architectures

Based on the seven-layer model, network management-related applications are also supported. Applications are implemented in layer 7. Layers 1 through 6 contribute to network management by offering the standard services to carry network management-related information. Systems management application entities (SMAE) have three key components—so-called application service elements—that are vital to network management (McCann 1989):

- ACSE (association control service elements) is responsible for an association establishment and a release establishment for an application association.
- ROSE (remote operation service elements) is responsible for connection establishment and release.
- CMISE (common management information service elements) is responsible for the logical part of communicating network management information.

The M-INITIALISE service is used by a CMISE service user, such as a managing process, to establish an association with a peer CMISE service user, such as a managed process. The M-INITIALISE service forms the first phase of an instance of management information service activity. It's only used to create an association and may not be issued on an established association. M-INITIALISE is defined as a confirmed service (e.g., meaning that the target CMISE acknowledges to the initiating CMISE that the service has been provided). It's routed to ACSE to establish an association with a peer CMISE service user.

The M-TERMINATE service is used by a CMISE service user to cause a normal release of an association with a peer CMISE user. M-TERMINATE is defined as a confirmed service. It's routed to ACSE to cause a normal release of an association with a peer CMISE service user.

The M-ABORT service is used by a CMISE service user to cause an abrupt release of an association with a peer CMISE service user. The M-ABORT is defined as a nonconfirmed service. It's routed to ACSE to cause an abort release of an association with a peer CMISE service user.

The M-EVENT-REPORT service is used by a CMISE service user to report an event associated with management information to a peer CMISE service user. M-EVENT-REPORT defined as either a confirmed or nonconfirmed service.

The service is used by a CMISE service user to retrieve management information values from a peer CMISE service user. M-GET is defined as a confirmed service.

The service is used by invoking CMISE service user to request the modification of management information values by a peer CMISE service user. M-SET is defined as a confirmed and a nonconfirmed service.

The M-ACTION service is used by a CMISE service user to request a peer CMISE service user to perform an action on a managed object. M-ACTION is defined as a confirmed and nonconfirmed service.

The M-CREATE service is used by an invoking CMISE service user to request a peer CMISE service user to create a representation of a new managed object instance, complete with its identification and the values of its associated management information, and simultaneously to register its identification. M-CREATE is defined as a confirmed service.

The M-DELETE service is used by an invoking CMISE service user to request a peer CMISE service user to delete a representation of a managed object instance, and to de-register its identification. M-DELETE is defined as a confirmed service.

It's expected that two additional services become part of this set of services. These are M-CANCELGET and M-ADD/REMOVE. Using these service elements, a variety of system management functions (SMF) can be supported (FIG. 4-3) (Collins 1989).

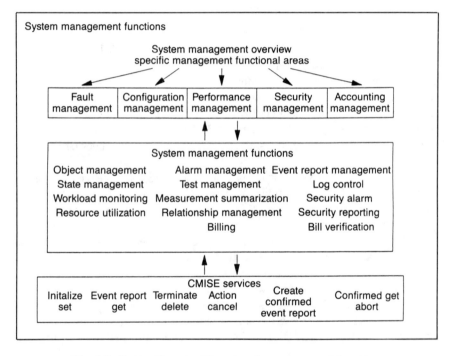

Fig. 4-3. Supporting specific network management functions.

SMFs carry out the management processes, or activities, specified by the various specific management functional areas (SMFA). It's clearly specified which of the SMFs are used by which SMFAs. For example, a state management SMF is used by the fault management and configuration management SMFAs. SMFs are defined in the SMF document (see FIG. 4-3 for examples). System management functions are detailed in the following section.

Object management

Object management uses OSI services, such as those specified in the Common Management Information Services (CMIS) standard, to perform actions on managed objects. For example, object management may invoke the CMISE service M-DELETE to delete a managed object from an open system.

Within object management definitions, services are specified that allow reports about object management activities to be communicated to other open systems. For example, an attribute change event report service can be used to send an event report to another open system if an object's attributes change.

In terms of modeling MIBs, there are two alternatives (Bapat 1991):

- Object-oriented (OO) modeling. The benefits of this technique are the well-structured class hierarchy, and the inheritance relationship from the superclass to the subclass.
- Entity-relationship (ER) modeling. This technique is well suited for defining generalized relations between MIB objects. Parts of the OO model can be subsumed within the ER model.

Both alternatives are well understood. Current OSI-based standardization efforts concentrate on OO modeling, with supplementary information from ER diagrams.

State management

State management describes services that allow the OSI Management user to monitor the past state of managed objects and receive notices, or alarms, in response to changes in the state of managed objects.

The State Reading service uses the M-GET service of CMIS to retrieve information from managed objects. For example, M-GET may be used to retrieve an indication of whether a managed object is accessible by the management system.

The State Change Reporting service calls on the attribute change event report service of Object Management to notify users of changes in either the administrative or operational state of managed objects.

Relationship management

Relationship management describes services that create, delete, change, and report relationships among managed objects. Relationships among managed objects is a complicated issue. In general, a *relationship* is a set of rules that describes how the operation of one managed object affects the operation of another managed object within an open system. For example, two managed objects in an open system may have a relationship in which one is activated in the event that the other fails as a result of a fault management diagnostic.

Error reporting and information retrieval

Error reporting and information retrieval allow various types of information to be reported and retrieved through the open system. Descriptions of error types, probable causes, and measures of severity are specified. This type of functionality will be essential in integrated network management scenarios where users have more than one network in place. For example, a single network-management system's ability to access information about errors occurring in two open systems could be important in situations where a relationship exists between the two open systems.

Types of errors defined by this SMF are: communication failure, quality of service failure, processing failure, environment failure, and equipment failure. Error reporting services for each type of error are defined in this SMF.

Probable cause information provided by this SMF would indicate the problem source that results in an error. For example, in the case of a communication failure, a probable cause might be a call establishment error.

Five severity parameters are defined: indeterminate, critical, major, minor, and warning. In a network management application of this SMF, the ability to categorize alarms by severity helps the network manager quickly decide which alarms must be responded to immediately and which ones can wait. This SMF uses the CMIS service M-GET to perform information retrieval.

Management service control

This describes services that allow the management system user to determine which event reports are to be sent where. For example, this SMF could play a key role in network management systems scenarios by allowing the network manager to specify which information can be exchanged between manager processes and agent processes. Consider a scenario in which a user has one manager process that centralizes management of multiple, separate agent processes.

As FIG. 4-3 illustrates, the management service control functions will allow the user to choose which types of event reports will be exchanged between the manager process and the individual agent process.

Confidence and diagnostic testing

Confidence and diagnostic testing allows tests to be performed on managed objects. The purpose of such tests is to allow the management system to determine the quality of services and to assist in the diagnosis of faults within the open system. For example, this SMF might be used to initiate bit error rate tests on remote modems.

Log control

This service allows users to choose which event reports the system will log. The log control function also enables an external managing system user to change the criteria used for logging event reports.

The application of the log control function in a network management scenario is very important. The network manager wants the ability to specify which events should be logged, but the ability to add or delete event reports to be logged is also very important. For example, the user may want to log only critical event reports, but at a later date, perhaps the need to track all reports on a historical basis will become important.

The implementation targets are SMFAs (specific management function areas), which represent the principal network management applications, including configuration, fault, performance, security, and accounting management. Figure 4-4 shows an example of fault management that includes two systems management functions and three different service elements for managing objects.

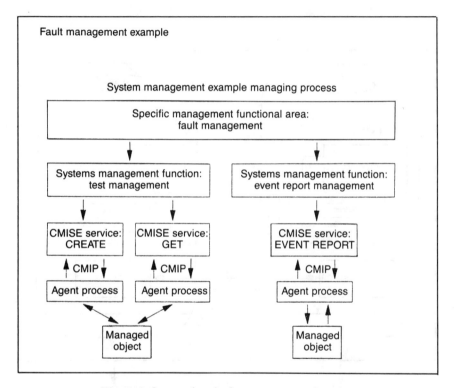

Fig. 4-4. Supporting fault management functions.

OSI includes the concept of managed objects. It specifies their attributes, operations that may be performed upon them, and the notification that may result. The set of managed objects in a system, together with their attributes, constitute that system's management information base (MIB). In addition to MIB, the structure of management information (SMI) defines the logical structure of OSI management information. Both MIB and SMI are subject to special customization by manufacturers and users.

The brief overview of OSI-based network management is shown in FIGS. 4-5 and 4-6. Figure 4-5 displays the relationship between manager and agent. Figure 4-6 illustrates the logical and physical peer-to-peer structures. As mentioned earlier, layers 1 through 6 serve as communication services providers.

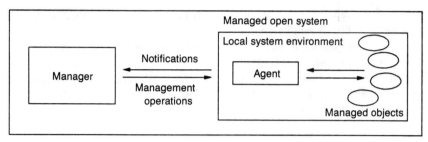

Fig. 4-5. Manager-agent relationship.

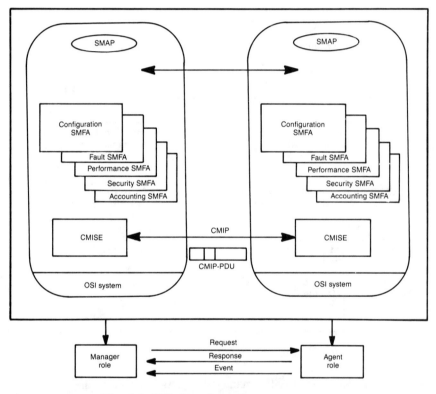

Fig. 4-6. OSI network management structure.

Simple Network Management Protocol (SNMP)

Simple Network Management Protocol (SNMP) originated in the Internet community as a means for managing TCP/IP networks and Ethernet networks. During 1990 and 1991, SNMP's appeal broadened rapidly beyond Internet, attracting waves of users searching for a proven, available method of monitoring multivendor networks. SNMP's monitoring and control transactions are actually completely independent of TCP/IP. SNMP only requires the datagram transport mechanism to operate. It can, therefore, be implemented over any network media or protocol suite, including OSI.

SNMP operates on three basic concepts; manager, agent, and the manage-- ment information base (MIB). (See FIG. 4-7.) (Datapro NM40 1990). Imagine FIG. 4-5 with different protocol data units and commands, and it's similar to SNMP.

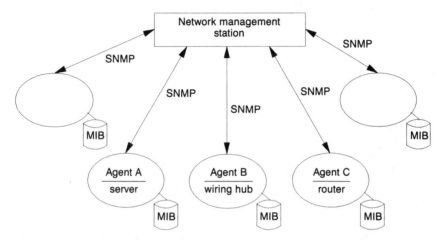

MIB = Management Information Base
SNMP = Simple Network Management Protocol

Fig. 4-7. SNMP structure.

An *agent* is a software program housed within a managed network device (such as a host, gateway, bridge, router, brouter, hub, or server). An agent stores management data and responds to the manager's request for this data.

A *manager* is a software program housed within a network management station. The manager has the ability to query agents using various SNMP commands.

The management information base (MIB) is a virtual database of managed objects, accessible to an agent and manipulated via SNMP to achieve network management.

Agent responsibilities

Each agent possesses its own MIB view, which includes the Internet standard MIB and, typically, other extensions. However, the agent's MIB doesn't have to implement every group of defined variables in MIB specification. This means, for example, that gateways need not support objects applicable only to hosts, and vice versa. This eliminates unnecessary overhead, facilitating

SNMP implementation in smaller LAN components that have little excess capacity for bearing overhead. An agent performs two basic functions:

- Inspects variables in its MIB.
- Alters variables in its MIB.

Inspecting variables usually means examining the values of counters, thresholds, states, and other parameters. Altering variables may mean resetting these counters, thresholds, and so on. It's possible to actually reboot a node, for example, by setting a variable.

An MIB implementation can be hosted on several types of platforms (Bapat 1991):

- Object-oriented databases.
- Relational databases.
- Flat-file databases.
- Proprietary-format databases.
- Firmware.

Basically, MIB information is distributed in agents. A typical configuration may include at the agent level a disk-based relational database, or a combination of PROM with static object attributes, and a RAM with dynamically changing information.

An agent with full functionality will typically require 50 or more KB of program code and memory. About fifty percent of the manufacturers have implemented SNMP agents in software, which means the agents are loaded into memory from an outside storage device or downloaded from a server after startup. Other manufacturers have implemented their agents in read-only memory chips, or programmable ROM. These implementations can be upgraded, usually by the user in the field. The most advanced implementations, electrically erasable PROM and flash PROM, can be reprogrammed without physically changing the module. Thus, they offer excellent flexibility at minimum interruption.

The trends of SNMP agents may be summarized as follows:

- The quality of agents is getting better because the SNMP technology is becoming better understood by implementors.
- Performance and speed depend on the agent's platform.
- Memory requirements depend on the functionality. (Case 1992)
  a. 32 KB without an MIB.
  b. Support of timers, drivers, operating system and protocol stacks, approximately 48 KB.
  c. Approximately .25 KB for each MIB variable that's supported by the agent.
- Penetration of new managed objects, such as traditional networking devices, packet switching nodes, FDDI nodes, frame relay nodes, networking infrastructures, voice components, and applications.

- Ability to run multiple agents from the same or different manufacturers on the same platform.
- More education for properly using the "SET" and "TRAP" commands to reduce unnecessary overhead due to polling and due to an increase in the control capabilities of the management station.

The MIB (management information base)

The MIB conforms to the structure of management information (SMI) for TCP/IP-based internets. This SMI, in turn, is modeled after OSI's SMI. While the SMI is equivalent for both SNMP and OSI environments, the actual objects defined in the MIB are different. SMI conformance is important, since it means that the MIB is capable of functioning in both current and future SNMP environments. In fact, the Internet SMI and the MIB are completely independent of any specific network management protocol, including SNMP.

MIB is documented as a chain of numbers in hierarchical order. Internet is in the middle of this hierarchy, as shown in FIG. 4-8.

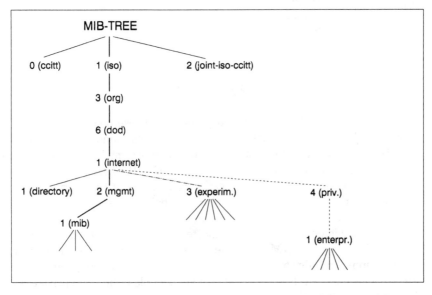

Fig. 4-8. Hierarchy of MIB components.

The SNMP-MIB repository is divided into four areas:

- Management attributes.
- Private attributes.
- Experimental attributes.
- Directory attributes.

All documentation is written in ASN.1 (Abstract Syntax Notation One). ASN.1 is no replacement for other programming languages, but it offers many benefits, such as flexibility, definition of new structures, and writing of new macros. The clear structure and ease of specification helped ASN.1 become the common denominator of SNMP documentation. Figure 4-9 shows a representative example.

```
Management information base entry example

—the interfaces group
ifNumber OBJECT-TYPE
SYNTAX INTEGER
ACCESS read-only
STATUS mandatory
:: = {interfaces 1}
—the IP group
UnixIpRouteEntry :: = SEQUENCE {
unixIpRouteFlags
INTEGER,
unixIpRouteRefCnt
INTEGER,
unixipRouteUses
Counter,
}
```

Fig. 4-9. ASN-1 example for MIBs.

MIB I includes a limited list of objects only. These objects deal with IP internetworking routing variables. MIB II, currently under consideration, extends the capabilities to a variety of media types, network devices, and SNMP statistics, not limited to the territory of TCP/IP. There have been many attempts to improve the performance of MIB accesses. A query language interface seems to offer a number of new capabilities such as a relational mask, and fast access (Datapro NM40 1991).

The management attributes are expected to be the same for all agents supporting SNMP. Thus, SNMP managers may work with agents from various manufacturers. In order to offer more functionality, vendors populate the private attributes as well. Figure 4-10 shows an example of how the private variables are structured by Cisco's NetCentral. It's similar to other vendors' structures, but may be completely different in the context of the indicators. As a result, the portability of solutions is somewhat limited.

Using MIBs, the partitioning will play a very important role in the future. The following discussion assumes that a minimal configuration for a network management product consists of a management station with some storage capability, and that this station is connected to managed objects equipped with agent capabilities.

Frequently, network resources are capable of being downloaded for certain management attributes (e.g., configuration, fault and performance attri-

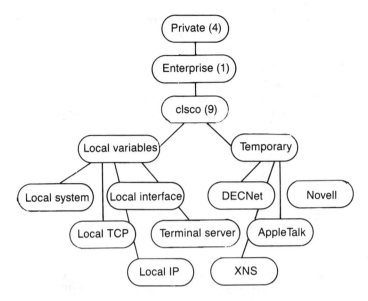

Fig. 4-10. Private attributes structure of Cisco.

butes). Further, they're capable of being polled and queried for current status. In such cases—the general idea of SNMP—it's not necessary to store this information in the central database of the network management station. Certain other network objects may be capable of storing MIB information, not only about themselves, but also about other managed objects as well. Good examples are multiplexer, PBXs, routers, and bridges. They maintain information about connected or owned components. This type of information doesn't need to be duplicated in the central database.

On the other hand, there are information groups that are optimally stored in a central database, including the central directory of managed objects, and LAN-wide topology information. The following architectural principles may be applied towards distributing MIB information (Bapat 1991).

The internal information storage capabilities of every managed object must be determined. If the resource can store nonvolatile information, and is capable of being queried for that, those attributes don't need to be stored centrally. If the managed object can store only volatile information that needs to be supplied to it, then copies of this information must be stored in a central database. Systemwide information, such as directory, connectivity, high-level security management functions, maintenance of historical data and accounting information is optimally stored in the central database.

In the hierarchy of management entities, where the intermediate entity also has storing capabilities, some of the data should be maintained in the intermediate entity. However, query requirement on behalf of the management station must not exceed a reasonable limit. Reliability and fault-tolerance requirements may result in maintaining two copies of relevant information.

LAN objects using wireless connection technologies are expected to use SNMP for management. Accessibility of objects by SNMP managers may be supported by both wireless and wire-based techniques.

The first SNMP-based products use a combination by maintaining information in both databases. In order to keep the price of a managed object low, just the necessary amount of information is stored in the objects. In terms of how much information should be stored in objects, OSI and SNMP guidelines strongly disagree.

Real MIB implementations may require extensions, incorporating other types of information to be stored for supporting operations. Such extensions may include (Bapat 1991):

- Improving security management by including security information about access to various managed objects, access to the network management system itself, and access to manipulating the MIB.
- Extended user data may help to manage users and groups of users. Users and user groups can themselves be managed objects that must be created, maintained, and eventually deleted in the MIB.
- Configuration histories and profiles support for retrieving past information, for reporting, or for supporting backup, and alternate routing as part of LAN fault and performance management.
- Trouble tracking helps to resolve networking problems more rapidly. The augmented MIB would provide the ability to translate event reports into trouble tickets, assign work codes to staff, recognize and categorize types of problems, relate problems, escalate problems by severity, and close trouble tickets after eliminating the problem and its causes.
- Extended set of performance indicators that supports more advanced performance management by reporting on resource use, on threshold violations, on trends, and on the quality of managing bandwidth between interconnected LANs. A concrete extension example is RMON.

Performance of MIBs and their counterpart at the network management station must be observed very carefully. Observation includes the registration of the actual frequency of command, number of traps, frequency of information retrievals by GetNextRequest, and the relation of positive to negative poll responses. MIBs are performing optimally only when tuned to special environments.

Manager responsibilities

Managers execute network manager station (NMS) applications, and often provide a graphical user interface that depicts a network map of agents. Typically, the manager also archives MIB data for trend analysis. The archivation may be implemented in two different ways (FIG. 4-11).

Each agent's MIB entries are copied into the dedicated MIB segment, or

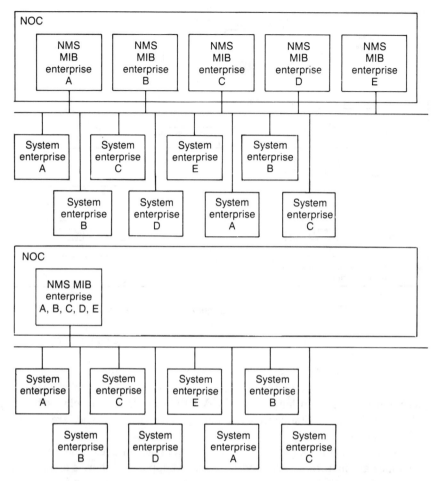

Fig. 4-11. MIB templates at the SNMP Manager.

MIB entries are copied into a common area for immediate correlation and analysis.

At the manager level, presentation services and database services are offered. Presentation services are most frequently implemented on SUN; databases are usually relational or object oriented. Figure 4-12 depicts a typical arrangement, indicating the wide opportunities of managing agents residing in file servers, bridges, routers, and X.25 gateways.

It's very important to choose the right database at the manager level. Some issues involved are the use of object-oriented database, the use of relational databases, and the use of other databases.

Object-oriented databases have several advantages (Bapat 1991).

They're naturally suited to an MIB because the MIB itself is formally described as a set of abstract data types in an object-oriented hierarchy.

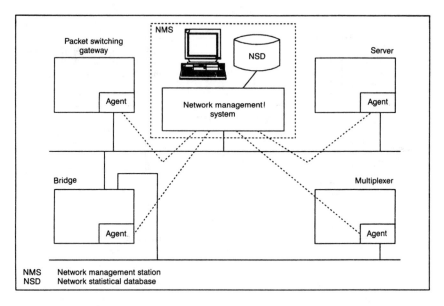

Fig. 4-12. Network management system structure.

Object-oriented databases have the ability to model interface behavior through the ability to store methods.

Object-oriented databases also have several disadvantages. The technique is not yet mature for product implementations; there are no standards yet for query and manipulation languages; the MIB object class hierarchy is broad and shallow in an inheritance tree, and performance characteristics are not yet well documented.

The use of relational databases also has several advantages. The relational techniques are mature, stable, and have many supporters; there's a standard access language (SQL); there are quality translators for translating ER models into relational schema, and there are many choices of applications.

The disadvantages of relational databases are: they're not well suited to store OO models; performance depends on tuning the database, and relational databases are highly application dependent.

Other types of databases can also be used. Flat-file databases and other proprietary formats can be tailored very specifically to MIBs, and can be optimized for performance. But, the design and implementation of network management applications may become more complex and time-consuming to develop and maintain.

The trends of SNMP managers may be summarized as follows:

- Many users and manufacturers have recognized that managers and agents from different suppliers could interoperate and have found it unnecessary to supply separate management stations for each family of agents.

- Many management stations are expensive and are hard to install, coordinate, and maintain.
- Low end, but still friendly, management systems are expected to be offered and implemented soon.
- More applications are needed in order to interpret and correlate data from MIBs; in particular, applications are needed to collect data, process it to produce information to answer questions, solve problems, and generate reports.
- Management stations are expected to augment control capabilities by properly using the "SET" command.

To carry out these duties, SNMP specifies five types of commands or verbs, called protocol data units (PDUs): GetRequest, GetNextRequest, SetRequest, GetResponse, and Trap.

GetRequest, GetNextRequest, and GetResponse

An agent will inspect the value of MIB variables after receiving either a GetRequest or GetNextRequest command (PDU) from a manager. Then, with a GetResponse verb, the agent then sends back the data it gathers.

The agent will alter MIB variables after receiving a SetRequest command. Using SetRequest, an NMS could, for example, instruct an agent to modify an IP route. SetRequest is a powerful command, and, if used improperly, could corrupt configuration parameters and seriously impair network service. Due to SNMP's lack of inherent security measures, some component vendors have not implemented or enabled SetRequest within their SNMP agent implementation. Many vendors are working to enhance security features within their products.

Traps

Trap is a special unsolicited command type that agents send to a manager after sensing a prespecified condition such as ColdStart, WarmStart, Link Down, LinkUp, AuthenticationFailure, EGPneighborLoss, or other enterprise-specific events. Traps are used to guide the timing and focus of polling, which SNMP employs to monitor the network's state.

Transport mechanisms

As mentioned previously, managers and agents exchange commands in the form of messages. There are currently two standard SNMP transport mechanisms: Unreliable Datagram Protocol (UDP) and Ethernet frames.

Other transport alternatives (e.g., OSI mechanisms) could also be implemented to carry the SNMP message. The message itself is constructed from data (type, request ID, error status, index, variables), the community string, and the version number. (See FIG. 4-13.)

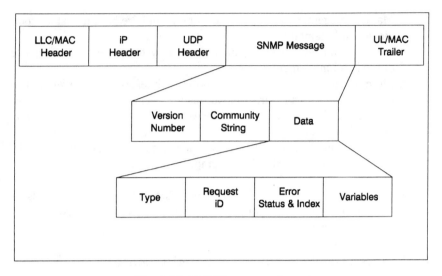

Fig. 4-13. SNMP message format.

SNMP is usually used in TCP/IP networks. SNMP operates over the transport and network layers of any protocol stack. Presently, UDP (User Data Protocol) is the most popular version of the transport protocol used. For the network layer, IP is the usual choice. But, users with multiple protocols are facing the question of the applicability of other protocols. Early implementation examples include Apple Talk instead of IP, IPX or DECnet. In these cases, a replacement in layers 3 and 4 may be observed. In other cases, SNMP is transported directly over the logical link control layer (LLC). Using this alternative, memory requirement savings are minimal.

SNMP proxy agents

Proxy agent software permits an SNMP manager to monitor and control network elements that are otherwise not addressable using SNMP. For example, a vendor wishes to migrate its network management scheme to SNMP, but has devices on the network that use a proprietary network management scheme. An SNMP proxy can manage those devices in their native mode. The SNMP proxy acts as a protocol converter to translate the SNMP manager's commands into the proprietary scheme. This strategy facilitates migration from the current proprietary environment, which is prevalent today, to the open SNMP equipment (see FIG. 4-14).

Proxy agents are well suited for vendors with an existing base of non-SNMP devices communicating efficiently under a proprietary scheme. By using a proxy agent, the vendor can reduce the investment risk of putting SNMP equipment in the field.

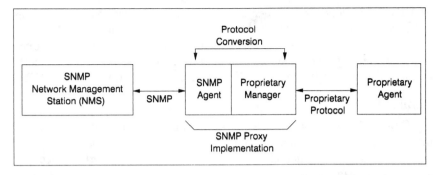

Fig. 4-14. SNMP proxy implementation.

In summary, SNMP's major advantages are:

- Its simplicity eases vendor implementation effort.
- It requires less memory and fewer CPU cycles than CMIP.
- It has been used and tested on the Internet.
- SNMP products are available now, and are affordable.
- Development kits are available free of charge.

SNMP has several disadvantages, including:

- Weak security features.
- Lack of global vision.
- Problems with the Trap command.

A lot of progress is expected in the area of security features. SNMP security specifications under development define a security architecture, protocols, and a new MIB variable that can be managed by SNMP. The security technology uses the MIT (Massachusetts Institute of Technology) algorithm for authentication, and can control who is authorized to access and change information. SNMP messages are divided into two basic components for safety purposes. The first component is constructed by the SNMP protocol data units, which transport management information. The second component is the authentication segment, which provides the authentication, authorization, and access control information. Changes to the second segment don't have any impact on the first. In particular, this new feature is very valuable when the "set" command is widely used.

Comparing CMIP and SNMP

For managing heterogeneous local area networks, two competing standards are under consideration; CMIP (Common Management Information Protocol), and

SNMP (Simple Network Management Protocol). Despite contradictory opinions and expectations, the coexistence of both protocols is in sight (Fisher 1991).

Since quite recently, more time has been spent on identifying the best-suited application areas for both alternatives. In order to promote availability of both, this section concentrates on similarities and differences of CMIP and SNMP.

Similarities

Goals   Both protocols have the same ultimate goal of moving network management-related information from one place to another. In order to execute network management functions, such as fault, configuration, performance, and accounting management.

Managed objects   Both protocols work with managed objects. (See again FIG. 4-5.) OSI objects are defined with attributes, with generated events, and performance options. Furthermore, objects are scoped by numerous hierarchies (e.g., for the purpose of inheritance or containment). ASN.1 is used as an object-oriented specification language to define this characteristic (Rose 1991).

In contrast, SNMP views managed objects as little more than simple variables in a virtual store. The SMI (structure of management information) is used as the schema for this database, and provides a naming relationship between managed objects. ASN.1 is used as a description language.

Management information base (MIB)   Both alternatives use the concept of a MIB, and allow for vendor-specific extensions to the MIB. These extensions could allow users to control devices more specifically, and implement more detailed performance metrication. It's likely that both products will borrow modules from each other. However, some differences will remain (Rose 1991).

- SNMP-based MIBs have no optional objects. Instead, related objects are grouped, and these groups form the basic unit of conformance.
- SNMP defines a core MIB first, containing only essential objects in the public area; later, other objects may be added from the private area.
- OSI-CMIP is using eventing for transporting MIB variables; SNMP is using traps very infrequently.

Commands   Although command sets are different, the targets of information retrieval, updates, reporting on events, and triggering actions are the same. TABLE 4-2 compares both command sets; this table doesn't include the confirmed-version of OSI commands.

Differences

Data access and retrieval   SNMP is oriented toward retrieving individual items of information; CMIP is more oriented to retrieving aggregate information. With SNMP, the manager has to be specific with the inquiry, issued as a "GET." With CMIP, more information can be transmitted easier for in-depth analysis at the manager level; most of this information is not needed. SNMP

Table 4-2.
Comparison of OSI-CMIP
and SNMP Command Sets

Commands	CMIP	SNMP
Get	x	x
Set	x	x
Event	x	
Create	x	
Delete	x	
Action	x	
Trap		x

tries to chain information retrieval units by "GET-NEXT." CMIP may require more resources; SNMP may fail in transmitting files at a reasonable performance level.

Polling versus eventing   SNMP works by polling or regularly inquiring on the status of objects, while CMIP uses eventing or has the objects inform the manager of their status when it changes. Eventing may require some intelligence built into the managed objects, which may not be the case with simple products. On the other hand, frequent polling may exceed reasonable overhead limits when many objects have to be polled for their status.

Number of managed objects to be supervised   Accurate calculations may help in both cases to determine the number of devices that may be continuously supervised by the manager. The number of managed objects depends on the SNMP polling interval (T) and the average duration (D) of each poll:

$$N < T/D$$

D can be calculated by adding up the delays caused in the management system, in the network, and in the managed objects. The delay component differs in LANs (around 1 ms) and WANs (around 500 ms). Assuming a polling interval of 15 minutes, a processing time in the manager and in the managed objects of 50 ms, 4,500 objects in a LAN, then just 750 objects in an interconnected LAN environment may be continuously supervised.

With eventing (CMIP), specific (filtered) events are sent to the manager in an unsolicited manner. The number of objects depends on the time interval between the generation of two consecutive event reports from the same managed object, and on the time required to interpret and process an incoming event:

$$N < 1/N \times 1/M)$$

Using the above formula, with eventing cycles of 1.5 minutes, and a processing demand of 50 ms, 18,000 managed objects may be continuously supervised.

Storage requirements   Considering the protocol stack and protocol encode/decode requirements (Datapro NM40 1991). SNMP needs considerably less storage; estimates indicate approximately 70 to 80 KB for SNMP, and over 300 KB for CMIP.

Functionality   Basically, CMIP offers more capability for network management functions support. In certain cases, in order to be comparable, SNMP implementations need more elaborate implementation work. But, most CMIP functions can be implemented by SNMP, as well.

Size and performance   There's less SNMP support code, and it's faster and less expensive than a CMIP implementation. Most of this is because of the polling-versus-eventing issue; eventing requires more intelligence in the managed objects: SNMP puts the intelligence into the manager; CMIP requests more functionality at the managed object level.

Transport services   For its underlying transport mechanisms, SNMP requires connectionless (CL) datagrams. This means that it can be used with Ethernet, IPX, UDP, XNS, and other simple communication protocols. CMIP requires a reliable transport layer, such as OSI's connection-oriented (CO) TP-4 transport protocol. CL techniques are more useful in fault cases; CO techniques are better suited for retrieving large amounts of data.

In both cases, however, other architectures may be used at lower layers. Even proprietary solutions may call for an interesting combination, such as CMOL, where IBM and 3Com try to reduce the need for the full OSI stack in managed objects. Another solution would be the use of a proxy that would accomplish the work outside the managed object.

Standards and testing   CMIP is controlled by international standard bodies such as the ISO. Vendors can test their implementations against a conformance test suite from the COS (Corporation for Open Systems). Vendors are offering to demonstrate the interoperability of their products at trade shows. SNMP is controlled by the Internet Activities Board. Vendors check their implementation with interoperability testing.

Availability of products   SNMP has in this respect an undeniable advantage. Most LAN interworking products support SNMP, either at the agent or the manager level. Many vendors support both. CMIP implementations are fewer, but it's only a matter of time before its use is more widespread.

TABLE 4-3 summarizes the strengths of both alternatives. It's likely that in the future they will be used in combination; CMIP will solve the problems of intercommunication between management systems, and SNMP will most likely concentrate on the manager and managed-objects area. SNMP support for the leading *de facto* and open standards will become a high-priority item.

As SNMP-applications are more widely used, vendors and users are interested in improving the performance and extending the functionality. The first customization examples include the extensive use of traps, use of dialogs, multilevel polling, compression of GETs, improved security functions, use of dynamic polling, and support of trouble tickets. Implementation examples may be seen with NCE (Network Control Engine) from SynOptics and MultiMan from Lannet.

Table 4-3. Strengths and
Weaknesses of OSI-CMIP and SNMP

Comparison Criteria	CMIP	SNMP
1. Functional		
Configuration management	+	+
Fault management	+ +	+ +
Performance management	+ +	+
Security management	+	
Accounting management		
Planning		
2. Operational		
Number of objects being supervised	+ +	+
Efficiency	+	+ +
Personnel required	+	+ +
Simplicity		+ +
User friendliness	+	+
3. Implementation		
Memory cost		+ + +
Processing cost	+	+ +
Application cost	+	+ +
4. Support by manufacturers of		
Processors	+	+ +
LAN software		+
Internet products		+ +
LAN hardware		+
Number of products		+ + +
5. Maintenance expenses	+	
6. Centralization		+ +
7. Decentralization	+ +	
8. Future trends		
Extensions	+ +	+
Scaleability	+ +	+
Inheritance of attributes	+ +	
Protocol dependability	+ +	

+ + + very strong
+ +   strong
+   fair
       weak

Leading manufacturers' strategy examples

Manufacturers are expected to support *de facto* network management standards, such as SNMP or open standards like CMIP, or even both. Proprietary solutions and products will only have limited use or limited life cycles. This section concentrates on leading manufacturers' architectures and standards implementation strategies. Products supporting these architectures will be addressed in chapter 5.

IBM network management architecture

Open network management (ONA) is intended as a framework for the development of IBM management products, which are aimed at managing large SNA networks. Through published interfaces and message formats, IBM is also inviting other vendors to implement compatibility with this architecture, in much the same way that most vendors implement at least limited SNA compatibility. Figure 4-15 summarizes the architecture. Under this framework, there are three major kinds of elements that perform management functions:

- Focal points, which provide centralized network management support. Focal points support the needs of human and programmed operators and provide a central point for collecting, analyzing, and storing network and system management data. The NetView family of products constitute IBM's strategic focal point products.
- Entry points, which are SNA devices capable of implementing the SNA management services architecture for themselves and other attached products. Most IBM data network products are capable of functioning as entry points.
- Service points, which provide SNA management services for themselves and for attached devices and networks that are not capable of being entry points.

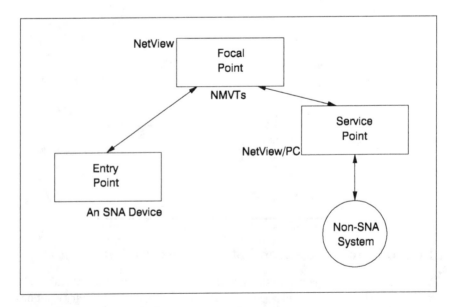

Fig. 4-15. SNA architecture.

The service point is capable of sending network management data about-non-SNA systems to a focal point, and it's capable of receiving commands from a focal point to be executed on the non-SNA systems. The service point is thus a network management gateway, translating between SNA formats and those of non-SNA devices. NetView/PC was the first implementation of a major service point product, although other management packages may contain embedded service point functions.

IBM's intention is to use the focal point to manage all the information resources of the enterprise, even those from other vendors, through the agency of the service point. IBM had a major marketing lead for about a year and a half. But other vendors are now actively competing with IBM for control of the enterprise-wide focal point.

In the early 1990s, IBM informally showed an expanded version of their open management architecture, as shown in FIG. 4-16. It adds the following

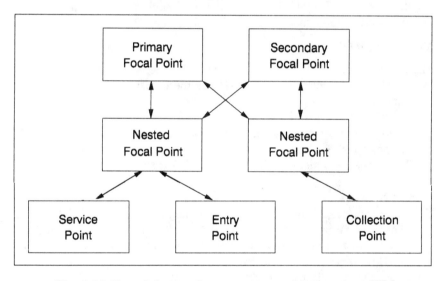

Fig. 4-16. Extended network management architecture from IBM.

architectural elements:

- Secondary focal points, which are redundant focal points that can take over in case the primary focal point fails. Reacting to the need for high availability of the focal point, IBM will be providing increased support for multiple focal points that are able to back each other up.
- Nested focal points, which provide distributed management support for segments of large networks, while still forwarding critical information up to more global focal points.
- Collection points, which provide a network management relay function from a self-contained SNA subnetwork to a standard focal point. It would appear that the AS/400 or System 88 will act as a collection point for IBM peer-to-peer networks of midrange systems.

The direction is clear with these architectural extensions: IBM is developing the capability for a more distributed approach to network and system management that allows many different IBM network management systems to work together to deliver enterprise-wide management.

In order to support the Graphic Monitor Facility with object-oriented data about multivendor network devices, a host-based Resource Object Data Manager (RODM) is used. RODM is a high-speed, high-performance, in-memory data manager designed to keep up with the status of the network in realtime.

A distributed systems management (DSM) platform will give users a single point of control over local area networks. The platform is based on OS/2, and will include base management software, and a graphical user interface. Both IBM, and third-party applications may be written to IBM-APIs; both NMS of Novell and LAN Network Manager may run on the same platform. Enterprise network management may be supported by porting this platform to AS/400, to mainframes, and to RISC/6000. A new set of applications for the platform includes configuration, installation and distribution (CID) services.

Xerox Network System

Many early solutions have been influenced by the Xerox Network System (XNS). Many companies have used XNS as the cornerstone of their network product offerings. The XNS layered approach is known to have been part of the OSI models. The XNS approach to networking and network management is well adapted to most office applications, with clear functional layers, clearly defined protocols, and easy-to-implement features. Due to its robustness and simplicity, it has become one of the favorite LAN architectures.

Novell

The other example is Novell with the LAN operating system called NetWare. Novell offers NetWare care for fault and performance monitoring of physical and data link layers, and there are accounting and security features in its operating system. However, the present software architecture doesn't include a special extension toward dedicated network management.

Novell has been forthcoming concerning specifics of its approach to LAN management. Recent statements on OSI indicate long-term commitment to OSI network management standards, CMISE, and CMIP. Novell's stated goal is to create standards-based management tools that will work with any OSI-compliant system. Initially, CMIP and CMIS will run over Novell's IPX transport protocols. Once Novell's multiprotocol architecture is fully implemented, CMIP and CMIS will run over the OSI transports and any other NetWare-supported transport protocol, such as TCP/IP, SNA, and X.25, in addition to its proprietary Internetwork Packet Exchange (IPX) and Sequenced Packet Exchange (SPX) protocols. Novell's Network Management Server will communicate using CMIP with both NetWare servers and with OSI-compatible hosts running network management systems that are CMIP/CMIS compliant. Novell is exploring links with integrated management systems from Hewlett-Packard,

IBM, AT&T, and DEC. Also, SNMP is going to be supported. The first results are visible with IBM; Novell is exporting network-related information from NetWare to NetView.

Both Novell and third parties are expected to use NetWare Diagnostic Protocol (NDP) more widely. NDP is the monitoring protocol—with similarities to SNMP-included in the IPX protocol stack. Decoding NDP, network managers receive valuable diagnostics about NetWare components. Vendors with products targeting NetWare use exclusively NDP as an information source.

In summary, Novell wants to maintain its leading position by gradually extending NetWare's management capabilities, by providing portable and remote monitoring devices, by supporting *de facto* standards such as NMVT, and SNMP, and by announcing future support for open standards.

Ungerman-Bass

Ungerman-Bass has recently enhanced its core network management system (NMS) and launched a new line of intelligent bridges that link with wide area networks. Integration with Tandem's network management architectures is expected soon. Ungerman-Bass has been successful with Access/One, which is providing a wide range of connectivity and internetworking capabilities with Ethernet, token ring, and FDDI-based high-speed LANs. On the way to more integration, the partnership with Advanced Computer Communications will help to add a multiprotocol router to its hub. Two other strategic alliances will help in penetrating the WAN management area as well. The alliance with British Telecom will lead to an interface with BT's Concert, supporting CMIP. With this interface, communication with many other managers will result. The network management product implementation (NetDirector) resides on PS/2 under OS/2. In addition, the Unix platform is supported.

3Com

3Com's network management strategy provides for simplified, flexible, and integrated network management based on standards. 3Com manufactures a broad range of products that are building blocks for a global data network, including adapters, intelligent wiring hubs, bridges, routers, and terminal servers. The company is committed to providing standards-based agents on all products and assuring that they're manageable by any standards-based manager or 3Com's standards-based management platforms.

Currently, 3Com products support SNMP. 3Com and IBM are in the process of defining the HLM specification, which will be the standard of future desktop management. 3Com has a two-pronged approach to providing a network management platform solution: ViewBuilder, a PC-based SNMP manager for small to medium-sized networks, and ViewBuilder Unix management applications for open Unix SNMP managers for management of large enterprise networks.

ViewBuilder is an OS/2 based SNMP manager that can integrate and centralize the management of network adapters, servers, intelligent hubs, bridges, routers, and terminal servers. It features a sophisticated graphical interface (Presentation Manager) that uses icons and bitmaps to give the administrator an overview of the realtime status, performance, and configuration of the entire network. What's unique to this product is its ability to proactively manage the network. The network operator can specify custom activity thresholds that can trigger scripted applications in case of abnormal or exception activity. These scripted applications can be used for automatic fault isolation and resolution.

ViewBuilder/Unix is a family of graphical network management applications for open Unix-based SNMP managers. Network administrators requiring true multivendor management of large enterprise networks can use 3Com applications for simplifying the management of 3Com products on their network. 3Com is targeting its first set of management applications for SunNet Manager, since Sun has the largest installed base among open Unix-based SNMP managers. 3Com will deliver management applications for its high-performance bridge/router NetBuilder II and its third generation hub LinkBuilder. These applications are integrated with SunNet Manager and simplify management by hiding the complexity of SNMP.

Banyan

Banyan's network management software option is a realtime network monitor that enables administrators to examine the performance of all network components, including LAN/WAN connections, system configuration, Vines software services server disk, and network routing. It provides diagnostic, performance, and use statistics from any network PC or server console (Herman 1991).

Vines-based geographically dispersed local area networks may be linked to each other using existing SNA backbones. It may mean the start of more cooperation between IBM and Banyan in the area of network management.

Banyan is supporting SNMP and optional LAN administration utilities under the Vines 4.X operating system. The company has mapped all the information from its proprietary M-Net management utility into the SNMP format. Banyan provides information about servers, services, peripherals, file systems, communication resources, and network interfaces. Most users want to tie Vines management to SNMP to be able to centralize management. A number of network management systems and protocol analyzers are generic, and able to decode Vines protocols. However, there are only a handful of vendors with special solutions for Vines. Those products are very similar because they are all based on information provided by Vines through its M-Net application programming interface. The SNMP support confines itself to an SNMP agent reporting on Vines network status. For security reasons, changes by the SNMP manager are not (yet) supported.

Proteon

Proteon provides simple but effective tools for the management of its LANs and of multivendor, multiprotocol internets. These tools address the management of the physical rather than logical networks. Proteon offers network management packages: TokenView for LANs and OverView for internets. At present, these systems don't interoperate. Currently based on SNMP, Over-View is designed to allow future support for CMOT (CMIS/CMIP on TCP). Their internetworking router products support SNMP, and they can migrate to CMOT if the market demands it.

Proteon continues to assess their network management strategy. Possible future directions include porting OverView to a Unix environment and/or distributing the current OverView functionality over multiple machines in order to avoid a single point of failure in the management system. Since they're primarily a networking and router vendor, they're also considering partnering with a management platform vendor such as Sun and placing less emphasis on OverView (Herman 1989).

AT&T's network management architecture

UNMA (Unified Network Management Architecture) is a general, OSI-based, multiple management system architecture (Gilbert 1988). It fits well with AT&T's product direction, which is also based on ISO and CCITT open protocols. One of the most distinctive aspects of AT&T's approach is the fact that it's not tied to particular network technology, but is intended to serve as an all-encompassing design for managing any type of network. It will cover networks of all types, including voice and data, public and private, wide area and local area, AT&T and non-AT&T. Based on vendor-independent interfaces defined by ISO, it provides a way of tying together network management systems from a variety of suppliers. UNMA will also guide the development of AT&T's future products for integrated management of diverse products and services.

UNMA consists of a three-tier architecture (see FIG. 4-17). The lowest tier

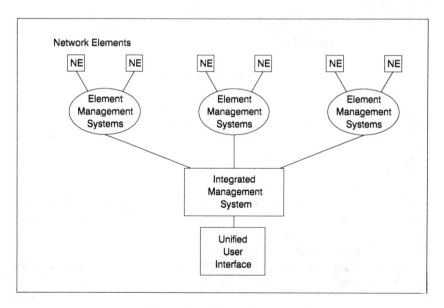

Fig. 4-17. UNMA architecture.

is composed of network elements, which are the logical and physical components that comprise the network(s) being managed. Network elements exist in three domains:

- Customer premises, which includes PBXs, computer systems, workstations and PCs, LANs, premise wiring, modems, multiplexers, DSUs, bandwidth managers, packet switches, and the like. AT&T seems to be focusing on management of premises equipment with UNMA.
- Local exchange carrier (LEC) networks, which provide intra-LATA communications services, including switched and private line services for both voice and data. Although AT&T always talks about intra-LATA elements being part of UNMA, there's little indication that any of the BOCs want to play along with AT&T.
- Interexchange carrier (IEX) networks, which provide long-distance, inter-LATA communications services, including switched and private line services for voice and/or data. AT&T, of course, is the major IEX on which UNMA is focused. By providing management of public network services to customers through UNMA, AT&T is hoping to improve the appeal of its services and make them more dynamic and responsive to customer needs.

The second tier of UNMA consists of the element management systems (EMS), which administer and manage network elements. EMSs can be located on customer's premises, at a LEC central office, or at an IEX central office. They might be located at a third-party site. Element management systems are designed to meet the needs of specific kinds of equipment and form a set of modular components for meeting the management requirements of different network environments. The EMS tier is necessary since network equipment exists in different administrative domains (e.g., LECs versus IEXs). In addition, the concept of an EMS allows AT&T to preserve its current investment in network management software and systems.

The third tier of UNMA consists of integrated management systems, which tie together the element management systems from the three domains. This tier concentrates on integrated applications and unified user interfaces. Although most AT&T diagrams show one integrated management system, the architecture is very general and allows for many.

Element management systems and integrated management systems communicate with and among each other using a standard management protocol, which AT&T calls the Network Management Protocol (NMP). Element management systems communicate with network elements using whatever protocols are best suited to the task. NMP is based on the ISO Common Management Information Protocol (CMIP). NMP is really the means for integration in the architecture and the vehicle for tying in management systems from other vendors.

AT&T has defined two basic models, which will guide the development of

NMP and the implementation of products that will operate under UNMA:

- The organizational model, which describes the ways in which network management can be distributed administratively across management domains and across management systems within a domain.
- The information model, which provides guidelines for defining managed objects in the communications network and their respective interrelationship, classes, attributes, methods, and names. It's the most concrete published example of how OSI management concepts might be put into practice.

One thing is immediately clear upon examining the definition of these models: AT&T is defining a multiple management system architecture, in which an essentially unlimited number of administratively separate management systems can cooperate to perform useful network management functions. This is evident when considering the definition of a management network, which is distinct from the network(s) being managed.

Leading LAN management platform examples

In the platform category, UNIX-based systems are leading the market. Eight alternatives will be briefly introduced:

- Enterprise Management Architecture from Digital.
- OpenView Network Management server from HP.
- SunNet Manager from Sun Microsystems.
- DualManager from Netlabs.
- NMC 3000 from Network Managers.
- NetExpert from Objective Systems Integrators.
- NMS/Core from Teknekron Communications Systems.
- Network Knowledge Systems from Applied Computing Devices.

DEC's network management architecture

Enterprise Management Architecture (EMA) from DEC incorporates a number of design goals and principles. Its primary function is to provide integrated network management: a consistent user interface, a common information repository, and integrated access to management functions and managed devices. Four distinguishing EMA characteristics in particular directly address current market needs: applicability for distributed environments, open interfaces, third-party support, and OSI compliance via a migration path (Datapro NM40 1989)

The structure of EMA is simple, yet flexible enough to be implemented in numerous ways. EMA is composed of several basic pieces that don't have to reside in one location. This flexibility is a major advantage, since it's adaptable to a distributed computing environment which, due to LAN and PC technology, is on the rise in more and more enterprise networks.

EMA employs a director-entity model to describe the relationship between the networking elements being managed (entities) and the systems managing them (directors). The entity is actually composed of two parts: the managed object (multiplexer, modem, line, control unit, and so on), and its agent (the management software) (FIG. 4-18). This software acts as a conduit for management operations such as events and directives, and may also provide a degree of management capability for the entity.

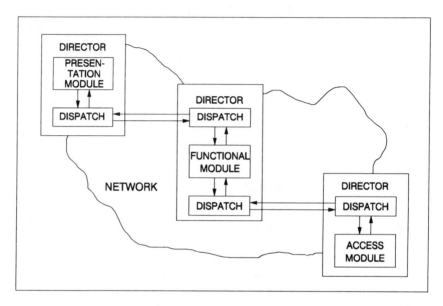

Fig. 4-18. EMA architecture.

Network management solutions are grouped into domains. Domains are described as user-defined spheres of management interest and control, adding another dimension of architecture flexibility. Domain may be defined according to function, organization, technology, geography, or a combination of all of these. Domains may be nested, overlapped, shared, or clearly fragmented. It's assumed that EMA will first be populated with existing DEC products in the WAN area, such as the NMCC/DECNetMon, Netpath, Netresponse, Netaval, and NIWatch; and in the LAN area, such as Ethernim, LAN Traffic Monitor, Terminal Server Manager, Remote System Manager and Remote Bridge Management Software.

Hewlett-Packard's network management architecture

HP's OpenView offers a comprehensive network management solution for managing local and wide area multivendor networks. The product is based on an OSI platform and integrates existing wide area HP AdvanceNet network management and LAN-based performance management products.

The center of OpenView is HP OpenWindows, a graphical user interface running on the HP Vectra PC or on Windows. For third-party integration, HP offers a developer's kit.

HP approaches the management of multiprotocol, multivendor LANs with a distributed architecture. In their view, a single enterprise-wide management system is impractical today given the lack of universally accepted standards and the complexity of networks. Thus, a distributed architecture allows for the management of a diverse set of networks and network elements.

Initial OpenView offerings build on HP's extensive experience with network diagnostic and monitoring equipment, network interfaces and routing devices, workstations, PC LANs, and network management services. HP's OpenView offerings focus on seven areas: fault management or problem isolation, accounting management, security management, configuration and change management, performance management, inventory management, and system management.

At present, OpenView focuses on management of HP systems and networks with current or future interfaces to equipment and systems due from other vendors. Although not yet a true multivendor management offering, OpenView is well positioned if HP decides to create interfaces to other vendors' equipment and systems, a task currently left to third parties.

The new releases of OpenView emphasize the development platform feature for users and developers to customize and build upon. The applications-related features include SingleView, a tool that lets developers integrate existing network management applications with OpenView. Another component is Dynamic Data Collection, which gathers and stores network-management related information into databases for historical processing. With the User-Defined Threshold feature, a user can set parameters for MIB variables to help them troubleshoot performance problems. Application Builder is intended for third-party developers and users who are interested in writing SNMP-based applications for OpenView. Offering an SNMP agent application for SUN workstations under OpenView, users receive an alternative solution to SunNet Manager.

Interconnect Manager is a UNIX-based application for OpenView Network Node Manager, emphasizing HP's goal of managing LAN interconnecting devices. In order to increase network management effectivity, a relational database from Ingres Corporation is also supported.

The OpenView architectural concepts are implemented in the design of HP's OpenView Network Node Manager. The server implements a standard set of management APIs that enables the distribution of applications across multiple servers, and it provides these applications with common services for data management, access to managed objects, and presentation. In each area, using the developer's kit, changes and extensions are possible. The server consists of five major components (Herman 1990):

- Presentation services.
- Data management services.
- Event management services.
- Communication protocols.
- Distributed communication infrastructure.

Presentation services implement the user interface. The server will support the X11 and OSF/Motif standards, which provide a windowing graphical user interface. The OpenView Windows dynamic network map interface from DOS OpenView is implemented on the server as well.

The OpenView Windows user interface is well organized, logical, and extensive. The OpenView Windows map is made up of a collection of pictures. A *picture* is a collection of symbols that represent network devices. Usually, a picture would represent the collection of devices on a single LAN. On the top-level map display, a picture is represented by an icon. Picture icons are linked together on the map using subnet symbols. There can be multiple independent maps. OpenView Windows provides facilities for editing maps and pictures. The multilevel display capability of maps and pictures helps handle the large number of devices in a big internet. The X11 implementation makes it possible for multiple operations to share a common map display.

SingleView allows management of the network from a single screen, rather than with multiple monitors. It allows user-developed or third-party applications to be integrated into the OpenView graphical user interface.

Data management services implement a common, shared data store for all applications and management services on the server. Access to stored data is through a set of APIs that protect developers from dependence on the actual physical structure of the database. The server's data manager stores and retrieves all data in object form (i.e., as instances of defined object classes). In fact, the APIs in the NM Server provide the set of services defined by the ISO CMIS standard.

As part of the developer's kit, HP will provide a metadata compiler that enables users and developers to define new object classes or extensions to existing object classes. Object classes, attributes, actions, and events are defined using templates that can be compiled into ISO ASN.1 notation, as is done in the OSI management standards.

References to stored data can make use of the scoping and filtering mechanism defined in CMIP/CMIS that allow for the selection of multiple object instances in a single reference. By making its API conform to CMIS, HP makes it possible for applications to retrieve information from the network or the database using the same syntax.

The actual database delivered with the server is specially engineered to meet the performance requirements of realtime network management. HP will provide a facility for exporting data from the database to an SQL-compatible RDBMS.

Although HP's Data Manager is a good first start, it does have some limitations. It can store the latest instance data about an object, but doesn't yet have the machinery to support storing a time series of data. Significant improvements are expected from the Dynamic Data Collection and the User-Defined Threshold features.

Event management services route and log events generated by network objects or other server components. Using these services, applications can request receipt of specific events by registering one or more event sieves. Event sieve managers determine which other server nodes should receive copies of particular events, and they also route events to registered applications. Routing of events across servers is controlled by a distribution list, which is a simple ASCII file that must be edited manually by operations administrators.

The communication protocols component implements communication between the server and managed objects. HP's first release of the server supports SNMP and CMOT. Interestingly, it will not support real CMIP, presumably because there are no managed objects that implement CMIP over a full OSI stack. HP's implementation of SNMP has some built-in features, such as automatic retry of requests that time out, and access to aggregate objects without having to make repeated "GET" requests. HP plans to include full CMIP in the server once the Network Management Forum (NMF) finishes specifying its first full Management Information Base (MIB) and other vendors start implementing the OSI management protocol interface.

The Distributed Communication Infrastructure is the key server building block that implements the intermodule communication mechanism, allowing pieces of the server to reside on different machines. The communication infrastructure defines a standard API that provides the services defined by ISO's CMIS. Applications and object managers refer to object classes and instances of their calls to the server, and the communication infrastructure maps these to network addresses and choices of management protocol for accessing the managed object.

The goal of these APIs is to shield applications from knowing the location of the objects they're manipulating or the protocols being used. Application developers do need to know if they're using SNMP, since only a subset of the calls can work over SNMP. The use of a CMIS API as the OpenView standard is in keeping with easier migration to standard OSI management for applications that are written to work with SNMP today. Application Builder gives further help in writing applications rapidly for the SNMP-based OpenView.

Although the communication infrastructure API separates location information from applications, this information is still needed at runtime. It's supplied through what HP calls local registration files (LRF). Similar to event distribution lists, LRFs seem like primitive mechanisms, which are prone to error and additional configuration confusion. Location information should be obtained through a general directory service shared by other network applications. (Figure 4-19 shows the principal components of the Network Management Server.)

OpenView evolves toward the OSF's DME in multiple steps. Starting with its own offering, the company will continue with segments provided by other contributors. Because the application programming interfaces between the various modules remain the same, users will probably not notice the changes; e.g., Network Logger from Banyan may replace the Event Manager in OpenView for both Unix and MS-DOS versions.

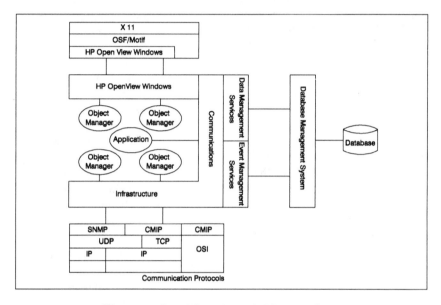

Fig. 4-19. OpenView Network Manager Server.

SunNet Manager (Sun)

Based on distributed computing architectures and protocols, Sun has created a set of tools to manage elements of a network rather than an enterprise-wide network. Sun has implemented a platform-based approach in which the platform is a Unix workstation with SunNet Manager software that monitors and controls devices and processes on TCP/IP and DECNet over Ethernet networks, with future support for managing FDDI networks announced. SunNet includes development tools so that third parties can create interfaces to devices and networks not supported by Sun and so that users can create customized reports and network management applications.

SunNet Manager manages TCP/IP and DECNet networks. Through network windowing and terminal emulation products, SunNet Manager also provides integration with systems such as IBM NetView and AT&T Accumaster Integrator, allowing them to be run from the same screen (Herman 1989).

SunNet Manager is a network system that provides user and development tools for administration of today's distributed work groups. These tools automatically monitor and analyze systems and networks, so users are notified when they need to be involved. SunNet Manager lets users manage more resources in less time and operate in larger networks. Network control is consistently integrated at the user interface.

SunNet Manager is an open, heterogeneous platform based on the OSI management framework. It offers expandability to third parties through well-known open protocols such as ONC (RPC/XDR), SNMP, and DECnet NICE (with SunLink DNI). Because SunNet Manager is built with distributed computing technologies, users can install it in a centralized or decentralized fashion to suit organizational preference.

Sun products make it easy for users to add their own managed objects, such as systems, OS resources, application and network services, communication protocol layers and interfaces, and other network devices. SunNet Manager employs a consistent Open Look Graphical User Interface (GUI), regardless of the type of resource being managed, so it's easy to use new tools. SunNet Manager runs on SunOS and the OpenWindows environment, offering integrated access to a variety of network windowing and terminal emulation products. SunNet Manager also provides integration with systems such as IBM NetView and AT&T Accumaster Integrator, allowing them to be run from the same screen.

Sun provides a wide range of agents written to manage SunNet objects. Because the OSI management framework is new, not every agent that users may require has been written. Many agents are available from third-party vendors for their equipment. These agents may be reachable through a standard protocol such as SNMP, but they're more commonly accessible through proprietary protocols. There are many ways users can add their own agents and managed objects or acquire them from a third party, so that SunNet Manager may apply to an entire distributed work group. Agents packaged with SunNet Manager include:

- Communication protocol layers and interfaces such as Internet MIB (RFC 1066) through SNMP, Ethernet, FDDI (to follow with SunNet FDDI/DX), and X.25 (through SunNet X.25).
- Network devices such as IP routers (e.g., SunNet IR) and MAC bridges.
- System and OS resource statistics.
  a. System mechanism such as CPU use and free memory buffers.
  b. Disk and file systems.
  c. Application, database, and network service statistics such as NFS or RPC.

Sun workstations, SunOS, and OpenWindows support a number of tools for SunNet work group management. SunNet Manager provides a centralized data and application platform for integration of these tools and creation of new tools. Applications for controlling network objects, logging in, or using XWindows to access other management systems may be specifically directed by the topology map selection service of SunNet Manager. In addition, SunNet Manager includes common tools for two well-defined, secure applications: event reporting and performance monitoring.

Event reporting   Events are notifications of user-defined conditions in the work group. Distributed agents monitor resources at a given sampling interval, and if the condition exists, an event notification is sent back to the manager console. This feature is extremely powerful because any condition may be defined against any defined object. It saves the administrator from the time-consuming task of personally monitoring the status of distributed systems. Examples of how to use events include:

- Fault notification: an alarm when a system fails.
- Warning notification: if a resource such as a network or a disk system is at 90% capacity, an event provides early warning so users can take remedial action.
- Security: notification of a network security break-in.
- Accounting: notification of resource use that may be logged for later reporting and billing.
- Configuration change: network can be monitored to determine if any new systems or users exist.

Events may signal users in a variety of ways, based on user selection. Events may highlight the node or subnet icon on the work group topology display; they may be received in the user's mail; they may initiate an audio signal. Also, they may be sent to a user program. This allows attachment of programs to automate responses to network events. It also provides a convenient mechanism for forwarding event messages to a central management system from another vendor. All events are logged for later statistical analysis.

Performance monitoring   Resource performance values may be sampled at a given rate for either realtime charting or logging for later analysis. Once a problem is identified, often by an event notification, administrators use this feature to look at current status or log a complete sampling interval for review.

All SunNet Manager tools use the Open Look graphical user interface and run in the OpenWindows environment as SunView applications. Sun recommends that all add-on tools be written in XView and that the entire program be run in the X11/NeWS environment, since this is the direction of the core tools.

SunNet Manager allows users to easily customize their operation. The tools provided are relevant and important for the SunNet work group, but users may integrate other tools. SunNet Manager was built with this in mind.

Users may add new managed objects in two ways (FIG. 4-20):

1. With Sun's Agent Services API, users can create a new agent or can quickly turn an existing program into an agent; Sun's target of simplicity is one agent in a day. Agent programs may use the ONC-based Agent Services libraries directly, gaining the benefits of security (through secure RPC authentication) and openness, since many ONC-licensed vendors and Unix System V Release 4.0 support the RPC/XDR interfaces.

2. If the new object supports an industry protocol, users may create an agent (sometimes called a proxy agent) that translates between it and the Agent Service. Proxies have access to all of the services in SunNet Manager. SNMP is implemented through a proxy agent, so events can be defined against SNMP agents from third parties, enhancing native SNMP functionality.

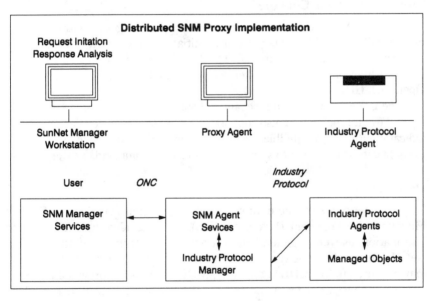

Fig. 4-20. SunNet Manager structure.

Analysis (trend analysis, accounting, security, and so on), automation, expert system, and control applications may be added in three ways:

1. Applications may be linked into a user interface through the selection service.

2. They may use any of the underlying services and data that are exposed in SunNet Manager. There are two APIs—Agent and Manager Services—that are open for all tool builders.
3. They may create or review historical logs, including the default log of all events. All data is kept in ASCII form for speed and ease of use by programmers.

Agents and custom programs/logs may be run or mounted on separate machines or on the SunNet Manager user workstation because they're built on ONC services. A simple configuration may house most of the distributed application on administrators' workstations, but a large configuration may house modules, such as an SNMP proxy, on a separate server. This arrangement lets the product be scaled affordably. And since agents may have open dialogs with multiple managers, it lets administration be implemented in a centralized or distributed fashion to suit local organizational preferences.

SunNet Manager Console

The SunNet Manager Console contains SunNet Manager's central management application. This is where the user initiates management tasks and management information is returned. The SunNet Manager Console presents users with an object-oriented interface that may be customized through the OpenLook GUI.

The Console provides a mechanism for initiating request-for-data reporting and event reporting. It also supports the display of reported data and event indications (including audible, visible, and programmatic mechanisms). The Console can be extended to support user-specified commands as well.

Database

The Console relies on the definition and information contained in SunNet Manager's Management Database (MDB). This includes the agent schema information, as well as general and user-supplied interface definitions. Sun-Net Manager's dynamic runtime databases are comprised of MDB data and may be stored to the MDB at any time; MDB flat files are provided in ASCII format. SunNet Manager supports SNMP, but is not identical to an SNMP-Manager.

DualManager (Netlabs)   NetLabs' product strategy is to provide a distributed network management platform that supports the available product today—Simple Network Management Protocol (SNMP)—as well as the emerging protocol of the future—Common Management Information Protocol (CMIP). This strategy reduces the customer's risk of investing in equipment.

OSI management may be the platform of the future, but SNMP is what's selling now—because it's available and affordable. DualManager's SNMP support makes it a product for managing today's networks. This support comes in the form of the standard Management Information Base (MIB), including both MIB I and MIB II. Standard MIB variables provide rudimentary network management for TCP/IP objects, such as ICMP message counts and TCP routing algorithms.

DualManager also includes private extended MIBs from over 10 vendors, including Cisco, Novell (LANtern), SynOptics, and Wellfleet. Private extensions provide fuller function network management for a specific vendor's devices. DualManager also provides a mechanism for adding MIB objects from other vendors' extended MIBS.

DualManager includes two types of APIs—for user applications and for remote object access. The user application interface supports customization of the user interface and allows third-party or user-written applications to use DualManager functions. In particular, the User Application interface supports an Alarm API, allowing users to add applications that can be triggered by network events. For example, an alarm-triggered application may set a device parameter, sound a console alarm, or send an alert to IBM's NetView.

The Remote Object Access API supports an SNMP/CMOT/Ping/CMIP switch, allowing the same user-written application to work with multiple protocol schemes. This switch represents the essence of DualManager's capability to transparently support both SNMP and CMOT, as well as specific user-defined protocol stacks. This allows users or OEMs to develop applications independently of the underlying protocols employed by various network devices. Figure 4-21 illustrates this "duality" of management capabilities.

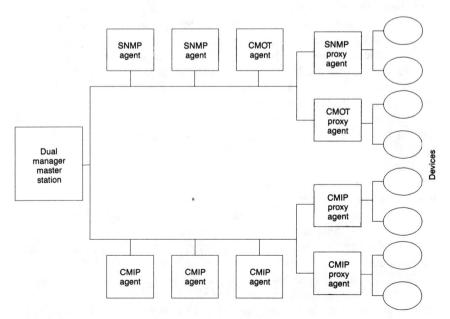

Fig. 4-21. DualManager architecture.

DualManager provides both SNMP-based and CMOT-based fault management capabilities. SNMP relies on polling and traps (asynchronous messages that are analogous to SNA alerts), while CMOT uses M-EventReport messages (events).

When DualManager detects network activity that exceeds a user-defined threshold, alarms are triggered. Depending upon the alarm, an alarm monitor program may initiate one of the following actions: log the alarm; sound an audible alarm; trigger an application to send a message, create a trouble ticket, or perform some user-defined action.

DualManager allows users to monitor performance as well as fault conditions through alarms. Alarm definitions are flexible and user defined. Also, DualManager allows users to specify at least six alarm severity levels: special, inform, warning, minor, major, and critical.

Users can define multistate alarms and program the system to automatically respond to changes in alarm conditions. The technology underlying this component is called a conditional-state machine model, which allows greater flexibility than a simple condition-action model. For example, DualManager detects a simple fault condition in a device and sounds a console alarm. If the fault is not corrected within a certain time period, the alarm may be escalated, triggering a major fault condition that pages the network administrator. Thus, the same condition (fault) triggers different actions, depending on the device state. States and actions are completely user defined.

Specifically, DualManager's alarm transition component can support up to four alarm states that determine the alarm's behavior pattern. The alarm transition component is a sophisticated feature that will be of most benefit to the knowledgeable user. By manipulating the alarm transition component, users can automate responses to trigger applications when an alarm changes state.

DualManager also allows users to display alarm and event information in a number of views, including top-level summaries, iconic views, lists of active/inactive polls, lists of active/inactive traps or events, and audit views.

Audit views provide a means of checking the consistency of the alarm policy. For example, the user can display a list of all devices that can trigger a given alarm or list all alarms that are unreachable.

DualManager doesn't provide a full-functioned auto topology facility; however, the product does assist users in depicting configurations via network maps. Background maps may be scanned in or drawn manually using the mouse and a map-editing function. Theoretically, DualManager allows an infinite number of submaps to be nested within maps or submaps.

DualManager has an automatic discovery utility that will automatically inform operators of changes to the network configuration. This utility relies on the polling, trap, and event mechanism discussed previously.

The map management feature allows the user to organize network information on three levels: Map Level—depicting network connections; Host Level—depicting managed devices (in DualManager's view, a host is any network node, including workstations, bridges, routers, terminal concentrators, gateways, and switches); Object Level—providing information about each managed device. This information is stored in a Network Configuration information file—an ASCII file which the user may browse through.

DualManager supports both manual and automatic performance management. To obtain automatic performance management, the user must configure the Alarm Management component to trigger actions or applications when parameter thresholds are crossed. For full-function automatic performance management, user-written applications are required.

Access to DualManager is controlled via a typical Unix-based scheme or permissions (user/group/all). Additionally, sophisticated users can manipulate the subviews.c file of the DualManager's Remote Object Access API to selectively restrict specific users from modifying device attributes through DualManager. DualManager provides no added security management applications; however, access control to managed devices can be enhanced via user-written programs.

DualManager operates several hardware platforms, including Sun Microsystems' SPARCstation and the IBM RS/6000 or PS/2. DualManager requires at least 20 Mbytes of main memory to support its own software as well as its Unix/X Windows software platform. The product supports a mouse-driven interface.

DualManager needs the following software environment:

- Unix-based operating systems, such as Unix System V, SCO Unix, IBM AIX, or SunOS.
- X Windows-based graphical user interface (GUI) using either Open-Look or Motif.
- Flat file configuration databases, supporting file export to Informix Wingz spreadsheet.

Optional software packages available include the following:

- OSI protocol stack.
- SNMP, CMOT, or CMIP agent or proxy agent implementations.
- NetCAD Planning/Simulation package.
- Informix database management system and Informix Wingz spreadsheet.

Due to dual support of both OSI- and TCP/IP-based management, DualManager is an interesting choice for many manufacturers and users.

NMC 3000 from Network Managers

With this platform, multivendor and multiprotocol applications are provided for a wide variety of users. It's a new concept in open and independent network management supported by highly modular system modules and software building blocks. The product is designed for growth and change (Network Managers 1991).

NMC 3000 Network Manager supports concurrent use of multiple management protocols to monitor and control any number of different devices from multiple vendors. Using special software modules for each product or management protocol used in the network, WAN/LAN-administration is in full control. Using a portable implementation running under Unix, both large and small networks may benefit from the solution. Up to 250 management systems may be supervised by a single NMC; large networks can be supported by multiple networked NMCs. Using distributed management centers, the load of network management may be shared, reducing network traffic and improving network management performance. Depending on the special customer requirements, the platform can be tailored, and multiple concurrent network operators with different access rights can be supported.

NMC 3000 may access the full range of different end systems via appropriate management stacks. There are a variety of protocols supported today, including SNMP, MAP/TOP, CMIP, CMOT, EMA, IPX, NMVT, etc.. But, the manufacturer targets an evolutionary migration path towards OSI in the future. The particular strengths of the product are in the following areas. (Also see FIG. 4-22.)

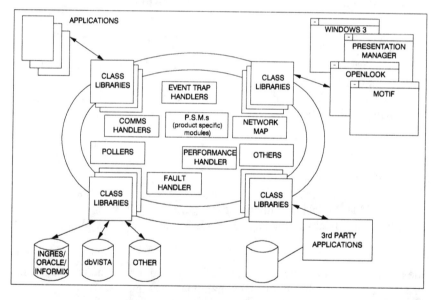

Fig. 4-22. NMC 3000 architecture.

Maps   There's an open palette from which to construct network maps. Maps may be nested to provide ordered and uncluttered views of the network. Multiple hierarchical levels for improving visibility are supported.

Configuration management   This offers a common denominator for various managed objects. Configuration details are uploaded directly from the device. Attributes may be meaningfully grouped for improving efficiency. Also, device parameter setting is supported from easy-to-use dialog boxes. Parameters can be changed dynamically without interrupting operations.

Fault management   This group of functions includes a seven-color network map symbol status display; fuzzy logic allows the network management system to conduct initial problem analysis; the function also provides the ability to mask trivial problems in order to focus on important issues. To build up the network management knowledge base, operators can keep track of faults and how they have been resolved.

Performance management   Continuous monitoring can identify problems before serious failures occur. In addition to monitoring the network for error and trap conditions, NMC 3000 can poll devices for statistics and performance information. Collected information may be displayed or also stored in an SQL database for further analysis and reporting.

Security management   Two levels of access security is provided. This gives general users and operators the ability to view the network, while limiting access to specific user applications. Special users get more access rights for monitoring, controlling, and changing the network.

The product supports MIB I, MIB II, and IEEE Hub-MIB. In addition, private MIBs from a number of vendors, such as Retix, Cisco, BICC, Novell, Chipcom are supported. The number of private MIBs supported is expected to increase, enabling NMC 3000 users to increase the depth of integration. In order to include an additional vendor, so-called Product Specific Modules (PSM) are required. The modules may be developed and implemented by the vendor or the customer. In both cases, an optional Developers Toolkit is recommended for use.

NetExpert from objective systems integrators

NetExpert system is a series of software modules, each of which performs a specific network management function. Users of this platform can build a full-featured network management system. The structure of the platform is shown in FIG. 4-23. The various modules are linked together by the InterProcess Message Handler (IPMH). An IPMH process is resident on each server that's supporting NetExpert processes. The platform is using industry-standard relational databases for the repository of information. The database provides storage of rule definitions, managed object information, device interface information, alert and event histories, and trouble reports. The database can be implemented on Ingres or Oracle; NetExpert can be converted to use any standard SQL database system. The principal components are the following (refer again to FIG. 4-23.)

Protocol agent   The protocol agents are responsible for the protocol conversion between the managed objects and the generic gateways. Protocol

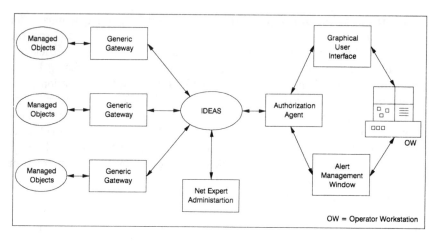

Fig. 4-23. NetExpert architecture.

agents take the ASCII stream input and output from generic gateways and convert it into the protocol (e.g., SNMP or proprietary) used by the managed objects.

Generic gateway   Generic gateways are responsible for message interchange between the managed objects and IDEAS. The communication protocol is CMIP. There are four kinds of rules that are downloaded to and compiled by the generic gateway; message identification rules, message parse rules, dialog command state rules, and dialog response state rules. These rules are composed of operators, operands, and attributes for the class of managed object that is being analyzed. Managed objects without eventing capabilities can be polled periodically, continuously, or on a scheduled basis. Generic gateways and IDEAS communicate via M-Event-Report, M-Action, M-Get, and M-Set.

Intelligent Dynamic Event Analysis Subsystem (IDEAS)
IDEAS is the central part of the platform. It's defined by the network expert using the Rule and Dialog Editor. Events sent by the Generic gateways are analyzed to determine further action. Possible actions include the creation of an alert for display in the operators window, incrementing a frequency or threshold counter, or deletion of the event due to subsequent information.

Authorization agent   This agent interacts with the Alert Management Window, NetExpert Administration, and with IDEAS processes. It's responsible for the dissemination of alerts from IDEAS to the appropriate operator. Alerts are displayed in the Alerts Management Window, based on login and authorization levels.

NetExpert Authorization   This function is responsible for systems management. NetExpert is started and stopped by this process. In addition, all NetExpert processes are monitored by NetExAdmin to ensure that they're operational.

Graphical user interface   There are three processes that make up NetExpert's graphical interface. Each has a responsibility for collecting and associating information so that the picture seen on the operators screen is a realtime collection of what's happening throughout the network. Graphics Database Machine is responsible for interaction with the NetExpert Database at runtime and when data is entered in the Graphics Editor. It's responsible for binding graphic objects with managed objects. Each managed object is represented on the network operators screen by several graphical objects. When IDEAS sends an alert to the machine, the alert is composed of the affected managed object, the severity of the alert, and the identification of the alert. The machine then collects a list of associated graphical objects and appropriate model files. It bundles this information with the alert and sends it to the Graphics State Machine.

The Graphic State Machine is responsible for maintaining a management information tree for the graphic objects. Each object can keep track of the current history of severities for each alert, which may be reflected by a graphic object on the operators screen. The alert with the highest severity is always percolated up in the tree. A graphical object will always depict the worst severity of any managed object associated with it. The information is forwarded to the Graphics Window, which is responsible for the presentation of graphics. It's used at runtime and in the Graphics Editor. There are two types of windows.

The overview window provides for a top-level view of the network. The top level is totally user defined and can contain whatever the user wants. Using context switching, different logical or physical network views can be presented. From any of these views, graphic objects may be selected for the focus window. The focus window supports multiple-level zooming as defined in the Graphics Editor.

Alert management   The Alert Management Window is responsible for the presentation and management of alerts by the operator. It interacts with the Graphics Database Machine, Authorization agent, and NetExpert administration. Alert management functions allow the operator to acknowledge an alert, clear the alert, pull up the Online Adviser Window, have the focus window display the graphical representation of the alert, or create a trouble ticket. In the case of related alerts, it's possible to associate multiple alerts with an existing trouble ticket.

After selecting an alert, the operator can then view additional information, specific to that alert, in the Online Adviser Window. An operator may create a trouble ticket for an alert or associate an alert with an existing trouble ticket. When a trouble ticket is created, most fields in the ticket form are automatically filled out.

There are different history forms that include alert, event and trouble-ticket history. Each of these history forms have many different fields that allow the operator to apply a scope and filter to the history information that is of interest.

NetExpert provides two separate ways to communicate with a device on demand. Cut through connects the operator to the managed object. It then opens a window where the operator can enter commands that are sent directly to the managed object. The Command and Response option allows the operator to conduct special sessions with the managed object. These sessions have to be previously developed.

Rules Editor   The Rules Editor provides the experienced expert with user-friendly menus and forms for specifying what information is of interest. The Rules Editor is programmerless. It uses a simple point-and-click mouse interface and requires minimal keyboard entry.

The product has a number of other system administration functions. Most of the routines are written in C and Objective-C. The product runs on Unix machines.

Network management systems from Teknekron

Teknekron Communication Systems (TSC) develops advanced element and integrated network management systems on the basis of their core platform. The functionality of these systems includes configuration, fault, trouble ticketing, security, performance, and systems administration. Teknekron's network management systems have distinctive features and capabilities. The most important are the following.

Advanced graphical user interfaces   User interfaces are often the key factor in determining whether a system is attractive to the marketplace and whether it's successfully used by its operators. The company has exceptional experience in developing advanced graphical user interfaces built on OSF-Motif and X.11 windows manager.

Network Management Forum interoperable interface   As a member of the Network Management Forum, the vendor contributes to the advance of interoperable standards and in now working with clients to develop NM Forum-compliant management systems using TCS-developed software.

Other communication interfaces   TCS supports a configurable communications interface to other NMSs and to specific network elements. This permits TCS to build network management systems that can communicate using protocols such as SNMP, other common industry communications protocols, and proprietary protocols. This also enables NMSs to cooperatively manage networks with other systems such as NetView.

Object-oriented programming   Industry experience shows that efficiently implemented object-oriented software can support greater structural complexity and permits development, maintenance, and extension of systems for a fraction of the time and cost required to enhance traditional, functionally oriented software. Accordingly, TCS has developed systems with extensive use of object-oriented programming techniques and methodology.

Rapid prototyping   Rapid prototyping is an essential technique that TCS uses for testing the initial concepts of the system's operation and presentation. In addition, early prototypes allow clients to preannounce capabilities and to gather support for projects internally by showing managers the potential of systems being developed.

Distributed Unix workstation deployment   Unix is becoming the *de facto* standard for network management and operations systems in most parts of the telecommunications industry. This allows easy portability of applications across diverse vendor hardware platforms. In addition, the competitive nature of the Unix workstation marketplace provides price-performance benefits to clients. Finally, the distributed nature of the network management systems allows clients to scale system hardware in accordance with their specific requirements.

Relational database integration   TCS's network management software integrates with SQL-based relational database management systems. This allows NMSs built by TCS to use the relational database management systems for persistent storage of information, as well as to access information from other relational databases.

The NMS/CORE   The company's experience in network management systems has led it to develop the NMS/Core (TM), an object-oriented platform that provides a proven foundation for the construction of advanced network management systems. TCS is therefore able to deliver network management solutions that meet the specific requirements of each of its clients' applications.

The NMS/Core (TM) is organized in a layered, modular design, as shown in FIG. 4-24. The foundation of the NMS/Core serves as the infrastructure that

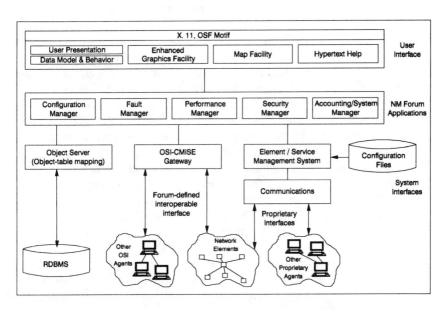

Fig. 4-24. Layered structure of NMS/Core.

provides all the processing capabilities required for the operation of the network management system. Such capabilities include event processing and the ability to distribute processing across workstations. In addition, modules are provided for developing interfaces such as graphical user interfaces and gateways to OSI-CMISE-conformant systems or to other NMSs and network elements communicating over nonstandard protocols. The NMS infrastructure is based upon the computing infrastructure, which includes industry standard software such as Unix, C, and C++. Finally, the specific customization that provides extended capabilities beyond the modules supplied with the NMS/Core are developed on a customized basis to complete the network management system.

Network management systems based on the NMS/Core follow a layered architecture. Broadly, NMS/Core-based systems have three distinct layers— user interface, applications, and system interfaces. Specific support provided by the NMS/Core in each of these layers is discussed later.

User interfaces   The company builds unique user interfaces for each project to meet the special "look and feel" requirement of its customers. The current generation of graphical user interfaces is built on the X.11 Window Management System and uses the OSF/Motif interface toolkit.

Among the features provided by the NMS/Core Graphical User Interface is the hypertext help system, which is associated with the user interface. Its hypertext capability allows the user to call up the Help System and easily browse through help information on related systems aspects in a nonlinear fashion. The Help System is object-oriented and can therefore be context-sensitive, automatically presenting information about the particular operations the user is performing.

The NMS/Core Graphical User Interface also provides an integrated database of world maps that can be displayed with the representations of the managed networks. These maps can be enlarged, reduced, or cut and pasted into other maps to let the operator manage portions of the network more easily.

The user interface also provides capabilities for supporting foreign language interfaces, including Japanese kanji characters. Supporting multiple languages in the user interface permits significant flexibility in distributing the developed network management system worldwide.

Applications   The central element of this architecture is the application layer. This layer embodies the functionality for the network management functional areas, which are analogous to the ISO-defined Specific Management Functional Areas (SMFA). The application functionality typically implemented using the NMS/Core objects includes:

- Object server. Persistent storage of information is a necessary element of any deployed network management system. The NMS/Core accomplishes this through an Object Server that interfaces with SQL-based relational database management systems. Since Network Management applications are written in an object-oriented paradigm, the Object Server provides the translation from objects to tables in the database.
- OSI-CMISE gateway. The OSI-CMISE gateway is the communication stack by which an NMS/Core-based network management system communicates with other NMSs or network elements over the OSI/NM

Forum interoperable interface. The NMS/Core provides software libraries for the construction of OSI-CMISE gateways. Using this software, TCS has built network management systems supporting the full OSI seven-layer communications stack, permitting the NMSs to receive full CMISE message sets.

System interfaces   This category includes the agent-manager structure, and the network elements interfaces. The agent-manager structure for designing cooperative network management systems is an important aspect of interoperability and goes hand-in-hand with the OSI-CMISE gateway. This structure, which TCS supports within NMS/Core-based systems, allows multiple network management systems to participate in the management of the network. The agent-manager relationship structure entails designating specific network management systems as agents of particular network elements. An agent is then responsible for communicating directly with its assigned network management systems. These other network management systems, which receive information about the network elements and which may participate in managing it, are called managers. This structure is particularly useful for implementing both customer network management systems and multidomain administration systems.

Not all network elements and network management systems can communicate over the OSI-CMISE interoperable interface. For this reason, the NMS/Core includes a module that provides a generalized network element interface gateway that can be tailored for proprietary communications protocols. The specification of these protocols is driven by configuration files, which are data files containing information on specific devices and message protocols. The configuration file approach allows the network element interface to be configured for a broad range of network elements without restructuring the module's internal software. Whether designing and implementing element management systems or integrators, the common platform may be used.

TCS builds network management systems for equipment manufacturers and service providers that enable its customers to have a consistent and conceptually intuitive view of their hybrid networks. Although the scope of each network management system varies with the client, all TCS systems share a common architecture (see FIG. 4-25).

Applications with support of the network management capabilities, such as configuration, fault, or performance management, reside on either central or distributed processors. The application processors maintain the management information base (MIB) for that portion of the managed network for which the network management system has responsibility. These application processors communicate with other network management systems, operations support systems and, in some cases, with network elements directly. The applications aggregate information on the status of the network, on customer billing, and on other events and data that pertain to the management of the equipment and services.

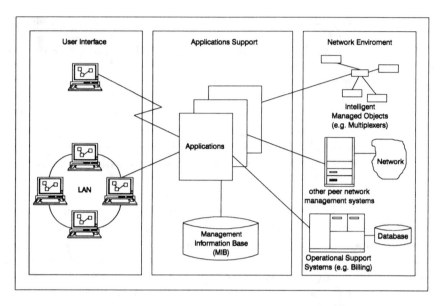

Fig. 4-25. Common architecture of TCS systems.

Another important aspect of the network management system is the user interface, which typically resides on graphical workstations to maximize the effectiveness of operation. The graphical user interfaces typically coexist with the application processors on a local area network.

There are two types of systems built using NMS/Core: element management systems and network management integrators. Element management systems function as the immediate managers of specific types of network equipment such as multiplexers, packet switches, cross connects and VSATs. An element manager also forwards status information about its portion of the network to an integrator.

A number of management operations are performed by the element manager. These operations usually include configuration, fault, and performance management of the physical equipment. As network elements have varying degrees of internal capabilities, the element manager may sometimes poll the network for the element's status. To perform these operations, the element manager maintains a representation of the managed elements and their status. In addition to the standard NM Forum Applications, element managers often include applications for the generation, editing, and downloading of routing control constants, as well as the automatic switching circuits around failed nodes or links (protective switching).

Network management integrators aggregate information from various element managers, from other network management systems, and from operations support systems. Information can be received via proprietary message protocols, in which case the integrator must have a gateway for each proprietary protocol. Increasingly, however, network management systems communicate messages based on interoperable standards and communications protocols such as the CMIS/CMIP messages defined by the NM Forum.

TCS develops network management integrators to provide a single consistent view of the network. These integrators are used to perform the complete control over management operations ranging from configuration management to accounting management and trouble ticketing for fault correction. An important feature of integrators is that they're able to abstract and represent services and to relate the services to the supporting physical equipment. Services are seldom supported by only one type of network equipment. The essential ability to integrate information from multivendor sources and thus accurately represent the services supported has to be built into the systems.

TCS integrators support the agent/manager model, which provides shared access to managed objects. As a result, different network views can be defined to support differing operational requirements. Service providers can partition responsibility for the managed objects into local, regional, or national views. Similarly, customer views can be configured to provide the operational behavior for a virtual private network.

The NMS/Core's NMS Application Object Classes consist of a set of managed objects that have been built using the NMS/Core's NMS Software Infrastructure. Objects in this set can be combined and extended to create network management functionality. The NMS Application Classes provide functionality for typical NMS behavior, and the classes include: Fault Management, Performance Management, Configuration Management, Security Management, and Accounting and System Administration.

The NMS/Core includes the 35 Managed Object class definitions as specified in the NM Forum Guidelines for the Definition of Managed Objects (GDMO). Also, other Managed Object classes have been built and are based in part on the NM Forum set, which provides the specialized and extended functionality necessary for the operation of a network management system. Some of the NM Forum object classes include: Agent Conformant Management Entity, Alarm record, Circuit, Enroll Object Event record, Equipment, Event Log, Event record, Event Reporting Sieve, Facility, Forum Test Object, Function, Network, Processing Entity, and Provider Service. Some of the specialized object classes defined by TCS include: Trouble Ticket, User Group, Domain, and Map.

TCS continues to track standards issued by the NM Forum and appropriately enhances the NMS/Core to support these standards. Thus, the NM Forum objects serve as a foundation for building NM Forum compliant systems, and they provide a pathway to future compliance as standards evolve. Note that the development of a network management system always entails extensions or additions to both the NM Forum-defined object classes and the specialized set of object classes defined by separate custom development projects. Programming tools are available as part of the NMS/Core to build the runtime NMS applications.

TCS is continually developing new technologies and applying them to the solution of technical challenge presented to it by its clients. Specifically, it plans to evaluate the NMS/Core in a number of directions in support of its client's requirements.

Support for new system interfaces   As the use of OSI application interfaces becomes more widespread, the NMS/Core will support such interfaces, including X.400 electronic mail and X.500 directory services. Bellcore's Sonet Interface will also be supported as it becomes an industry standard.

Multimedia human interfaces   As demonstrated by NMSs, TCS has developed and now it sees itself at the forefront of human interface technology. The next step in NMS human interfaces is the use of multimedia technology—including voice, video, and image—to enhance the ease of use of NMSs. TCS expects that network management services offered by telecommunications service providers will incorporate multimedia interfaces with the ability to replicate the display contents of customer screens at the service provider's network management centers. The NMS/Core will support such cooperative problem solving through the use of multimedia human interfaces.

Object-oriented databases   The NMS/Core application environment is completely object-oriented; however, persistent objects are stored in relational database management systems. The next logical step is towards object-oriented databases, which now exist, and TCS will adopt object-oriented databases as an optional means of managing persistent objects. This technology will provide significant advantages in flexibility of information management, as well as in the overall efficiency of the resultant network management systems.

Automated network operations   Automated network operations enable network management end users to specify operations or series of operations to be performed automatically. These operations can be triggered by time, by events, received by the network management system, and by user instructions. Any of these events can cause, for example, networks to be automatically reconfigured, or pager alerts or mail messages to be sent in response to given conditions. The NMS/Core's object-oriented software architecture allows TCS to easily add such capabilities into the NMS/Core.

Network planning   TCS intends to incorporate network design and planning modules with the NMS/Core to produce network management systems capable of performing failure analysis, traffic loading analysis, and performance evolutions in software without affecting the live network. In addition, this module will allow the user of a network management system to perform topological reconfigurations of the networks and evaluate cost trade-offs of proposed changes by modeling representation of the physical network in the network management system.

Network knowledge systems from Applied Computing Devices

Unlike traditional network management suppliers who normally develop systems primarily to manage their own proprietary mainstream network element hardware products, ACD's origin was and remains in integrated network management. Consequently, one of ACD's strengths has been the ability to manage and integrate diverse network elements and element managers from a multitude of suppliers. These requirements have resulted in powerful, flexible systems comprised of ACD-developed Unix-based platform software and hardware.

Target customers with the tool set are: owners of large private networks, regional Bell holding companies, independent telcos, interexchange carriers, and major industry value-added resellers. Managed objects include: central office switches, digital cross connects, operations support systems, private branch exchanges, T-type multiplexers, modems, packet switches, third-parties' network managers, and standalone components (e.g., fiber-optic terminals).

Network knowledge systems consist of three dimensions (FIG. 4-26):

- Dimension one—customer-defined applications, including:
  a. Digital connection management (cross-connect, mux).
  b. Data network management.
  c. Integrated computer application and network management.
  d. Network management system elements and operating systems elements.
  e. Umbrella integration.
  f. Digital loop carrier management.
  g. Network design management/NMS integration.
  h. Toll fraud prevention.
  i. Network performance management.
  j. Switching control center management.
  k. Circuit test.
  l. Centrex management services.
  m. Billing data management.
  n. Work-force management.
  o. Switched traffic engineering.
  p. Facilities records management.
  q. T1 multiplexer management.
- Dimension two: network knowledge platforms, including:
  a. MLA for event modeling.
  b. NRM for configuration modeling.
  c. MTA for work modeling.
  d. RDC for performance modeling.
- Dimension three: physical architectural elements, including:
  a. Unix.
  b. SuperLayer.
  c. Engines & peripherals.
  d. Universal network architecture.
  e. Fault management architecture.
  f. MegArray neural processing.
  g. System management architecture.
  h. Workstation architecture.

i. Presentation architecture.
j. Database architecture.
k. Transaction interface manager.

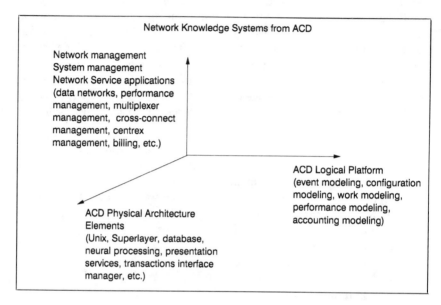

Fig. 4-26. Dimensions of Network Knowledge Systems.

The ultimate goal is to support both networks and systems management. Figure 4-27 displays the principal components of the integrated architecture. Altogether, the product offers one of the most advanced architectures in the industry, with many innovative features such as expert systems, neural networks, and hypermedia.

The future of network and systems management technology is difficult or impossible to predict. ACD's Future Bridge Framework provides a safe, predictable way to prepare for the challenges of the future while taking care of present integration problems today.

Some basic concerns have always faced the network administrator: reacting to network faults, improving application performance, configuring and securing the system, accounting for system usage. Questions centered around the compatibility of network elements. Today, network administrators face a greater problem with more far-reaching implications: how to integrate multiple network management systems.

The rapid expansion of complex voice, data, video and graphics/imaging networks, plus the soaring numbers of central and distributed information systems and their applications, have thrust the network administrator into a new world of multiple networks, systems, network/entity layers, and applications.

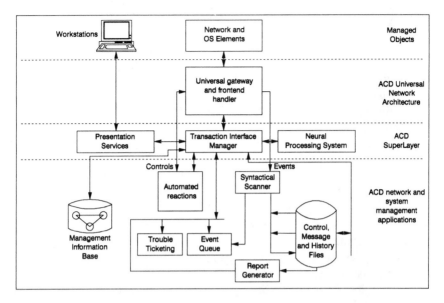

Fig. 4-27. Principal components of the integrated architecture.

Network administrators are responsible for delivering the benefits of this exploding technology to their companies—while handling multiple network management systems to control it—against a backdrop of ever-tighter margins and shrinking resources.

Network administrators now must resolve several major concerns. They need the integration offered by emerging standards and specifications, but they can't justify the cost of quickly replacing or redesigning all of their networks and systems to conform to these standards. Even if new, standards-compliant elements are added, they must be integrated into a nonstandards-compliant embedded base.

ACD is actively committed to standards compliance. It has long been a member of the NMF and has actively incorporated IAB application models into its products. ACD is also committed to providing standards-compliant protocol capabilities such as Common Management Information Protocol/Service (CMIP/CMIS), Synchronous Optical Network (SONET), Simple Network Management Protocol (SNMP), OSF Distributed Management/Computing Environment (DME/DCE) and others. However, ACD's products also allow its customers to preserve their investments in embedded multivendor systems, while enabling clients to derive optimal benefits from new standards as they're adopted.

FutureBridge, part of ACD's architecture for evolution, provides a single, unified framework that allows network managers and planners to effectively integrate compliant and noncompliant networks, systems, and elements. The

FutureBridge Framework offers three solutions:

1. Integrates noncompliant systems and networks using FutureBridge tools and components that adapt to nonstandard protocols without changing or replacing them; it means integration without conformance.
2. Uses FutureBridge tools and components to take noncompliant systems/networks and render them compliant; it means proxy agent conformance.
3. Integrates new, standards-compliant systems/networks; it means fully conforming integration.

The Simple Network Management Protocol (SNMP) Application Starter Kit enhances the capabilities of ACD's Unix-based software platform products to integrate diverse industry standard and nonstandard protocols into a system to manage networks and other systems. The SNMP Starter Kit, built from ACD's NRM Object-Oriented Configuration Manager, MLA Event Analysis Modeling Platform, and SuperLayer Finite State machine controls, delivers time-saving integration of SNMP-compliant elements into the Network Manager while still enabling users to manage other protocols, both standard and nonstandard embedded base.

This object-oriented, knowledge-base-derived SNMP kit supports the five SNMP operations with ACD's Advanced MetaVision Presentation Architecture offering a standard Motif interface. The kit allows users to initiate operations with prepackaged options and/or tailor the kit itself to meet their specific applications.

Most companies that sell SNMP sell only SNMP—potentially locking users into SNMP on a long-term basis, without the ability to manage non-SNMP protocols.

Application Starter Kits provide a blueprint for effective network management by substantially speeding the development of applications, or by establishing structures, directions, or techniques for part or all of an application. This can reduce start-up time frames and thus enable customers to more quickly benefit from advanced technology. ACD is a business partner of IBM, thus, most products developed with the platform offer two-way communication to NetView.

Impacts of Distributed Management Environment from OSF

In order to improve distributed management capabilities, OSF/DME will combine the most advanced features of various leading solutions. The ultimate structure is a layered one, dealing with: network management protocols; naming, location, security and registration services; protocol APIs; programming interfaces; applications; and user interfaces. Different APIs are implemented for different requirements: low-level protocol access API; high-level, object-oriented API for ANSI-C programmers; high-level, object-oriented API for C++ programmers; template language and compiler for convenience.

In order to improve service quality and implementation speed, common services will be supported for authentication and authorization, for naming and location schemes, for consistent event management, and for graphical user interfaces. In summary, DME tries to use existing components on a consistent and future-proof platform. DME enables businesses to dynamically configure LAN management policies by providing the basis for distributed systems and networks management.

The technologies selected are:

- IBM's forthcoming data engine, an object-oriented relational database environment that includes an SQL interface. IBM will also supply its AIX operating system's System Resource Controller, which helps manage tasks and applications.
- HP's OpenView Network Manager Server is responsible for the graphical user interface.
- Groupe Bull's Consolidated Management application programming interface will give application developers a common interface to the data engine and the protocol engine.
- Tivoli Systems contributes with the Wizdom object-oriented framework that governs managed object interaction and provides the graphical and command-line user interface.
- Event filtering, forwarding, and logging is solved with Network Logger from Banyan. Network Logger will be integrated with every other DME component to log its actions and retrieve information from logs.
- Remote software management services will be supported by HP's software distribution utilities.
- Gradient Technologies contributes to software licensing management and to remote PC access and communication by using NetLS PC.
- Printing management services are going to be supported by MIT's project Athena's Palladium System.

The prerequisites are good for an industry standard. Leading platform vendors are expected to support DME, enabling existing solutions to be ported to DME.

Summary

Standardization of local area networks management has recently been significantly accelerated by available SNMP solutions. At the moment, over 70% of router vendors, over 60% of bridge vendors, over 40% of hub vendors, and over 50% of server vendors are supporting SNMP with their products, at least at the agent level. Many of them are supporting users by offering applications such as alert logs, filtering, reporting, diagnostics, autotopology, electronic mail, and trouble ticketing at the manager level. SNMP is, however, not the ultimate goal, due to obvious shortcomings such as performance, excess overhead, and limited functionality. Open standards will slowly spread throughout the market, introducing more functionality and interoperability. Implementation speed is affected by overhead, volume of changes needed, performance, and user acceptance. Proprietary solutions that are not supporting *de facto* or open standards will have significantly limited usage and life cycles.

In many cases, the strategy and architecture of leading manufacturers will not differentiate between LANs and WANs, but will embed both. MAN management will follow almost automatically.

Two principal enhancements will significantly increase the life expectations of SNMP: Emanate and SMP. A new API called Enhanced Management Agent (Emanate) defines how one master SNMP agent can communicate with multiple subagents on the same managed object. It consists of interface specifications, master agent source code and subagent source code. This new arrangement will simplify SNMP structures and reduce the overhead of polling to single subagents. SMP (Simple Management Protocol) offers a broader view of managing networks and systems. The improvements include security features, a bulk data retrieval capability to support performance management, manager-to-manager interaction supporting flexible hierarchies of management structures, better error handling by including meaningful error messages, exception reporting, better definition of managed objects, and expanded network protocol support. Both manufacturers and users are very satisfied with these extensions.

5

Local area network management products

A brief look at the applicability of LAN management products shows the following:

- LAN management functions are well understood and categorized.
- There are a number of instruments that are able to support single LAN management functions or even a group of functions.
- The allocation of tools to functions is not yet well understood; experiences stemming from WANs are expected to help.
- There are no special LAN management integrators available yet. In most cases, users are considering general integrators to manage LANs and interconnected LANs.

Instrumentation of local area network segments and interconnected LANs starts with fragmented products that address individual functions providing monitoring, testing, and analyzing services, or providing databases or front ends to user administration. LAN instrumentation trends may be summarized as follows:

- SNMP (Simple Network Management Protocol) is continuing to make inroads into network management systems. Support by virtually all vendors for LANs and for internetworked LANs can be assumed.
- Hundreds of products will incorporate SNMP agent capabilities. Fewer companies will provide generic or specific SNMP management capabilities.
- UNIX seems to be the delivery platform for many network management products. The most popular combination is with Sun. Also, an integrated relational database with SQL is offered.

- A GUI (graphical user interface) provides color-coded alarms, click-and-zoom capability, and manipulatable icons.
- IBM is becoming very active in this area. Besides solutions for their offerings, the company has teamed up with 3Com to offer CMOL—a *de facto* protocol for layer 2 below LLC. IBM implements CMIP between LAN Network Manager and its agents.
- OSF (Open Systems Foundation) is a consortium of users and vendors cooperating to achieve a standard implementation of Unix. Distributed management environment (DME) has received a lot of attention from leading vendors. DME may influence future network management standards.
- With time, dual interfaces will be supported. In other words, not only SNMP agents, but also CMIP and CMOT agents will be supported by generic network management solutions. The very same management station may also support proprietary agents using simple or complex protocol converters, called proxy-agents.

This chapter addresses the following subjects: categorization of LAN management products, LAN management platforms and platform independent applications, standalone products, PC LAN management capabilities, LAN element management systems, integrated LAN management solutions, and LAN management services.

Categorization of products

There's a variety of products available to manage LAN segments and interconnected LANs. For the sake of simplicity, this chapter discusses the following groups:

- Standalone products addressing special monitoring, testing analysis, security, and accounting needs.
- Network management platforms providing an environment in which applications can be developed, enhanced, and exchanged.
- PC LAN management tools, including special-purpose solutions as a combination of LAN operating systems features and special add-ons.
- LAN element management systems based on *de facto* or open standards offering acceptable functionality to LAN elements, such as LAN segments, wiring hubs, LAN interconnecting devices, FDDI, PBXs, and connection to network management integrators.
- Integrators that most likely support LAN, MAN, and WAN element management systems on the same platform.

The product has to provide certain basic attributes that are independent from the product category under consideration: a user-friendly interface that's based on standards such as a GUI (graphical user interface), which offers reasonable presentation solutions that allow users to customize icons, windows, layouts, color codes, and combinations with acoustic alarms; powerful applications, including those that address major LAN management functions; system techniques that allow future extensions and the ability to be scaled based on LAN-management needs (factors are processing power, memory, and peripherals); database supporting object-oriented or relational techniques that offer access via SQL (Structured Query Language); reasonable performance in use with real networks; gateways to open, *de facto*, and proprietary agents. Figure 5-1 shows the generic architecture of a product with the principal attributes just listed.

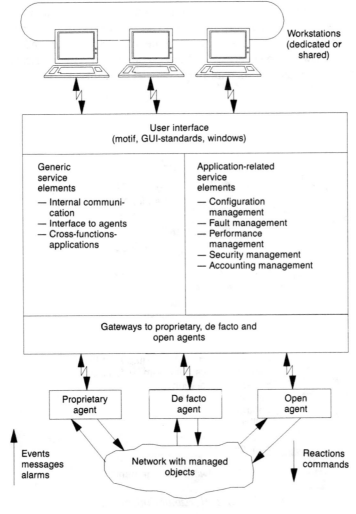

Fig. 5-1. Generic architecture of a LAN management product.

LAN management concepts

LAN management concepts are expected to support an enterprise's strategic network management implementation decisions, such as integration, automation, centralization, and database support. From the perspective of instrumentation, integration is usually addressed first.

Most managed-objects-level vendors provide products that engender useful individual functionality, but they're limited in that they can't easily be integrated into a system vendor's network management offering. Future integrated solutions are expected to solve this problem by offering horizontal integration across (Terplan 1991): communication forms (data, voice, image, video); WANs, MANs, and LANs; private, public, and virtual networks; multivendor architectures; processing and communication systems.

Figure 5-2 shows an example of horizontal integration. System vendors have developed single network management protocols (e.g., NMVT from IBM) to facilitate data collection and integration about both physical and logical components, as long as data may be collected from the components sup-

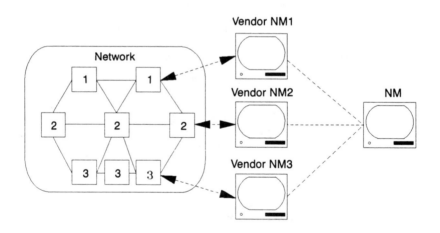

Horizontal integration of equipment from
multiple vendors doing similar functions
Degree of Integration
　displays
　controls
Intelligence
　displays
　controls

NM = Network Management

Fig. 5-2. Horizontal integration.

ported by the protocol. But this type of vertical integration is not easy, in particular owing to the proprietary nature of applications and logical session management. Future integrated solutions are expected to solve this problem by offering vertically integrated applications across logical and physical network components, and across applications and network components.

Figure 5-3 shows an example of vertical integration. In addition, users and suppliers are expected to work more closely together by co-managing their instruments (e.g., by using electronic data interchange techniques).

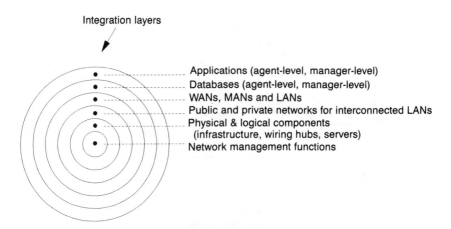

Integration layers

Applications (agent-level, manager-level)
Databases (agent-level, manager-level)
WANs, MANs and LANs
Public and private networks for interconnected LANs
Physical & logical components
(infrastructure, wiring hubs, servers)
Network management functions

Fig. 5-3. Vertical integration.

Integration will require multiple steps in terms of depth of integration. One will start at the physical terminal level by emulating multiple consoles' images in various windows of an intelligent workstation. In this case, the native protocols, messages, and commands of the emulated vendors are in use. But, concentrating the screens in one area on a few workstations helps to substantially improve efficiency. Next, the emulated third party or the integrator, or both, will convert to a unique protocol or format, such as NMP from AT&T or NMVT from IBM. In this case, messages and commands are unique up to the third parties' demarcation line. Ultimately, real integration is achieved with two approaches (FIG. 5-4), both offering either horizontal or vertical integration, or both (Herman 1991). In this case, information from various sources is integrated.

The first approach is the manager of managers, a hierarchical approach in which an integrated manager interfaces to a lower-level element management system. The premier examples of such systems are NetView from IBM, the AT&T Accumaster Integrator, and the Nynex Allink products. The second general approach is the platform approach, in which multiple vendors write

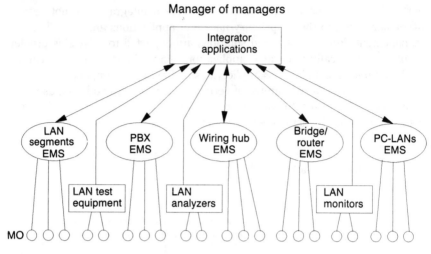

EMS = Element Management System
MO = Managed Object

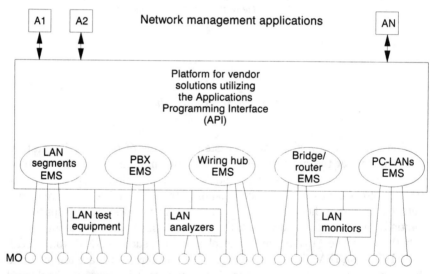

EMS = Element Management System
MO = Managed Object

Fig. 5-4. Hierarchical versus platform LAN management integration.

network management applications to a standard set of application programming interfaces (APIs). The premier examples of this approach are the DEC Enterprise Management Architecture (EMA), SunNet Manager from Sun, OpenView from Hewlett-Packard, and DualManager from Netlabs.

The platform approach to integrated management offers the possibility of a greater degree of multivendor integration than the manager of managers scheme. In the manager of managers architecture, interactions among management systems from different vendors are accomplished through a standardized protocol interface and a standardized set of management data definitions. This hierarchical way of aggregating management information requires that a single vendor—the provider of the integrator—develop all the multivendor network management application software. Other vendors merely provide raw data to the integrated manager through open interfaces and accept commands through open interfaces.

In practice today, only a few applications of the integrated manager exist, so most functionality is obtained through windowed access to device manager applications, called cut-through or terminal emulation. Moreover, this approach multiplies management systems at a time when operations centers are looking to reduce the number of management systems they use. It may also result in multiple network management databases.

In the platform strategy, the eventual goal is to develop a single management system that can handle a diverse, multivendor network. Rather than do it alone, the platform vendor creates an open development environment in which multiple vendors can write software that shares common user views and a common data repository. If the platform offers a rich set of services and advanced capabilities, such as an object-oriented user interface or relational database, many vendors may find it attractive to implement their management software on such platforms rather than developing their own base at considerable cost and risk.

The advantage of the manager of managers approach is that it builds on existing management systems. Using this approach, IBM shows how to integrate WAN and LAN management. Token Ring has a standalone management capability using the LAN Network Manager. Fault, performance, and configuration management are also supported without NetView. But a more complete solution is using NetView as the focal point. In this structure, bidirectional information exchange is supported. The platform strategy in its pure form requires writing all new management software. In practice, the two approaches can be combined, if necessary. But the platform strategy aims at reducing the number of management systems, which is highly appealing to network owners. The manager of managers approach, on the other hand, is necessary in order to reserve an installed base of management systems. The platform concept is most appealing when new software has to be written anyway.

Another argument against proprietary or OSI-based manager of managers solutions to multivendor network management is that no one vendor can meet all the management application needs of a large enterprise. With the platform approach, many vendors can simultaneously work on management software that will play together. If a particular platform achieves a critical mass of important applications, then there's a good chance that users will choose it, since applications are what the user really wants. If users start buying a particular platform, then more application software developers will want to write for that platform since the market for their creations will be large.

Leading integrator products from IBM, AT&T, and DEC will be addressed later in this chapter. In the platform category, Unix-based systems are leading the market. The most important alternatives were discussed in chapter 4.

Independently, whether the manager of managers or the platform approach is selected, the ultimate goal is multivendor management. Vendors may support proprietary, *de facto*, or open standards at the managed-objects or management-application level. Figures 5-5 and 5-6 (Datapro NM40 1990) show examples with SNMP and CMIP, indicating also that proprietary solutions—in form of proprietary MIBs—are supported. Cross connection via gateways (proxy agents) is expected to be supported, as illustrated in FIG. 5-7.

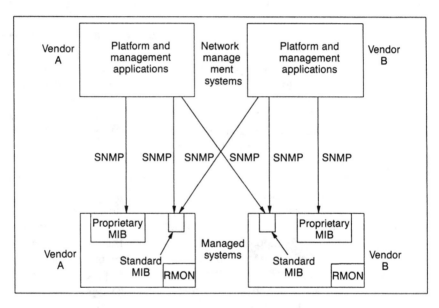

Fig. 5-5. Emerging SNMP network management systems.

Other Unix-based platforms are offered under other norms, such as AIX (IBM) and SINIX (Siemens). In particular, the AIX platform on RISC/6000 puters from IBM is a source of contradiction. Which is IBM's strategic platform: AIX or OS/2? The company populates both with network management-related solutions. In any case, either one of IBM's platform solutions will help to build hierarchical or peer-to-peer network management architectures, and to offload the usually centrally located NetView. MS-DOS-based solutions still exist with LAN element management systems, but their importance is decreasing.

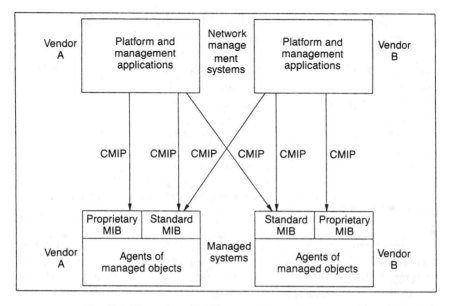

Fig. 5-6. Emerging CMIP network management systems.

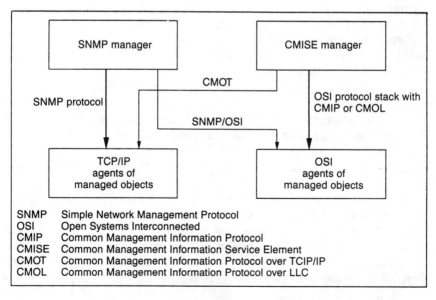

Fig. 5-7. Management of heterogeneous LANs.

In order to increase flexibility, distributed architectures may help. They're still immature, but they improve the reliability of the network management system by distributing functions to multiple servers. The vulnerable point of distributed architectures is the process manager, which is responsible for coordinating between various agents and managers. This coordination task includes the following:

- Unwrapping protocol headers and trailers in order to interpret the "useful" information of protocol data units.
- Forwarding this information to managers, which are responsible for processing and forwarding the results to applications.
- Ensuring that final results have reached the user using presentation services.

This coordinator function has been implemented by the manufacturers differently. Hewlett-Packard is using CMIP as a common denominator between communicating modules. DEC and Sun use remote procedure calls (RPC) to export and import messages between communicating modules. WizardWare from Tivoli is an example of an object-oriented message-passing approach. Other systems use a combination of the three techniques discussed. Almost in all cases, proprietary features are added. RPC implementations seem to lead the market now; object orientation will increase, but its penetration speed is hard to predict. This speed will be largely influenced by how inventory and configuration databases are implemented. Despite databases, a coexistence of relational techniques (e.g., fault and performance management), and object-oriented techniques (e.g., configuration and fault management) is likely. More details may be found in (Herman 1991).

The platforms enable vendors and users to write applications for supporting network management. Such support is provided by MONET (Managing Open Networks) from Hughes LAN systems. MONET links a management information base compiler to a Structured Query Language (SQL) relational database. As a result, multiple vendors' private SNMP MIB extensions can be automatically and dynamically installed in a central repository and accessed by all MONET applications. These capabilities significantly reduce the time and work required to configure an SNMP-based system to manage multivendor devices. Most SNMP-based systems today use a flat-file storage method, which doesn't automatically recognize relationships between stored information. When they do support a relational database, it has not been connected to a MIB compiler, and adding private variables requires manual work.

Two MONET applications seem to be valuable to users. MONET logs network fault messages to the SQL database for third-party applications to access. It includes a configuration discovery feature that automatically identifies devices on the LANs that support SNMP, and enters their configuration parameters in the relational database.

A flat-file, rules-based system is used to automatically generate probable causes and recommended actions based on alerts. The rules-base can be updated and expanded by the users.

The uncertainty of platforms may be lifted when applications are available. The first series of applications that work independently from platforms may be seen from Remedy (Remedy 1991).

The first example is a trouble management system for LANs, called Action Request System (ARS). The application will run on a number of platforms making it vendor independent. Actually, ARS gathers network information and stores it in an SQL database. Both vendors and users can add information to the database on a selected number of common problems and how to solve them. ARS is playing a middle-ware role of a clearing house for LAN-related problems. When problems occur, ARS automatically generates a trouble ticket. It can open a ticket for any network resource that can send alert messages via SNMP traps, CMIP events, or proprietary mechanisms. Also, end users can submit messages to ARS, which generates an alarm to the designated network manager. When the problem is eliminated, ARS will notify all the end users impacted by the problem. This application shields the end users from the platforms. Furthermore, this type of application may move network management functions closer to end users, helping to stabilize the number of human resources required to manage LANs.

Similar offers are expected from INA/Proxar. The first application introduced is an auto-discovery application for network topologies. The application observes network traffic and records the different types of devices residing on the network.

Microsoft is offering a standard set of programming interfaces called WinSNMP, which developers can use to build SNMP support into applications running under Windows and Windows NT. The APIs fall into the categories of agent, manager, trap, general, and utility. As vendors and users do for other SNMP-managed devices, developers need to define MIB-entries for both public and private areas.

The expectations of users are high; most likely, applications will be provided in the following areas:

- Trouble ticketing for multivendor LAN environments.
- Performance management applications for early recognition of bottlenecks.
- LAN accounting packages.
- Automated problem determination by observing LAN events and taking actions automatically to eliminate routine problems, and alerting LAN management about subtle problems.

Standalone LAN management products

Standalone products serve special functional areas without aiming at the general applicability of LAN management integration. Standalone products are characterized and evaluated according to a number of criteria, as listed:

- User interface.
- What protocols are supported.
- The decode level.
- What kind of LANs are supported.
- What kind of WANs are supported.
- Capture buffers.
- Filtering.
- Support for distributed monitoring.
- Triggers.
- Search.
- Time-stamping.
- Traffic generators.
- Cable checks.
- Naming conventions.
- Self-test diagnostics.
- Hard-copy printing.
- Password protection.

TABLE 5-1 shows the principle ones in table form (Datapro NM50 1989).

**Table 5-1. Common Features
of Standalone LAN Products**

User interface
Capture buffers
Filtering
Triggers
Search capabilities
Time stamping
Traffic generation
Use of symbolic station names
Self-test diagnostics
Hardcopy printing
Password protection

The most frequently used LAN analyzer features have been summarized elsewhere in the book. Differences in methods of implementation and degree of functionality, for both hardware and software, distinguish one product from another. These differences vary in importance with users and their networks. Practically no product is equipped with all features, making it difficult to decide which product is best for a given environment. Standalone products may be further subdivided into test instruments, analyzers, monitors, and special instruments.

LAN test instruments

The most important test instruments include ohmmeters, outlet testers, coax connectors, T-connectors, terminators, oscilloscopes, and time domain reflectometers.

Ohmmeters   An ohmmeter is a simple tool that gives impedance measurement. You can use an ohmmeter to locate open or shorted cable. If the impedance reading matches the rated impedance of the cable, the cable is fine. If the reading doesn't match the rated impedance, then the LAN has a short, a crashed cable, or a cable break somewhere along the cable run. Ohmmeters can't be used in fiber-based LANs. Ohmmeters are typically quite inexpensive.

Outlet testers   Sometimes the problem is not the cable, but the electrical outlet. For example, if an outlet is not grounded properly, noise or even current may be introduced through the power supply into the workstation, and then through the network interface card onto the copper-based (twisted pair or coaxial) LAN cable. An outlet tester, which is very inexpensive, can help detect this type of problem.

Coax connectors, T-connectors, and terminators   Extra terminators are a basic requirement, particularly on the bus network. Extra terminators can be used to isolate sections of the cable for testing.

Oscilloscope   An oscilloscope allows the network manager to examine the cable's waveform. An oscilloscope helps detect the existence of noise or other disturbances on the wire, such as continuous voltage spikes. Again, this applies only to copper-based LANs.

Time domain reflectometers (TDRs)   A time domain reflectometer operates by sending an electrical pulse over the LAN cable, monitoring for signal reflections. On a good cable there will be no reflections, indicating that the cable is clean, with no breaks or shorts. If there's a break or short in the cable, however, the time it takes for the pulse reflection to return gives the TDR a very accurate idea of where the fault is located. Many TDRs can locate cable breaks to within a few feet. TDRs have traditionally been relatively expensive instruments.

A new, less expensive generation of TDR equipment is now available. These new instruments are more compact than their predecessors, often measuring about the size of a paperback book or smaller. The newer TDRs are also easier to use and still accurate to within a few feet. A time domain reflectometer (TDR) is built as a combination of a pulse generator, a voltage sampler, and an output amplifier, supplying either a display or an oscilloscope.

Because of their distributed-star topologies, ARCNET, token ring, StarLAN, and IEEE 10BASE-T networks are easiest to test when a specific cable segment is isolated and inactive. A TDR can be used on a live Ethernet, however, if a very short pulse (of less than 10 nanoseconds duration) is used, and if that pulse is of a negative polarity. Positive pulse TDRs have to be avoided, since they can affect transceiver operation.

The TDR's operation is similar to radar. An electrical pulse of known amplitude and duration is transmitted from one end of the cable. Any changes in the cable's characteristic impedance will cause reflections of the transmitted pulse. If no cable faults exist, and the cable is terminated at the far end in its characteristic impedance, no pulse reflection will occur.

A variety of cable problems, such as shorts, opens, faults, or improper terminations, kinks, bends, crimps, shorted taps, or impedance mismatches (from mixing different types of coaxial cable), produce a unique signal reflection, known as a TDR fault signature. Typical results include the display of shorted, open, crimped, and frayed cables. Troubleshooting LANs requires a tool set (Miller 1989), addressing various types of instruments.

Here are some guidelines for assembling a toolkit (Miller 1989):

1. Obtain any network-specific tools such as the NIC diagnostic disk from the manufacturer. These tools are the least expensive, and provide a great amount of diagnostic power at a very nominal cost.
2. Prepare for cable failures. Surveys indicate that a high percentage of network failures are related to the network wiring. Therefore, have the tools required to test your twisted-pair, coax, or fiber-optic cables.
3. Be able to test the network interfaces. Compile a list of all the various interfaces (EIA-232, EIA-422, Centronics, etc.) on your LAN, and purchase test equipment that can test these points.
4. Consider software analyzers if either multiple LAN protocols or gateways are part of your network. If the network is relatively large (100 or more workstations) or heavily used, a LAN protocol analyzer can also assist with network optimization.

LAN analyzers

These are sophisticated instruments whose ultimate goal is to support performance or fault management, or both. They usually offer measurement for a large number of indicators. Measurements are conducted with high accuracy. In order to avoid having unnecessarily large amounts of data to deal with, analyzers are not used continuously. Chapter 3 gave examples for compressing data and generating reports. Without differentiation, products offer indicators for:

- Service (delay time, transfer time, dialog time).
- Use (global use of bandwidth, specific use by applications and/or by users. Figure 5-8 shows bandwidth and station activities with Sniffer).
- User profiles (what applications, what activities).
- Server profiles (internal use, queuing delays in most cases). (Cooperation is required by the operating system.)

Novell's LANalyzer (Novell 1990) network analyzer is a precision monitoring and diagnostic tool for network managers, software developers, and ser-

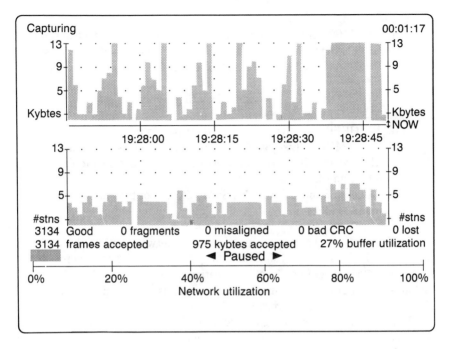

Fig. 5-8. Bandwidth and station statistics captured by Sniffer.

vice organizations. Because it was designed with a problem-solving focus, the LANalyzer not only troubleshoots system difficulties in real time, but it also helps users anticipate and prevent future problems, and plan for continued growth.

The LANalyzer owes its ease of use to its unique Application Test Suite (ATS), which embodies "expert" knowledge for performing specific common tasks. With a few simple keystrokes, users can launch any of these applications, and find expert guidance to help solve their problems. Dozens of these applications have already been written, with more on the way, and they're included free of charge with each LANalyzer system or kit. What's more, it's easy to add site-specific applications as the need arises.

Both Ethernet and Token Ring LANs may be measured and analyzed. Important applications include:

- Ethernet.
  - a. LOOKNET: Collection, filtering and processing errors, such as local collision, late collision, remote collision, CRC/alignment, too-long, and too-short packets.
  - b. TRACKCOL: Localization of the source of collision in both the local and remote segment.

- Token Ring.
  a. ERRMON: Intercepting and analyzing information sent to the Ring Error Monitor. Categorization of errors into isolation errors (line, lost, and abort), and nonisolating errors (lost frames, receive congestion, frequency, token).
  b. NONISOER: Analysis of nonisolating errors.
  c. MAP: Listing active station in ring.
  d. PRIORITY: Analysis of traffic distribution in ring.
  e. PARAMCHG: Listing all or selected parameters as set in the ring.
  f. RINGMON: Evaluation of overhead due to ring polling error monitoring and LLC managements.
  g. IN-CROSS and SEGMENTS: Monitoring of typical packet paths in multisegment rings.

The LANalyzer displays multiple views of network activity by means of nine channels. Each channel simultaneously collects statistics on network traffic based on criteria defined by an application or user, and displays the data as an easy-to-read graph. By comparing these graphs side by side, it becomes a simple matter to isolate network trouble spots.

When used as a monitoring device, the LANalyzer can generate separate alarms for each channel to notify users when network activity exceeds desired levels. Network managers can adjust the threshold for each alarm, creating an extremely flexible warning system.

Today's LANalyzer offers full seven-layer decoders for a large and growing number of the industry's most popular protocols. This feature is especially useful for developers, who often need a detailed view of network packets when they're debugging their software and hardware.

Other significant features include user-definable triggers and filters, automatic name table generation, and the ability to export captured data to popular spreadsheets for further graphic analysis and detailed, printed reports. In particular, these features include help in eliminating bottlenecks and in gaining insight into network trends:

- Overview (NetWare traffic in real time).
- Nodeview (verification of connectivity and troubleshooting).
- Fileview (file activities in real time).
- Brigview (verification of connectivity and delay measurements).
- Srvrview (hardware test for server and load simulation).

Figure 5-9 shows an example of nodeview, Due to its capability of measuring both Ethernet and Token Ring, the LANAnalyzer has been receiving very favorable evaluation results.

LANAnalyzer 3.11 is able to decode NetWare 3.11 protocols in addition to the total of 12 other protocols on both Token Ring and Ethernet. Decoding protocols provides the basis of data processing and performance interpretation.

```
 00:00:38, Collecting. . .                                    Run Station      14:58

         ┌──────────────────────────────────────────────────────┐
         │ c: \ xln \ lanz \ 802.3 \ netware \ config \ nodeview │
 131 stations └──────────────────────────────────────────────────┘

                                Packets:              Avg size:    Errors:
 No.    In station address    Out  Receive  Transmit  Rev  Xmt    Rev  Xmt
  1    114 > Hayes                 1050*      0        67
  2          radhika         1 >     0        9*             64
  3          joannd                 0        8*             64
  4          clay            1 >     0        9*             64
  5          judyj           1 >     0        9*             64
  6          ken                    0        9*             64
  7          08 00 14 52 69 55      0        7*             64
  8          kaajal          1 >     0        9*             64
  9          OSD-TS-TIDB     1 >     0        9*             70
 10          delyne          1 >     0        9*             68
 11          steveb          1 >     0        7*             64
 12          johnj2          1 >     0        9*             64
 13          08 00 14 C1 36 70 1 >  0        8*             64
 14          wen3                   0        8*             64
 15          cj              1 >     0        7*             64
 16          08 00 14 50 68 79 1 >  0        8*             64

                                               32 stations

 F1     F2     F3       F4     F5     F6       F7    F8       F9    F10
                Global    Rate           Station   Util   TxStats  More   Stop
```

Fig. 5-9. LANalyzer measurement results.

Also, the applications test suite (ATS) has been augmented by numerous predefined tests. These tests capture network traffic, filter specific types of packets, and interpret the results accordingly. Besides the new protocols and test added, the new features include summary display mode, which gives users an online description of each packet and its function, new entries for MIBs, filtering capabilities for MIB-indicators, and SNMP support for transmitting monitored data from the MIB to the manager's database.

The increased deployment of FDDI networks has motivated vendors to develop, and implement special FDDI-analyzers. Digital Technologies' LANHawk Network Analyzer functions as a passive monitor or, with an optional simulation module, as an FDDI station generating traffic. Channel-LAN 100 from Tekelec acts as an FDDI repeater and connects to the network as dual—or single—attached station. Simulation is supported with a special option. Evaluation criteria for LAN analyzers are shown in TABLE 5-2.

LAN monitoring systems

This family of tools supports continuous monitoring by offering a data collection unit in each LAN segment. The master monitor's capabilities are similar to a LAN analyzer's, but they're extended by control software to communicate with the remote data collection units.

Incorporating fault management functions for LANs into centralized fault

Table 5-2. Evaluation Criteria for LAN Analyzers

General features

Dedicated device or PC
Standards supported
    Ethernet
    Token Ring
    Token Bus
    FDDI
Scaleability for WAN analysis
Dimensions
Weight

Hardware architecture

What hardware
On board memory
On board CPU
Memory size
What printer and plotter
Ability to analyze
    Ethernet (cabling, reflectometer, collisions, wrong packets)
    Token Ring (media test, rotating time and recovery time
                measurements)
    Support of remote monitoring and analysis

Software features

Number of input channels
Filtering
Time stamps
Monitoring stations
Buffering
Triggering
Presentation
List of alarms
Protocols measured
Overhead
Statistics and performance reports
Interface to spreadsheets and databases
SNMP support

Screen and handling

Size of screen
Color codes
Resolution
What graphic cards are supported
Use of function keys
Use of maps
Use of pop-up menus

References

Number of installations
Price
Conditions
Training

management applications is not easy. Downtime and delayed service may severely impact targeted service-level agreements. There are fragmented monitoring applications supporting performance management, but continuous monitoring for supporting fault management is still very rare. A growing number of manufacturers have recognized the need and offer solutions for remote monitoring LANs. The central station or focal point may reach across via network or dial-up connections, providing the equivalent of very remote terminal and keybord operations. They may also have additional filtering and analysis capabilities.

Figure 5-10 (Network General 1991) shows a distributed Sniffer architecture. This first release of SniffMaster software runs on any Sun SPARCstation or Sun 4 workstation, and it provides central monitoring and control of one or more Model 300 and 500 Sniffers (which are Network General's line of PC-based protocol analyzer/monitors for LANs) (Dem 1989).

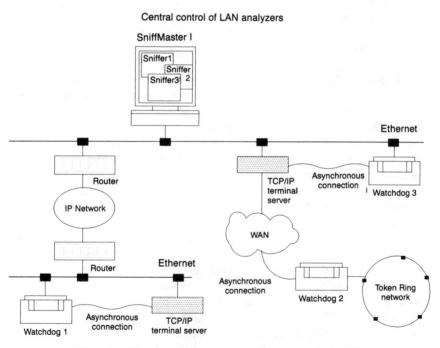

Fig. 5-10. Distributed monitoring structure with Sniffer.

Each individual Sniffer (called Watchdog) attaches locally to the desired Ethernet segment; using SniffMaster, central operators can view and control these Sniffers either across a 19.2 Kbps TCP/IP network connection or RS-232 dial-up link, rather than having to be on-site (see again FIG. 5-10). The remote Sniffer sends only data whose change would cause a screen update, rather than simply forwarding all its monitored knowledge. Between this selective filtering and Network General's data compression techniques, the amount of actual traffic can run as low as a packet per second.

A copy of SniffMaster I software is currently priced at a reasonable level. It needs a Sun workstation to operate, but Network General assumes that its current user base will be using one for their network operations centers. The wide screen and multiwindowing, multiprocess power make this class of workstation platform well suited for network management. Users don't necessarily need to dedicate a workstation solely to SniffMaster. They're also likely to be running software from Synoptics, NET, and others, WAN management software, and perhaps even word processing software (Dem 1989).

Two applications run the servers:

- The analysis application collects and analyzes packets and thus provides troubleshooting, performance analysis, and network optimization. Detailed seven-layer protocol analysis gives users an integrated view of LAN segment activity.
- The monitoring application tracks network traffic, keeps detailed network and station statistics, and generates alarms and customizable reports. It may send alarms to SniffMaster or to SNMP-based network management stations.

The new generation of Sniffer will support problem interpretation and provide recommended actions for probable problem causes. These two functions will be supported by artificial intelligence based on computer-aided software design technology. Expert Sniffer implements the most important pieces of expert-system technology, and does not try to solve all LAN-related problems. The system translates complex information about traffic and protocol analysis into high-level problem diagnosis and recommended resolutions. It's expected that a combination of products from the LAN and WAN area will help to monitor interconnected LANs from the same Sniff-Master platform.

Spider System's Remote Monitor Option (Spider Systems 1991) is a software module that needs to be loaded onto Model 220 Spider Monitors and Model 320 Spider Analyzers that a user wants to monitor remotely. A user can then configure any analyzer to act as the central monitoring point.

Digilog (Digilog 1990) offers central monitoring of its remote LAN analyzer with its recently introduced LANVista, which runs on any DOS PC with 640 Kbytes of RAM. LANVista is available in three configurations: standalone, integrated, and distributed. In the standalone and integrated configurations, the unit monitors a LAN.

In the distributed configuration, LANVista has a master-slave architecture. A central PC running the diagnostic and management software communicates through bridges, gateways, or wide area networks with slave boxes installed on each of the remote LANs.

The slave boxes perform hardware filtering; up to eight 2048-byte filters can be set. The boxes include sufficient memory on which to store captured data. Slave boxes also test cabling, using a built-in time-domain reflectometer. Thus, network administrators can locate cable breaks on remote LANs. LAN-

Vista includes slave boxes for Token Ring and Ethernet LANs. From the central master PC, network administrators can monitor up through all the layers of a number of different protocol stacks. Initially available from Digilog are TCP/IP, XNS, DECnet, and NetWare monitors.

The master software can be duplicated and then distributed to any PC on any of the LANs. Thus, the network administrator could theoretically monitor any of the LANs from any of the others. That means that local and remote fault management become meaningless in terms of defining responsibilities.

Because all product examples support either inband or outband connection techniques, they may use a variety of configuration alternatives. Some of the products are using both by sending events to the destination address. It's then up to the destination address—usually the management station—to eliminate the redundant messages. However, different instrumentation is used for Ethernet and Token Ring. Outband management may offer an additional benefit; the same physical link may be used as an outband power supply to the sensors of managed objects. Thus, the supervisory function remains uninterrupted even in cases when the main supply to the managed object has broken down. At this time, SNMP is not yet used for exporting or importing information to and from central and remote locations. This is because neither the MIB, nor the SNMP-commands are able to support the rich set of indicators and data volumes at reasonable levels of performance. RMON implementations will soon change this.

Concord's Trakker (Concord Communications 1991) is important because it seeks to bridge the gap between fault detection and fault diagnosis. Typical segment monitors look at passing traffic and trigger alarms when thresholds are exceeded, but provide little assistance in diagnosing problems. Often, a technician is dispatched to the faulty segment with a network analyzer. The technician decides which filters to set and what tests to run to uncover the root cause. This solution has three weaknesses—it's time-consuming; it depends upon expensive and relatively scarce human expertise; and it can't be easily integrated into an overall, automated network management strategy.

Recently, the market produced two new products aimed at overcoming one or more of these weaknesses. First, Network General announced its Distributed Sniffer, which allows a technician to perform traditional protocol analysis from a central console. Permanently attached Remote Sniffer units (80386-based) forward protocol packets and alarms to the console. Although this reduces the need for dispatching technicians, the central operator must still know how to set filters and run tests to effectively use the analyzer.

Second, Hewlett-Packard introduced its "Network Advisor" line of portable testers that interpret collected data using a rule-based expert system capability called "Fault Finder." This feature provides suggested causes for detected problems, such as error rates exceeding given thresholds or fluctuations in network traffic patterns. While Fault Finder allows an organization to rely less on human expertise, each network is unique and is in a constant state of flux—generic rules can't pinpoint exact causes most of the time.

Now, Concord has chosen to tackle this dilemma by adding automation software that doesn't employ rule-based design. Rather than estimate problem causes, Concord's strategy is to process and correlate the data before presenting it to the user, then making it easier for the user to diagnose faults.

A Trakker smart monitor resides on each segment, continuously capturing network packets—parsing each one, processing it through an algorithm that extracts the useful information from it, and storing it in a temporary data structure right in the monitor (see FIG. 5-11).

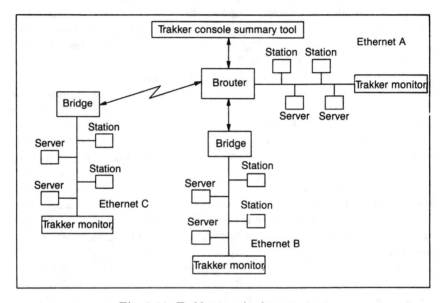

Fig. 5-11. Trakker monitoring structure.

Collectively, these data structures—residing in monitors scattered across various LAN segments—create a realtime logical map of protocol interactions (using counters, and so on). A central operator uses a menu-driven tool to query the monitor responses by sending abbreviated facts. The operator can descend further down in a menu tree to request more specific information, to which the monitor responds. The operators need not set filters or run traces to obtain results. Altogether, Trakker supports 4,000 extensions of the private MIB.

Concord is positioning Trakker as a tool for the LAN internetworked help desk—not just for a few skilled technicians. Concord views the smart monitors as application processors for value-added services such as preventing security violations, tuning/designing networks, and cost-modeling performance management. Currently, Trakker provides a basis for cost-accounting (chargeback) activities by providing data on: users relative to IP addresses, duration of node-to-node conversations, usage of application services (Telnet, FTP, NFS), and amount of data transferred (bytes, packets). To perform chargeback, the user must define this or a similar data set, put it in a Unix file and export it to another application for formatting and/or further processing.

Trakker is capable of providing information for capacity planning and performance assessment, as well as problem diagnosis. Examples of Trakker functions are shown in TABLE 5-3.

Table 5-3. Indicators Collected by Trakkers

Translates flow control messages
Examines traffic sources by network address
Reports duplicate addresses
Notifies operator of time-outs, disconnects, and failed
    connection attempts
Detects new station network addresses
Sees router-issued "source quench" message, indicating
    overload
Tracks NFS traffic outages on a server
Alarms on unauthorized stations accessing a network resource
Sees a node issuing excessive retransmissions
Reports server usage by application protocol
Monitors all protocol layers simultaneously

Other continuous monitoring products are from Cabletron, Experdata, and Novell. In all cases, two options are available to the LAN designer and planner: inband monitoring indicating the use of productive channels to exchange network management information (events, replies to polls, and commands); outband monitoring indicating the use of secondary channels or independent communication facilities to exchange network management information.

The ultimate choice depends on the following factors: availability of communication channels, bandwidth allocation options, overhead in production channels, message storms due to alerts, cost of outband, and availability of media and services.

Special instruments

Special instruments support specific LAN-management areas. Accounting management is supported in particular by two types of products: Software meters, and audit trail management tools.

Software meters   PC software vendors are particularly concerned about product licensing; they want to keep tight control over illegal copying of their software. Obviously, a vendor doesn't want to sell one copy of a product to a large company, only to have hundreds of employees copy it. On the other hand, it would be quite inefficient for the LAN manager to buy as many copies of the software as there are employees. At any time, it's unlikely that thousands, or even hundreds, of people need a given application. Vendors have devised software meters as a way of deterring illegal copying. Certain PC applications now come with built-in meters. A meter works on the same principle as a lending library. When a user starts an application, he or she checks it out of the license library and returns it when finished. If all copies are lent out, the meter returns a temporary denial.

The LAN manager may consider using meters to monitor and control software usage, as well as to provide users with enough copies without purchasing volumes of software. The LAN manager can also use the meter to keep usage statistics; this can assist "traffic engineering" of the software library.

Audit trail management tools   Audit trail systems are a key component of security management, although the function can be considered part of accounting management. Audit trail systems provide information on user activity on the LAN. Additionally, these systems can assist in billing management by providing the data needed to charge back usage.

For an audit trail system to be effective, it must provide LAN management with streamlined and useful information. The manager may wish to audit only certain users, operations on files with certain extensions or in certain subdirectories, certain types of operations, or certain servers. All file and directory creations, deletions, and renames may need to be reported. A system error log report, listing all system error messages to alert the LAN manager of potential problems, may be advantageous. A sophisticated audit tool must allow this management flexibility.

Most vendors provide some form of support for accounting management, but the level of sophistication is much lower than with SMDR Station Message Detail Record. Substantial future development is needed and expected in this area.

Documentation tools   Large-scale or interconnected LANs require powerful documentation systems or, in other words, an enterprise-wide library of data accessible by any user on the LAN. A user should be able to access any document without prior knowledge of where it physically resides. On the basis of basic information about a document, a user should be able to formulate a query, and the document management system is expected to search, find, retrieve, and route the document to the requester. The documents may be in image or in coded formats (Network Management, Inc., 1990). LANfolio is one example offering support for document management. LANfolio is structured around a three-tiered, client/server model. The ultimate goal of this product is to solve two common problems: the successful accommodation of large numbers of users requiring simultaneous access to an enterprise-wide resource (e.g., the document database), and remote offices querying a centrally located database without performance bottlenecks.

The three tiers are:

- Workstation. This is the front-end section of LANfolio and the part that interacts with users. The Document Profile Screen displays fields into which critical information about a document is entered. Any of the fields can be used to formulate a query. Also, a combination of fields may be used as search criteria.

- Document request server. This is an interface between users and the database server executing distributed control tasks and syntax conversion. Each document request server can be configured to query one or several database servers in a user-defined sequence, based on what the probability is of a given document's location.
- Database server. This is an SQL-based database engine. LANfolio can span multiple disk volumes and even multiple file servers. Due to SQL, other SQL-based minis and micros may be integrated into the "directory" service capabilities of LANfolio.

LANfolio first and foremost supports configuration management and user administration. LANfolio is, however, not connected to realtime network status supervision and displays that are key components of fault management. The LAN support product family focuses on three LAN management issues: software control (protection against viruses), network printing (sharing printers and pop-up access amongst all users), and user support (control of all PCs residing on the LAN segment from one workstation). (TABLE 5-4 lists examples of standalone products, categorized by principal application areas.

Table 5-4. List of Standalone LAN Management Products

Configuration management

• Interpoll	(Apple)
• LAN Automatic Inventory	(Brightwork Development, Inc.)
• Monitrix	(Cheyenne Software)
• Communications Resource Management Systems	(Chi Cor Information Management)
• LANTools	(Computer Communication, Inc.)
• LANscope Resource Manager	(Connect Computers)
• Network SuperVisor	(CSG Technologies)
• LAN Command	(Dolphin)
• CheckNet and NetAtlas	(Farallon Computing)
• Net Vision	(Fresh Technology Group)
• LAN Directory	(Frye Computer Systems)
• LAN Auditor	(Horizon Technology)
• Command 2000	(Isicad)
• LANSight	(LAN Systems)
• Network H.Q.	(Magee Enterprises)
• LAN Track	(NetWave)
• Planet	(Network & Communication Technology)
• CAD/COM Cable Management System	(Network Facilities Professionals)
• SnapNET	(Network Monitoring, Inc.)
• Status*Mac	(Pharos Technologies, Inc.)
• Origen	(Preferred Systems, Inc.)
• LANcentral Express	(Racal)
• NetVisualizer	(Silicon Graphics)
• VisiNET	(Technology Dynamics, Inc.)
• GraceLAN Network Manager	(Technology Works)
• Cable Master	(The Angeles Group)
• The Aperture Networker and The Graphic Networker	(The Graphic Management Group)

Table 5-4. Continued

- Netbuild   (Trilogy)
- ARGUS/n   (Triticom)
- Dpware   (Vycor Corporation)
- Telecommunications Management Systems   (Xiox Corporation)

Fault and performance management

Analyzers:

- Net Watchman   (AG Group)
- ARCAN   (Analysis, Inc.)
- Trakker   (Concord Systems)
- LAN Traffic Monitor   (DEC)
- Ethernim   (DEC)
- Network Quality Analyzer   (Digicom)
- LANVista   (Digilog)
- NetWare Early Warning System   (Frye Computer Systems)
- 4972 LAN Analyzer   (Hewlett-Packard)
- LAN Probe   (Hewlett-Packard)
- Trace and Performance Program   (IBM)
- LANSight Sentry   (Intel)
- Sherlock LW   (International Data Sciences)
- LAN Ranger   (Kinetics, Inc.)
- LANSpy   (Legent)
- Comtest LAN Analyzer   (M-Test Equipment)
- Netalarm for Netware   (Mayer & Associates)
- NetScanner   (Microtest, Inc.)
- Ethermeter   (Network Application Technology)
- Sniffer   (Network General)
- LANAlert   (Network Computing, Inc.)
- Ethernex   (Network Corporation)
- SnapProbe   (Network Monitoring, Inc.)
- LANAnalyzer   (Novell)
- LANterm   (Novell)
- Evergreen   (Oneac Corporation)
- Protolyzer   (ProTools)
- POWERScope   (Performance Technology)
- Prodatest   (Prodatel Communications)
- LAN Detector   (Racal Interlan)
- AlertView   (Shany Computers)
- SpiderProbe, Spider Analyzer   (Spider)
- Interview 1000   (Telenex)
- TRW-NMS   (TRW)

SW-diagnostic tools

- E-Monitor, ARC-Monitor   (Brightwork Software)
- NetVision   (Fresh Technology Group)
- Traffic Watch   (Farallon)
- Network Advisor   (Hewlett-Packard)
- LANtraffic   (LANTools)
- LAN Patrol   (Legend Software)
- Carbon Copy   (Microcom)
- Fault Finder   (Network Advisor)
- Network Ranger   (Sarbec)

Time domain reflectometers

- Experdata E10-N   (Experdata)
- Universal tool   (Tektronix)

Accounting management

- LT Auditor   (Blue Lance)

Table 5-4. Continued

• LANScope	(Connect Computers)
• LANtrail	(LAN Services)
• NM 2000	(TRW)

Security management

• Antivirus	(Central Point Software)
• NetBack	(Cheyenne Software)
• Virus Clean	(Computer Consulting Group)
• Turnstyle	(Connect Computer)
• SecureMax	(Demax Software)
• F-Prot	(Fridrik Skulason)
• LANAuditor	(Horizon Technology)
• Sitelock	(Integrity Software)
• AntiVirus Plus	(IRIS Software & Computers)
• LAN Shadow	(LAN Services)
• Virus Buster	(Leprechaun Software International)
• Scan Clean	(McAfee Associates)
• Virex PC	(Microcom)
• Saber Meter	(Saber Software)
• ACE Server	(Security Dynamics)
• Norton Antivirus	(Symamec)
• Dr. Solomon Toolkit	(S&S)
• Annex	(Xylogics, Inc.)
• ViruSafe	(XTree Company)

User Administration

• Network Navigator	(Annatek Systems, Inc.)
• Windows Menu	(Automated Design)
• Help Desk	(Blue Lance)
• LAN Support Center, Netremote	(Brightwork Software)
• SuperVisor	(CSG Technologies, Inc.)
• LANScope	(Connect Computers)
• Cybertek Pro Menu	(Cybertek)
• LANAuditor	(Horizon Technology)
• LANSightSupport	(Intel)
• BuildView	(LAN Support Group)
• LAN Shell	(LAN Systems)
• Reference Point	(LAN Systems)
• Lanshare	(Micronet)
• WorkGroup	(Ncompass Software)
• NETMenu	(NetInc)
• Action Request System	(Remedy, Inc.)
• Saber Menu	(Saber Software)
• GraceLAN	(Technology Works, Inc.)

Management of PC LANs

PC LANs are specialized solutions implemented by smaller user groups or departments. Principal implementation criteria are low cost, ease of installation, and transparent maintenance. They're generally built around the client-server model of computing. Products have been tuned for high performance—mostly in the MS-DOS area—within severe memory and processing power limitations. PC LANs were in the past rarely interconnected. As a result, the number of LAN management instruments was limited. Solutions focused on status supervision, fault determination, and very basic administration capabilities. Most of these functions have been incorporated into the LAN operating systems of market-leading companies.

Besides IBM, products from Novell, 3Com and Banyan have dominated the market. Until recently, these dominating players have resisted opening their architectures and products to multiprotocol applications, interoperability, and to leading network management protocols, such as SNMP, CMOT, and CMIP. Other interesting products in the PC LAN area are StarLAN from AT&T and LocalTalk from Apple.

As a result of tremendous user pressure, leading companies have been reacting in the following ways:

- Offering gateways to TCP/IP.
- Cooperative agreements (e.g., IBM and Novell, IBM and 3Com, Banyan and Novell).
- Support of SNMP over a short range.
- Support of CMOT over a longer range.
- Acquisition of monitoring products in order to immediately provide users with enhanced monitoring and management.

The following discussion centers on LANtern, which is a monitoring extension of Novell operating systems. LANtern is a permanently installed remote network monitor, with specialized hardware designed for network managers. It provides the information needed most to maintain, manage, and diagnose networking problems. The information is made available at a centralized SNMP-based network management console. LANtern is a complimentary product of the LAN-analyzer, and of NetWare. The specialized monitor detects events, such as collisions or ring recoveries, and provides a picture of true network use. LANtern's basic components include hardware for information collection and management software.

Specialized hardware technology enables the LANtern to accomplish special supervisory and measurement functions. For example, by sensing collision rates and true use of the network, it can assist users in isolating faulty transceivers or cabling, jabbering stations, or Ethernets extended beyond their maximum legal length.

A PC extended by a LAN board and running under Windows 3.0 is used as a management console. The management station displays information collected from LANtern agents, to alert management when thresholds are violated (e.g., duplicate IP addresses, dead stations, new stations, abnormal traffic levels, cable failures), and to support proactive performance management with statistical evaluations. Figure 5-12 shows the structure of LANtern.

LANtern is designed to monitor only the networks they're attached to. Since LANtern is a remote device and uses the SNMP protocol, which is IP-based, the LANtern can be placed anywhere on the network and report information about that segment across both bridges and routers to the central management facility. LANtern has a serial port that may be used for outband

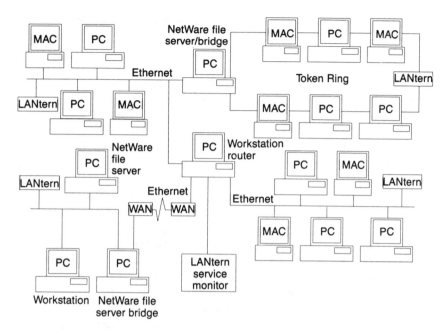

Fig. 5-12. LANtern structure.

monitoring, providing information to the central facility even when the productive communication channels are down.

Leading vendors of LAN operating systems are expected to make status information on principal servers available to external LAN management entities. Novell was the first to provide a NetWare Management Agent that provides two types of alerts to NetView:

- Token ring alerts: lobe problem, beaconing condition, insertion process has failed, remove ring station during insertion, error during insertion, wire fault condition, self-test unsuccessful, reporting station has left the LAN, beaconing longer than error detection timer.
- LAN logical link control alerts. For various reasons, logical link has been lost is indicated by the following symptoms: remote link station doesn't respond, remote link station sends a disconnect mode message, remote link station sends an SABME command, local link station sends an invalid or unsupported command, local link station sends an I field that's not permitted, local link station sends a frame with an invalid N(r), local link station sends a frame with an I-field that's too long, local link station returns a frame reject response, remote link station sends an I field that's not permitted, remote link station sends a frame with invalid N(r), remote link station sends a frame with an I-field that's too long.

After proper customization, NetView can display, and further process these alerts.

On the way to a fully integrated network management product, Novell offers NetWare Management System (NMS). This product provides an open, extensive, object-oriented environment to administer and manage hubs, links, switches, routers, and components of the NetWare environment. NMS includes the following elements:

- NetWare Services Manager, available for either Microsoft's Windows or OS/2, lets network administrators monitor and control NetWare environments and develop NMS-compatible applications. It includes the NetWare Management Map that automatically discovers NetWare devices on the network, displays them graphically, and lets administrators see detailed information or set thresholds for each device.
- Netware Management Agents, which are NetWare Loadable Modules (NLM), relay statistics about the server to NetWare Services Manager.
- NetWare Management Enhanced Map lets administrators combine images of actual corporate locations with the NMS' logical network map. The Enhanced Map also can automatically map Internet Protocol-based routers and hub management interface-compliant hub cards, and support management of SNMP-compatible devices from the NMS console.
- NetWare Network Management Toolkit helps developers write NMS-compatible NLMs using either SNMP or NetWare Management Agents.
- NetWare Management System Software Development Kit provides application programming interfaces to the NMS.

Support of both *de facto* and open standards is expected. At the moment, NMS is considered another platform with relatively rich functionality. The arrangement with LANtern (FIG. 5-12) prepares customers for migrating to NMS. Future work has to concentrate on integrating LANAnalyzer to offer powerful customization assistance to third-parties.

In order to support various network management activities, Banyan offers VINES Assistant, a set of seventeen utilities for online diagnostics, alert notification, and performance tuning. Among the utilities are server capacity and connectivity alert monitors, server configuration inventory, routing table reporters, and a list analyzer that eases access to entries in Banyan StreetTalk directory service.

LAN element management systems

LAN element management systems manage general-purpose LANs. Such LANs serve an entire enterprise consisting of large departments with various and usually powerful servers. General-purpose LANs are likely to be interconnected. Element management systems in this section are grouped around

Ethernet, Token Ring, wiring concentrators, interconnecting devices, and LAN backbones such as FDDI. Also, generic solutions are addressed that are derived from LAN management platforms.

Ethernet element management systems

Ethernet-based LAN segments still lead the market. It's extremely important to provide monitoring and management capabilities for these segments. Two leading products from DEC, and a product combination from Hewlett-Packard, will be addressed next.

Ethernim has been built with modularity, flexibility, and expandability in mind. In terms of the user interface, DEC has targeted the following criteria (Morrison 1989):

- Easily learned by novice user.
- Windowing.
- Presentation of meaningful data only.
- Easy navigation within menus.
- Zooming in on information segments.
- Status line for displaying relevant system messages.

Ethernim's principal components are (FIG. 5-13).

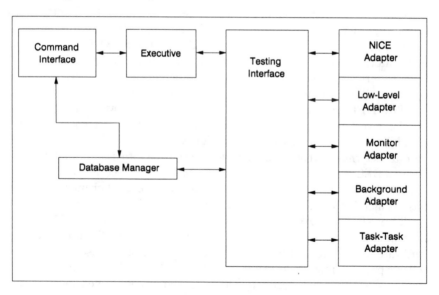

Fig. 5-13. Ethernim components overview.

The database   As with the design of the user interface, a key database design point revolved around whether or not to use a layered product on which to build the functionality. DEC has chosen to build their own database from scratch. The NMCC/VAX Ethernim data is stored in two separate indexed files: one contains information about the nodes that reside on those segments. Each record contains internal pointers to other records to which they're related.

The Testing Interface   While most programs revolve around the Executive, this design evolved another module that performed most of the generalized services. This module, the "Testing Interface," became the "socket" where the individual protocol-dependent modules were plugged in. While the actual Executive handles top-level scheduling, the Testing Interface runs a subset for the protocol modules, along with providing services such as address translation.

The Testing Interface also has a direct interface to the database services, allowing the data collected from the protocol modules to be stored or retrieved as needed during normal operation, and providing a single point of access for all the various adapters. It also has the task of finding additional information for DECnet nodes. If NMCC/VAX Ethernim has only a node name, it will "ask" the DECnet Adapter for the address. If only the address is known, it will "ask" for the node name. This new information is then automatically added to the database.

The Ethernet Adapter   This module is responsible for direct Ethernet-level operations (data link layer). The functions provided by the Ethernet Adapter include Ethernet loopback, sending of Digital MOP REQUEST ID messages and reception of response, and a "listener" for SYSTEM-ID messages that allows automated collection of the Digital nodes on the Ethernet. The Digital REQUEST ID/SYSTEM ID messages are similar in concept to 802.2 XID messages, although the SYSTEM-ID contains more information about the node. Items of interest include: Ethernet port type, Ethernet address(es), and device-specific information such as terminal server name and number.

The DECnet Adapter   The DECnet Adapter provides a higher level (session layer) interface to the network. Using the NICE protocol, it provides the ability to query the local or the designated routing node's DECnet database to determine what DECnet nodes are on the Ethernet. In addition, it allows a DECnet level loopback message to be sent and received, and provides a function that queries a target DECnet node for its DECnet characteristics. In this manner, both testing and information collection is facilitated.

The Monitor Adapter   The Monitor Adapter allows NMCC/VAX Ethernim to selectively monitor Ethernet traffic, without the use of special hardware. Using the host machine's Ethernet device in promiscuous mode, it collects packets from the local area network. Looking only at the header information (source address, destination address, and protocol type/length), it provides several different filters for analyzing the traffic patterns: the six nodes having the largest number of packets addressed to/from them, the six nodes sending/receiving the most packets to/from a specific node, the six multicast source addresses seen most often, the six protocol types in greatest use.

The Background Adapter   The Background Adapter is a special module that provides users with the ability to have certain repetitive functions performed automatically, while the product is in use. New or charged information is automatically updated in the database. It controls the "listening" for Digital MOP SYSTEM-ID messages, and in addition allows the user to do the following: send a REQUEST ID message to each node in the network that supports it (the data in the SYSTEM-ID message provides valuable information for the network manager); send a REQUEST ID message repeatedly to a specific node for testing purposes; send a request for DECnet Information to each node in the network that supports it (again providing important information for the user).

The Remote Task   The Remote Task Adapter (also called the Task-to-Task Adapter) is the final protocol module component. Requiring an executable image residing on the target node, it provides two simple functions: a user-level loopback to allow testing throughout the entire multilayer stack, and a function that queries for several valuable pieces of information from the target node, such as operating system type/version, CPU type, and so on.

The types of information that NMCC/VAX Ethernim collects fall into four major categories: Digital SYSTEM ID message, DECnet information, system information, and user-supplied reference data.

SYSTEM IDs   Digital SYSTEM ID messages, which are multicast on the Ethernet at periodic intervals, contain information about the Ethernet device type, Ethernet hardware address, and DECnet Ethernet address (if the node is running DECnet). Some devices provide additional data such as terminal server name/number, ROM version, and so on.

DECnet information   In keeping with a Digital product, several fields in the NMCC/VAX Ethernim database are devoted to DECnet information. These include: DECnet node name, the node's own name (which may be different from DECnet node name), DECnet address, DECnet management version, DECnet router type, DECnet router version, DECnet network Services Protocol Version, and a list of communication devices.

System information   NMCC/VAX Ethernim data fields that are gathered from system information include: CPU type, CPU serial number, microcode revision level, hardware revision level, operating system type/version.

User information   While any of the previous NMCC/VAX Ethernim data fields may be manually modified by the user, several fields can't be automatically gathered, and (if used) must be entered by the user. These are: system location, responsible person, phone number, modem phone number, modem speed, and additional line(s) of descriptive text of the user's choosing.

Many of the pieces of equipment that have appeared on Ethernets have been built with network management in mind. But some of them don't have any way to indicate via a remote protocol that they exist. The only hope for automatically finding these types of devices is via time domain reflectometry, or some similar mechanism for detecting them via the electrical characteristics that they impart to the wire. NMCC/VAX Ethernim allows these "transparent devices" to be edited into the topology by the user. Clearly, if you're attempting to build a database of the network topology, it's essential to learn about every major connecting device out there, not just those that are devised to provide the necessary information.

The LAN Traffic Monitor is an Ethernet monitor that uses Digital LAN Bridge 100 as a base for gathering network traffic data. This data is periodically forwarded to the VAX/VMS system for compilation and analysis.

The information is presented to the manager in a graphical format when requested (using a Digital VT340 or VT240/241 color graphics terminal). This information may be provided in tabular form when requested, for users with VT 220 nongraphics terminals.

LAN Traffic Monitor (Digital 1989) has been designed for easy use, with an integrated online help facility. This means that a new user doesn't need to constantly refer to the accompanying user documentation. The product can also report statistics to any node residing on the network, provided suitable access privileges have been granted. LAN Traffic Monitor collects data on any type of user on Ethernet (e.g., 802.3, TCP/IP, LAT, and so on).

From the data frames that pass along Ethernet, the Monitor learns source addresses, multicast addresses, and type fields. The information is used to classify each frame sent in terms of these categories. Each frame's type of address, whether single destination or multicast, is also recorded. The counters that collect the statistics allow for continuous operation without wraparound for approximately 50 days, assuming a continuous rate of 1000 frames per second. LAN Traffic Monitor is composed of two components:

- Special monitoring software that has been downline loaded from any VAX computer on the LAN to a specified LAN Bridge 100 or 150.
- User interface software that's installed on any VAX/VMS system with an Ethernet controller and associated driver.

The LAN Traffic Monitor may be configured in a number of ways:

- To monitor selected Ethernet segments.
- To monitor multiple segments.

LAN Bridge 100 can't be operated as an LTM listener and a bridge at the same time. However, if the bridges break down, the listener can be switched immediately to the switch function, serving in this way as a hot bridge backup. Both products will be incorporated into DECmcc, DEC's integrator product.

In order to enhance its Ethernet element management capabilities, Hewlett-Packard has acquired LANProbe. LANProbe is an analysis tool that allows detailed testing and traffic analysis of remote Ethernet segments. Stand-alone monitors and analyzers are too expensive for this purpose. The segment monitor is attached directly to an Ethernet (FIG. 5-14). There, it monitors all frames on the LAN and relays the information it collects to the node location, running under ProbeView. The connection between LANProbe and the node locator could be either dial-up or dedicated lines, or Ethernet itself. It's expected that both will be incorporated into the OpenView platform.

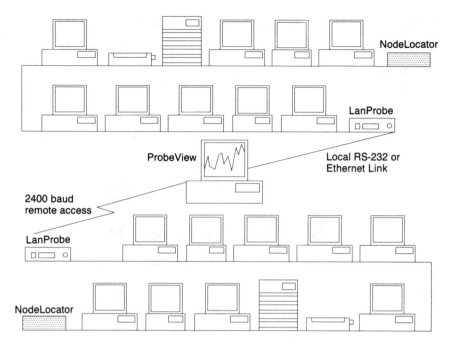

Fig. 5-14. ProbeView and LANProbe from Hewlett-Packard.

Hewlett-Packard supports software applications and computer systems by OpenView Extensible SNMP Agent software. This augmentation includes over 60 new managed objects. The functions supported include the status of foreground and background application and printer processes. Specific users may be searched and found, as well. Using this extension, correlation of network-related and applications-related events are much easier than using separate tools. Using the Application Builder, LAN managers can define the actions to be performed or the data to be collected without specifically programming. The Extensible Agent works with any SNMP-compliant SNMP management station, as far as public entries of the MIB are required. For including private MIB entries, case by case agreements are necessary.

In order to further support LAN performance management functions, Hewlett-Packard is providing a systems management tool that monitors server and workstation performance in real time and alerts LAN administrators when thresholds are exceeded. PerfView runs under Unix and the OSF/Motif graphical user interface. Intelligent Collections Agents are responsible for extracting data, and sending it to PerfView. PerfView and OpenView are expected to communicate with each other. The monitored indicators include CPU utilization, memory utilization, transaction processing rates, disk input/output rates, and the individual processes of applications. Agents will be implemented beside HP components into IBM mainframes, AS/400s, VAX minis, ATX processors, Ultrix processors, Novel servers. PerfView is using eventing instead of SNMP-like polling, with the result of low overhead continuous monitoring.

Token Ring element management systems

IBM is leading this market with individual Token Ring management tools and with the umbrella product called LAN Network Manager. There are two basic management options: standalone management of connected components, or centralized and integrated management via NetView. Figure 5-15 shows the structure of management with all managed objects (Datapro NS30 1990).

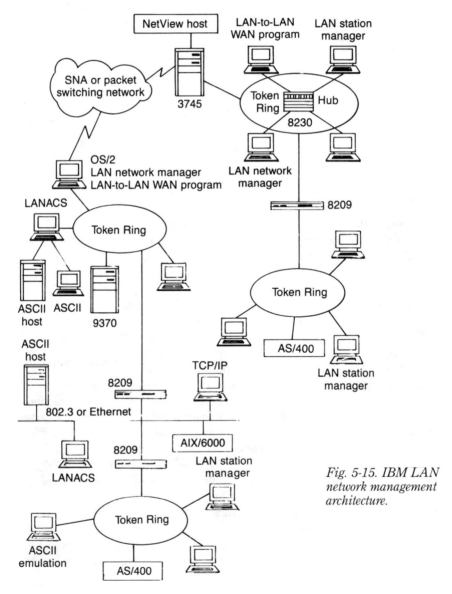

Fig. 5-15. IBM LAN network management architecture.

IBM's LAN network management products manage LANs at the workstation level and, with NetView, on a host computer. They track and control access to devices on each LAN. IBM has five major LAN management products:

1. IBM LAN Network Management Version 1.0.
2. IBM LAN Network Management Version 1.1.
3. IBM LAN Network Management Entry.
4. IBM LAN Station Manager.
5. IBM 8230 Controlled Access Unit (CAU).

IBM LAN Network Version 1.0

IBM LAN Network Management Version 1.0 (Datapro NS30 1990) is written as an application under OS/2 EE and uses the Presentation Manager operator interface. It enhances LAN media and LAN attachment management using the OS/2 EE SQL-based database manager for building the LAN configuration database.

Version 1.0 provides an event log and configuration database using the OS/2 EE database manager. Users can tailor applications for detailed analysis of the configuration data collected and maintained by the program. Working with CAU, Version 1.0 provides flexibility in controlling the network's access level. Access control can be based on adapter address, CAU identifier, attachment module adapter, CAU lobe identifier, office number, time of day, or day of week.

When a CAU-attached device inserts into the ring, the CAU reports its identifying information to the program, either directly or via the IBM LAN Station Manager. This information is compared with the information in Version 1.0's database, such as user-defined restrictions, to determine if the adapter is authorized to access the LAN. Discrepancies can be configured to generate an alert. Unauthorized adapters can be removed, or the lobe at the CAU can be disabled so the adapter can't be reinserted without operator assistance.

Also in conjunction with the CAU, Version 1.0 can increase network availability by providing automatic recovery from a cable or access unit failure in a token ring network. If the cable between two CAUs breaks, the CAU provides an automatic wrap-out, and the program identifies the fault domain. Version 1.0 can also issue wrap/unwrap commands to the CAU from the operator console for reconfiguration or troubleshooting purposes.

Version 1.0, working with NetView Version 2.1, provides most of the NetView LAN commands available using the older IBM LAN Manager Version 2.0 working with NetView Version 1.3. A LAN alert filtering capability is another feature of Version 1.0. Alerts that are not critical to managing the network with NetView can be filtered at the LAN. User-defined filters to customize LAN management are possible. There's also the capability of defining the frequency and number of retries when the program adapter is unable to insert into the network because of a disabled token ring segment. The number of retries and other parameters can be set by the user.

IBM LAN Network Manager Version 1.1

IBM LAN Network Manager Version 1.1 provides an expanded set of commands that can be issued from NetView Version 2.2, allowing full integration of LAN management into a comprehensive enterprise-wide management system. With these commands, users can add, delete, query, list, and set parameters for LAN-attached devices. This command/response communication between NetView and IBM LAN Network Manager Version 1.1 is provided by the OS/2 EE communication manager host interface.

Version 1.1 also has a facility for issuing commands at the OS/2 command line to invoke the various LAN management functions. Responses are provided to the screen interface at the LAN workstation. This facility can be used for providing local automation capabilities for LAN users.

Version 1.1 enhances the capability of Version 1.0's alert filtering facility, permitting the user to set filters from a NetView console. The program also collects additional statistics on network collision, late collision, CRC errors, and framing errors for the 8209 Ethernet port. An alert is generated if the Ethernet bus becomes inoperative, and the alert reports and logs the status if the bus recovers after the failure. With IBM GraphicsView/2, users can view the LAN topology and configuration pictorially. Status of network objects is indicated by colors.

IBM LAN Network Manager Entry

IBM LAN Network Manager Entry is also written as an application under OS/2 EE and allows management of remote single-segment IBM Token Ring Networks or IBM PC Networks (broadband or baseband). Since the program doesn't provide a user interface at the LAN workstation, users must manage single-segment remote LANs installed in a central NetView branch.

This program also provides a subset of IBM LAN Network Manager Version 1.1 command/response facilities for managing the network from NetView Version 2.2; this consolidates LAN/WAN management into a central management facility with NetView. It communicates with NetView at the host using the OS/2 EE communications manager via an existing LAN SNA gateway.

IBM LAN Station Manager

IBM LAN Station Manager is a licensed program providing LAN configuration and environment data to IBM LAN Network Manager Version 1.1 from DOS and OS/2 LAN stations. This capability improves LAN administration, security, and the ability to audit.

LAN Station Manager allows the IBM LAN Network Manager programs to set station configuration values. It also supports the emerging industry-standard protocol ISO/CMIP (Common Management Information Protocol). The management protocol between IBM LAN Network Manager Version 1.1 and IBM LAN Station Manager is based on OSI standards.

Station identifying information provided by IBM LAN Station Manager, combined with attachment information from the 8230 CAU, allows IBM LAN Network Manager Version 1.1 to build a LAN topology that can provide information on active and inactive network stations. The program supports existing DOS and OS/2 LAN stations.

IBM 8230 Token Ring Network Controlled Address Unit (CAU)

IBM 8230 Token Ring Network Controlled Access Unit is an intelligent access concentrator that allows connection of up to 80 workstations, via pluggable lobe attachment modules, to a token ring network. The unit can identify and isolate a malfunctioning node, automatically recovering or removing and bypassing the failing component so the network remains functional. Through IBM LAN Network Manager, the 8230 can notify the NetView operator of the problem.

The 8230 can be switched between 4 Mbps and 16 Mbps operation and has a media access control appearance on both the main and backup rings. A lobe length of 375 meters is possible with 4 Mbps data grade media. A length of 145 meters is possible with 16 Mbps data grade media. The integrated 16 Mbps copper repeater supports a longer drive distance between concentrators. In some cases, this could eliminate the need for standalone repeaters, reducing network complexity and cost.

The unit has interchangeable copper and/or fiber-optic ring-in and ring-out interface modules. If the main ring changes from copper to fiber, the converter modules can be changed from copper to fiber, or one side can be copper and the other fiber, without replacing the base unit or lobe attachment modules (LAMs).

The 8230's systems management capabilities permit automatic wrap/reconfiguration of a failing ring segment, a failing lobe, a LAM, or the 8230 itself. The unit also supports the IBM LAN Network Manager's configuration table, providing the adapter address, 8230 number, LAM number, and lobe number, so a particular workstation can easily be located to provide maintenance or attention to a problem area.

Other products contributing to integrated LAN management include the LAN-to-LAN wide area network program, IBM 8309 LAN Bridge, which connects Token Ring and Ethernet, and the LAN asynchronous connection server.

Token Ring management functions are distributed. Basically, all components play the role of agents, as shown in FIG. 5-16. The sources of information are the tokens generated and passed to control the operation. Those tokens are hidden to the user. TABLE 5-5 lists the available Token Ring management functions, their descriptions, and the location of the information source that supports the functions. Fault management plays a key role in managing token rings. Errors may be subdivided into hard and soft errors.

A *hard error* is a permanent fault that stops normal traffic of the ring. It's detected at the receive side of the ring, downstream of the fault. A change in

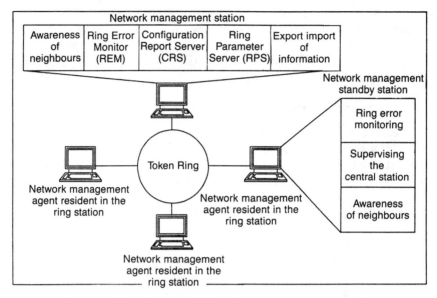

Fig. 5-16. Distribution of Token Ring measurement functions.

ring configuration is required to bypass such a fault and to restore normal operation. Reconfiguration may be the result of automatic recovery or, if this automatic recovery failed to bypass the error, it may require some manual intervention.

When a ring station detects a hard error, it starts transmitting at specified time intervals Beacon MAC frames until its input signal is restored or until it's removed from the ring. The detecting station also starts a Beacon MAC frame. A beacon frame identifies the address of the nearest active upstream neighbor (NAUN) of the beaconing station, as well as error type information.

When the beaconing station's NAUN copies three of these beacon frames, the NAUN will go offline and perform microcode and lobe tests. If the tests are successful, the station reattaches to the ring immediately. If the tests fail, the station stays offline.

When the Beacon timer expires and normal traffic has not been restored, the beaconing station assumes that its NAUN went offline, found no errors, and came back online. It will now go through the same process as its NAUN. If the tests fail, the beaconing station remains detached. If successful, the station reattaches immediately. In this case, normal traffic has not been restored during automatic recovery. Network Management will be informed, and manual intervention is required. While reporting a permanent hard error, a set of adapter addresses is provided, limiting the faulty part of the ring to a small fault domain.

Intermittent faults that temporarily disrupt normal operation of the ring are called soft errors. They're usually tolerated by error recovery procedures, but they impair normal ring operation if excessive or nonrandom.

Table 5-5. Available Token Ring Management Functions

Function	Description	Located	Election
Active monitor	Monitor the local ring for missing tokens, duplicate tokens, streaming, etc.	All adapters	Token claiming
Ring error monitor	Collects and analyzes hard errors and soft errors sent by ring stations on a single ring	Bridge 3174 9370, AS/400 LAN mgr 3270EM Lnmgt Ring diagn.	SW definition Addressing through functional address
Ring parameter server	Sends initialization info to new stations on the ring. Forwards registration info from new stations to the LAN manager	Bridge	SW definition Addressing through func. address
Ring configur. server	Collects and forwards config reports generated by stations on the ring. Accepts commands from LAN Mg. to get info from stations, set parameters and remove stations from the ring.	Bridge LAN mgr	SW definition Addressing through func. address
LAN Bridge Server	Keeps statistical information about traffic across the bridge. Forwards this information to LAN manager.	Bridge	
Trace and Performance	Traces some or all messages on the local ring and stores. Analyzes the stored trace. Measures performance statistics about traffic.	Specific adapter	Specific SW
Station manager	Collects the data from a name server. Sends statistics to manager.	PC or PS/2	SW program
Controlled Access Unit	Controls access to the ring. Acts as name server to stations. Controls the IAU to IAU link.	Access unit	SW defined
LAN manager	Collects the data from different servers. Analyzes it and takes management actions.	PC or PS/2	SW program
Netview (SNA control point)	Collects data being from either LAN manager, some REM stations, or applications (alerts).	SNA host	SW program

The most critical soft errors are monitored in each ring station by means of a set of counters. Every two seconds the values of soft error counters are sent as soft error report MAC frames to the ring error monitor functional address (typically residing in a bridge), where the values for each counter are accumulated. If a soft error counter exceeds a predefined threshold, LAN Network Manager will be informed through its link with the LAN reporting mechanism. The LAN Network Manager may reconfigure the ring to bypass a faulty node, if the fault can be located. Soft errors are said to be isolating if a fault domain can be specified. If not, they're called nonisolating soft errors. The most important functions are summarized in the next section.

Alert functions   An *alert* is a notification of a security violation on the network or of an interruption or a potential interruption in the flow of data around the network. The loss may have already occurred, or may be imminent. For example, a print server is considered by a particular work group to be a critical resource on the network. Accordingly, the print server should be monitored by the LAN Manager. If the print server's adapter is lost from the network, an alert is generated by the LAN Manager. Figure 5-17 shows an example of an alerts list. Recommended actions are supported, as well.

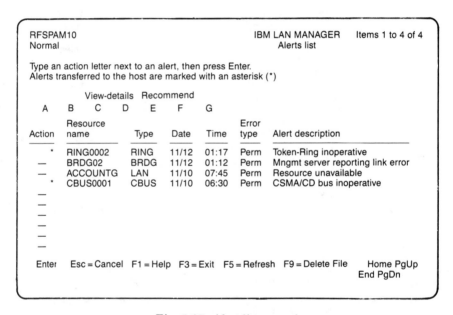

Fig. 5-17. Alert list example.

Event logging and reporting   The LAN Manager logs the following types of network events: configuration changes, alerts, invalid frames, soft errors, and notifications (such as "network recovered"). Configuration logging may be turned on/off for all LAN segments, or for a single LAN segment. Soft error reporting may be enabled and disabled for each LAN segment on the network.

Logged events may be retrieved for reporting by one or more of the following categories: data and time, adapter name, adapter address, LAN segment number, message number, or bridge name. Figure 5-18 (Goehring 1990) shows an event log report, including code point explanation and message detail.

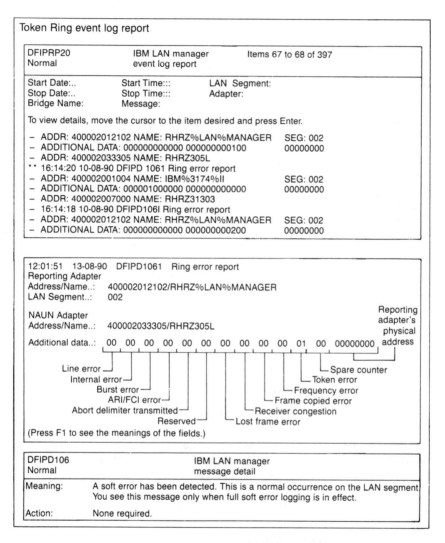

Fig. 5-18. Event log report example.

Adapter functions   Adapter function options allow the performance of the following: add an adapter definition, remove an adapter from the network, query an adapter profile on the network. Each computer in a LAN has an adapter to interface with the network. An adapter definition is needed for each adapter to be recognized by the LAN Network Manager by name. An adapter definition consists of the following information: adapter name, adapter address, whether the adapter is to be monitored, and comments about the adapter.

The monitoring of an adapter begins when the LAN manager is started or when an address is defined as monitored, using adapter definition. When the LAN Network Manager monitors an adapter, it generates an alert if any of the following conditions occurs: the adapter leaves the network or doesn't respond to the LAN Manager; the adapter is not currently active on the network when monitoring begins. Figure 5-19 shows an adapter profile panel for Token Ring.

```
┌─────────────────────────────────────────────────────────────────────┐
│  DFIPAP20                      IBM LAN MANAGER          Page 1 of 1    │
│  Normal                        Adapter profile                        │
│                                                                       │
│  A  Adapter address/name.....................:  4000000000A1/ADAPT01   │
│  B  LAN segment number ......................:  001                    │
│  C  LAN segment type ........................:  Token-Ring 16 Mbps     │
│  D  NAUN address/name .......................:  10005A100112/BR21AD1   │
│  E  Microcode level..........................:  010000CAP0000          │
│  F  Product ID...............................:  434F5246554656542000   │
│  G  Adapter monitored? ......................:  No                     │
│  H  Universal address........................:  10005A082461           │
│  I  Group address ...........................:  00000000               │
│  J  Functional addresses.....................:  0002008                │
│                                                 LAN Manager            │
│                                                 Ring error monitor     │
│                                                                       │
│                                                                       │
│  Esc = Cancel  F1 = Help  F3 = Exit                                    │
│                                                        End  PgDn       │
└─────────────────────────────────────────────────────────────────────┘
```

Fig. 5-19. Adapter profile example for Token Ring.

Bridge functions A *bridge* is a logical and physical connection between two LAN segments. A bridge consists of a dedicated computer which has two separate adapters, one for each LAN segment. The bridge computer runs a bridge program that handles the passing of information from one LAN segment to the other and the processing of LAN management frames. Bridge function options allow the following: add, change, or delete a bridge definition; change a bridge's configuration parameters; link a bridge; unlink a bridge; query a bridge profile.

A bridge consists of the following information: bridge name, bridge number, whether the bridge is to be linked automatically to the LAN Network Manager at startup (start or reset of the LAN Network Manager), the LAN segment number for each LAN segment attached to the bridge, and the adapter name or address for each LAN segment attached to the bridge.

Bridge configuration parameters include the following: bridge number, LAN segment connected to each adapter, frame forwarding active, performance notification interval, percent frame lost threshold, hop count limit, single-route broadcast, and link passwords. Figure 3-26 showed an example of bridge traffic indicators.

Network functions   The LAN manager provides the following network functions: network status, configuration list, path test, LAN segment test, and soft error conditions. Network status allows displaying the status of all LAN segments that are being monitored by the LAN manager. The net-

```
LAN segment configuration list
          example

 DFIPTO20                    IBM LAN MANAGER           Items 1 to 3 of 26
 Normal                      LAN Segment configuration list

 Type an action letter next to an adapter address and press Enter, or type an action letter
 and adapter address or name and press Enter.
 LAN segment type: Token Ring 4Mbps                    Date..: 13.08.90
 LAN segment..:  001                                   Time..: 12:55:57
                             Find query remove
            Adapter          Adapter                                   Group
 Action     address          name                     Function         address

 [ ]           [                  ]
 [ ]        400002012102     RHRZ%LAN%MANAGER   Active monitor          00000000
 [ ]                                            Ring error monitor
 [ ]                                            Configuration report server
 [ ]                                            LAN manager
 [ ]        400002033305     RHRZ305L           NETBIOS                 00000000
 [ ]        400002006000     DRUCKER%ETA3       NETBIOS                 00000000
 [ ]        400001001004     IBM%3174%I                                 00000000
 [ ]        400001057124     AVZCIPPOOLR124     NETBIOS                 00000000
 ........
 ........
```

Fig. 5-20. LAN segment configuration overview.

work status display includes the following information: LAN segment number; LAN segment status (possible status conditions are normal, soft error, beaconing, continuous carrier); and bridge names linked to the segment.

An asterisk beside the LAN segment number identifies the local LAN segment. The local LAN segment is the segment in which the LAN Network Manager is running. Those segments that are linked to the local LAN segment through bridges are called *remote LAN segments*. Figure 5-20 (Goehring 1990) gives a configuration example indicating the adapter address, adapter name, functions, and the group address.

System definition   The system definition functions allow you to set various system parameters: adapter number, security, reporting link, LAN name, trace option, and host connection. The adapter number specifies whether the LAN Manager uses the primary or alternate adapter. The security function allows you to set the password for access to LAN Network Manager.

The reporting link specifies the reporting link number and password used when LAN Network Manager links with bridges. The LAN name is the name assigned to the local area network being managed by the LAN Network Manager.

The trace option allows you to control which adapters can perform tracing. All adapters, no adapters, or a list of adapters may be allowed to perform tracing. Tracing results are shown for Token Ring in FIG. 5-21 (Goehring 1990); both short-range, and long-range measurement results are shown. As can be seen, use levels are very low.

LAN network management is supported by IBM LAN Management Utilities/2, which enables users to get support for configuration and fault management of DOS and OS/2 client workstations. Data are collected on processor

---

Typical examples for Token Ring
    performance

PERF01.CT0

PMON Performance analysis summary

Date 01/04/1989 Start 10:43 End 10:45 Sample period is 1 minute.
Number of intervals with unreliable data 0.

	Frames/sec	6 its/sec	Utilization %	% Non-MAC BW
Total	149	394,557	9.86	
MAC frames	2	625	0.02	
Non-MAC frames	147	393,932	9.85	100.00
LLC control	77	37,466	0.94	9.51
User data	70	356,467	8.91	90.49

Frame size distribution as a percent of total frames

0 - 128 - 256 - 512 - 1024 - 2048 - 32767
  81   3   0.   2   14   0

PERF031.CT0

PMON Performance analysis summary

Date 01/11/1989 Start 9:57 End 16:11 Sample period is 1 minute.
Number of intervals with unreliable data 0.

	Frames/sec	Bits/sec	Utilization	Non-MAC BW
Total	11	11,395	0.28	
MAC frames	2	620	0.02	
Non-MAC frames	9	10,775	0.27	100.00
LLC control	8	9,280	0.23	86.13
User data	1	1,495	0.04	13.87

Frame size distribution as a percent of total frames

0 - 128 - 256 - 512 - 1024 - 2048 - 32767
  81   0.   1   0.   9   0

Fig. 5-21. Tracing results for Token Ring.

use, workstation memory, and physical disk activity. Users can set thresholds for such items, and LMU/2 will generate an alert when the thresholds are exceeded. In addition, C or REXX programs may be written to automatically generate alerts. The product runs on a token-ring-attached OS/2 server running IBM's OS/2 LAN Server. But, no data are forwarded to LAN Network Manager. However, alerts can be forwarded to NetView. Future versions are expected to work with Ethernet LANs and other operating systems. IBM is considering offering LAN Network Manager also on the AIX platform, running on the RICS/6000 processor.

Wiring hub element management systems

Wiring hubs and concentrators are becoming increasingly popular for structuring enterprise wiring schemes. The concentrator market is competitive, and network management is a factor that can differentiate manufacturers. In fact, wiring concentrators are becoming the focus of network management in a local area. Many analysts predict that bridge-based and router-based network management will give way to hub-based solutions.

Four product families are representative examples. SynOptics is transitioning its DOS-based network management solution to a SunNet management platform called Lattisnet network management under Unix. This emerging network management philosophy of using a platform and putting more network management intelligence out on the network contrasts sharply with Cabletron's method of using its own developed platform. This architecture allows the use of generic components for connectivity and internetworking for all key areas, such as Ethernet, Token Ring, FDDI, and LAN wiring concentrators.

Figure 5-22 shows the objects to be managed by the hierarchical network

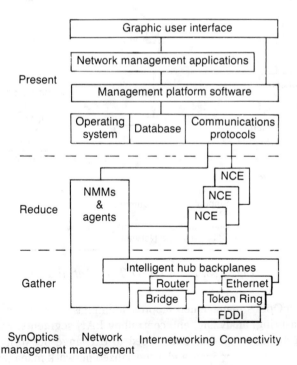

Fig. 5-22. LattisNet management by SynOptics.

management architecture. This architecture fully supports SNMP agents residing in LAN segments, routers, bridges, and FDDI nodes. SNMP agents collect
information. In order to reduce data, Network Control Engines (NCEs) are residing in strategically important locations. After compression, NCEs forward the
information to network management applications. Network management applications are based on SunNet Manager. The first two of NetMetrix applications—running on NCE—are the Protocol Analyzer and the load monitor.
They're designed to assist managers in capturing, viewing, and analyzing traffic
for Ethernet, Token Ring, and FDDI networks. Figure 5-23 displays Lattisnet
with NetView links that are optional. NETMAP is responsible for protocol conversion, representing one-way or two-way communication with designed and
implemented NetView/PC applications.

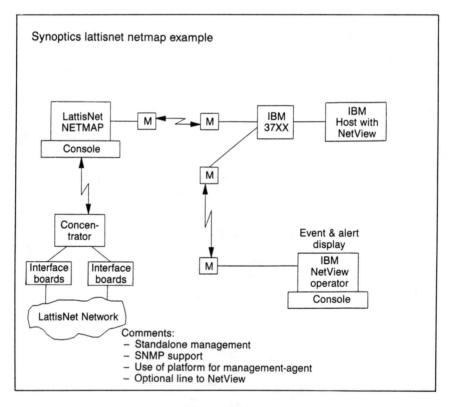

Fig. 5-23. LattisNet NETMAP application.

The SynOptics management approach emphasizes the role of the wiring
hub in measuring, analyzing, and controlling LAN segments. Each enclosure
includes a management bus that's used to exchange network management
information between modules and a specialized network management module

(NMM). Specialized circuitry in every module collects per-module and per-port data and forwards it to NMM. This dedication makes detailed measurement and control possible.

SynOptics offers three types of LAN management stations. LattisNet Basic Network Management is based on DOS and implemented on top of the DOS version of OpenView. This solution supports a graphical view of the hub, with the ability to analyze statistics, configuration and control ports. Lattisnet Advanced Network Management is an upgraded version featuring auto-topology and port address association. Also included is a generic SNMP manager that supports managing third-party SNMP agents with standard MIB. Lattisnet Network Management on SunNet Manager offers all functions of the DOS version, plus the foundation of a flexible, distributed architecture with Network Control Engine (NCE). SynOptics is working to interface Lattisnet Network Management to the leading network management integrator products, including Net-View, DECmcc and OpenView.

In order to help users with more complete solutions, the following applications are supported:

- MIBman is responsible for information collection from connected devices that may or may not support device-level MIBs.
- METERman depicts MIB data in graphical form to generate status and performance reports.
- TRENDman uses existing performance data to predict future performance.
- POLICYman evaluates thresholds and dynamically enables and disables ports of wiring hubs.
- FAULTman administers trouble tickets for tracking and resolving network problems.
- SynOptics extends the scope of the manageability of hubs by offering LattisViews. LattisViews will run as applications on DECmcc, Open-View, and on AIX NetView/6000. The functions available represent a subset of those offered with LattisNet Manager under Unix.

Cabletron Systems offer new avenues by combining an SNMP-based management system and expert systems technology for managing enterprise networks. Spectrum uses inductive modeling technology, creating programming models that define the intelligence and interrelationship of each network element and build an object-oriented knowledge base. As a result, the product can correlate information such as multiple alarms for multivendor network elements to identify the cause of a problem and solve it. Spectrum is very user-friendly for this type of maintenance and for changing network configuration and its graphical mapping.

Cabletron integrates all products under INA (Integrated Network Architecture). The LANView network analyzer has been designed and implemented for Ethernet networks. LANView is applicable for continuous monitoring. Its principal features include:

- Multiprotocol support: ISO/OSI, DECnet, TCP/IP, XNS, Novell Banyan, Appletalk.
- Powerful filtering of the large amounts of data.
- Capturing individual packets with packet tracing.
- Built-in time domain reflectometer tests.
- Support of network load generation.
- Generating controlled network traffic to force a suspected problem to occur.
- Built-in SNMP agent capabilities connected to SunNet Manager.

The LAN Analyzer board has been licensed from Novell and is based on LANtern.

Spectrum is sold as a new enterprise network management system to integrate a number of vendors' products. To a certain extent, Spectrum may also be considered a platform. Spectrum offers an extremely flexible, extended architecture based on highly intelligent software modeling of each and every network element, including equipment, users, privileges, and much more. By adding new induction rules to its model-based reasoning scheme, Spectrum can even capture and systemize the knowledge and preferences of a network administrator.

The heart of Spectrum is the virtual network machine (VNM) (FIG. 5-24). The VNM embodies an intelligent, comprehensive model of the overall enterprise network and each of its subelements. The VNM is based on Cabletron's breakthrough inductive modeling technology. The company's reasoning-capable technology provides an extremely agile, adaptive, and automatic way to model and control complex entities with software; Spectrum is its first commercial application.

Inductive modeling embraces model-based reasoning—one form of artificial intelligence. It creates programmatic models of each individual subfunction of a larger entity. Each of these "molecular" subfunction models understands the attributes and behavior of its real-world counterpart, essentially defining its intelligence. These molecular models are context-aware, interacting with each other to self-adjust their behavior as other subfunction models change status, appear, or disappear. This adaptive integration is similar to some synaptic processes of the brain. Through these adaptive subfunction responses, large-entity system models exhibit some traits of inductive reasoning. They can follow a logical progression from symptoms and effects to conclusions and actions.

Through inductive modeling technology, the VNM models everything that makes up the enterprise network—every network interface card, cable, workstation, node, user application, bridge, or other connection, and more.

The device communication manager supplies protocol support, which

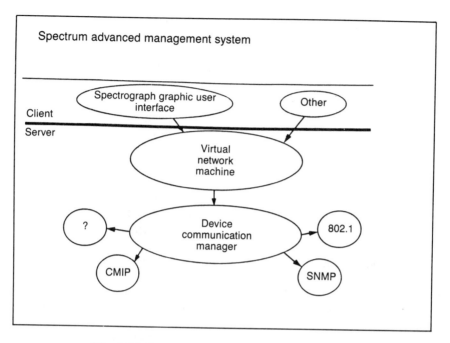

Fig. 5-24. Spectrum advanced management system.

includes SNMP, 802.1, CMIP, and ASCII. ASCII support enables nonstandard managed objects to send alarms to Spectrum. The graphical user interface offers many view levels and complex icons that enable it to create new views and to generate statistics. However, too many views may be difficult to learn and to use for an average help-desk person or LAN-operator. Integrating NetVisualyzer will add considerable graphical and realtime network monitoring capabilities to Spectrum. The combination represents the integration of passive monitoring capabilities with active control features.

Cabletron, Remedy, and Isicad have shown that Spectrum network management software, Remedy's Action Request System trouble ticket software, and Isicad's Command physical network management software can work together on a Sun workstation. With such a product's combination, alarm information identified by Spectrum can be fed into the Command system, which will locate the problem; and into the Action Request System, which will help the LAN administrator track and resolve the problem.

In conjunction with the Concert network management strategy from BT, Ungermann-Bass has delivered the Access/One management system, called NetDirector. The product is based on a client-server architecture, and is designed to provide an open platform for the management of multiple-vendor devices in an enterprise LAN environment. It's distinguished by its use of an SQL database as its core repository of network data, allowing access to network data and control via standard APIs to off-the-shell applications to managers of managers. A CMIP interface has been demonstrated connecting NetDirector to Concert, completing enterprise management offered by WAN and LAN management components.

The architecture of NetDirector is modular to allow for the support of multiple standard MIBs; it currently supports XNS management protocols and SNMP, and will support CMIS/CMIP as well. It provides a powerful topographical mapping and user interface via Presentation Manager/Windows through which a network administrator can readily identify and isolate network faults and performance status.

NetDirector is deployed to manage large, LAN-based, enterprise networks that are built around the Access/One intelligent hubs and include a variety of third-party devices as well. Access/One has been very successful, as it offers a very broad range of desktop connectivity and internetworking capabilities, with Ethernet, Token Ring, and FDDI-based high-speed LANs. These capabilities include device concentration, terminal service, bridging and routing covering the spectrum of device, protocol, media, and speed requirements of the enterprise user. The LAN-based backplane of Access/One can be equipped with a high-speed switching-based backplane and with extensions to standard bus architectures allowing network service applications to be integrated into the managed hub environment. This capability is built into the infrastructure of current systems, allowing customers to migrate by simply inserting new modules. With this capability, LAN, MAN, WAN, and routing functions will be made far more efficient and manageable, and support of multimedia (voice, data, video) applications to the desktop will be possible.

Also, MultiMan from Lannet (Lannet 1991) may be considered here as an alternative solution for multivendor LAN/WAN management. MultiMan is a powerful SNMP-based system that allows effective and optimal use of network devices and resources.

It allows enterprise-wide monitoring, control, and administration of active network devices in the internetworking environment. The system is implemented under state-of-the-art X-Windows and OSF/Motif on a Unix platform, providing powerful, flexible, and realistic representations of internetworking hardware, configuration, and status.

The console requests, sends, or traps information from the internetworking devices, relating to the states, parameters and option settings of each device. Management data is transmitted to the console on an interrupt basis when faults or critical events occur. This enables the system to continuously keep the network manager informed and to dynamically display changes and site modifications. When a fault in a managed device occurs, a visual alarm is immediately displayed, allowing the network manager to respond accordingly.

In particular, the following features distinguish MultiMan from other products:

- Auto-configuration through automatic recognition of manageable objects.

- Multilayer management of hubs, bridges, and routers.
- Support of multiconsole management, with regional or type-specific submanagers.
- Support of both inband and outband management.
- Diagnostics and tests without interrupting LAN operations.

The manufacturer intends to integrate OSI-CMIP capabilities into a future version of MultiMan.

Hub market and network management alternatives are expected to boom soon. Many small companies are expected to enter the market with specific solutions, but network management capabilities will be limited to a general-purpose SNMP agent. This agent is expected to support certain indicators of MIB II and RMON.

Also, powerful players, such as AT&T, IBM, and DEC, will likely invest in this market due to its strategic importance and pressure from their major accounts. IBM has introduced its first active hub product, called Controlled Access Unit (CAU). The technological capabilities of this hub are limited, but IBM is strong in the area of network management offerings. The integration of hub management and NetView will be an interesting solution for many IBM users.

DEC has entered this market with DEChub, which offers modular expansion opportunities. Management of these hubs is supported by built-in SNMP agent software, leaving the door open for SNMP managers, perhaps DECmcc or third-party managers.

Hewlett-Packard competes in the hub market with EtherTwist, which is equipped with SNMP agent software. The recommended management uses OpenView Interconnect Manager, which runs under the Unix version of Open-View. Other innovative solutions are expected from electronic matrix switch vendors; the first example is Maestro from Bytex.

In hubless LANs, it's still very important to learn about server and client status. Agents residing in the workstation help to identify the configuration and generate events. The latest solutions offer SNMP agents for the workstations without the requirement of installing TCP/IP protocol stacks. This reduces the agent memory demand to a few Kbytes. In order not to lose management capabilities, security has to be tougher at the managed-objects (server, client, workstation, interface card) level. In summary, system vendors offer less hub functionality, but more integration with other managed objects using their own platforms or manager stations.

Element management systems
for LAN backbones and high-speed LANs

LAN backbones and high-speed LANs are identified as FDDI. Its management has proprietary characteristics, because the management part, called station management (SMT), has not yet been standardized. As examples,

Finex Network Management System from Fibronix, and Viewplex LAN management tools are briefly discussed. Finex NMS is an existing product, while Viewplex may be considered a platform for unified FDDI management.

Fibronics offers a powerful FDDI monitoring, control and diagnostics system called Finex NMS (FIG. 5-25). Each Finex NMS consists of an FX 8510 software package and system management application process (SMAP). The software provides centralized network management and runs on IBM PC-compatible hardware under DOS 3.0 or later, with EGA or VGA color.

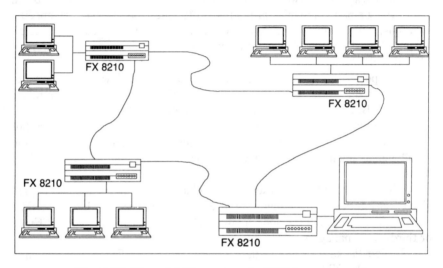

Fig. 5-25. Finex-NMS structure for FDDI management.

Each System Finex product includes embedded software for supporting the station management (SMT) portion of FDDI. This SMT software communicates with the network management station (NMS). The NMS can be installed at any Finex FDDI station, and supports a network events database, which logs user-defined performance parameters on the PC's hard disk. The Unix version of Finex NMS consists of software applications running under Unix and X-Windows on a Sun workstation.

Finex NMS supports remote management as well as implementations using multiple managers, when partitioning is required. The central station uses a standard Motif interface and supports SNMP. Existing Finex modules don't require upgrades to support the newer Unix NMS.

Forthcoming Fibronics products will include SNMP agent capabilities in addition to standard FDDI SMT support. Important features of the new Unix-based Finex NMS include:

- Graphical interface for depicting logical network connections.
- Click-and-zoom on interconnection components.
- Automated event message generation.

- Autoconfiguration for the physical LAN configuration.
- Browsing the event log.
- Setting alarm filters.
- Monitoring and reporting traffic and exceptions.
- Graphical reports.
- Flexible window management.
- Other customization capabilities.

The forthcoming Unix-based SNMP Manager will use proxy agents (protocol conversion software) to communicate with older existing Finex FDDI components. The conversion will be implemented in the Sun workstation console. The table-driven procedure is easy to customize. The SNMP console may also be used for displaying alarms and network management messages from third-party devices. The Unix-based SNMP Manager will support IBM's NetView via SNMP and, in the future, AT&T's Accumaster Integrator and DECmcc via the OSI protocol CMIP.

Viewplex (Datapro NS05 1991) consists of one or more software modules running under Unix on a user's Sun SPARCstation 1 or Sun 380. Possibly, the vendor will support other Sun workstations and other Unix platforms later on. Software modules comprise a base application, providing a number of general-purpose LAN management tools, and application modules are added to provide automation and intelligence. The base module is a mouse-driven, interactive program controlled by the user.

Additional modules, which are also software, run on the same workstation as the base program and provide functions such as scripting, which can speed up processes or allow the system to run unattended.

The user interface uses the OpenLook graphical interface based on X-Windows, providing a consistent look and feel among management tools and application modules. The workstation screen displays object-oriented icons that can be customized by the user. Color is used to indicate stressed areas of the LAN and fault severity.

Any operational statistic can be displayed in a variety of formats, including graphs, bar charts, and color-coded icons. Viewplex allows users to customize operations by defining new managed objects, managing vendor-specific MIB extensions, defining events and filters, writing scripted responses to various events or network conditions, and changing the appearance of icons. Shared system resources and applications, such as the database and a statistical analysis application, can supplement Viewplex operations. Figure 5-26 shows a typical Viewplex-based LAN management topology.

Viewplex can manage FDDI stations, such as concentrator hubs or high-speed terminal interface units SMT. In addition, by using SNMP it can manage LAN devices located on subnetworks connected to the FDDI fiber ring but beyond the management capabilities of SMT. Viewplex's base module consists of three general-purpose LAN management tools: LAN Navigator Tool, Configuration Tools, and Information Director Tools.

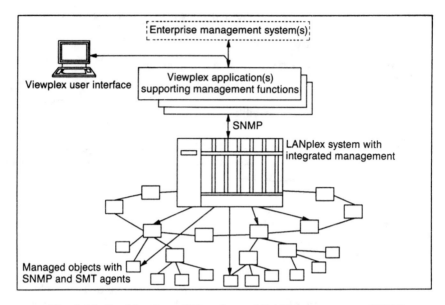

Fig. 5-26. Combination of Viewplex and LANplex to manage FDDI.

The LAN Navigator Tool presents a dynamically updated network map that displays information at a number of levels: the LAN system, network segment, LANplex system, board, port or end-station levels. It presents a hierarchical view of the network; windows allow a user to zoom in on points of interest, with each window representing a different level in the hierarchy. When configured with Synernetics' LANplexer family of products, it automatically learns the network topology without the need to manually configure the network map.

Configuration Tools allow an operator to modify the network, set up operation of Information Director Tools, and view lower-level information not displayed by the Navigator Tool. Using Configuration Tools, a user can change all MIB attributes that can be set, such as LAN connections, path assignments for individual LANplexer components, and various network operating parameters. Users can also define events and event filters and attach probes to monitor specific information about particular LAN objects.

Information Director Tools pass general network information and specific probe and event data to the display tools, database tools (logger), or management application modules (such as fault management or alarm reporting). They also set up information retrieval parameters such as updated period. Optional management application modules include fault management, performance management, alarm reporting, physical plant management, report generator, and others yet to be identified.

The interface between the Viewplex workstation and LANplex concentrators is SNMP; because SNMP frames can travel across any kind of network, the two devices need not be colocated. In other words, Viewplex can be located anywhere in an enterprise network, communicating with a LANplexer via SNMP. Viewplex doesn't work just with Synernetics products, however. Through the LANplex hubs, it can manage any FDDI station, regardless of manufacturer.

The LANplex concentrators contain SNMP agents as standard equipment. Synernetics SNMP products support FDDI station management (SMT), the SNMP "SET" command Management Information Base I (MIB I), while also providing over 100 proprietary (private MIB) SNMP variables. Support for SNMP standard MIB II variables is planned.

FiberCom's ViewMaster is a standards-based network management system to configure and monitor each network device, and to detect and isolate faults, as well as resolve those faults from a central management station. It uses SNMP to issue queries and commands to SNMP agents residing within managed objects such as bridges, routers, FDDI nodes, servers, and wiring hubs. The first implementation examples are available with the RingMaster FDDI bridge. This configuration supports MIB-I, offers APIs to customize applications, and accesses an SQL interface to the network management database, to alerting facilities, to hierarchical network maps, and to private MIB-I variables.

Element management systems for interconnected LANs

As stated earlier, the number of interconnected LANs is increasing. In order to increase the attractiveness of product lines, leading vendors are offering element management systems. These systems place both on-site LAN management and WAN management in the control of the Network Management Center. Each individual managed object, such as a repeater, extender, bridge, brouter, router, and gateway is part of the local LAN segment. But, at the same time, the very same components are part of the MAN and/or WAN topology.

A good example is the CrossComm bridge offering an integrated management system (IMS) on an MS-DOS base. This basic version supports simple fault, configuration, and performance management functions. In order to expand the scope of management capabilities, an interface to NetView from IBM has been implemented. The interface is actually a NetView/PC application called Network Management Access Program (NAP), which supports two-way communication with NetView (FIG. 5-27). The host alert facility supports the processing and display of IMS alarms on NetView screens. The service point command facility converts and executes NetView commands for the bridges. In most cases, the RUN command (TABLE 5-6) is applied in the CLISTS in the host, which are then invoked by the bridge operator or by specific events.

NetCentral Station from Cisco is a high-performance set of software tools designed to monitor complex, multiprotocol, multimedia, multivendor internetworks and to facilitate in-depth network planning and analysis. To achieve these goals, NetCentral Station employs a dynamic, user-configurable visual

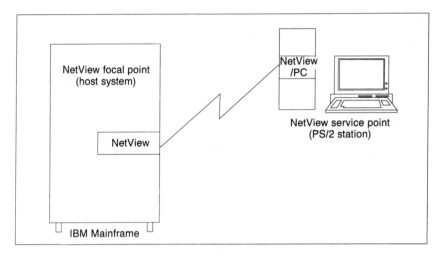

Fig. 5-27. NetView support for CrossComm bridge management.

Table 5-6. Run-Command CLIST Examples for CrossComm Bridges

File	Use	CLIST Text
DIAL	Dial up the IMS station or a node (if using RDCS).	RUNCMD SP = *NVPCPU01*,APPL = NAP,DIAL,&PARMSTR &EXIT ↑
HANGUP	Disconnect a dial-up line (above).	RUNCMD SP = *NVPCPU01*,APPL = NAP,HANGUP &EXIT ↑
IMS	Make IMS requests.	RUNCMD SP = *NVPCPU01*,APPL = NAP,IMSHST,&PARMSTR &EXIT ↑
DIAG	Communicate via the Remote Diagnostic Console Support (RDCS) facility.	RUNCMD SP = *NVPCPU01*,APPL = NAP,DIAGHST,&PARMSTR &EXIT ↑

network map and a fully integrated relational database management system (DBMS). The DBMS also provides a detailed historical record of network events and can produce customized reports for convenient, effective management of networks.

The NetCentral Station's realtime monitoring capabilities alert network managers to internetwork problems, including traffic congestion, line flapping, marginal performance, and other network conditions.

Using a menu-driven interface and a standard mouse point-and-select system, NetCentral Station simplifies network monitoring. NetCentral Station can query any device on the internetwork that implements the Simple Network Management Protocol (SNMP). SNMP provides the foundation from which network managers can monitor and control their networks. As NetCentral Station queries and controls devices throughout the internetwork, these devices respond with the requested information through the use of an "agent."

Network devices can also be configured to send traps to the NetCentral Station software. Events, such as host and server warm boot, cold boot, interface up, interface down, wrong community string, and exterior gateway neighbor loss, generate traps. A collection of SNMP standard object definitions, or the Management Information Base (MIB), provides a basis for communication between the agent and the network management system. The MIB is the repository for device parameters and network data.

SNMP allows vendors to add vendor-specific variables to the standard MIB. These private extensions can help optimize management of a particular vendor's product. For instance, Cisco has added more than 200 variables to the private branch of the MIB to support multiple networking protocols and other features for its routers.

The variables that Cisco has added allow network management support of:

- Apple Talk.
- DECnet.
- Local interface.
- Local IP.
- Local system.
- Local TCP.
- Novell.
- Terminal server.
- XNS.

Figure 5-28 is a symbolic depiction of NetCentral's multivendor, multidevice capability.

Cisco's NetCentral Station provides the following status windows:

- Device status—displays software details and cumulative uptime since last reload.
- Interface status—lists interfaces, status, and packet statistics for a device.
- ICMP statistics—displays the contents of the Internet Control Message Protocol table for a device.
- ARP table—displays the ARP cache of a device for mapping network and hardware addresses.
- Routing table—shows the graphical path of the data flow.
- Performance meter—provides a line graph of continually updated performance information.
- User-defined windows—allows network managers to design custom windows.

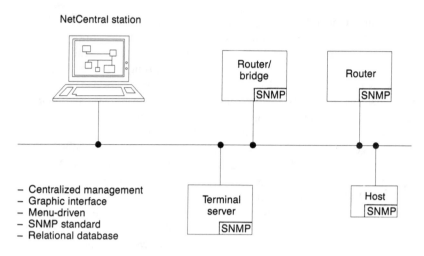

NetCentral station

Router/bridge SNMP

Router SNMP

– Centralized management
– Graphic interface
– Menu-driven
– SNMP standard
– Relational database

Terminal server SNMP

Host SNMP

SNMP agents respond to queries from the NetCentral station network management system.

Fig. 5-28. NetCentral as a manager for various LAN components.

Particularly useful is NetCentral Station's performance meter, which presents continuously updated information. This realtime network monitor provides a graphic display of performance parameters as they accumulate. The performance meter displays the number of input and output packets, input and output bytes, input and output errors, cyclic redundancy check (CRG) errors, and interface resets. Figure 5-29 shows examples of the performance meter. These results may be displayed in dedicated windows, or printed as part of the report generation function.

The dynamic map monitoring utility provides a starting point for tracking problems. For more information, the network manager then begins interactive querying of the problem device. NetCentral Station's network status windows provide detailed information for problem diagnosis.

Using a full-featured integrated relational database, the user has all the support functions necessary to manage and effectively use the data available to easily turn raw data into usable information, which is essential for accounting, determining traffic patterns, identifying potential problem areas, and logging security violations.

NetCentral Station's "device contacts" feature offers quick access to a list of the internetworked administrative personnel, as well as a central location for tracking network inventory. The database software provides a number of useful tools. For example, the Report Writing capability is used to create custom reports using standard Structured Query Language (SQL) commands. In addition, a utility program allows you to create a custom report format of virtually any collection of data elements available in the database. This graphics editor provides users with the tools to create and position graphic images of

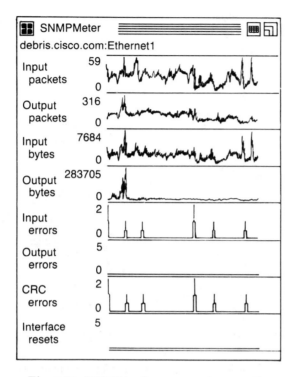

Fig. 5-29. SNMP performance meter example.

routers, bridges, hosts, and links. Using this drawing tool, users can create a completely customized map layout.

This graphics editor resides in NetCentral Station's map construction mode. It's used to create an accurate representation of an internetwork topology. The toolbox facilitates drawing both simple and complex graphics, duplicating, resizing and moving objects, and adding text blocks. Full implementation of a three-button mouse and convenient pull-down menus greatly enhances system flexibility for even novice users.

Figure 5-30 summarizes the features of NetCentral. The product uses SUN3/XX series or Sparc workstations, running SUNOS 4.0.3 or 4.1, and the X-Windows standard. NetCentral is easily portable to other Unix platforms.

The particular strengths of the Advanced Internetwork Management strategy from Wellfleet is the support of auto-configuration. This feature is supported for both its own SNMP network management system or customers' SUN-OS-based SNMP management station. The SQL-based solution allows centrally configuring a network of Wellfleet multiprotocol bridges and routers by defining a single configuration rather than connecting to each node's configuration file. After entering the network number and encapsulation type, NCU (Network Configuration Utility) supplies global information, such as software

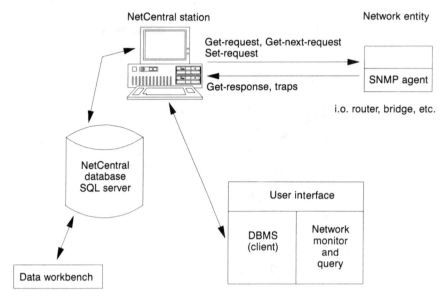

Fig. 5-30. NetCentral architecture.

versions, session information, circuit data, and protocol-specific parameters. The application is portable to any Sybase SQL relational database.

Offering a multiprotocol router to support TCP/IP in addition or instead of SNA will definitely change the topology of many SNA networks. The router is expected to play a peer role to centrally or remotely located front-end processors. The router may even replace front-end processors in remote sites, depending upon applications. The router runs on RISC/6000, and supports token ring, Ethernet, T-1s, X.25, and SDLC. The common denominator of routing SNA-Token Ring, SNA-SDLC, and NetBios is DLS (Data Link Switching), which converts the three protocols into TCP/IP frames. Also, other protocols, such as XNS, IPX, DECnet, and native TCP/IP are supported. Placing the router into SNA networks will influence the network management architecture, as well.

The AIX NetView/6000 is a graphics-based SNMP manager that runs on the RISC-AIX platform. In particular, it is intended to manage TCP/IP and Ethernet LANs and routers, as well as other devices that support SNMP agents. The product incorporates pieces of the OpenView platform from Hewlett-Packard. As an SNMP manager, this product has the following attributes that differentiate it from other SNMP managers:

- Very friendly graphics-based user interface.
- Management of IBM's AIX systems.
- Bidirectional link to NetView, functioning as a service point.
- Willingness to manage various agents, supporting both private and public MIBs.

This product will play an important role in managing heterogeneous networks. It is, however, still unclear how management capabilities of IBM LAN-Network Manager and NetView/PC-applications can be integrated with AIX NetView/6000 without involving host NetView as a master integrator. Figure 5-31 shows the structure and connectivity of this product.

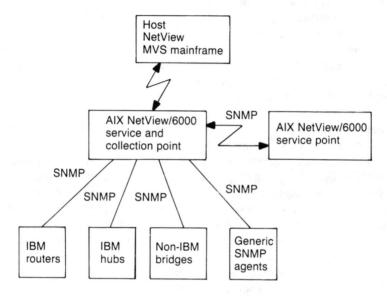

Fig. 5-31. AIX NetView/6000 structure.

Multisegment element management systems

Most of the element management systems have the capability of offering multisegment management from proprietary or standardized platform. LANCE from Micro Technology is a multisegment distributed network management system operating on a powerful VMS, Ultrix, or Unix-based platform that supports windows. LANCE provides internetwork "see-through" visibility of bridges, routers, T1s, and all other types of SNMP-based agents.

LANCE consists of LANCE/NMS, a powerful software application, working in conjunction with one or more LANCE/Tap distributed collectors. At the heart of the LANCE/TAP is a powerful 2-MIPS Motorola 68020 microprocessor for processing network segment statistics. A LANCE/Tap is required for each segment of the network to be monitored.

From a single central workstation, LANCE gives access to every aspect of operation, from close-up inspection of individual network segments to a comprehensive overview of the entire network, with the power of simultaneously viewing multiple segments via the X Windows System or DECwindows. LANCE communicates directly via the SNMP with its distributed LANCE/Tap collectors and other SNMP-based agents. Both now and in the future, customers will be able to monitor diverse, multivendor networking environments because LANCE will continue to conform to successive standards. LANCE already has pathways to CMIP and CMOT.

LANCE is designed to accommodate both large and small networks with a great degree of efficiency. For example, it can be set up on a small network with just one LANCE/NMS and one LANCE/Tap. On a large network, it can be set up as a structured system with numerous LANCE/NMSs, communicating to numerous LANCE/Taps.

Acting as the "eyes and ears" of the LANCE/NMS the LANCE/Taps see, count, and record all vital statistics, while maintaining network and data security. Each LANCE/Tap records statistics on all traffic on its segment, such as typical operating conditions, traffic patterns, packet problems, as well as peak load situations.

Since the LANCE/Tap doesn't gather any data from within packets, the sensitive data is never exposed, nor is the existing network security compromised. However, when data capture and in-depth protocol analysis are required, the LANager—Micro Technology's portable single-segment monitor and protocol analyzer—may be employed to explore and decode all seven layers of the OSI model. Since cables are the most frequent source of network problems, one of the most valuable functions of LANCE is a built-in cable tester. Customers predetermine the time interval at which TDRs are automatically performed, and whenever the TDR (Time Domain Reflectometer) built into each LANCE/Tap detects a fault, short, or open, then an alarm is generated.

LANCE alerts LAN management of segment conditions that indicate potential trouble. Segments use gauges for percent of bandwidth use, and collision and errors inform the user that it's time to alert the network troubleshooter.

Furthermore, built-in reporting capabilities are supported to enable LAN management to conduct trend analysis. LANCE's ASCII-formatted data may also be exported to spreadsheet programs for further processing and analysis. LANCE may also be categorized as a platform for multisegment network management.

A new combination of integrated managed objects is expected to be implemented. These will combine fast packet, switching, and routing technologies with FDDI, Ethernet, and Token Ring hubs that are managed from a common platform and offer better performance for less price. The first combination of this kind is called RubSystem and is supported by Cisco, SynOptics and Sun-Connect. The management platform is SunNetManager.

Integrators for LAN management

Integration may be accomplished in two different ways: use of an integrator or use of a platform. Platforms were introduced and evaluated in chapter 4. With integrator products, two major groups may be identified: console emulation products and advanced integrators.

Console emulation products

Users just beginning to integrate their network management facilities are typically attracted to console management-based solutions. Console management offers an integrated workstation for "cutting through" to any existing network management systems. Usually, console management enables users to issue commands as well as receive messages from one console.

Net/Command (Boole and Babbage) is a network center control system. Its architecture allows the user to select from a range of facilities to form a tailored system to be upgraded as future network control tools are introduced. Net/Command can examine the logging printer message stream from a network control tool and select from the stream those messages that an individual network control center decides are important to it. The rules for selecting messages are declared using a software package called Alert Logic Filter Editor (ALFE). A customized version of this product is considered by IBM as a third-party integrator for NetView. IBM intends to integrate this solution from International Telemanagement, with the Graphical Network Monitor under its AIX operating system. Figure 5-32 shows the functions and structure of the product.

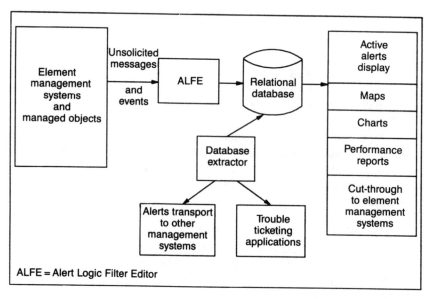

Fig. 5-32. Net/Command functions and structure.

Net/Command can monitor any equipment that outputs control information through an ASCII port, including servers, communication equipment, and network management systems. The device library of ported alerts is expected to include a very high percentage of all alerts that most users need to perform fault management. However, interfaces are lacking to widely used LAN-operating systems, such as NetWare and VINES. Configuration and fault management are performed by terminal emulation, requiring operators' expertise in other systems. The product incorporates very strong alert management, supporting fault detection, fault correlation, filtering alerts, grouping and prioritizing alerts, in addition to maintaining an alert log. Configuration management is supported by a graphical map, updated by active alarms. But the map must be constructed manually from configuration-related data of emulated systems and network management products.

MultiTerminal ASCII Emulator (MTAE) from IBM offers console management on an OS/2 platform. Besides NetView, products for systems management and network administration may be connected. Also, third-party devices may be included via NetView/PC.

Further examples include: TIC (The Integrated Control) architecture from VOTEK, the recent announcement from DEC of the consolidated workstation as its first step of EMA-implementation, Allink from Nynex, and the fully customized console management architecture from International Telemanagement. All of these solutions help simplify the network control center and the customer support desk area.

Console emulation doesn't change native, proprietary architectures and protocols. In the future, the presentation for all connected consoles will be unified. Following that, integration and correlation will also be supported, as seen in the next section.

Also, DEC and AT&T incorporate console emulation into their product offerings. For supporting site-management, including LAN and WAN element management systems, FECOS (Frederick Engineering 1991) may be considered as well.

Fecos is a network management workstation that provides information collection, monitoring, and control. It allows the consolidation of up to eight communication applications into one platform via a multitasking windowing environment running on an 80386 DOS-based platform under DESQview. Its three applications are:

- Consolidation of equipment: FETERM provides ASCII terminal emulations for use in configurations with asynchronous, serial communication links. Terminal emulations are defined in a FECOS database. Screens can be adjusted to suit the requirements of each piece of emulated equipment.
- Centralization of alarms and events: FELERM collects and processes alarms and events from different sources. These alarms and events are logged in the SERMON (Status Error Monitor) window. As a result of consolidated alarms, corrective action may be taken through FECOS.
- Dataline monitoring of networks: FEDAC provides local and remote dataline monitoring and protocol analysis for wide area networks. FEDAC allows the user to look at raw data or run protocol decode packages on the data.

For managing LANs, terminal emulation and alarm centralization are important. At the moment, FECOS is limited to smaller networks. In summary, console emulation is considered in many cases the first step towards larger-scale LAN management integration.

For supporting integrated WAN and LAN management, Codex adds SNMP capabilities to the 9800 management system. Thus, integration of systems on the basis of RS-232 serial or printer port interface, X.25-switches, modems, multiplexers, and LANs is applicable. In order to support all these systems at reasonable performance, the HP Apollo platform has been substantially upgraded.

NetView (IBM)

Figure 5-33 illustrates the NetView Architecture (Datapro NM40 1989).

NetView's Command Facility includes and enhances the Network Communication Control Facility's (NCCF) functions. The session monitor contains the network logical data manager's (NLDM) functions. The hardware monitor includes the network problem determination application's (NPDA) functions.

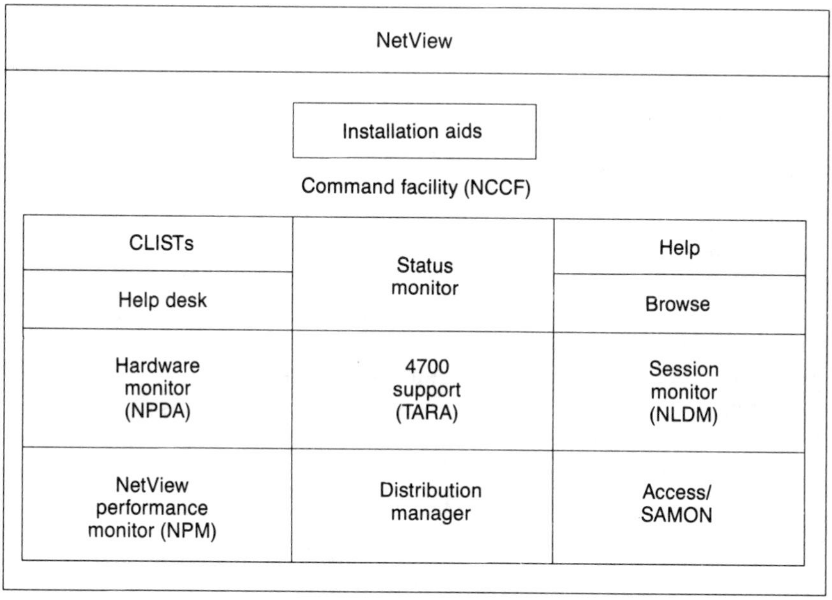

NetView		
Installation aids		
Command facility (NCCF)		
CLISTs	Status monitor	Help
Help desk		Browse
Hardware monitor (NPDA)	4700 support (TARA)	Session monitor (NLDM)
NetView performance monitor (NPM)	Distribution manager	Access/ SAMON

Fig. 5-33. NetView structure.

The status monitor (STATMON) allows network operators to look at the status of network resources and issue commands for any displayed resource.

Graphic Monitoring Facility (GMF) is an OS/2-based system that displays the status of SNA, and eventually non-SNA, non-IBM elements. With the multitasking features of OS/2, users can access other interfaces such as Net-

View Performance Monitor, Info/System, MVS-Automated Operations Controller, and NetView/PC. For a certain period of time, GMF is expected to coexist with the NetCenter product family.

The online help facility supplies data about NetView commands and many of the NetView display panels. A help desk facility offers an online guide to network problem diagnosis. The browse facility allows operators to look through libraries and the network log.

The NetView Performance Monitor (NPM) collects, analyzes, displays, and reports NCP-related information as well as data online use, response time, transaction, message, and retransmission counts. Release 3 includes TSO measurements, dynamic activation/deactivation of definite response, and collection of session-level and gateway-level accounting records. NPM is growing closer to the NetView nucleus by generating performance alarms, such as PIU traffic, line use, and error counts, and sending them to NetView for further processing, correlation, and display.

Release 2 also added an access facility for connecting to other host-based monitors offering terminal access facility features. IBM added the Distribution Manager (DM) feature, which has functions comparable with previous HCF and DSX products. The DM supports realtime diagnostics and collects error files from remote locations. The new release also enhanced the NetView File Transfer Program (FTP).

The network asset management facility collects vital product data from network elements. Release 3 also includes support for REXX, the SAA procedural language. System programmers can now customize NetView using REXX instead of the more cumbersome command lists.

Third-party systems, PBXs, multiplexers, and LANs may also be integrated using NetView/PC as a service point. NetView/PC is a multitasking personal computer subsystem that supplies the facilities to support communication of network management data between a personal computer and NetView on a host. NetView/PC was designed to be used in conjunction with NetView to provide services that permit user-written programs to extend SNA Management Services (SNA-MS) to non-IBM communications devices. Using NetView/PC, SNA-MS support can be extended to non-IBM and non-SNA communications devices, voice networks (CBX/PBX), and IBM Token Ring networks. It offers the basic services needed by a device-dependent SNA-MS application program and a network operator (Terplan 1991).

The four separate functions supported in Application Programming Interface/Communication Services (API/CS) are: host alert facility, operator communication facility, service point command facility, and host data facility.

NetView/PC doesn't seem to be the strategic solution for integrating non-SNA and non-IBM devices. Offering LU 6.2 capabilities in addition to or instead of the NetView/PC platform will bypass the writing of network management applications by third parties. The 6.2 interface is much easier to use and better performing, and is a more secure base for implementing applications. LU 6.2 will also be used for internetworking NetView and Net/Master.

Management data flows throughout SNA sessions, which provide reliable, connection-oriented network transport. The basic SNA message unit—called request/response unit (RU), which supports network management—is called the network management vector transport (NMVT). SNA-MS can flow on either LU 6.2 or SSCP-PU sessions.

For improving automation features, table-driven rules have been implemented based on converted NMVT messages. During the conversion, however, messages and data could be lost. The new alarm architecture, called message service units (MSU), will trigger automated actions without having to convert each MSU into a message.

In order to speed up the implementation process, IBM has entered into a number of partnerships. For voice applications, TSB's HubView/PC application can collect alerts and traffic statistics from a variety of PBX vendors. Also, CDMR (call detail maintenance records) may be collected and processed. Carl Vanderbeck and Associates has designed and implemented a development toolkit for NetView/PC applications. The first implementation is available for the VAX alarms. Most vendors of network management products are going to support NetView. However, the depth of support varies considerably, ranging from forwarding alerts all the way to giving away complete control of their own device family to IBM. Successful NetView/PC implementations are, for instance, operational with MCIView (supervising network services) and LattisNet NetMap (supervising SynOptics' Ethernet local area networks). Many companies consider a more efficient, peer-to-peer, solution for the NMVT conversion.

The fastest progress is expected with integrating Token Ring's management using NetView/PC emulation within the LAN Network Manager. Management responsibilities include:

- Automatic detection and bypass of media and station adapter failures through a mechanism embedded in the adapters.
- Controlling distributed management servers, which collect error statistics and report on resource utilization, changes, and parameter settings.
- Local LAN management applications, including fault, configuration, and performance management functions for stations and bridges.
- The Host Alert Facility of the IBM LAN Network Manager as service point for NetView (FIG. 5-34).
- Direct centralized management of SNA devices residing on the LAN from NetView, using Service Point Command Facility and optionally SolutionPac for automation.

LAN Network Manager lets customers manage multisegment Token Ring LANs, broadband and baseband PC networks, and—through the 8209 LAN Bridge—Ethernet segments. The application runs under OS/2 and uses both the presentation manager graphical user interface and relational database manager. Local management support is provided by LAN Station Managers.

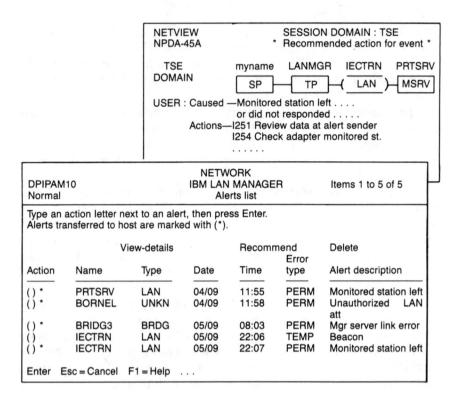

Fig. 5-34. Token Ring alerts to NetView.

Internally, CMIP is used for information exchange between the manager and managed objects.

IBM plans to correlate fault and configuration management via a network management repository. There's widespread speculation that the repository is assumed to support administrative and planning environments with inventory data, physical and logical configurations, accounting, user data, performance indicators, problem histories, application and change management information, and, simultaneously, realtime operations management by supporting automated systems' operations functions. It's very likely that the repository database will not be implemented in one step, but in many, starting with the operational part under the coordination of NetView developers.

IBM offers support for OSI network management. The initial OSI network-management interface for IBM systems will be part of IBM's newly announced OSI/Communication Subsystem (OSI/CS), which will provide a full implementation of the seven layers of the OSI model.

IBM has implemented the OSI Common Management Information Protocol (CMIP) under OSI/CS. This will allow OSI/CS to report events to other OSI management systems and/or to receive CMIP messages. OSI/CS will also be able to translate a CMIP event message into an SNA NMVT generic alert, which can be forwarded to NetView.

The extension of functionality of OS/2 for supporting network-management applications may mean that the OSI/CS gateway can be implemented under OS/2 as well. This implementation would offer a very powerful distributed integration capability at the site level.

IBM supports SNMP at both the agent and manager level. SNMP agents are available for OS/2, MVS, VM and S/6000 systems. Managers have been implemented on MVS, VM and on RISC/6000 under AIX.

The AIX solution is a graphics-based station with X-Windows, and as such, is comparable with other SNMP manager solutions. The mainframe-based solution is very important for customers who are thinking about integration. NetView is the focal point, and plays the role of an SNMP manager. The gateway between NetView and TCP/IP is the Query Engine. A usual dialog has the following steps:

1. SNMP command is issued by operator or CLIST/REXX.
2. SNMP command processor passes the command to the Query Engine.
3. The Query Engine validates, encodes and creates an SNMP PDU.
4. TCP/IP sends the SNMP PDU to the agent and receives response(s).
5. Response is passed to the Query Engine.
6. The Query Engine decodes the response(s) and sends it to NetView.
7. Responses are sent to operator or to other receiving task.

In order to offer service-level control up to the end user of SNA networks, the combination of NetSpy and LANSpy is extremely important. LANSpy resides on a single personal computer on each LAN segment. It collects LAN performance information such as response time (local and remote), client and server utilization, control-layer traffic, elapsed time from request to reply, inbound/outbound queue length, and sends them to NetSpy residing on the central mainframe. From NetSpy, users can set performance thresholds for LANSpy for any of the parameters. When a threshold is exceeded, LANSpy sends an alert to NetSpy that may be displayed in real time along with host alerts.

LANSpy may also be connected to NetView and to the Accumaster Integrator. LANSpy is time-division multiplexing network management data into the productive channels used between the host, front ends, and control units, respectively. Those connections may be local or remote. Future extensions include support for Ethernet, TCP/IP, DECnet, and NetWare IPX protocols. Also, a standalone monitoring version is under consideration under an SNMP manager.

In order to offer more capabilities to Novell users, IBM has designed and implemented the LAN Resource Extension and Services (LANRES) Series. This product family provides software for IBM PS/2 Micro Channel Servers running under Novell's NetWare Operating System, and software for IBM VM and MVS hosts. By means of LANRES, Novell servers can use mainframe resources for printing and for backup. Also, LAN administration tasks may be supported by the product.

LAN Automation Option (LANAO) is a mainframe package that lets network managers monitor the physical components of multiple token ring LANs from a centrally located NetView console. LANAO runs with IBM's Automated Network Operations (ANO), a NetView program that automates VTAM and MVS operations. It is intended to link LANAO to LAN Management Utilities/2(LMU/2), a set of applications that collects information on OS/2 activities.

LAN Network Manager (LNM) is still the best way to manage token ring LANs and IBM bridges; SNMP is a better for routers, hubs and non-IBM bridges. Since most internetworks require a combination of all those devices, two network manager stations are required. Solution alternatives include writing MIBs for token ring LANs and IBM bridges, redefining the station manager or writing integrative applications for LNM.

As an alternative, Net/Master may be implemented instead of NetView as a host product. In terms of integration and management of LANs, there are, however, no architectural differences. A detailed comparison of NetView and Net/Master may be found in (Terplan 1992).

In order to support Net/Master with LAN-based NMVTs, Systems Center offers Solve: LAN for OS/2. This product supports both IBM's and Microsoft's OS/2 operating systems. It's able to monitor a range of LAN alerts and send them to NEWS of Net/Master or to Hardware Monitor of NetView. Also, control commands are supported from the mainframe console. This facility can be used to configure, monitor, add, or delete network adapters from the LAN automatically, if required.

Accumaster Integration (AT&T)

Figure 5-35 diagrams Accumaster (Datapro NM40 1989), AT&T's network management strategy that addresses the three network management domains that exist in current communication networks: customer locations, local exchange carrier's network, and the interexchange network. Corporate customers maintain voice and data equipment on the premises, use local exchange carriers (LECs) for intra-LATA services and connections, and transmit network traffic across the country through an interexchange network. AT&T provides equipment and network management systems for customer premises and develops many interexchange services, often with customer interfaces to the built-in network management capabilities. Typically, these customer networks are mixed vendor environments. Accumaster concentrates on configuration and fault management solutions. The fault management functions and features include:

- Alarm management through differentiating and processing new alarms, active alarms, historical alarms, correlated alarms, and severity alarm logs.
- Alarm conditioning and synchronization, with the following features: error message analysis, threshold definition, and filtering and supporting alarm recognition.

- Alarm correlation, with links to the configuration database and to third-party management systems that support the Network Management Protocol.
- Traces for selected activities at the integrator or network element management level.
- Reports on alarms and trouble tickets, and their resolution.

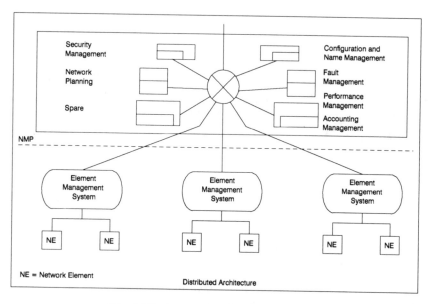

Fig. 5-35. Accumaster Integrator architecture.

Figure 5-36 shows the presently supported interfaces:

- Alarm interface—element management systems for alarm consolidation.
- Network management protocol—two-way OSI-based communication support from/to element management systems.
- SNA management application—links to NetView or Net/Master for information exchange using NMP and SNA carrier services.
- Terminal emulation—cuts through to any element management system.

The basic server is 3B2/600 from AT&T or Sun equipped with Unix System V operating system. The basic software includes the core software and software for the integrated workstation. The minimum configuration includes one integrated workstation, one server, and two element management systems (EMS). The maximum configuration includes five workstations and one 3B2/600. The number of element management systems that can be supported depends on the number of network elements each EMS is managing. These EMSs can be colocated with the integrator or may be at remote locations.

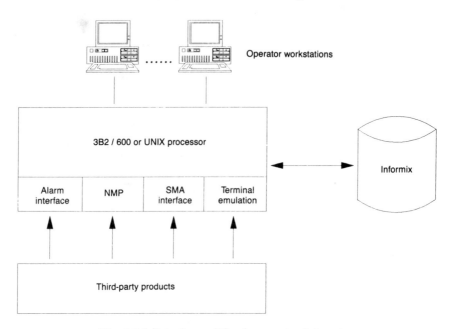

Fig. 5-36. Interfaces of the Accumaster Integrator.

The Accumaster Service Workstation (ASW) provides a single, powerful, user-friendly interface to give greater control and functionality in managing and monitoring network services. Both common applications such as ticket manager, traffic manager, call information manager, and electronic mail, and service-specific applications such as AT&T 800 services, Software Defined Network, and Accunet Digital Services are supported. With the workstation, users can access Accumaster Network Management Services, including configuration, fault, and performance management for AT&T's networking services. The workstation helps in the following ways:

- Improving network availability by controlling call routing.
- Minimizing downtime with realtime delivery of alarms and other fault management information.
- Using timely traffic and performance data to identify potential problems.
- Communicating with AT&T work centers to create, track, and resolve trouble tickets.
- Controlling and allocating costs efficiently with detailed call information.
- Maximizing performance with comprehensive network planning tools.

The platform is the same as with other network management products: Sun SPARCstation under Unix, connected to an Informix database. Similar services are provided or envisioned by INMS (Integrated Network Management Services) from MCI, and Insite from US Sprint.

DECmcc (DEC)

DECmcc is the product implementation of the Enterprise Management Architecture of DEC. DECmcc Director products provide the Application Programming Interfaces (APIs), basic management applications, consistent user interface, common structure for management information, flexibility to operate in a distributed and/or centralized fashion, and extensibility required to manage the enterprise environment. The implementation is centered around the director. The director is a software system that acts as an interface between the user and the managed network devices and systems. It's made up of five parts (FIG. 5-37).

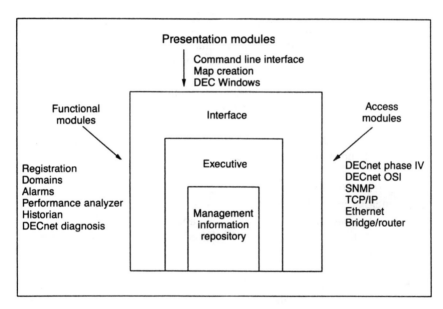

Fig. 5-37. DECmcc Director.

The executive is a master control program for coordinating all activities within the director. The management information repository (MIR) is an object-oriented configuration database for information about devices, management activities, and historical information. DECmcc management modules tap into the MIR to perform the required management functions for DEC and the other vendors' components.

The presentation modules (PM) create the user interface for EMA directors. These modules can be written to support a specific console or presentation format or to interface with non-EMA applications and other management systems. Presentation modules use the entity class information in the dictionary of the MIR to determine which commands, syntax, and attributes are appropriate and available for the entity selected. PMs display and operate across the full range of multivendor elements that make up the enterprise. The following modules have been implemented:

- DECmcc forms and command line PM. This module provides two user interfaces, a DECnet Phase V-compatible command line interface and a forms interface with scroll regions. Input is generally through the keyboard; output is to the terminal, a designated device, or a file. The standard DCL command line feature such as command recall, command line editing, and command abbreviations are supported.
- DECmcc iconic map PM. This module's interaction style provides a greater range of input and output capabilities than the previous module. Based on DECwindows, it supports keyboard, mouse, and menus as input mechanisms and makes use of the full range of graphical capabilities including iconic maps of networks. The iconic map PM features relationship-driven navigation and, using information provided by the Notification Service, displays visual color-coded alarm and status indicators.
- DECmcc notification services. This capability enhances PMs by providing notification of occurrences generated inside the DECmcc Director by managed entities or by applications external to the DECmcc Director (such as NMCC/DECnet monitor or another vendor's applications). Select and filter capabilities are included, as well.

The access modules communicate directly with typical network components, such as multiplexer, PBXs, modems, DSUs/CSUs, LANs, and non-network components, such as systems, applications, and databases. To accomplish this, various protocols are offered. The following access modules (AM) are offered:

- DECmcc DECnet Phase IV AM. This module provides the management pathway that allows a DECmcc user to control and monitor DECnet Phase IV implementations, including the DECnet side of the SNA Gateway and X25router 2000.
- DECmcc DECnet/OSI Phase V AM. This module provides the management pathway that allows a DECmcc user to control and monitor DECnet/OSI Phase V implementations, including the DECdns and the X.25 router.
- DECmcc TCP/IP (SNMP) AM. This module allows the DECmcc user to control and monitor TCP/IP network devices that support SNMP. MIB I and II objects are fully supported.
- DECmcc Ethernet station AM. This module provides the pathway to manage any multivendor device on the Ethernet that conforms to Ethernet V2 or ISO 8802-3 protocols.

- DECmcc LAN bridge AM. This module allows a DECmcc user to control and monitor any LAN Bridge 100, 150, or 200 in an extended local area network. The LAN Bridge AM goes beyond the basic Ethernet station AM capabilities, providing access to specific bridge attributes such as the forwarding database.

The functional modules provide configuration, fault, performance, accounting, and security management services. Functional modules can be developed by Digital or by third parties wishing to build on the EMA platform. Key modules include:

- DECmcc alarms FM. This module supplies the ability to detect and notify network managers of alarm conditions. Alarm conditions, as well as thresholds for these conditions, can be defined by the network manager with the help of rules. Alarm rules can be tested on specified entities at specified times (polled alarms), or they can execute when an unexpected fault occurs (unsolicited alarms). The network manager can also identify the notification mechanisms to be used when the alarm rule "fires."
- DECmcc registration FM. This module registers and maintains the set of known entities within the managed environment. Registration provides the "entity name to network address" translation, enabling the network manager to refer to entities by easy-to-remember names rather than being required to supply accurate hexadecimal physical addresses. Registration makes use of DECdns so that an entity registered by one DECmcc Director is known to all Directors in the network.
- DECmcc domains FM. This module provides the ability to collect entities into focused, user-defined groups to establish a span of control or view of the enterprise. Using domains, networks can be divided into logical and manageable subsets. Domains can overlap with and/or contain other domains. This module permits graceful scaling of management functions from small to large networks.
- DECmcc DECnet diagnosis FM. This module is used to diagnose common DECnet faults such as network partner exited, remote node is unreachable, and circuit on-synchronizing. When a problem is observed, the network manager involves this FM, which uses a series of diagnostic actions and test procedures to assist in determining the source of the problem.
- DECmcc historian FM. This module provides DECmcc users with an integrated set of facilities for collecting, purging, archiving, and exporting historical management data. This FM periodically collects attribute data and records them to the MIR. This allows the data to be operated on by the various DECmcc functional modules. This FM also supports export of data to databases external to DECmcc. This permits offline analysis of the data using various tools.

- DECmcc performance analyzer FM. This module provides important management information on various aspects of performance, such as error rates, throughput, and resource use. It obtains raw traffic and error data from managed entities or historically recorded information and processes the data into meaningful statistical information. This FM interoperates with alarm FM and notification services to permit logging of performance-related alarms, dynamic map updates, and messages to the network manager concerning performance threshold violations.

DECmcc is expected to be populated with existing DEC network management related products first. NMCC/DECnet Monitor, NMCC/VAX, LAN Traffic Monitor, Terminal Server Manager, DECelms, Remote System Manager, and Ethernim represent the beginning, followed by analyzers and SNMP agents. The next phase may involve bridges, routers, and other wide area networking products from Digital and from other vendors. Finally, PBXs and voice-related products are expected for integration.

Other products

Integrated LAN management is a very dynamic area with a number of new products expected. Users may team up with vendors, and vendors with each other. Interesting solutions are from Concert (British Telecom), MAXM (International Telemanagement), and Allink (Nynex). All three product families would be able to integrate many LAN element management systems.

SNMP-based network management may get add-ons in the form of expert systems at the management stations level. One example is Netcortex (Bim 1992). Netcortex runs on Sun Sparcstations, and collects SNMP information from managed objects via standard TCP/IP connections. Its workstations can be set up at multiple locations in distributed networks. The core of the product was written in Prolog. The core obtains live data by continuously polling to check for alarm conditions. It then compares the data against a conceptual model of the network. The correlation between the actual network conditions and the conceptual model enables Netcortex to interpret data and recommend solutions, not just display data. The core interacts with the presentation service module and with the Sybase relational database. Post processors may be used to generate statistical and historical reports. Bim directly manages equipment using MIB II variables; in certain cases, Bim has added MIB extensions. To manage non-TCP/IP devices, the company is using its own SNMP proxy agents, which are protocol conversion programs. Proxies are offered for a number of WAN element management systems, enabling customers to integrate WAN and LAN management on the basis of SNMP.

Selection of LAN management instruments

In order to select the right instrument, prior to making a decision, both the selection criteria and products must be carefully evaluated. To do so, use the criteria listed in the following section.

Functional criteria

Functional criteria focus on LAN management functions, integration capabilities, and conformance to standards.

Support of configuration management Configuration management is a set of mid-range and long-range activities for controlling physical, electrical, and logical inventories, maintaining vendor files and trouble tickets, supporting provisioning and order processing, managing changes, and distributing software. Directory service and help for generating different network generations are also provided.

Support of fault management Fault management is a collection of activities required to dynamically maintain the network service level. These activities ensure high availability by quickly recognizing problems and performance degradation, and by initiating controlling functions when necessary, which may include diagnosis, repair, testing, recovery, workaround, and backup. Log control and information distribution techniques are also supported.

Support of performance management Performance management defines the ongoing evaluation of the network in order to verify that service levels are maintained, to identify actual and potential bottlenecks, and establish and report on trends for management decision making and planning. Building and maintaining the performance database and automation procedures for operational control are also included.

Support of security management Security management is a set of functions to ensure the ongoing protection of the network by analyzing risks, minimizing risks, implementing a network security plan, and monitoring success of the strategy. Special functions include surveillance of security indicators, partitioning, password administration, and warning or alarm messages on violations.

Support of accounting management Accounting management is the process of collecting, interpreting, processing, and reporting cost-oriented and charge-oriented information on resource usage. In particular, processing of SMDRs, bill notification, and chargeback procedures are included for voice and data.

Support of LAN design and planning Network planning is the process of determining the optimal network, based on data for network performance, traffic flow, resource use, networking requirements, technological trade-offs, and estimated growth of present and future applications. Sizing rules and interfaces to modeling devices are also parts of the planning process.

Integration capabilities These capabilities include the ability of interfacing different kinds of products that use proprietary or standard architectures.

- Multivendor capability—ability to integrate other vendors' products.
- Space covered that needs integration—WAN, LAN, MAN; private, public; logical, physical; processing and networking components; data and voice.
- Depth of integration—(physical terminal level, protocol conversion, full integration).

- Conformance to standards, including support of CMISEs from OSI and TCP/IP management capabilities (SNMP).
- Electronic Data Interchange used for improving communications with customers.
- Peer-to-peer to other network management systems—capability of interconnection to other vendors' network management systems using advanced communication techniques.

Database support   Repository support summarizes information about integrity across network management functions, what sort of data is included in the repository, and the techniques used. The criteria are:

- Static and dynamic support.
- Relational or object-oriented techniques.
- Integrity across network management subsystems.
- Performance.

Database support includes the capability of defining and maintaining MIBs and their variables. MIB public contains only generic, or nonimplementation-specific objects that the Internet working group has determined as essential to managing components. From this minimal set of objects, all other variables specific to a product and to an implementation can be derived. These variables constitute the private branches of MIBs. The support of the public branch is absolutely necessary; the content of the private branch is negotiable.

Operational criteria

The operational and maintainability criteria focus on the product's installation, performance, and use. These criteria provide support of judging a product's applicability to the user's environment apart from its functionality and conformance to standards.

Ease of installation   Most products are user-installed software, meaning that the users are responsible for software installation. Ease of installation means the use of automated or semiautomated procedures assisted by high-quality documentation.

User interface   The user interface defines the quality level for presenting network-related information, and characterizes the flexibility of changing product features:

- Platform—hardware and software that refer to the actual machine and operating system that perform the management tasks.
- Presentation services—features that characterize what level of user support is needed from the network management workstations, including graphics, zooms, windowing, business graphics combined with text windows, colors keyed to content, automated generation of network pictures, standardized commands, and information reports.

- Programmability—defines the language supported for customizing and value-added functions.
- Main memory and disk storage capacity—defines the resource capabilities that may influence configuration, generation, and sizing.

Performance   Performance of a network management system may be defined as its ability to effectively process large amounts of requests and responses in an acceptable manner. Performance also includes the demand of using as little as possible bandwidth to exchange network management-related information. Distribution of LAN management functions may help in this respect. In order to guarantee improved service, multiple workstations may be installed, each of them serving certain users or certain applications.

Reliability   Because the LAN management product provides the focal point of controlling and monitoring the LANs, the product should be robust enough to minimize LAN crashes. If the management product fails, it should not affect the LANs being managed in any way.

Security   The security criteria focuses on access control and authentication for using the product, its database, and its communication connections. *Authentication* means to determine the identity of the requester, while access control is determining whether the requester has the authority to issue a given request. A different level of access is desirable.

Scalability   This criteria refers to use in larger and more complex LANs than the original environment. It means that the product should handle higher volumes of information, use more sophisticated maps, be able to partition the complex network, and provide for manager-to-manager (product-to-product) communication if necessary.

General purchase criteria

Besides the functional and operational criteria, other more general criteria must be used to evaluate the merits of the network management product. These criteria embed purchase conditions.

- Customer support—differentiates manufacturers on the basis of product customization and whether they provide consulting services.
- Development kit—help for design, development, and implementation.
- Customizing—ability to tailor applications.
- Consulting—service provided by the manufacturer for supporting, planning, configuring, sizing, and testing the network management system.
- Costs—includes all components of purchasing, implementing, and operating the product.
- Availability of products—indicates what features are applicable now and in the near future and how easy the migration will be. Installation records, and efficiency of use on many networks may be included as well.
- Documentation—the existence of well organized and easily readable documentation is essential to installing and maintaining a network man-

agement product. State-of-the-art techniques, such as the use of hyper-text may be considered.

- Training requirements—Because the skill level of LAN management personnel varies from enterprise to enterprise, training requirements are essential. Questions about type of training, duration of training, and technical level of training must become part of the evaluation process.
- Financial stability—The business environment and financial viability of the vendor is evaluated here. In certain cases, this criterion receives a lot of attention and a high weight.

TABLE 5-7 summarizes the criteria for selecting LAN management products.

Table 5-7. Network Management Systems' Evaluation Criteria

Functional criteria
- Support of configuration management
- Support of fault management
- Support of performance management
- Support of security management
- Support of accounting management
- Support of LAN design and planning
- Integration capabilities
- Database support

Operational criteria
- Ease of installation
- User interface
- Performance
- Reliability
- Security
- Scaleability

General purpose criteria
- Customer support
- Costs
- Availability
- Documentation
- Training requirements
- Financial

In order to facilitate the selection process, I have provided three tables. TABLE 5-8 identifies leading products, their managed objects, such as bridges, FDDI-nodes, DQDB-nodes, servers, routers, LAN hubs, extenders, repeaters, adapters, and processors, and network management capabilities. TABLE 5-9 shows physical and logical interfaces, support of leading network architectures, support of new networking services, such as fast packet, SMDS, and

B-ISDN for the same products. Finally, TABLE 5-10 summarizes LAN management capabilities such as protocols supported, element manager, integrator, and support of integrators for the same product.

Summary

The instrumentation of LAN management is becoming more visible. Also, the number of alternatives is increasing, making implementation easier, but selection more difficult.

Instrumentation trends may be summarized as follows:

- LAN management requires a combination of tools.
- Most manufacturers implement SNMP agent capabilities into their products, offering both public and private MIBs.
- Some manufacturers also offer SNMP manager capabilities, including the management of third-party agents.
- Platforms are getting more popular; some of them will support SNMP, CMOT, and CMIP capabilities.
- Most vendors will offer gateways to leading network management integrators, such as NetView, NetMaster, Accumaster, DECmcc, and OpenView.
- There is more cooperation between vendors of LAN-related products in the area of LAN management.

Table 5-8. Products/Capabilities Matrix

Support of managed objects

Company	Product	Wiring Hub and Repeater	Router	Bridge	Extender	Brouter	Terminal Server	File Server	Print Server	Processor	Cable and NIC	FDDI Node	DQDB Node	Concentrator	Multiplexer
Advanced Computer Communications	ACS 4800 Network Management System	×	×	×		×	×							×	
Applied Computing Devices	ACCs Network Knowledge Platforms	×	×	×			×	×	×	×		×			×
AT&T	StarGroup Router Manager		×												
	Systems Manager									×					
BICC Data Network	ISOView	×		×											
Bytex Corp.	ATS 1000		×	×		×	×	×		×					
	Maestro NMS		×	×		×	×	×		×		×		×	×
Cabletron Systems	LANView, Spectrum	×	×	×		×	×	×		×	×	×		×	×
Chipcom	Online NCS		×	×	×	×	×	×	×						
Data General Corp.	Eye*Node, AViiON		×	×		×	×	×		×		×			×
Cisco Systems	NetCentral	×	×	×		×	×	×		×					
David Systems	ExpressView		×	×		×	×	×							
Digilog	LANVista		×	×		×	×	×							
FiberCom	ViewMaster	×	×	×	×	×	×	×	×	×	×	×		×	×
Fibermux	Lightwatch	×	×					×			×			×	×
Fibronics	FX 8510-Interview	×	×									×			
General DataComm	Mega*Bridge			×											
Halley Systems	ConnectView			×											
Hewlett-Packard	OpenView	×	×	×		×	×	×	×	×				×	×

Company	Product
Hughes LAN Systems	MONET
Infotron-Dowty	LANSpan
IBM	LAN Network Manager
IBM	LMU/2
IBM	AIX NetView/6000
	WatchTower
Intercon	LANCE
Micro Technology-Lexcel	Star*Sentry
NCR Corp.	MultiGate Manager
Network Resources	8001 LAN Manager
Newbridge	OverView
Proteon	CMS Express
Racal Milgo	NetVisualyzer
Silicon Graphics	SunNet Manager
Sun Connect	Lattisnet Network Manager
SynOptics	Time/LAN 100 EMS
Timeplex	Net Director
Ungermann-Bass	WAN Manager
Vitalink	PC LAN Network Manager
WANG	SNMP-NMS
Wellfleet Communications	WIN Management Station
Wollongong Group	Enterprise Network Manager
Zenith	

Table 5-9. Products/Interfaces Matrix

Support of interfaces

Company	Product	ISO	Ethernet	Token Ring	Token Bus	X.25	TCP/IP	FDDI	DQDB	IPX	NFS	Kermit	NetBios	LLC 1, 2	SNA	DCA	DNA	DSA	Fast Packet	SMDS	ISDN, B-ISDN
Advanced Computer Communications	ACS 4800 Network Management System		×			×															
Applied Computing Devices	ACCs Network Knowledge Platforms	×	×	×		×				×	×						×				
AT&T	StarGroup Router Manager		×	×																	
	Systems Manager		×	×			×	×							×						
BICC Data Network	ISOView		×	×			×	×													
Bytex Corp.	ATS 1000		×	×		×	×	×					×	×							
	Maestro NMS		×	×		×	×						×	×							
Cabletron Systems	LANView, Spectrum		×	×			×	×		×	×				×						
Chipcom	Online NCS		×	×		×	×														
Cisco Systems	NetCentral		×	×		×															
Data General Corp.	Eye*Node, AViiON		×				×	×													
	ExpressView		×																		
David Systems	LANVista		×	×			×			×	×										
Digilog	ViewMaster		×	×		×		×		×	×										
FiberCom	Lightwatch		×	×											×						
Fibermux			×	×	×																
Fibronics	FX 8510-Interview		×		×																
General DataComm	Mega*Bridge		×	×		×		×													
Halley Systems	ConnectView		×							×	×										
Hewlett-Packard	OpenView	×	×	×		×	×	×							×						

Vendor	Product
Hughes LAN Systems	MONET
Infotron-Dowty	LANSpan
IBM	LAN Network Manager
IBM	LMU/2
IBM	AIX NetView/6000
Intercon	WatchTower
Micro Technology-Lexcel	LANCE
NCR Corp.	Star*Sentry
Network Resources	MultiGate Manager
Newbridge	8001 LAN Manager
Proteon	OverView
Racal Milgo	CMS Express
Silicon Graphics	NetVisualyzer
Sun Connect	SunNet Manager
SynOptics	Lattisnet Network Manager
Timeplex	Time/LAN 100 EMS
Ungermann-Bass	Net Director
Vitalink	WAN Manager
WANG	PC LAN Network Manager
Wellfleet Communications	SNMP-NMS
Wollongong Group	WIN Management Station
Zenith	Enterprise Network Manager

Table 5-10. LAN management capabilities

Company	Product	Protocols Supported	Element Management	Integration	Support of Integrators
3Com	ViewBuilder	SNMP	Yes	No	NetView
Advanced Comp. Comm.	ACS 4800 NMS	SNMP (SNMP Res.)	Yes	Yes	Concert
Applied Computing Decices	ACD Network Knowledge Platform	CMIP, NMVT DECnet, CMOT, SNMP CMOL	Yes	No	NetView, DECmcc Accumaster-Integrator OpenView
AT&T	Computer Manager	Proprie- tary	Yes	No	NetView, Accumaster- Integrator
	StarGroup Manager	OSI	Yes	No	NetView, Accumaster- Integrator
	StarGroup Router	OSI	Yes	No	NetView, Accumaster- Integrator
	System Manager (NetLabs)	CMOT, SNMP	Yes	Yes	
BICC Data Networks	IsoView	CMIP, SNMP	Yes	Yes	Accumaster-Integrator, DECmcc, OpenView, SunNet Manager
BIM	Netcortex	SNMP	Yes	Yes	
Bytex	ATS 1000	IEEE 802.5 MAC Frames			
	Maestro NMS	SNMP	Yes	No	NetView
Cabletron	LanView	Proprie- tary	Yes	No	
	Spectrum	CMIP, SNMP DECnet, NMVT	Yes	Yes	NetView, Accumaster- Integrator, DECmcc
Chipcom Corp.	Online NCS	SNMP (SNMP Res.)	Yes	No	
Cisco Systems	NetCentral	SNMP	Yes	No	SunNet Manager
Codex Corp.	9800 SNMP Processor	SNMP (MIT)	Yes	Yes	
Concord	Trakker	SNMP	Yes	No	SunNet Manager
Data General	Eye*Node	SNMP (SNMP Res.)	Yes	No	
	AViiON	SNMP, CMIP	Yes	No	
David Systems	ExpressView	SNMP (Epilogue)	Yes	No	
Digilog	LanVista	Proprie- tary, NICE DECnet	Yes	No	DECmcc
Digital Equip.	DECmcc TCP/IP	Proprie- tary, SNMP	Yes	Yes	DECmcc

Table 5-10. Continued

Company	Product	Protocols Supported	Element Management	Integration	Support of Integrators
Digital Equip.	DECmcc Ultrix	Proprie-tary,SNMP	Yes	Yes	DECmcc
Fibercom	Viewmaster	SNMP (Carnegie)	Yes	Yes	
Fibermux	Lightwatch	Proprie-tary, SNMP (SNMP Res.)	Yes	No	Accumaster-Integrator, OpenView, NetView, SunNet Manager
Fibronics	FX-8510 Interview	SNMP	Yes	No	NetView
Gandalf	Access Manager	SNMP (NetLabs)	Yes	No	NetView, Accumaster-Integrator
General Datacom	Mega*Bridge	SNMP	Yes	No	NetView
Halley Systems	ConnectView	Proprie-tary	Yes	No	
Hewlett-Packard	OpenView Bridge Manager	SNMP (Carnegie, MIT)	Yes	Yes	OpenView
	OpenView Hub Manager	SNMP (Carnegie, MIT)	Yes	Yes	OpenView
	OpenView Interconnect Manager	SNMP (Carnegie, MIT)	Yes	Yes	OpenView
	OpenView NM Server Manager	SNMP (Carnegie, MIT)	Yes	Yes	OpenView
	OpenView Network Node Manager	SNMP (Carnegie, MIT)	Yes	Yes	OpenView
Hughes LAN Systems	Monet	SNMP (Epilogue)	Yes	Yes	NetView, Accumaster-Integrator
IBM	AIX NetView/6000	SNMP	Yes	Yes	NetView
	LAN Network Manager	NMVT, CMIP	Yes	No	NetView
Infotron (Dowty)	LANSpan	Proprie-tary, SNMP	Yes	No	NetView, Accumaster-Integrator
Interlan	WatchTower	SNMP	Yes	No	
Lannet	MultiMan	SNMP (MIT)	Yes	Yes	NetView
Micro Techn. Lextel	Lance	SNMP (PSI)	Yes	Yes	DECmcc, NetView Accumaster-Integrator
NetLabs	DualManager	SNMP, CMIP CMOT	Yes	Yes	
NCR Corp.	Star*Sentry Manager	CMIP, NMVT CMOT, SNMP	Yes	Yes	Accumaster-Integrator, NetView, DECmcc

Table 5-10. Continued

Company	Product	Protocols Supported	Element Management	Integration	Support of Integrators
Network Managers	NMC 3000	SNMP, CMOT	Yes	Yes	NetView, OpenView, DECmcc
Network Systems Corp.	SNMP Manager	SNMP (SNMP Res.)	Yes	No	
Network Resources Corp.	MultiGate Manager	Proprie- tary	Yes	No	
Newbridge	LAN Manager	SNMP (SNMP Res.)	Yes	No	NetView, Accumaster- Integrator
Northern Telecom	LANScope	SNMP	Yes	No	NetView
Novell	LANtern NMS	SNMP (Carnegie)	Yes Yes	No Yes	NetView NetView
Objective Systems Integeators	NetExpert	CMIP SNMP	Yes	Yes	NetView, DECmcc, OpenView
Proteon	OverView	SNMP	Yes	No	NetView
Retix	5025 Network Management Center	SNMP, CMIP (Epilogue)	Yes	No	SunNet Manager
Silicon Graphics	NetVisualizer	Proprie- tary	Yes	No	Spectrum
SynOptics	Lattisnet	SNMP, NMVT (Epilogue)	Yes	Yes	NetView, SunNet Manager, DECmcc, OpenView
Teknekron	NMS/Core	Proprie- tary	Yes	No	
Timeplex	Time/LAN	SNMP	Yes	No	NetView, Accumaster- Integrator
Ungermann Bass	NetDirector	SNMP	Yes	No	NetView, Concert
Vitalink	WAN Manager	SNMP (SNMP Res.)	Yes	No	DECmcc
Wang Labs	PC LAN Net- work Manager	Vines	Yes	No	
Wellfleet Comm.	SNMP-NMS	SNMP	Yes	No	DECmcc, SunNet Manager
Wollongong Group	WIN Manage- ment Station	SNMP (PSI)	Yes	No	
Zenith	Enterprise Network Manager	SNMP	Yes	Yes	

6

Design
and planning
of LANs

LAN design and capacity planning is the process of determining the optimal local area network, based on data for networking and internetworking requirements, technological trade-offs, existing and estimated traffic flows, current resource use, and estimated growth of present and future applications. Sizing rules, and information export/import are considered parts of the planning process. The most important functions are:

- Determining and quantifying current work load and resource use.
- Estimating future user demand, volume by communication form, location, and user groups.
- Design and sizing of servers, communication facilities, and workstations, including backup and recovery plans.
- Implementation of local area networks, including wiring plans, conformance and stress testing, tuning, paralleling existing and new LANs, and cutover.

Local area network design and planning don't receive enough attention. In most cases, they're an afterthought, usually considered a continuation of LAN tuning work. LAN design and planning are understood in only a limited sense. It's understood as the installation of the infrastructure. After introducing the basics of the LAN design and planning process, this chapter will address the principal functions and design criteria. Instrumentation will also be analyzed in some depth, with particular attention to modeling instruments.

The process of
LAN design and capacity planning

Figure 6-1 shows the basic steps in the design and capacity planning process. In the first step—assuming LANs are in operation—the current work load is

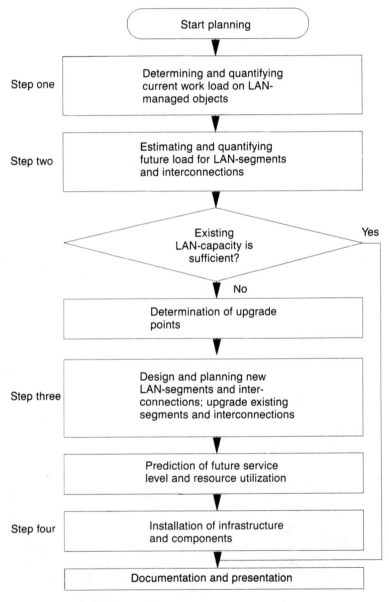

Fig. 6-1. Basic steps of LAN design and planning.

identified and quantified. Measured and modeled results may help to calibrate modeling instruments and determine communication overhead. Step one offers as a final result the quantified resource demand by application, workstation, and users.

Step two deals with estimating and quantifying future load. This step starts with identifying locations for LAN segments and their components, respectively. Also included are activities that determine user requirements for communication services by communication form, volume, and application. Step two offers as a final result the quantified resource demand by application and user. For new LANs, step two is the entry point into the design and planning process.

Step three addresses the design of new LAN segments, upgrades, cabling plans, and internetworking components. To optimize design, various criteria, such as performance, availability, and cost, are considered. Also, backup and recovery plans need to be elaborated in this step. Step three offers as a final result the complete design of local area networks, including their components with sizing specifications and emergency procedures. Step three provides information to be included in requests for proposals to vendors.

Step four includes sending out requests for proposals, evaluating their responses, selecting products and vendors, physically installing the infrastructure and LAN components, preparing operations and conversion plans, conformance, feasibility and stress testing, and, finally the cutover to a completely installed and tested LAN. This chapter concentrates on steps two and three. However, recommendations are also provided for steps one and four.

The ultimate goal of LAN design and planning is to meet service-level agreements using optimal resource capacity at a reasonable cost. LAN optimization can be viewed as a process of balancing design factors to attain the best LAN configuration within the constraints of such factors as transport, service, performance, and cost indicators. During the design and optimization process, when one factor is held constant, the interaction of the others must be quantified, since each indicator, when held constant, affects all the others.

Figure 6-2 shows a simple example illustrating the interaction of the indicators mentioned. The first diagram displays cost as a function of the expected level of availability; the performance indicator—number of collisions—is kept constant (CSMA/CD access-method is assumed). Redundant cabling may improve availability by increasing cost. The same is true for backup. The overall load is assumed to remain constant, and user behavior is not expected to change significantly. The second diagram shows the relationship between availability and number of collisions, while cost is kept constant. Cost may represent the total bandwidth considered for the LAN segment. Requirements for increasing availability may mean separation of the bandwidth into parallel channels supporting production, and offering backup. Finally, the third diagram displays the number of collisions as a function of cost, while availability is constrained. As shown, the number of collisions may be significantly reduced by increasing bandwidth migration from baseband to broadband.

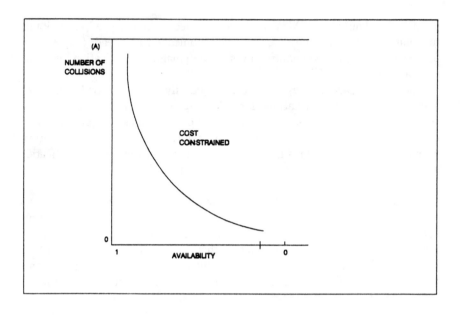

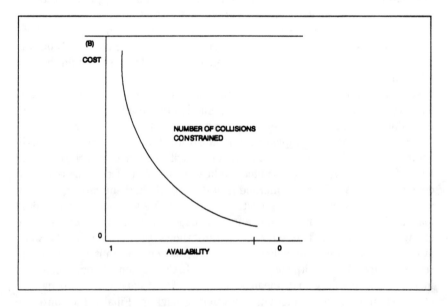

Fig. 6-2. Interaction of planning indicators.

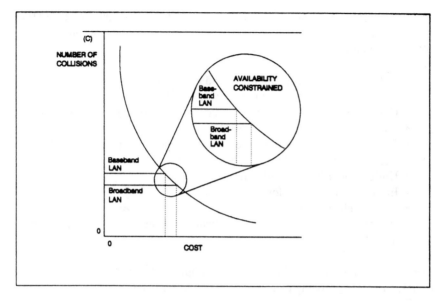

Fig. 6-2. Continued.

Design and planning functions

This section summarizes the principal functions of designing and planning of LANs.

Determination and quantification of current work load

The principal goal is to determine resource demand by application, by user, or by both. Resource demand means bits and bytes when considering transmission resources, and it means the processing demand for all kinds of servers. Resource demand may be measured by LAN analyzers, which were addressed in a previous chapter. Resource demand may be determined by sampling the use of LAN resources. In order to break down global resource use, volume indicators have to be collected, as well. In this case, continuous monitoring is required. Examples of continuous monitoring include products like Sniffer, Spider, LANtern and Trakker, discussed in chapter 5.

Work load volumes have to be collected in representative time periods. If monthly and weekly volume are fairly constant, then the representative day should be chosen. The concept of the busy (peak) hour is helpful in designing LANs. This refers to a continuous period of any day when the intensity of traffic is at its maximum. The busy (peak) hour is a statistical tool that allows the system planner to accommodate and engineer for peak traffic and avoid long delays during WAN peaks. There are two common ways to determine the busy hour (Terplan 1991): time constant busy hour, and bouncing busy hour.

After aggregating individual load components by user and by application, computed and measured results have to be compared. For deviations, multiple reasons should be evaluated. Examples are:

- Data that's too global for work load projection.
- Underestimation of contingency work load.
- Overestimation of the impact of data compression and compaction.
- Forecasting errors for the work load volumes.
- Planning errors in terms of selecting the base month, week, or hour.
- Resource capacities have not been accurately estimated.
- Underestimation of overhead.
- Inaccurate estimates for the resources.
- Wrong selection of quantities.
- Wrong characterization of application groups and communication forms.

In most cases, a combination of reasons apply. After several LAN planning cycles, the most probable causes for the deviation become easier to identify.
This process helps to:

- Increase the visibility of applications and their resource demand.
- Quantify typical volumes by application and user.
- Choose the right instruments for planning-related data collection.
- Identify resource demand components that can't be allocated to work load groups.
- Verify computations of LAN resource demand.

Estimation and quantification of future work load

This function should start with identifying locations for LAN segments and their components, such as servers, interconnecting devices, and workstations. This activity usually involves drawing maps based on information that's usually submitted. With existing LANs, the inventory or configuration database could serve as the basis. Other functions have to address the collection of service-related, work load-related, and volume-related information. In LANs, communication no longer means simply transmitting data between various locations. Figure 6-3 gives an overview of how to start identifying desired or existing services (e.g. E-mail, Voice-mail, Teleconferencing) with network traffic requirements. TABLE 6-1 defines all cells of FIG. 6-3. In the first phase, users identify the services they want to implement during the planning cycle. In the second phase, users are expected to identify volume ranges for the services they're requesting. As a result of these phases, the separation into cable-oriented LANs and PBXs may be very clearly identified.

LAN designers and planners have to identify the quantities of each service item. To determine the individual resource demand on transmission facilities,

Output Input	Video	Data	Voice	Facsimile
Video	Television 1	Radar analysis 2	Surveillance system 3	Freeze frame video 4
Data	Computer aided design videotex 5	Data processing 6	Voice response credit author 7	Hard-copy terminal 8
Voice	Voice-actuated system 9	Voice compression and storage 10	Phone voice mail 11	Voice-actuated system 12
Facsimile (word & fixed image)	Computer aided design videotex 13	Pattern recognition 14	Voice response (output) 15	Document transmission 16

Teleconferencing:	1, 9, 10, 11, 16
Computer aided design:	5, 6, 8, 13, 14
Credit author:	10, 11, 14, 15, 16
Videotex:	5, 6, 11, 13

Fig. 6-3. Matrix of user needs.

Table 6-1. Categories of Users' Needs

1. *Television:* Video-Video with expected quality and bandwidth
2. *Radar analysis:* Video-Data for military applications, in particular
3. *Surveillance system:* Video-Voice for supervising installations including alarm and alert management
4. *Freeze-frame video:* Video-Fax for transmitting information framewise
5. *CAD-Videotex:* Data-Video for information distribution
6. *Data processing:* Data-Data for processing information
7. *Voice response credit author:* Data-Voice for output processing or decision making results
8. *Hard-copy terminal:* Data-Fax for displaying and storing data displays on paper
9. *Voice actuated system:* Voice-Video, using voice as a trigger for displaying and distributing information
10. *Voice compression and storage:* Voice-Data for storing voice-based information in computing systems
11. *Phone, voice mail:* Voice-Voice for straight or delayed transmission of voice
12. *Voice actuated system:* Voice-Fax, s. item 9
13. *CAD videotex:* Fax-Video, s. item 5
14. *Pattern recognition:* Fax-Data for analyzing word or fixed images using data output for results
15. *Voice response:* Fax-Voice, whereby voice output will be triggered by Fax
16. *Document transmission:* Fax-Fax for serving office automation in particular

TABLES 6-2 and 6-3 are very helpful. These tables do represent only general guidelines. But, at least some resource demand ranges by user and by application may be determined.

Consolidation of the workload means to aggregate the resource demand

Table 6-2. Resource Demand by Communication Forms

Communication Form	Application Area	Throughput Rates
Data	Low volume	4.8 Kbps
	Medium volume (Data entry, word processing)	9.6 Kbps
	Line printer	19.2 Kbps
	High volume (Data enquiry, laser printer)	64 – 256 Kbps
	Net server/hosts	100 Kbps – 20 Mbps
Voice	Digital voice	32 Kbps
	Analog voice	64 Kbps
	Store and forward	8 – 32 Kbps
Image	OCR	2.4 Kbps
	Facsimile	9.6 Kbps
	Compressed graphics	64 Kbps
	Non-compressed graphics	256 Kbps
Video	Freeze-frame	64 Kbps
	Compressed motion	400 Kbps – 1.5 Mbps
	Non-compressed motion	30 Mbps
	Digital video	30 Mbps
	Television-grade color video	92 Mbps

Table 6-3. Resource Demand by Typical Messages

Message Type	Volume (Bits)
Color picture	2,000,000
Television picture	1,000,000
Short phone message	1,000,000
One-page document	200,000
Newspaper picture	100,000
One-page document (coded)	10,000
Typical interoffice memo	3,000
Typical telegram	2,000
Transaction inbound	500
Transaction outbound	1,500
Airline reservation	200
Fire alarm	40

from: current locations and current applications/services after growth factor adoption, current locations and new application/services, new locations and current application/services after growth factor adoption, and new locations and new application/services.

The aggregated results have to be extended by overhead figures, by contingency work load reserves, and by the pent-up demand (Terplan 1991). The results of this function may be summarized as follows:

- Realistic concept of user requirements.
- Realistic range (not precise value) of resources demand broken down by location, application/service, and user.
- Consideration of contingency work load elements for backups and emergencies.
- Phased plan for implementing new applications on LAN segments.

Design, planning, and sizing LAN components

The previous step has provided the consolidated work load and its aggregated resource demand for all significant LAN resources. Those are, in most cases, communication facilities and servers. This consolidated demand has then to be compared with existing or ordered resources. In this comparison, practical capacity limits have to be considered instead of theoretical throughput limits. For communication facilities, peak throughput limits can be determined by stress testing. Industry standards indicate:

- Ethernet with CSMA/CD—up to 40% use.
- Token Ring—up to 80% use.
- FDDI—up to 85% use.

The remaining part can't be used due to the inefficiency of the access control mechanism, frame/message sizes, and physical layout of the LAN segments.

In interconnecting LANs, the same or similar rules apply as for wide area networks. Due to use ceilings, unscheduled downtime, and overhead, portions of the bandwidth can't be used for productive traffic. Depending on the communication protocols, the practical limit's between 50% and 70%. Practical examples are computed in (Terplan 1991).

The ultimate goal of internetworking LAN segments is to economically connect local area networks to each other and to an enterprise's various information sources. The interconnection strategy depends on many facts, including the level of distributed processing, traffic concentration by sharing communication resources, and the availability of networking services.

Despite the fact that processing power and databases are now gradually becoming distributed, investment in central resources will remain substantial over the next few years. Those resources have to remain accessible to LAN segments.

Depending on the LAN locations—few large sites or many small sites—existing communication facilities may be used, or new ones may have to be provisioned. In the latter case, transmission costs need to be included in the budget.

The internetworking decision depends to a large extent on the availability of networking services within the corporation, or in a broader sense, in the geographical area of the LAN segments and processing entities. These services include: leased lines, virtual networks, and circuit, packet, or frame switching.

The LAN designer and planner faces several alternatives: centralized processing and support of a few LAN sites, distributed processing and support of a few LAN sites, centralized processing and support of many smaller LAN sites, or distributed processing and support of many smaller LAN sites.

With centralized processing and support of a few LAN sites, there are no basic changes to the existing hierarchical network. LANs are gatewayed to the central or remote communication controller. In most cases, private networks are in operation. But, it's highly unlikely that the same physical channel is shared between internetworked LAN traffic and traffic supported by proprietary protocols.

With distributed processing and support of a few LAN sites, it would be desirable to use the same LAN operating systems. The solution is the use of open or at least *de facto* standards. When migrating to a standard, the common denominator is usually found with TCP/IP, XNS, or NFS. The best solution is to link the local LANs to a premise backbone, and then to network the backbones via current private network facilities.

With centralized processing and support of many smaller LAN sites, the overall star topology will remain. LANs are gatewayed to the central or remote controllers or concentrators. In most cases, virtual networking services are used to internetwork the LAN segments with the central processing entity.

With distributed processing and support of many smaller LAN sites, each LAN segment works relatively independently from the other. Standards for the operating systems would be advantageous, but are not a prerequisite. Information exchange is occasional; most likely support is via frame-relay with public/private packet switching.

Although FDDI or DQDB could cover larger metropolitan area distances, the majority of interconnected LANs will involve a remote bridge or router connection. Whether to choose bridges or routers will depend on the type of internetwork traffic, and on the overall network configuration.

In general, routers are the best choice for applications in which the interlinked network connects many independent networks that occasionally exchange information with each other. In such cases, the intra-LAN traffic is considerably higher than the inter-LAN traffic. Local LAN administration is required. TCP/IP internets are good examples of those applications. When traffic volumes are higher and more directed, local LAN administration is not required, and bridges offer better performance. Bridges allow support of multiple operating systems and protocols, a critical requirement not met by routers.

Corporations with highly distributed geography dedicated to distributed processing will find routers the best solution for interconnection. Routers allow local control of LANs, and offer a more flexible network, with future high growth and change in mind.

TABLE 6-4 compares the most important attributes of bridges and routers from a LAN designer perspective. It's assumed that the differences will disappear as more brouters appear on the market.

Table 6-4. Comparison of Bridges and Routers

Attributes	Bridges	Routers
Function	Device for offering connectivity at layer 2 between various access protocols and media	Device for offering connectivity at layer 3 for networks with the same protocol at layer 3 and higher
Traffic volumes	High	Low to medium
Directed traffic	Good	Fair
Multiple protocols	Not sensitive	Sensitive
Address interpretation	Fast	Fair
Flexibility	Fair	High
Robustness	Fair	High
Management capabilities	Fair	Good
Route selection and path optimization	Not supported	Supported
Address analysis & filtering	Yes	Yes
Combination with wiring hubs	Yes	Yes
Backup and alternate routes support	Weak	Strong
Number of devices required	High	Moderate
Number of hops	Fair	Fair to good
Costs	Low	High

Usually, the decision of whether to use the spanning tree or source routing algorithms for bridging networks is beyond the LAN design and planning activity. But, depending on the standards and products selected, the impact of the algorithms has to be quantified by the designer and planner. Spanning tree may cause some performance bottlenecks unless the WAN portion of the interconnection is sized correctly or unless vendors provide additional features for bandwidth increase and load balancing among available channels. But, spanning tree would not cause electronic storms or flooding of the interconnected LAN network. In the case of heavily meshed and bridged LANs, source routing may seriously degrade overall performance and impact all applications using the same WAN connection. While source routing broadcast messages are small—generally only 30 to 40 characters—their numbers can significantly increase the load on communication facilities connecting remote bridges to each other. Worst-case considerations are summarized in TABLE 6-5.

TABLE 6-5 takes the theoretical bandwidth as a basis. Practical examples from Travelers, Inc. show that the saturation level is reached earlier. LAN designers and planners have to limit the hop count by not sacrificing alternate routing capabilities. As the table shows, the maximum number of messages increases exponentially with the number of hop counts.

Table 6-5. Source Routing in a Meshed Network

Number of Nodes	Maximum Number of Broadcast Messages Per Connection Request	Line utilization			
		9.6 Kbps	56 Kbps	128 Kbps	1.5 Mbps
5	5	14%	2%	1%	0.1%
6	16	46%	8%	4%	0.3%
7	65	184%	32%	14%	1.1%
8	328	929%	159%	74%	5.8%

These facts require building partitioned mesh networks with limited numbers of connections to each other. Practical examples show that corporations are unlikely to build bridged networks with so many connections to each other, increasing performance risks due to source routing overhead. When a number of parallel connections is required, routers may be implemented instead.

Basically, there are two alternatives to carrying the traffic of internetworked LANs:

1. Physical and logical connections of network architectures serving other applications; SNA, DNA, DCA, Expand, and so on could be chosen. This solution requires that gateways be at the locations of the LANs to be connected. Both the gateways and the communication links may become the bottlenecks.
2. Separate LAN-LAN internetwork using bridges, routers, or brouters for directing the traffic between the LAN locations. By selecting adequate bandwidth, performance bottlenecks are unlikely.

Recent surveys show that approximately 25% choose solution 1, and 75% choose solution 2. Solution 2 is more expensive, due to the dedicated nature of the communication links.

In sizing servers, certain server computation cycles are used for administration that can't be allocated to any particular station or application. Factors such as overhead, downtime and queuing at high use levels reduce the practical server utilization limit to 75% to 85%.

RAD is enhancing its routers to handle SNA and LAN protocols, including

SDLC, NetBios, and LU 6.2, using a new combination of routing/bridging schemes. The protocols are transmitted at the MAC layer, but the bridges exchange information in order to find the best path through the network. The new technique, called shortest-path first (SPF), is replacing source routing. In terms of bandwidth utilization, using SPF is more economical than encapsulating protocols into TCP/IP packets.

Figure 6-4 shows how upgrade points can be identified for LAN resources. With new design, this consideration starts at the upgrade point. This figure offers a generic view that's applicable for all LAN managed objects.

The design stage is accomplished in a hierarchical manner:

1. Designing and sizing LAN segments at floors.
2. Designing and sizing building distribution systems.
3. Designing and sizing premise (campus) distribution systems.
4. Designing and sizing LAN interconnection facilities.

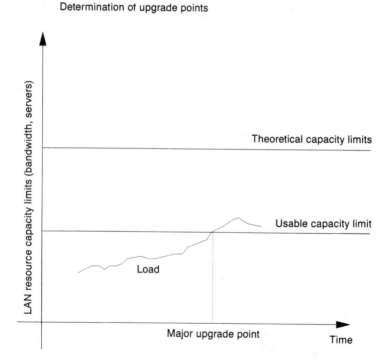

Fig. 6-4. Upgrade points for LAN resources.

Design includes the wiring concentrators and wiring connections to the network interface cards in the servers and stations. Figure 6-5 shows the result of the "logical" design, indicating Ethernet and Token Rings at the floors, Token Ring for connecting floors and FDDI for the campus backbone. The same logical topology is mapped into the "physical" layout, as shown in FIG. 6-6.

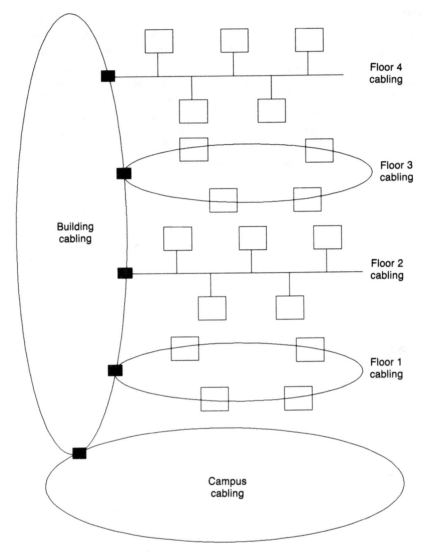

Fig. 6-5. Results of logical network design.

In order to improve fault tolerance of hub topologies, redundancy needs to be planned very carefully. Hubs may be networked by using the tree, ring, or bus topology. Figure 6-7 (Lannet 1991) shows the three structures, indicating a decision point for redundant links with an "R." It's assumed that Ethernet transceivers are equipped with redundant link connections. In the event of any link or hub breakdown, the network is still fully functional.

Figure 6-8 (Lannet 1991) offers a full fault-tolerant network. Synchronous Ethernet is assumed due to the number of hubs traversed between stations on

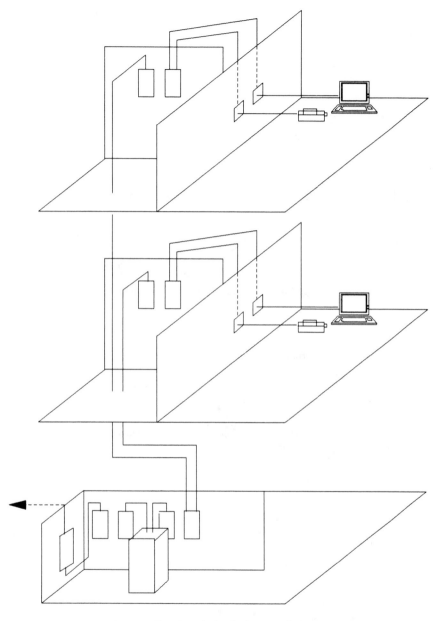

Fig. 6-6. Results of physical network design.

the maximum path. Figure 6-9 (Lannet 1991) shows a ring solution with redundant links. The media of this arrangement could be copper or fiber. Part of the aim of designing and planning is to provide management access to the hubs. Either outband access has to be guaranteed to each of the hubs, or parts connecting backbone hubs must be retained in a manual (nonmanageable) mode.

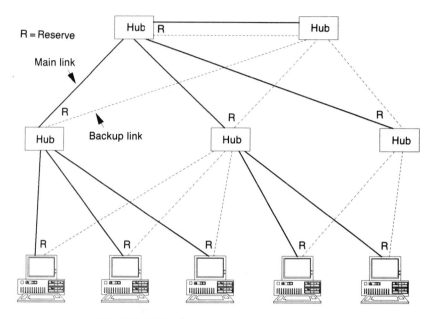

Fig. 6-7. *Full tolerant tree topology with hubs.*

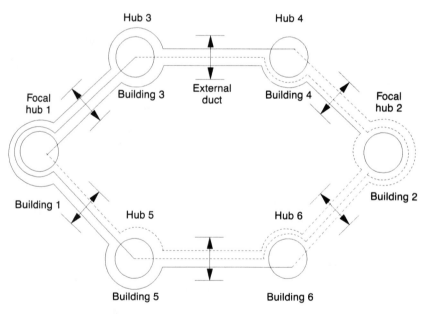

Fig. 6-8. *Full tolerant ring topology with hubs.*

In planning and implementing LANs, the question of power supply must not be ignored. There are two options: online uninterrupted power supply (UPS), or a standby UPS. As part of the design process, careful consideration

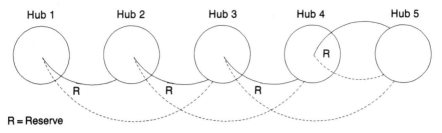

Hub 1   Hub 2   Hub 3   Hub 4   Hub 5

R = Reserve

Fig. 6-9. Full tolerant bus topology with hubs.

is needed to determine which components need special protection. The availability of inexpensive UPSs makes protection of each managed object attractive, but the planner should make sure not to sacrifice quality for price. UPSs only stop electrical transients from the wall outlet, and they don't provide protection against the potentially harmful transients—surges and spikes—that enter into peripheral pacts via the cables connecting components, such as hiring hubs, concentrators, adapter cards, modems, and principal servers with other LAN segments or CPUs.

LAN cables act like antennas, attracting all forms of transients: secondary lightning hits, electrostatic discharges, equipment power transients, and switching and environmentally caused transients may enter into the connected equipment part and bring expensive circuitry down.

UPSs may be configured in a distributed or central manner. Opinions vary on which is the best approach. The ultimate solution will probably be a combination of both basic techniques. Figure 6-10 shows an implementation example, with support for the file server and all the attached nodes. Ideally, a smart

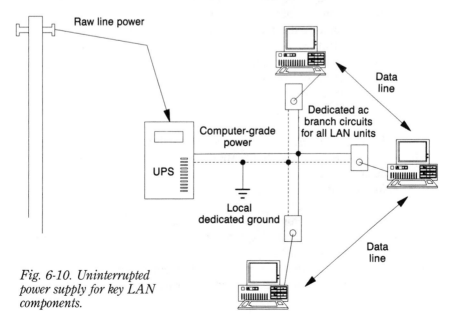

Fig. 6-10. Uninterrupted power supply for key LAN components.

UPS offers monitoring and auto-shutdown capabilities. In the event of a power breakdown, the software will initiate a countdown and proceed with an orderly termination of the program and a shutdown of the system to ensure the protection of all information. An intelligent UPS also adjusts for overloaded, defective, or aging batteries and closes down critical programs before the batteries are exhausted. Links to wiring concentrators are expected.

For each planning phase, several criteria have to be considered. Those criteria may be grouped as follows:

1. Transport-oriented criteria.
   - Fairness: all stations have the same rights to transmit.
   - Priority of transmission: certain frames/messages may be transmitted in an expedited manner.
   - Flexibility: reconfiguration of station without interrupting operations.
   - Expandability: additional stations may be connected without interrupting operations.
   - Connectivity: any-to-any connections have to be supported.
   - Throughput rates: practical throughput limits between stations, which may be supported independently from the overall traffic in the LAN segments, or in the LAN interconnecting segments.

2. Service-oriented criteria.
   - Throughput rates: practical throughput rates that may be offered to users.
   - Elapsed time: transmission time of frames/messages within the LAN segment, or in the interconnected LAN environment.
   - Access delay: elapsed time between transmission intention and actual "control" of transmission devices.
   - Use: dynamic indicators showing the ratio between offered and supportable traffic.
   - Performance in saturation: metric for quantifying how rapidly congested traffic can be accommodated and serviced.

3. Quality-oriented criteria.
   - Availability: LANs are expected to be available when users want service.
   - Reliability: metric to characterize the ability of individual objects to sustain service; usually MTBF (mean time between failures) is used as an indicator.
   - Maintainability: metric to express the ability for detecting, determining and eliminating problems; usually MTTR (mean time to repair) is used as indicator.
   - Accuracy: LANs are expected to offer error-free transmission of frames/messages.
   - Data security: this indicator offers the transmission of frames/messages without the risk of being read or manipulated.

- User friendliness: handling of applications has to be as simple as possible; usually help functions, front ends, and menus are offered and implemented.
4. Cost-oriented criteria.
   - Installation costs: one-time costs to implement the LAN segment or segments.
   - Operational costs: recurring cost of operating the WAN segment or segments.
   - Maintenance costs: recurring cost of preventing maintenance activities.

Cabling selection is very important to ensure good economics and reasonable performance at the same time. The demarcation lines between technologies can't be drawn very easily. In terms of applicability, the following recommendations may work well (Mier 1991):

1. Unshielded twisted pair in use: telecommunication connections, analog voice, analog PBX, dial-up modems for data.
2. New unshielded twisted pair: same as for #1, plus digital PBX for voice, ISDN, data/voice between 64 Kbps to T1 rates.
3. Data-grade unshielded twisted pair: all the applications listed for #2, plus low-speed Token Ring (4 Mbps), 10BaseT Ethernet, LANs up to 10 Mbps.
4. Shielded-twisted-pair: all LANs between 4 and 16 Mbps (and eventually above).
5. Optical fiber: all LANs above 16 Mbps, FDDI data rates, and any applications beyond 100 Mpbs.

Besides technological feasibility, cabling costs have to be evaluated very carefully. Cable costs per foot are approximately 10 times higher for optical fiber than for unshielded twisted pair; for wall plates, this ratio could be as high as 40. In case of comparing typical installations, the ratio is decreasing to two to three. The installation cost per station is approximately $900 with unshielded twisted pair, and $1,800 with optical fiber (Mier 1991).

Shielded twisted pair is between those prices. Outside the United States, prices are much different. Examples of how some of the criteria interact with each other were discussed earlier in this chapter.

Implementation of local area networks

Implementation is the planning and execution of all activities related to upgrades or new installations. Activities are partly clerical and partly technical.

Requests for proposals   Companies ask vendors for specific information on products. This information is then used to select facilities and equipment, interconnecting devices, WAN communication services (optional), wiring solutions, and interrupted power supply components. Potential suppliers are expected to detail the products' functions, price, availability, support, security, and conformance with international standards.

Selection and weighting criteria   Selection criteria, and the priority weighting of each criterion, should be determined prior to evaluation. For weighting criteria, the preference matrix technique is very useful. Rather than comparing each criterion against all others at the same time, the preference matrix compares only two criteria at a time (Terplan 1991). Expert systems may be used as well for configuring complex networks, considering a fairly large number of design alternatives.

Operational manuals   Operational manuals should be prepared based on guidelines from planning steps. They will describe how the LAN is going to be used. An operational manual is extremely useful in helping someone to understand what he or she is supposed to accomplish in the operational control and administration areas. In particular, standards and procedures for the following areas may be included: problem determination and LAN management, version control of server software, fallback or failure planning, inventory control and name management, financial analysis and budgeting, configuration and management, change management.

Conversion plans   Assuming that you're dealing with a complex interconnected LAN, whereby the operation of the larger organization may be impaired once the network has broken down, it's quite unlikely that the network will be implemented without careful scrutiny. It will more likely need a step-by-step approach, perhaps running parallel, doubling volumes and operation for a certain period of time. That means that the old network (most likely a hierarchical structure with a powerful host computer) should remain operational until the new one has been thoroughly tested and proven. These functions involve plans detailing the necessary products to be installed and time frames for the development of standards and procedures, education, and installation management.

Prototyping   When the user has custom engineering and/or custom software development, he or she is expected to take responsibility for testing by using prototypes of the network. Based on the testing results, the principal requirements may or may not be met. If not, the capacity planner must go back to step 2 in order to do more planning, and the engineering effort must continue. The whole planning process is strongly iterative (in other words, previous phases and steps within the phases may be repeated many times). When the functionality and/or the service requirements are not met, there are several alternatives to be implemented: return to the planning phase and include more alternatives; return to the optimization and modeling phase and evaluate additional alternatives within the original hardware or software capabilities; tune the prototype, evaluate the results, and decide on further actions. This procedure may be observed again in FIG. 6-1 as part of the overall capacity planning methodology.

Backup and recovery plan   Due to the reliability behavior of a complex LAN, it's not a matter of whether the LAN(s) will break down as much as when. When the LAN does fail, LAN operational control must be ready with a preconceived action plan. Contingency and recovery planning become key elements of operating a LAN with online service. Since the various components are relied upon so heavily by the users, it's essential that there are predefined plans for restoring service in the case of adverse circumstances. The two plans required are as follows.

Contingency plan   A contingency plan must deal with ways for temporarily reconfiguring to overcome individually failing LAN components and allow for continued operation during the time taken to resolve the problem. Each operational level of the network should be considered in this plan and a full range of automated and manual methods included. There will be some situations that can be handled by network operations alone through dynamic reconfiguration; others will require a combination of automated and manual steps to be performed both centrally and remotely. Contingency plans should prescribe the various combinations of these steps and should also define alternate procedures in the event that the primary method is unworkable. Examples of situations that should be addressed in the plan include handling of the following situations: a failing cable; a failing regional concentrator, node, gateway, router or bridge; a failing communication server; a failing wiring hub; a failing power supply; an errant application or system program.

Any significant change in the LAN components will require that the contingency plan be reevaluated and updated as appropriate. The addition or deletion of hardware or software components in the LAN could have an impact on the alternatives available in contingency planning. The impact of such changes should be reflected in the contingency plan. "Dry run" testing of the plan should be used to verify its workability and to train the LAN staff in the identified methods. The complexity of the contingency plan becomes a reflection of how well the components are isolated from one another. The network should be designed to minimize the impact of network failures. Such a network will result in fewer variables to be considered in the contingency plan and perhaps simplify modeling if the independence also applies to the component's functionality. In this respect, segmentation by using local and remote bridges may contribute to lower vulnerability.

Recovery plan   The recovery plan differs from the contingency plan in that it defines methods available to restore either a single component of the network or the entire network to operational status. The recovery plan should contain detailed procedures to be used in returning the component back to service. Topics that should be covered in this plan include preferred approach, acceptable alternatives, critical steps to be performed (along with their priorities), personnel responsibilities, and target deadlines. The plan should take into account the fact that system failure may result from equipment malfunction, natural disaster, fire, and sabotage, as well as from other, unforeseen causes. Therefore, the identified procedures must be able to deal with single components all the way up to the entire network. Procedures developed as a result of the recovery planning process should become a permanent portion of guides for LAN operational control. To the extent possible, the recovery plan should also be tested to familiarize personnel with the effort involved and to validate the plan's effectiveness.

Examples of issues that should be covered in the recovery plan are the following:

- Emergency procedures for the recovery of critical items such as online files and programs.
- Assignment of responsibilities to human resources.
- Who should be contacted first in the escalation procedure.
- Recovery procedures for operator errors that destroy files and programs.
- Recovery from application software failures on servers.
- Availability of backup computer facilities.
- Recovery from power failures.
- Implementing continuous backup systems.
- Availability of backup power.
- How to diagnose the problem.
- Off-site storage of duplicates of customer-sensitive information.
- How to guarantee LAN security.
- How to inform customers about anomalies.

Cutover scheduling   Based on the conversion plan, implementation usually takes several steps. The best way is to phase in implementation by location or application. The cutover must be prepared with great care and should be accomplished overnight or over a weekend that gives time for debugging. For extensive debugging, test transactions are expected to be ready for trial runs. These could be the same transactions used previously in the prototyping phase. They may be generated and composed as part of the remote terminal emulation.

Stress testing   LAN design and planning are iterative processes. Using remote terminal emulation for existing subsets of communication networks (e.g., for prototypes) is a promising technique for reducing the time requirements for designing and modeling. A remote terminal emulator is an external, independent driver that's connected to the system and LAN under test via standard communication interfaces. The emulator generates messages and transactions for the network under test, based on a set of representative scripts defined by the user's application.

Using this technique, not only the functionality but also the service-level requirements can be evaluated. By attempting to use as many of the new LAN facilities as possible, the chances of identifying potential bottlenecks are significantly improved. Operations and communication networks personnel must be trained to face all eventualities before actual cutover. Help desk, administration, and technical support personnel should be prepared as well. As a result, tuning activities may be initiated. Examples include placement of bridges or routers, splitting LAN segments, consolidating LAN segments, changing the logical sequence of stations, upgrading and downgrading servers, re-allocating stations to servers, and many others. Links to performance management are options. CPM and PERT techniques are useful in timing the cutover.

Paralleling actual volumes and cutover It's recommended that actual volumes and transaction types be emulated as closely as possible prior to cutover. The new LAN and the old LAN (or old procedures) should work simultaneously for a defined period of time. If results are satisfactory, service levels are met, and personnel are properly trained, complete cutover may be executed.

Instruments for planning local area networks

Recently, designing LANs has been a more or less intuitive process. Due to the price of products and human time requirements, users were not really eager to design and size local area networks. Connectivity and compatibility items were much more highly prioritized than properly sizing the servers and properly determining the bandwidth required for satisfactory performance. But load and local area networks are increasing, topologies are getting more complex, and performance is being evaluated more critically.

LAN design tools is a fairly new product area. There are many wide area network design tools on the market, but few address the LAN design marketplace. Outside of design guidelines provided by vendors, which are usually not available to users, there are only a handful of tools that can be purchased for in-house planning and ongoing network management. The present obstacles of using such tools are:

- There's no budget for such tools.
- They require a computer that may not be part of the installation.
- Performance information is required, but is not available.
- They require monitoring instruments that may not be part of the installation.

In order to evaluate products, the following criteria should be considered (Datapro NS30 1990): system requirements, input data requirements, control parameter extensions, technology used, applicability of live data, postprocessing, animated displays, and maturity of product.

System requirements The processing power should be enough to meet needs of simulation techniques, which can be very extensive for large segments or interconnected LANs. At least an EGA display is generally required for PC-based systems. However, some of the design systems are based on more powerful platforms, such as Sun Microsystems workstations.

Input data requirements This includes what data the user should provide prior to starting a "what-if" evaluation. Input parameters may be grouped by LAN segment and interconnecting parameters. Modeling parameters may be classified into two groups: LAN parameters and internetwork parameters.

LAN segments parameters are: sizes (average packet and message sizes), protocols (lower, middle, and high level), application and network operating systems, measure of LAN power and its background load index of average workstations on a local LAN, and number of workstations on a remote LAN.

Internetwork parameters are: network architecture; bridge, router, and gateway transfer rates; lower level protocol on the interlink; number of hops between two LANs; background load on links between LANs.

Control parameter extensions   Users may be interested in changing or extending modeling to new operating systems, unsupported protocols, and to new transmission media. This criterion checks on the openness of the modeling process. Also, programmability may be included here.

Technology used   The answers here impact the accuracy of modeling results. Queuing equations allow for quick evaluations of expected performance ranges. Complex simulation allows modeling in greater detail, and guarantees much higher accuracy. Some products combine both techniques.

Applicability of live data   Once the LAN is running, LAN analyzers (see chapter 5 for more details) may be used to collect actual traffic data. Some performance models can read in this collected data and use it to augment the modeling capabilities. It helps model calibration and validation. Also, the effects of growth may be observed more accurately.

Postprocessing   The right presentation form helps to interpret modeling results. It's extremely important to re-examine the modeling results without completely rerunning the model. Graphics and colors help to better understand the results.

Animated displays   This capability allows designers and planners to get a feel for the impact of certain modeling parameters, such as queuing delays at congestion points or collisions in certain LAN segments. Some products provide both a step mode and an automatic mode in support of this type of visual display. In many circumstances, this graphical support accelerates the evaluation process by highlighting potential performance bottlenecks.

Maturity of product   It's extremely important to collect implementation experiences from other users. Most products are recent developments, and just a few products are based on mature products that have been around in the WAN area for many years. Also, the integration of existing solutions for LAN segments and for interconnected LANs would be a positive sign of maturity.

The following segment offers a brief review of existing products for modeling LANs.

LANNET II.5 (C.A.C.I.)

Basically, a LAN is expected to support clients, servers, and gateways (C.A.C.I. 1990). A client is a generic user without explicit storage capability.

Each client or client group has an action list representing the application initiated by the client; frequency and resource demand have to be identified. A server represents all common types of LAN servers, files, printers, and administrations. Servers have storage capacity and, like clients, have a server action list, each having a unique name, with a generation time, length, and destination. A gateway is the generic element used to model a link to another LAN, MAN, or WAN.

The local area network to be simulated is described in LANNET II by the data structure consisting of the LAN backbone, clients, servers, and gateways. The baseline model is built by a powerful menu hierarchy supported by graphics. Besides work load identification, the architecture, such as Ethernet, Token Ring, and Token Bus, the backbone bandwidth, and overhead, also have to be identified. LANNET II offers the following reports:

- LAN statistics, including transfer time, transit, system waiting time, overhead time, information overhead, information throughput, system throughput, message loss, and time to complete.
- Client statistics, showing queue length, waiting time, and blocking.
- Server statistics, concentrating on queue length, waiting time, blocking, use, and storage capacity.
- Gateway statistics, focusing on queue length and blocking.

Graphs and plots can be generated showing throughput, delay, and resource use.

LANNET offers a number of summary reports for user analysis. The reports consist of statistics about LANs, clients, servers, and gateways. Figure 6-11 shows the evaluation results of collision statistics (Datapro NS30 1990). A related program, Network II.5 permits modeling of more complex computer and networking systems. This package also has a LAN capability, allowing users to analyze mixed networks. Network II.5 is a superset of LANNET 11.5.

Metasan (Industrial Technology Institute)

Metasan, from the Industrial Technology Institute, is a Unix-based network modeling tool, and is applicable to any type of local area network. It may be expanded to accommodate wide area networks as well. Metasan uses stochastic activity networks (SANs), which are an extension of Petri-nets, and which permit the representation of timeliness (realtime requirements), fault tolerance, degradable performance, and parallelism in a single model. Models developed with Metasan consist of descriptions of network structure and desired performance and solution options to be used in the evaluation process.

LANSIM, Softbench, and LANAI (Internetix)

Internetix offers two network modeling products for LANs: LANSIM and Softbench (Datapro NS30 1990). LANSIM models the major LAN protocols,

Collision LAN utilization statistics
from 0. to 120. seconds
(all times reported in microseconds)

LAN name	Ethernet
Collison episodes	7
Collided transfers	19
Deferrals	81
Avg deferral delay	1694.140
Max deferral delay	1873.000
Std dev deferral delay	468.075
Avg deferral queue	1.019
Max queue size	3.000
Std dev queue size	.635
Multiple collisions	4
Avg mult collisions	2
Max mult collisions	2
Successful transfers	
Avg usage time	2443.990
Max usage time	2450.000
Std dev usage time	7.552
Percent of time busy	28.453

Fig. 6-11. LANNET collision statistics.

including Ethernet, Token Bus, Token Ring, FDDI, and TCP/IP, through the transport layer of the OSI model. LANSIM is a bottom-up simulation offering in-depth modeling of traffic flows in LANs.

LANSIM is a more sophisticated tool than Softbench. LANSIM is a full discrete event simulator that uses the power of the computer to calculate the time for the various components of a LAN to perform each functional step. By simulating thousands of transactions and computing statistics on the times and queue lengths recorded, performance can be predicted accurately.

Softbench is an analytical model that assists in computing throughput and delays. It includes message and packet sizes, but it can't model actual traffic. The best results may be accomplished when both PC-based products are used in combination.

Figure 6-12 shows an example of LANSIM graphic output indicating the simulated end-to-end delays for various transaction types, such as downloading an application from the server to a workstation. LANSIM simulates many LAN operating conditions as specified by the planner, and prepares a variety of graphical screens.

LAN SoftBench is similar to an analytical model, but is more an empirical one, calibrated using test data. The SoftBench product has been calibrated

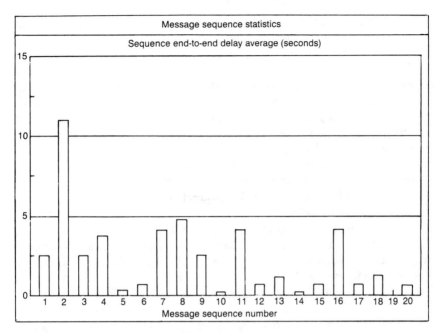

Fig. 6-12. LANSIM graphical output example.

using actual performance data obtained from various vendors and independent testing sources, as well as being verified against detailed simulation runs. The latest versions allow the planner to describe each LAN segment with 12 parameters. An additional five parameters allow specifying how the LAN segments are interconnected. These features also allow decomposing complex LANs, analyzing pairs of LAN segments, and then reassembling the result for ultimate analysis. Planners can also conduct rapid "what if" prototyping on the LAN's variables. Based on a calibrated baseline model, new announcements can be more rapidly incorporated and evaluated.

Internetix tries to link LAN design and modeling tools to LAN monitors. If it's applicable, the LAN monitor will provide live work load to the model. Also, expert system extensions are under consideration. The first implementation experiences are expected from Network General with the Sniffer product family.

BONeS (Comdisco)

BONeS provides a graphical environment for the description and simulation of a range of communication networks, including LANs and WANs, ISDN, packet- and circuit-switched networks, store and forward networks, packet radio networks, and computer buses and architectures (Comdisco 1991). It also provides a user-extendible model library and a set of analysis tools. It minimizes the amount of code you have to write, and it offers online help, documentation aids, and error checking.

The BONeS architecture features several key components: the block diagram editor creates and edits documents and stores block diagrams; the data structure editor creates and edits documents and stores data structures; the model library contains programmed models in a data structure database and protocol functions in a model database; the code generator transforms a simulation model into a simulation program in C; the database manager and consistency checker organizes, stores, retrieves and checks block diagrams, data structures, simulation code and documentation; the post processor analyzes and displays simulation results.

The planner constructs the network model graphically and hierarchically using building blocks from the BONeS model library. Components of a network model can be written in C and incorporated into a BONeS model. BONeS translates the network model into a C program, executes an event-driven Monte Carlo simulation, computes statistical measures of performance, and displays the result graphically. BONeS can be used to evaluate the performance of a network with a given topology and protocols (standard or user-defined) and to analyze the impact of changes in network topology, traffic, and protocols on the overall performance of the network.

BONeS is based on a unified graphical framework for specification of network topology, data structures, and protocol functions. This provides a clear indication of the transformation that messages and packets undergo as they flow through the network. The data-flow block diagram approach minimizes the amount of code to be written and provides a mechanism for ensuring consistency of interconnections in a network model.

BONeS provides a variety of database management services, including storage retrieval and checking of modules and data structures and maintenance of revision histories. Simulation results are organized and stored along with models and parameter files so that they can be compared with the results of multiple simulations. Figure 6-13 shows the multiple layers of the BONeS model using an Ethernet example.

OPNET (MIL 3, Inc.)

OPNET is a workstation-based network simulation tool. The product brings the advantages of computer-aided engineering (CAE) technology to communication network modeling and analysis. OPNET incorporates the latest technologies from the fields of object-oriented modeling, simulation performance enhancement, and graphical user interfaces, and removes costly and time-consuming simulation software development from the network modeling and analysis cycle. Because OPNET provides a modeling and simulation infrastructure, communication engineers can focus on modeling the specifics under study.

The power of OPNET lies in its ability to support the development of complicated network and protocol models in a structured and logical manner. It uses a hierarchical and modular specification approach to break down model complexity. Design specification is tightly coupled with simulation and advanced postprocessing within an integrated environment.

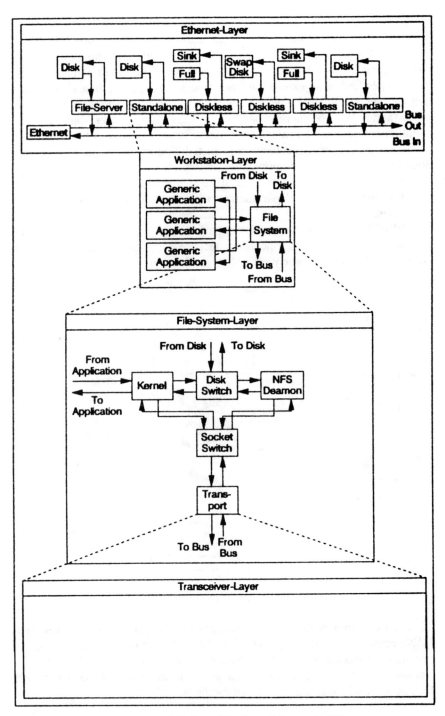

Fig. 6-13. BONeS model of an Ethernet LAN.

OPNET differs in many respects from other commercially available network (or general distributed system) simulation tools: it supports full modeling flexibility for application-specific protocols and algorithms rather than constraining the user to hard-wired protocol types; protocols and algorithms can be specified in an extensible-state machine language, instead of a rudimentary set of inflexible blocks; packets that flow between nodes on the network model are not merely bandwidth-occupying entities, but also can contain user-determined values and data structures necessary to realistically model the operation of protocols and distributed algorithms; the modeling domain of OPNET is communication networks, and all OPNET tools and features are based on the nomenclature and conventions of this domain; OPNET provides detailed parametriced physical layer models of common link types.

OPNET is available on a variety of hardware platforms in several versions, optimized for different applications. Figure 6-14 shows the structure of OPNET, detailing the three principal steps of design, test, and evaluation.

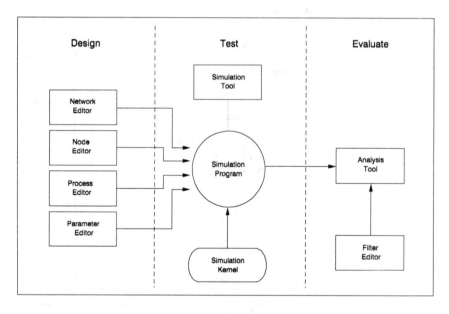

Fig. 6-14. Structure of OPNET.

LAN modeling tools have matured, particularly those that are PC-based. LAN segments can be adequately modeled now; the real void is the lack of products composing models for interconnected LANs. TABLE 6-6 compares leading products, using criteria such as platform, transmission and access techniques, and modeling and output-methods.

Table 6-6. Product Comparison of LAN Modeling Tools

Vendor	CACI	COMDISCO	INTERNETIX	MIL3
Product	Lannet II.5	BONeS	Lansim Softbench	OpNet
Systems				
Platforms	80286/80386	Sun 3 & 4 Digital 2100 Digital 3100	80286, 80386	Sun; others are negotiable
DOS	Yes	No	Yes	No, but negotiable
OS/2	Yes	No	Yes	No, but negotiable
Unix	Yes	Yes	No	Yes
Coprocessor	Required	Not required	Recommended	Not specified
Hard disk	3 M	100 M	10 M	100 M
Graphics	EGA/VGA	Standard	EGA/VGA	Windows
Transmission & access				
Ethernet	Yes	Yes	Yes	Yes
Token Ring	Yes	Yes	Yes	Yes
FDDI	Yes	Yes	Yes	Yes, but customization
Modeling				
Modeling technique	Discrete event	Discrete event	Discrete event analytical	Discrete event
Input	Menus	Menus	Menus or LAN monitor	Editor
Printed reports	Yes	Yes	Yes	Yes
Graphic displays	Yes	Yes	Yes	Yes
Animation	Yes	No	No	Yes

Summary

Designing and planning LANs are activities that are usually still limited to the infrastructure. Performance metrics and service indicators are not included. For LAN segments that have a limited geographical area and stable work load and user profiles, change is not expected soon. However, when LAN segments have to be interconnected, serving a wider user base and occasionally including wide area networks, more objective design and planning are urgently needed. In particular, in cases when LAN segments are extending or replacing the traditionally hierarchical networking structures, users are very familiar with service-level agreements, including service and use indicators. In terms of the planning process, there are many similarities between LAN and WAN design and planning. LAN modeling tools have matured, but offer little for interconnected LANs. For improving planning quality, the LAN designer and planner are expected to combine various models from both the WAN and LAN area.

LAN design and optimization tools run on a wide variety of processors, from minicomputers to powerful mainframes. At the low end are tools such as SoftBench (Internetix) and NetMod (University of Michigan), both of which estimate feasibility and performance without going into detail at the LAN protocol levels. At the high end, there are simulators that emulate and simulate a lot of the details of protocols, access methods, and LAN configurations. This category includes SES (Scientific and Engineering Software, Inc.), Lannet and Network II (CACI), Lansim (Internetix), BONeS (Comdisco) and Optimized Network Engineering Tools (MIL3).

Performance of LAN interconnecting devices can be predicted by NeTool (Make Systems), which simulates specific vendors' bridge, router and brouter devices using an approach similar to computer-aided engineering. Performance of individual software applications running on specific LANs can be modeled by QASE (Quantitative Aided Software Engineering from Advanced Systems Technologies, Inc.). This product uses computer-aided engineering technology, as well.

7

LAN management organizational structure

LAN management functions are assigned to various people who are hired and educated to manage LANs. The same is true of the instruments addressed in previous chapters; typical groups of instruments are used by certain organizational units of the enterprise. The LAN management organizational structure is not yet mature, but installation and operation do seem to be clearly segregated from each other. At the moment, the following human resources can be identified. A LAN management supervisor is responsible for supervising design, planning, installation, and operation. Reporting to the LAN management supervisor are:

- Design, planning, and installation.
  a. LAN designers and planners.
  b. LAN installer.
- Operations.
  a. LAN help-desk operator.
  b. LAN administrator.
  c. LAN analyst.

TABLE 7-1 shows an organizational chart of a hypothetical LAN environment. If WANs and LANs are going to be managed together, there will be some overlap. Otherwise, interconnecting devices such as bridges, routers, and gateways represent demarcation lines between the WAN and LAN management organizations (refer again to FIG. 1-1). These components are expected to provide information to both management entities. Sharing responsibilities between the management entities depends on the environment and its service expectations.

Table 7-1. Organizational Structure of LAN Management

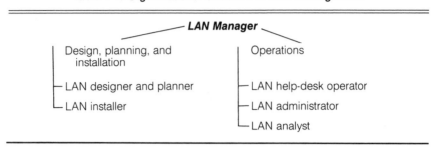

LAN Manager	
Design, planning, and installation	Operations
├─ LAN designer and planner	├─ LAN help-desk operator
└─ LAN installer	├─ LAN administrator
	└─ LAN analyst

But, in any case, it's recommended to use outband communication techniques between those entities to ensure management capabilities when objects, segments, or communication links have broken down.

TABLE 7-2 shows the clearly defined responsibilities for each human resource involved in LAN management. As can be seen, there are overlaps in the functions each group/person is responsible for. In order to identify the right instruments for each LAN management group, TABLE 7-3 displays the allocation of typical instruments. This table represents the most likely allocations.

The number of human resources needed to execute LAN management functions depends on many factors, such as: the number and educational level of users, the number of workstations to be managed, the number of servers to be managed, the number of interconnecting devices to be managed, the geography of and distances within LAN segments, the density of station and servers, the communication media used, the availability of instruments for continuous monitoring, the availability of instruments for troubleshooting, the skill levels of the LAN management group, and the level of support from the control (WAN) network management organization.

TABLE 7-4 summarizes the number ranges that may be applicable in a typical LAN environment. This table uses two different numbers for the server/station ratio: one server for thirty workstations, or two servers for seventy workstations. Furthermore, both standalone LANs and internetworked LANs are considered.

The assumptions on which this table is based include:

1. Geographical distances not exceeding a typical campus of approximately two miles in diameter.
2. Skill levels of the LAN management staff are average.
3. Instrumentation.
   - Console emulation for the LAN help desk.
   - Relational database for administration.
   - LAN analyzers for LAN help desk (for use by analysts and installers).
   - Unsophisticated modeling tools for LAN designers and planners.
4. LAN segments and LAN interconnecting devices provide raw data for both WAN and LAN management.
5. Basic LAN services include spreadsheet applications, E-mail, printing, and connections to other LAN segments or to mainframes.

Table 7-2. Allocation of LAN Management Functions to Human Resources

LAN Management Functions	Organization					
	LM	DS	LI	HD	AD	AN
Configuration management						
• Inventory control			x		x	
• Configuration control	x	x	x	x	x	x
• Naming and addressing			x			x
• Change control			x		x	
• Cabling control			x		x	
• Directory services	x					x
Fault management						
• Status supervision				x		
• Fault detection and alarming				x		
• Diagnosis and testing						x
• Isolation and correction						x
• Trouble ticketing				x	x	
• Help-desk support				x	x	
Performance management						
• Defining performance indicators						x
• Performance monitoring						x
• Traffic analysis	x	x				x
• Network modeling		x				x
• Network optimization						x
Security management						
• Defining security indicators	x	x			x	
• Access authorization					x	
• Password administration					x	
• Ensuring hardware/software integrity					x	
• Ensuring data integrity					x	
• Warnings and alarms about violations				x		
Accounting management						
• Collecting resource usage statistics					x	
• Software license compliance					x	
• Billing and chargeback services					x	
Design and planning						
• Strategic planning	x	x				
• Capacity planning		x				
• Analyzing needs		x				
• Logical and physical design		x	x			
• Contingency planning	x	x				
• Installation			x			
• Testing			x			x
User administration						
• Enhancing ease of use	x					x
• Maintenance of user data					x	
• Help to users					x	
• Training						x

Table 7-3. Allocation of Typical
Instruments to LAN Management Groups

Instrument Types	Organization					
	LM	DS	LI	HD	AD	AN
Databases	x	x	x		x	x
Document managers			x		x	
Configuration trailing products			x		x	
Document and file organizers			x		x	
Management information base	x	x			x	x
User tracking products				x	x	
Audit trail utilities	x				x	x
Virus safeguards					x	
Disk usage utilities		x			x	x
Protocol analyzers				x		x
Network monitors		x		x		x
NOS monitors		x		x		x
Time domain reflectometers				x		x
Software diagnostic tools			x	x		x
Ohmmeters			x	x		
Outlet testers			x	x		
Terminator testers			x	x		
Oscilloscopes			x	x		
Power meters			x	x		
Optical bandwidth testers			x	x		
Network usage meters		x			x	x
Traffic monitors	x	x			x	x
Emulators		x				x
Simulators		x				x
Access surveillance tools	x				x	x
Backup utilities				x	x	
Remote end-user support tools				x	x	
Help-desk utilities				x		
Front-end utilities				x		
Console emulation tools	x			x		x
Trouble ticketing systems	x	x	x	x	x	x
Modeling devices		x				x
LAN management systems	x	x	x	x	x	x

LM   LAN manager
DS   LAN designer and planner
LI   LAN installer
HD   LAN help-desk operator
AD   LAN administrator
AN   LAN analyst

Table 7-4. Quantification of Human Resources Needs

LANs	Standalone		Networked	
Number of segments	30 segments	30 segments	30 segments	30 segments
Server to stations	1/30	2/70	1/30	2/70
Supervisor	1	1	1	1
Operations				
LAN help-desk operator	2	2	2	3
LAN administrator	1	2	2	3
LAN analyst	1	1	1	2
Design, planning, and installation				
LAN designer and planner	1	2	1	2
LAN installer (*)	1	3	2	4
Total demand	7	11	9	15

(*) not a continuous activity

TABLES 7-5 to 7-10 summarize the human resources profiles for each LAN management organizational unit, including the manager of the group. Each profile includes a job description, responsibilities, interfaces, qualifying experiences, training requirements, and compensation ranges.

The process of creating or expanding the LAN management staff is complicated by a number of factors. Here are the most important ones: scarce technical resources, no standard job descriptions and responsibilities, few specific academic training programs, rapidly changing LAN technology, short career paths, and few upward mobility alternatives.

These factors complicate the hiring process by making it very difficult to write job descriptions and analyze candidates' background materials. The following is a list of recommended criteria when hiring LAN management staff.

Identify team members.   TABLE 7-1 gave an overview on functions to be supported for managing LANs. Depending on the size of LANs, the human resources demand may be computed (TABLE 7-4). After subtracting the available staff from the total demand for each activity, the demand on new hires can be quantified.

Recruit candidates.   Advertisements, conferences, headhunters and individual contacts to colleges, universities, and other companies help to find candidates to be interviewed.

Establish interview criteria.   Guidelines and evaluation criteria have to be set prior to starting the interviews. In order to keep investment for both

Table 7-5. Profile of a LAN Network Manager

Job description: Allocation and coordination of work in the area of LAN design, planning, installation, and operations.

Responsibilities:

1. Allocates work to staff.
2. Coordinates work among staff members.
3. Resolves problems between staff members.
4. Selects instruments.
5. Oversees all functions.
6. Works out processes and procedures.
7. Reviews staff performance.
8. Assists in evaluating LAN performance.
9. Supervises planning and change management.
10. Sets priorities for work orders.
11. Schedules installation work.
12. Consults on which applications may be ported to LANs.
13. Provision vision.
14. Provides overall architectures for LAN management.

Interfaces:

1. Network manager.
2. LAN designers and planners.
3. Users.
4. Vendors.
5. Group leaders.

Qualifying experiences:

1. Some know-how of LAN applications, servers, workstations, LAN media, and internetworking alternatives.
2. Communication and negotiation skills.
3. Some know-how of LAN management tools.
4. Decision-making skills.
5. Project management experiences.
6. People management skills.
7. The person is expected to have a degree (B.S. or B.A.).

Training:

1. Continuing education toward a B.S. in business administration.
2. Overview courses on LAN technology.
3. Overview courses on LAN instrumentation.

Compensation: $45 – $55 K.

parties low, written applications must be filtered carefully. Occasional phone conversations may fill existing gaps. Invitations to personal interviews should be sent out to candidates whose applications are matching the expectations.

Hire properly qualified candidates. Hiring has to be for mutual benefits, and not just to fill the job. Future turnover can be avoided this way.

Table 7-6. Profile of a LAN Designer and Planner

Job description: Technically oriented activities resulting in an optimal LAN configuration within reasonable budgetary limits.

Responsibilities:
1. Reviews user needs.
2. Quantifies user needs.
3. Evaluates current LAN utilization.
4. Evaluates technology.
5. Conducts LAN design.
6. Sizes principal LAN resources.
7. Models LANs, and evaluates modeling results.
8. Writes specifications and operational manuals.
9. Helps in selecting LAN instruments.
10. Presents funding to management in a clearly understandable manner.

Interfaces:
1. LAN network manager.
2. Users.
3. Vendors.
4. LAN analysts.
5. Other designers and planners from the WAN area.

Qualifying experiences:
1. Detailed knowledge of LAN applications.
2. Detailed knowledge of LAN components, such as servers, workstations, media, access methods, protocols, interconnecting devices, and interconnecting networking alternatives.
3. Some background in statistics.
4. Communication skills.
5. Patience in pursuing planning projects.
6. This person is expected to have a degree (B.S. or B.A.).

Training:
1. Continuing education toward a B.S. or M.S.
2. In-depth courses on technology.
3. In-depth courses on LAN modeling.
4. Overview courses on LAN instrumentation.

Compensation: $40 – $50 K.

Assign and/or reassign responsibilities. Static job descriptions should serve as a guideline, only. Within this framework, more dynamic descriptions with rotation in mind are necessary.

Institute performance evaluations. Periodic reviews are most widely used. If possible, upward performance appraisals should be agreed upon as early as possible in the team-building phase.

Promote openness and handle complaints. In order to emphasize team spirit, opinions, even complaints must be encouraged on behalf of

Table 7-7. Profile of a LAN Installer

Job description: Based on accurate specifications, installation of LAN segments, inter-connected WANs, and LAN management instruments.

Responsibilities:
1. Tests LAN components prior to installation.
2. Installs LANs.
3. Conducts integration tests.
4. Maintains and coordinates subcontractors and their data.
5. Assists in problem determination.
6. Activates and deactivates LAN segments.
7. Customizes LAN test instruments.
8. Interprets and reviews LAN configuration documentation.
9. Conducts stress tests.
10. Assists in writing troubleshooting checklists for LAN help-desk operators.
11. Maintains LAN database.

Interfaces:
1. Vendors.
2. Suppliers.
3. Users.
4. LAN designers and planners.

Qualifying experiences:
1. Detailed knowledge of LAN components to be installed.
2. Knowledge of LAN software.
3. Detailed knowledge of LAN media, their testing, and their measurement.
4. Detailed knowledge of test instruments.

Training:
1. Continuing education toward an engineering degree.
2. In-depth briefings on new LAN hardware and WAN media.
3. Updates on LAN test instruments.

Compensation: $30 – $40 K.

LAN management supervisors. The employees must have the feeling that their comments and suggestions are handled at the earliest convenience of managers.

Resolve personnel problems quickly. In order to avoid tensions within the LAN management organization, problems must be resolved for mutual benefits as quickly as possible. The reward system must provide opportunities to do so. More often, visibility of how the reward system works resolves problems almost automatically.

Institute systematic training and development programs. Systematic education should include training for LAN management functions, LAN management instruments, and for personal skills. A curriculum in coordination with vendors and educational institutes would guarantee high quality and employee satisfaction.

Table 7-8. Profile of a LAN Help-Desk Operator

Job description: Accepting and prediagnosing user calls and monitored events in order to properly solve problems.

Responsibilities:

1. Supervises LAN operations.
2. Registers troubles identified by users and monitors.
3. Opens trouble tickets.
4. Implements procedures for "tier one" problem determination.
5. Invokes corrections.
6. Solves problems, depending on priorities, to central network management center or to peer help desks.
7. Communicates with users.
8. Communicates with vendors.
9. Activates and deactivates local area networks.
10. Generates reports on network problems.
11. Closes trouble tickets.
12. Reviews documentation of change management.
13. Sets priorities for problem diagnosis.
14. Registers security management problems.

Interfaces:

1. Users.
2. Vendors.
3. Central help-desk operators.
4. LAN administrators.
5. LAN analysts.
6. LAN installers.

Qualifying experiences:

1. Some knowledge of applications, servers, and workstations.
2. Very good communication skills.
3. Background in dealing with trouble-ticketing systems.
4. At least one year's experience with LANs.
5. Know-how of instruments that help monitor LAN status and performance.
6. Experience judging what problems need escalation.
7. Negotiation skills.
8. Some knowledge about how to execute changes.
9. Experience handling powerful workstations.

Training:

1. Continuing education toward a college degree.
2. In-depth courses on LAN instrumentation.
3. Course on interpersonal communication skills.

Compensation: $25 – $35 K.

Regularly interface LAN management staff with LAN users.
In order to promote mutual understanding of working conditions and problems, both parties should exchange views and opinions. The level of formality may vary from very informal to very formal; in the second case, written service-level agreements are evaluated.

Table 7-9. Profile of a LAN Administrator

Job description: An administration-oriented specialist that combines clerical and project control capabilities.

Responsibilities:
1. Administers LAN configuration, including logical, electrical, and physical attributes.
2. Maintains LAN database.
3. Maintains vendor data.
4. Coordinates planning and executing changes.
5. Administers names and addresses.
6. Defines and supervises authorizations.
7. Maintains trouble tickets and trouble files.
8. Coordinates complex problem solving.
9. Helps to establish powerful security policy.
10. Organizes data export and import with central database.

Interfaces:
1. LAN help-desk operators.
2. Users.
3. Vendors.
4. LAN analysts.
5. LAN installers.

Qualifying experiences:
1. Know-how of applications, servers, workstations, cables, and internetworking devices.
2. Experience with inventory management.
3. Some experience with project management.
4. Some communications skills.
5. Detailed knowledge of database or file management systems in use.
6. Experience handling powerful workstations.

Training:
1. Continuing education toward a B.S. in business administration.
2. In-depth courses in the area of inventory management.
3. Project management courses.

Compensation: $30 – $40 K.

Evaluate new technologies. As part of the motivation process, LAN management renovation opportunities must be evaluated continuously. This process includes new management platforms, new technologies of LAN processing and internetworking, feasibility of new and existing solutions, new monitors, change in supporting *de facto* and open standards, simplification of management processes, changes in the offerings of leading manufacturers, and monitoring the needs of LAN users. Thus, enrichment of lower-level jobs may easily be accomplished.

Table 7-10. Profile of a LAN Analyst

Job description: A technically-oriented specialist to measure, interpret, analyze, and optimize LAN performance.

Responsibilities:

1. Conducts LAN tuning studies.
2. Executes specific LAN measurements.
3. Designs and executes performance and functionality tests.
4. Defines performance indicators.
5. Selects LAN management instruments.
6. Surveys performance needs of LAN users.
7. Maintains the LAN performance database.
8. Generates reports.
9. Maintains the LAN baseline models.
10. Sizes LAN resources.
11. Customizes LAN instruments.
12. Analyzes work load and utilization trends.
13. Prepares checklists and processes for LAN help desk.
14. Helps install LAN management instruments.
15. Specifies and documents LAN configurations.

Interfaces:

1. Vendors.
2. Users.
3. LAN designers and planners.
4. LAN administrators.
5. LAN help-desk operators.
6. Other companies.

Qualifying experiences:

1. Detailed knowledge of media, protocols, access methods, servers, bridges, brouters, routers, gateways, wiring hubs, interconnecting alternatives, and LAN network operating systems.
2. Detailed knowledge of LAN measurement, and management instruments.
3. Some know-how of LAN modeling instruments.
4. Communication skills.
5. Some experience with project management.

Training:

1. Continuing education toward a B.S. degree.
2. In-depth briefings on new technology.
3. Updates on LAN management instruments.

Compensation: $40 – $50 K.

In order to keep the LAN management team together, expectations of employers and employees must match to a certain degree. TABLE 7-11 shows a sample of expectations on both sides. The individual-organization contract is termed psychological because much of it is often unwritten and unspoken.

Table 7-11. Expectations in the Employer/Employee Contract

Expectations of the Individual	Expectations of the Employer
1. Compensation	1. An honest day's work
2. Personal development opportunities	2. Loyalty to organization
3. Recognition and approval for good work	3. Initiative
4. Security through fringe benefits	4. Conformity to organizational norms
5. Friendly, supportive environment	5. Job effectiveness
6. Fair treatment	6. Flexibility and willingness to learn and develop
7. Meaningful or purposeful job	7. No security violations

There are several reasons why this may be so:

- Both parties may not be entirely clear about their expectations and how they wish them to be met. They may not want to define the contract until they have a better feel for what they want.
- Neither of the parties are aware of their expectations. For example, organizations are hardly able to define loyalty.
- Some expectations may be perceived as so natural and basic that they're taken for granted, e.g., expectations of not stealing and an honest day's work for a day's pay.
- Cultural norms may inhibit verbalization.

At a given time, there will be some relatively fulfilled and unfulfilled expectations; however, each party has to have a minimum acceptance level of fulfillment. If either party concludes that the fulfillment of its needs is below this minimum level, it will view the contract as having been violated.

Turnover in LAN management can be very disadvantageous for maintaining service levels to end users. Corporate and business units management should try to avoid overaverage turnover by implementing rewards to satisfy employees. Gaining satisfaction with the rewards given is not a simple matter. It's a function of several factors that organizations must learn to manage.

The individual's satisfaction with rewards is, in part, related to what's expected and how much is received. Feelings of satisfaction or dissatisfaction arise when individuals compare their input (knowledge, skills, experience) to output (mix of rewards) they receive.

Employee satisfaction is also affected by comparisons with other people in similar jobs and organizations. People vary considerably in how they weight various inputs and outputs in that comparison. They tend to weigh their strong points more heavily, such as certain skills or a recent performance peak. Individuals also tend to correlate their own performance compared with the rating they receive from their supervisors. The problem of unrealistic self-ratings exists partly because supervisors in most organizations don't communicate a candid evaluation of their subordinates' performance to them.

Employees often misperceive the rewards of others; their misperception can cause the employees to become dissatisfied. Evidence shows that individuals tend to overestimate the pay of colleagues doing similar jobs and to underestimate their colleagues' performance.

Finally, overall satisfaction results from a mix of rewards rather than from any single reward. The evidence suggests that intrinsic rewards and extrinsic rewards are both important, and that they can't be directly substituted for each other.

Rewards mean motivation. To be useful, rewards must be tied as timely as possible to effective performance. Success factors of motivation are: employees must believe in effective performance; employees must feel that the rewards offered are attractive; employees must believe that a certain level of individual effort will lead to achieving the corporation's standards of performance.

Rewards fall into two principal categories: extrinsic and intrinsic. Extrinsic rewards come from the employer as compensation, benefits, job security, training, promotions, effective LAN management instruments, and recognition. Intrinsic rewards come from performing the task itself, and may include job satisfaction, sense of influence, quality of environment, and quality of assignment. The priority of extrinsic and intrinsic rewards depends on the individual person. The following list tries to give a frequently seen priority sequence.

Compensation   Payment is still the most important motivation factor. Organizations try to use a number of person-based or skill-based compensation techniques combined with the dependence of sales revenues of the larger organization, if applicable. Pay is a matter of perception and values that often generates conflict.

Benefits   Benefits take special forms, depending on the employer's business; e.g., company car, life insurance, lower interest rates, housing. The cost of benefits at companies can be as high as 30-40 % of pay dollars.

Job security   Seniority with job assignments is a very valuable management practice, in particular, when the economy is stressed. Job security policies include retirement plans, options for early retirement, and agreements of nonlayoff. Job security packages are more advanced in Europe and Japan than in the United States.

Recognition   Recognition may come from the organization or from fellow employees. The periodic form of recognition is the performance appraisal conducted by the supervisor. A relatively new form, the so-called upward appraisal is considered a form of recognition. It's difficult because most managers don't want to be evaluated by their subordinates. For the subordinates, it's a forum to articulate ideas for improvement.

Career path and creation of dual ladders   In order to keep motivation high, managerial and technical assignments must be compensated equally. Promoting technically interested persons into managerial positions may not have the desired results; these persons are usually high in affiliation motivation and low in power motivation. Helpful activities include career counseling and exploration, increased company career opportunity information, improving career feedback, enhancing linear career, slower early-career advancement, and enrichment of lower-level jobs with more challenges.

Effective training   This type of motivation helps to keep the specific and generic knowledge of the employees at the most advanced level. Three to six weeks of training and education per annum is considered adequate in the dynamically changing LAN management environment.

Quality of assignments   Job descriptions are expected to give the framework for expectations. But, dynamic job descriptions may help to avoid monotony and promote job rotation. The help desk, LAN administration, and LAN analysis may be rotated periodically.

Use of adequate tools   Better instrumented LAN environments facilitate the jobs of the LAN staff, increase the service quality to LAN users, and improve the image of the LAN management organization. At the same time, persons working with advanced tools are proud of their special knowledge, and of their employer. They're highly motivated to continue with the company.

Realistic performance goals   As part of dynamic job descriptions and job rotation, realistic performance expectations may help to stabilize the position of the LAN management team. Management must find the balance between quantifiable and nonquantifiable goals. Average time spent on trouble calls, response time to problems, time of repair, and end-user satisfaction/dissatisfaction are examples for both types of goals.

Quality of environment   This is more or less a generic term expressing the mix of LAN-related instruments, pleasant working atmosphere, comfortable furniture, adequate legroom, easy access to filing cabinets or to hypermedia, acceptance of opinions on shortcomings, and team spirit.

Employee control   Despite high team spirit, individuals need certain levels of control that can only be determined by managerial skills. Depending on the person, use positive or negative motivation, or a combination of both.

The preceding list has tried to concentrate on key motivation alternatives, only. There are many more. In order to find the optimal combination for individual LAN installations, a human resources management audit is recommended.

When considering outsourcing LAN management, customers are investigating the feasibility of farming out LAN management functions. Before deciding for or against outsourcing, the following criteria should be evaluated very carefully (Terplan 1991):

1. In the first step, present costs of LAN management equipment, communications, and people have to be quantified.
2. Full analysis of all existing processes, instruments, and human resources in order to decide which functions may be considered appropriate for outsourcing. Considering outsourcing is a good excuse for

auditing present operations and addressing areas that need improvement. The result of considering outsourcing may be insourcing. Analysis by internal or external analysts may result in substantial savings in operating expenses (30% to 40%), in staff reduction (25% to 50%), and in a network budget's stabilization.

3. Determination of the company's dependence on network availability, indicating highest levels by critical LAN applications. The company should include the key indicators into the service contract; many times, vendors will fall short from the very beginning, not being able to guarantee the target availability levels.

4. Determination of the service grade required by users and applications. Perhaps the outsourcing company should even be solely dedicated to the user company, and not share its resources among multiple clients.

5. Security standards and risk levels may prohibit a company from allowing third-party vendors to gain access to the network and to its carried traffic.

6. Because the business may need to concentrate its main energy and resources on its own business, it may simply not be a practical priority to it to build a sophisticated LAN management system and organization.

7. Availability of LAN management instruments may facilitate the decision. If the company had to invest substantial amounts into instrumentation, outsourcing should be favored; if not, outsourcing may still be considered, but with a lower priority.

8. Availability of skilled LAN management personnel is one of the most critical issues; most frequently, it's the only driving factor for outsourcing. Not only the present status, but the satisfaction of future needs has to be quantified prior to the outsourcing decision.

9. Stability of environment and growth rates has serious impacts on the contract with the vendor. Acquisitions, mergers, business unit sales, and application portfolio changes need special and careful treatment in vendor contracts.

10. Consideration of the intention to offer value-added services to other third parties needs to be made. In certain corporations, the underused bandwidth of communication resources may be used for offering "low-priority" services to third parties who can't afford to build a network on their own (e.g., point-of-sale applications).

11. The ability to construct good outsourcing contracts is one of the key issues. The length of outsourcing contracts—often seven to ten years—means that the wording of the contract is extremely important. Adequate legal support is required from the very beginning.

12. Consideration of the philosophy of a company's LAN management approach, including consideration of whether to use horizontal or vertical integration, centralization, automation and/or the use of a network management repository, should be in concert with the offer and capabilities of the outsourcer.

The final decision of the right outsourcing partner depends on the networking environment and the budget for third-party network management. Summarizing the expectations, outsourcers are expected to meet the following requirements:

- Financial strength and stability over a long period of time.
- Proven experience in managing domestic and multinational networks.
- Availability of a powerful pool of skilled personnel.
- Tailored LAN management instruments that may be used exclusively for one client or shared between multiple clients.
- Proven ability of implementing the most advanced technology.
- Outstanding reputation in conducting business.
- Willingness for revenue sharing.
- Fair employee transfers.

The user community is still divided. There are strong opinions against outsourcing LAN management. Frequently used arguments are: LAN management can easily be handled by in-house staff; outsourcing involves losing control to "unknown" third parties; problems can be solved cheaper in house; business is better known by in-house staff; in-house staff is more responsible and more easily motivated. It seems likely that LAN maintenance functions will be farmed out at first. In summary, it's many times easier to build than to keep the LAN management team.

8
Future trends
for managing LANs

Local area networks and interconnected local area networks are becoming mission critical to many corporations, who need to: provide the end user with computing power, supply bandwidth for integrating communication forms and databases, support better service levels, decrease risks due to fatal outages of focal point resources, and speed up application design cycles.

LAN technology shows a number of dynamic changes. In terms of expectations, keep attuned to the following developments: Ethernet technology will stay, but market share is expected to dip, and use of token ring and token bus technologies will rise to share more equally in the market; fast LANs and MANs will penetrate the market rapidly; in terms of media, twisted-pair may penetrate new areas when radiation reduction techniques are more effective; wiring hubs will take on the responsibility for being the local management entity, incorporating both physical and logical management; wireless LANs will be used for certain environments and applications, particularly as a backup alternative, but they will remain limited, and a major breakthrough is not expected soon; due to higher flexibility, routers and brouters will take implementation away from bridges, particularly in complex and geographically widespread environments; with bridges, the spanning tree technique or its enhanced versions will most likely be preferred to source routing algorithms. However, new source routing algorithms seem to be more efficient and may delay this process; interconnecting devices will house multiple functions, integrating the capabilities of a multiplexer, router, packet switch, and eventually of a matrix switch; from the management point of view, these devices will offer a multifunctional, integrated element management system, representing attributes of distributed element management; interconnecting LANs technology will show a number of alternatives; fast packet (frame and cell relay), SMDS, B-ISDN and T1/T3 services seem to be the most popular ones.

LAN management has always been concerned with minimizing costs and improving operator efficiency. Various factors will make these goals more challenging in the near future (Swanson 1991):

- Growth of LANs. Enterprise networks continue to expand, both domestically and internationally. In particular, the number of interconnected LANs will grow substantially. In the LAN management control center, this growth adds to the volume of status and alarm data that an operator must monitor and analyze. LAN instrumentation must allow operators to easily and comprehensively monitor the large interconnected LANs, determine the troubles, and rapidly focus on a magnified portion of the network. At the highest level of monitoring, a several-hundred-segments network must be reduced to a graphic display with well-designed icons and symbols for key network elements.
- Continuous operations. Most enterprise networks will operate continuously, around the clock. The challenge for network management system vendors is to maintain operators' attention, and focus their activities on the most relevant actions in emergencies.
- Automation. LAN management systems must begin to automate routine functions by improving their capabilities for automated decision making. Thus, LAN administrators can focus on traffic analysis, trend analysis, and planning.
- Multimedia and multivendor networks. Proprietary designs, separate workstations, dissimilar operator interfaces, and unique command structures can prevent LAN operators from becoming experienced users in all LAN management products they operate.
- High cost of reactive LAN management. The majority of monitors and management systems support reactive techniques instead of proactive ones. Instruments are not yet powerful enough to perform realtime trend analysis on parallel, seemingly unrelated information streams.

The success of LANs and interconnected LAN management will depend on three critical success factors; a well-organized set of LAN management functions, allocated and assigned to instruments and to human skill levels; proper instrumentation, with the ability to extract integrated information, to export and import it, to maintain databases, and to provide analysis and performance prediction; personnel who understand their job responsibilities and possess the necessary qualifying skills.

Over a long period of time, it will remain valid to expand LAN management processes to include configuration, fault, performance, security, accounting management, and LAN design and capacity planning concerns. Naturally, functions will be constantly added and deleted, depending on actual user needs. However, a core with standard functions and features will remain.

Figure 8-1 shows the various layers of a generic LAN management architecture on the example of OSF/DME. The key is how applications are going to be developed and implemented for the six principal LAN management functional areas. The following trends are very likely.

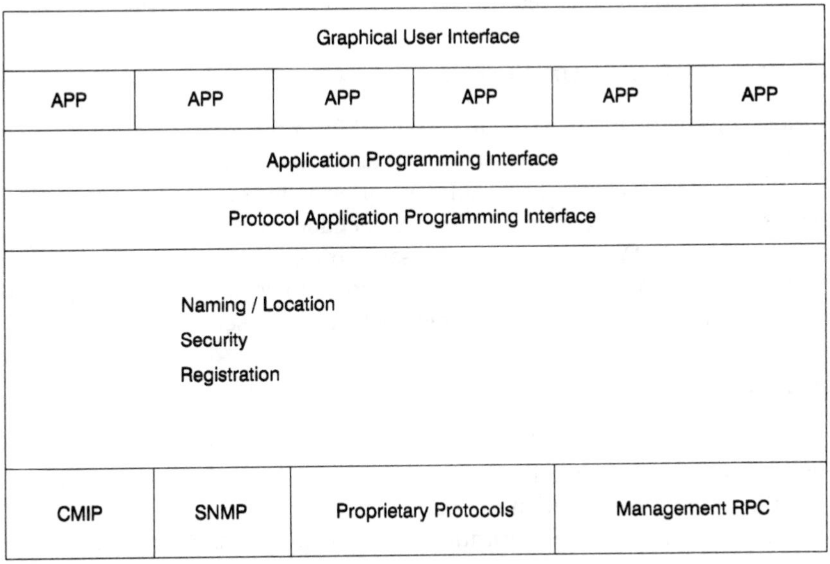

Graphical User Interface					
APP	APP	APP	APP	APP	APP
Application Programming Interface					
Protocol Application Programming Interface					
Naming / Location Security Registration					
CMIP	SNMP	Proprietary Protocols		Management RPC	

Fig. 8-1. Simplified architecture of DME.

Configuration management

Recommendations for managed objects and their must-and-can attributes will be widely accepted by users. They will slowly convert existing fragmented files and databases into a more integrated structure. More graphics are expected for supporting inventory and configuration management by a meaningful combination of a relational database and computer aided design. However, the migration to a relational database may be delayed due to the fact of existing products that serve certain architectures in the wide area; examples are Info/System, Info/Master, PNMS, and Netman in the IBM environment. More integrity is expected between configuration and fault management via auto-configuration features that will be offered by various vendors.

Fault management

In order to accelerate problem determination and diagnosis, new trouble-ticketing applications are expected. They will provide the flexibility of entering, exporting and importing trouble tickets, using advanced electronic mail features. The same systems will simplify the trouble-ownership question.

More automation is expected, where examples from mainframes will show the directions; NetView with REXX extensions or Net/Master with NCL applications will embed LAN automation procedures into existing WAN-automation solutions. Existing and new monitors will be equipped with polling and eventing features, or with a combination of both. Fine-tuning polling and eventing will help to reduce the overhead in communications channels.

Performance management

Performance data are expected to be ported from the MIBs of LAN management stations into existing performance databases, such as SLR, SAS, and MICS. For a more comprehensive LAN performance evaluation, more help is expected from LAN operating systems; vendors will offer alternatives—in most cases via NetView—but not necessarily by external and internal monitoring capabilities. Performance evaluation is going to be made easier by continuous and distributed monitoring in practically all LAN segments.

Security management

Security management in LANs will definitively get a face-lift; there will simply be too many mission-critical applications on LANs. Companies will try to find the optimal combination of organizational, physical, and logical protection; authentication and authorization are becoming equally important. Within a short period of time, a breakthrough is expected with using biometrics as the basis of authentication. Virus detection and removal will remain very high on the priority list.

Accounting management

Accounting management will receive higher priority treatment due to the high cost of interconnecting LAN segments. In addition, as a preparation for evaluating outsourcing, LAN managers will try to estimate the costs of LAN ownership.

User administration

User administration is expected to receive more attention and more utilities to simplify the use of LANs. But, most of the features will incorporate some sort of authentication check in order to avoid security violations. More advanced tools are expected for the help desk, as well.

When expanding and redesigning processes, several innovative design principles must be considered: (Herman 1991)

- Information sharing. Information must be made available to anyone who can effectively use it to perform their work. Sharing captured knowledge will avoid having to rediscover problems and changes.

- Responsibility of individuals. The responsibility for the quality of process execution should lie with a single individual. That person should also be responsible for the integrity of the data they create or update. This way, additional integrity checks may be eliminated.
- Simplification. Processes should be performed in as simple a fashion as possible, eliminating all steps that don't clearly add value.
- Stratification. After defining levels of process complexity, the lowest level is the primary target for automation. In future steps, process experiences have to be used to derive from the highest level to the lowest possible level, and to continue automation.

LAN management standards will help in accelerating the implementation of functions and in selecting future proof instruments. Specific management application areas that are supported by system management functions and by common management information service elements (CMIP) have been clearly defined by ISO groups. Their implementation in LANs, however, depends on how *de facto* standards perform. OSI network management may include LAN management, but the estimated overhead scares both vendors and users away. Similar definitions for the management dialog have been provided for the TCP/IP environment (SNMP). Users have turned to SNMP, and hope to have found a common denominator for at least a number of years. For standardizing the manager-agent dialog, the following three items have to be carefully considered (Herman 1991).

How will the management information be formatted and how will the information exchange be regulated? This is actually the protocol definition problem. How will the management information be transported between manager and agent? The OSI standards are using OSI protocol stack, and the TCP/IP standards use TCP/IP protocol stack. In both cases, the management protocol is defined as an application-layer protocol that uses the underlying transport services of the protocol stack. What management information will be exchanged? The collection of management data definitions that a manager or agent knows about is called the management information base. MIBs have to be known to both.

In terms of SNMP, the following trends are expected. SNMP agent-level support will be provided by the greatest number of vendors. This support is coming very soon. SNMP manager-level support will be provided by some vendors who most likely will implement on a well-accepted platform, leaving customization and the development of additional applications to vendors and users. Leading manufacturers with network management integrator products such as NetView, Net/Master, Accumaster, DECmcc, and OpenView will enable vendors to link their SNMP managers to the integrators. Competition for SNMP manager products and platforms will be significant over the next few years. The MIB private areas are expected to move slowly to the public area and support heterogeneous LAN management on an SNMP basis. The RMON MIB will bridge the gap between the functionality of LAN manage-

ment systems and analyzers with rich functionality. It defines the next generation of network monitoring with more comprehensive network fault diagnosis,
planning, and performance tuning features than any current monitoring solution. It uses SNMP and its standard MIB design to provide multivendor interoperability between monitoring products and management stations, allowing
users to mix and match network monitors and management stations from different vendors.

The number of SNMP-based managers and objects is increasing. It's not
easy to decide which product is best suited to the customers environment. To
help to select, the following items will become important. What LAN management functions are supported by the agents and manager(s)? What security
features are supported? What non-LAN objects and services can be managed.
What platforms are supported. Is the product helpful for determining any
LAN troubles? Is the product able to determine whether the managed object is
operating at its potential? Is the product helpful in assessing whether the LAN
is operating at its best performance capabilities?

Figure 8-2 illustrates migration alternatives for everyone using proprietary
architectures. There are two ways: migration to an open standard, and migration to a *de facto* standard first, then migration to an open standard. At this
point in time, the second alternative is preferred by the majority of vendors
and users.

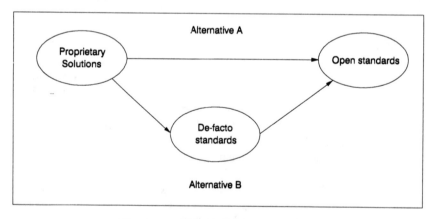

Fig. 8-2. Migration to open standards.

As more LAN management application software gets written, it's important to define standardized APIs so that the software can be easily ported to
different platforms, and so that software developed by different vendors can be
easily combined on a single platform. The platforms provide a standardized
environment for developing and implementing applications, and they also separate management application software from the usual system-level services.
Users and vendors do not have to deal with the details of protocols, data definitions, user interfaces, and presentation services.

On the basis of platforms, it's expected that independent companies will offer network and system management applications designed to provide real multivendor solutions while taking advantage of the system-level services of platforms. This way, vendors can concentrate on their specific hardware and software, and users can focus on the customization and fine-tuning of LAN management applications.

In order to provide supervision of LAN segments, there will be more continuous monitoring supported by inexpensive sensors residing in each segment. At least at the beginning, they will communicate with their master monitor using proprietary protocols. In such environments, both eventing and polling structures and inband and outband transmission options may be implemented. In addition to fault management, structures may also support performance management by distributing analysis capabilities to remote sites. In order to maximize the uptime of LAN segments, outband channels are preferred as carriers of LAN management information. Depending on budget limits, outband channels may be dedicated or switched. Figure 8-3 shows a typical example for outband LAN management. Not only the independence from communication facilities can be guaranteed, but also the power supply for the sensor is supplied to the sensor residing in the managed object. Health-check recording doesn't stop when the managed object breaks down.

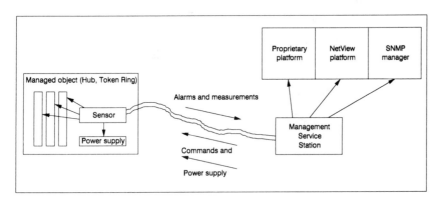

Fig. 8-3. Outband LAN management.

Monitoring devices may become part of network management structures. These devices expand the capability of managed objects to provide status and performance indicators. The structures of the future may follow one of the following three basic alternatives:

- LAN Integrator. Hierarchical LAN management structure with a network management service station in the middle. This station supervises all the managed objects through polling and eventing techniques. A typical example is an arrangement of an SNMP manager and SNMP agents. A LAN-specific example includes the central manager of Cabletron with the product Spectrum.

- Manager of the managers. Hierarchical LAN management structure with a network management service station in the middle. This station supervises LAN element management systems that are responsible for managing a family of managed objects, such as hubs, segments, routers and bridges. In this case, investment in an installed base can be preserved. The interfaces are well defined, but the number of managers will probably not be reduced. Typical examples are NetView, Accumaster-Integrator, Net/Master and Allink. A LAN-specific example is from SynOptics using the network control engine as an element manager for reducing the SNMP message volume and polling overhead.

- Management platform. In this case, system services and clearly defined application programming interfaces are provided by the suppliers, enabling other vendors to develop, implement, and port applications. Typical examples are: DEC—EMA, HP—OpenView, Network Managers—NMC 3000, NetLabs—DualManager, Sun—SunNet, and OSI—NetExpert. Most of the companies are not eager to offer products for the element management system level. The main goal is to offer integration capabilities.

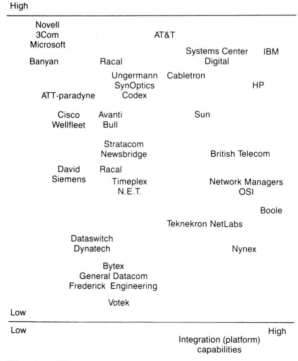

Fig. 8-4. Element management and integrator capabilities of leading manufacturers.

Figure 8-4 displays the position of leading companies in a two-dimensional table. It investigates the capabilities of various vendors to offer element management and integration capabilities. Due to the dynamic nature of the industry, this table needs frequent updates. Completely new technologies for supporting various LAN management functions are likely. Examples may include: hypermedia and hypertext for the help desk, training, and problem sectionalization and design; voice annotation of trouble tickets and voice messaging; optical storage for documentation and raw LAN analyzer data; storage of graphical images for assisting trouble storage at remote/local LAN help desks; intelligent user interfaces with flexible customization features; and expert systems for fault isolation and diagnosis.

In the future, progress is expected in the following areas: (Swanson 1991)

- Graphical user interfaces. Progress has been made with various tools, including X-Windows (low-level window manager running on Unix), OpenLook (high-level graphic toolkit from Sun), Motif (high-level graphic toolkit from DEC and HP), and GMS (Graphics Modeling Systems for providing graphics routines for all the others). As a result, GUIs can draw complex network diagrams that allow an operator to view the status of hundreds of network nodes and elements simultaneously. Within a short period of time, operators can focus on particular managed objects. In addition, the animation of icons, along with digital speech processing, can attract an operator's attention to a problem.
- Expert systems and neural networks. In order to support proactive LAN management, many measurements have to be taken at different points in the LAN segments and at interconnecting devices. These measurement results must be correlated and analyzed in realtime. Figure 8-5 shows the combination of both tools. The neural network is a

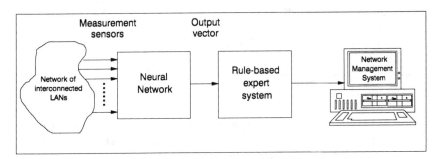

Fig. 8-5. Combination of neural networks and expert systems.

fundamentally new form of computer processor to collect and correlate high volumes of measurement data and to provide appropriate input to the rule-based expert system. Unlike traditional processors, neural networks are trained to recognize patterns by running simple data through them. They can also process many inputs simultaneously. In managing local area networks, neural networks can correlate multiple measurement data streams against preprogrammed measurement data ranges that will cause network faults unless corrected proactively. The output from the neural networks is then used by the rule-based expert system to select a corrective action.

- Distributed element management. Managed objects are equipped with enough processing power to manage their own environment, to self-diagnose, and to initiate status reports to the network management center. This trend supports the implementation of robust OSI-based network management standards in the future.
- Database technology. LANs are expected to be modelled as objects. Objects interact by sending messages between each other. The called object (e.g., any network element) executes the processes prescribed in the message against its attributes (configuration data and status), and reports the results back to the calling object (e.g., network management station). Object-oriented databases are supporting this type of dialogue with high efficiency. For some applications, they offer considerably better performance than relational databases.

The distribution of human responsibilities will follow the same path as the functions of LAN management. Depending on the size of LAN segments, and their interconnection, staffing will vary greatly. In terms of LAN management teams, two subjects have to be remembered: building the team, and keeping the team together. These require considerable managerial skills. The LAN area supervisors will report to the LAN manager, who may also be the WAN manager, who may report to the information system manager or the chief information officer of the corporation. In a completely decentralized environment, the LAN manager most likely reports to business unit management.

LAN management directions may be summarized as follows. There will be integration of LAN-element management systems by a platform, SNMP manager, or with a manager of managers. In very complex and interconnected LANs, multiple integrators may be implemented. These integrators will use standard protocols for peer-to-peer communication.

There will be integration of LAN and WAN management, first by SNMP, then by CMIP; dual support is expected by integrators and platform providers. This step of integration will take place in multiple steps; in case of MANs and interconnected LANs, the integration speed is expected to be higher. The integration is expected to be demand driven.

Expect more centralized LAN management that will centralize control, but distribute certain functions. In particular, monitoring, filtering functions, and reactions to routine messages will be distributed to remote sites. The practical implementation may follow OSI standards or hierarchical SNMP standards.

Due to limited human resources, automation of routine LAN management functions is absolutely necessary; support is expected by providers of integrated WAN/MAN management solutions. Automation packages may migrate to expert systems that can be used offline and then online, offloading LAN management personnel from routine tasks.

There will be implementation of more powerful databases as support for the LAN management stations, which will consolidate many templates from various LAN and WAN MIBs. Object-orientation is obvious, but relational databases will not lose their importance, in particular, not for fault management.

Expect a slow move to outsource LAN management functions, if at all. The decision making will depend on the country, industry, and on the importance of LANs for critical applications. WAN network management outsourcing is expected to provide positive and negative examples.

The expenses of managing LANs and interconnected LANs will increase due to the demand for constantly improved service levels and enhanced management capabilities. The LAN management market is expected to face a serious shakeout; only products and companies with the best responses to strategic direction demands will survive.

Appendix A

Abbreviations

ACD   automated call distributor
ACSE   association control service element
ANSI   American National Standards Institute
ARP   Address Resolution Protocol
ARPA   Advanced Research Projects Agency
ARPANET ARPA computer network
AS   autonomous system (connection between IGP and EGP)
ASN.1   Abstract Syntax Notation One
ATM   association transfer mode
AUI   attachment unit interface
BHCA   busy hour call attempt
B-ISDN   Broadband ISDN
BU   business unit
CAD   computer aided design
CATV   coaxial community antenna television
CAU   controlled access unit
CCITT   *Commitee Consultatif International Telegraphique et Telephonique*
CLNP   Connectionless Network Protocol
CMIP   Common Management Information Protocol
CMISE   common management information service element
CMOL   CMIP over logical link control
CMOT   CMIP over TCP/IP
CMS   cable management system
CSMA/CD carrier sense multiple access/collision detect
CSU   channel service unit
CSV   comma separated value
CU   call Unix (remote session)
DAP   Data Access Protocol (DEC)
DARPA   ARPA of DoD
DAS   double attached station
DEE   data circuit-terminating equipment
DDN   Defense Data Network

DME	Distributed Management Environment (from OSF)
DNA	Digital Network Architecture (DEC)
DQDB	dual queue dual bus
DSA	Distributed Systems Architecture (Bull)
DSAP	destination service access point
DSU	data service unit
DTE	data terminal equipment
EDI	electronic data interchange
EGP	Exterior Gateway Protocol
EMS	element management system
ETN	electronic tandem network
FADU	file access data unit
FAT	file allocation table
FCS	frame check sum
FDDI	fiber distributed data interface
FDM	frequency division multiplexing
FIFO	first in first out
FOIRL	fiber optic inter repeater link
FOMAU	fiber optic medium attach unit
FSK	frequency shift keying
FTP	file transfer protocol
GGP	Gateway Gateway Protocol
GNMP	Government Network Management Profile
GOS	global operating system
GUI	graphical user interface
HDLC	High-level Data Link Protocol
IAB	Internet Activities Board
ICMP	Internet Control Message Protocol
IEEE	Institute of Electrical and Electronic Engineers
IETF	Internet Engineering Task Force
IGP	Internet Gateway Routing Protocol
IIVR	integrated interactive voice response
IMP	interface messages processors
IP	Internet Protocol
IPX	internet packet exchange
IS	intermediate system (ISO for IP-router)
ISDN	Integrated Services Digital Network
ISN	initial sequence number
ISO	International Organization for Standardization
LAN	local area network
LAT	Local Area Transport Protocol (DEC)
LED	light emitting device
LLC	logical link control
LM	LAN manager
LMU	LAN management utilities

LM/X	LAN manager on Unix
MAC	media access control
MAN	metropolitan area network
MAP	manufacturing automation protocol
MAU	media attachment unit or multiple access unit
MIB	management information base
MIS	management information system
MO	managed object
MTA	message transfer agent
MTBF	mean time between failures
MTOR	mean time of repair
MTTD	mean time to diagnosis
MTTR	mean time to repair
MTU	maximum transmission unit
NCB	Network Control Block (IBM—NetBIOS)
NCE	network control engine
NCP	network control program
NCL	network control language
NE	network element
NetBIOS	network basic input-output system
NFS	Network File System (Sun)
NIC	network interface card
NMF	Network Management Forum
NMM	network management module
NMP	Network Management Protocol
NMS	network management station or network management system
NMVT	network management vector transport
NOS	network operating system
NVT	network virtual terminal
OSF	Open Systems Foundation
OSI	open system interconnected
OTDR	optical time domain reflectometer
PAD	packet assembler disassembler
PBX	private branch exchange
PDU	protocol data unit
PC	personal computer
PCM	pulse code modulation
PHY	physical layer (FDDI)
PIN	personal identification number or positive intrinsic negative
PING	packet inter net grouper
PLS	physical signalling
PMD	physical medium dependent
PSM	product specific module
RFC	request for comments
RFS	Remote File System (AT&T)

RMON	Remote MONitoring standard for SNMP-MIBs
RODM	resource object data manager
ROSE	remote operating service element
RPC	remote procedure call
SAS	single attached station
SDH	synchronous digital hierarchy
SFD	start frame delimiter
SGMP	Simple Gateway Monitoring Protocol
SLIP	IP over serial lines
SMAE	systems management application entities
SMAP	specific management application protocol
SMF	systems management function
SMFA	specific management functional area
SMB	Server Message Block (IBM—NetBIOS)
SMI	structure of management information
SMDR	station message detailed recording
SMP	Station or Simple Management Protocol (FDDI)
SMTP	Simple Mail Transfer Protocol
SNA	Systems Network Architecture (IBM)
SNI	Systems Network Interconnected (IBM)
SNMP	Simple Network Management Protocol
SNP	Sub Network Protocol
SPF	shortest path first
SPX	sequenced packet exchange
SQE	Signal Quality Error (Heartbeat)
SRB	source routing bridge
SSAP	source service access point
STA	spanning tree algorithms
TB	token bus
TCP	Transmission Control Protocol
TDM	time division multiplexing
TDR	time domain reflectometer
TFTP	Trivial File Transfer Protocol
TLI	Transport Level Interface (AT&T)
TR	token ring
TTRT	target token ring rotation time
UA	user agent
UDP	User Datagram Protocol
ULP	Upper Layer Protocol
UPS	uninterrupted power supply
VNM	Virtual Network Machine
VT	virtual terminal
VTAM	Virtual Telecommunication Access Method (IBM)
WAN	wide area network
XNS	Xerox Network Services

Appendix B
Bibliography

Applied Computer Devices. Network Knowledge Tool Implementation Manual, Terre Haute, Indiana, USA, 1992.

AT&T. Premises Distribution System, Product Implementation Guide, Basking Ridge, NJ, USA, 1989.

Autrata, M. Technologies and support in the OSF/DME offering Network & Distributed Systems Management '91, Washington, D.C., September 1991.

Axner, D.H. Tools for analyzing LAN performance, *Business Communication Review*, August 1991, pp. 46 – 52.

Banyan Systems Inc. VINES System Guide, Westboro, USA, 1991.

Bapat, S. OSI Management Information Base Implementation, Integrated Network Management II, Washington, D.C., 1991.

BICC Data Networks. ISOLAN Product Guide, Westborough, USA, 1990.

BIM. Netcortex Operational Guide, Bruxelles, 1992.

Bloom, G. An End to Cable Chaos, *Telecommunications*, February, 1990.

Boell, H.P. *Lokale Netze (Local Area Networks)*, McGraw-Hill Book Company GmbH, Hamburg, Germany, 1989.

Brady, S. Management User Interfaces, IEEE Network Management and Control Workshop, Tarrytown, 1989, pp. 329 – 334.

Brigth J. The smart card: An application in search of a technology, *Telecommunications*, March, 1990, pp. 63 – 68.

Bytex Corporation. Maestro—Intelligent Switching Hub, Product Guide, Southborough, USA, 1991.

Cabletron Systems. LanceView Product Guide, Rochester, New York, USA, 1990.

Cabletron Systems. Spectrum Product Guide, Rochester, New York, USA, 1991.

CACI, Inc. SIMLAN II Local Area Network Analysis Product Guide, La Jolla, California, USA, 1990.

Carter, E.H., Dia, P.G. Evaluating Network Management Systems: Criteria and observations, Integrated Network Management II, Washington, D.C., 1991.

Case, J.D. SNMP: Making the Standards work in today's heterogenous networks, ComNet '92, Washington, D.C., 1992.

Chiong, J. UNIX can play a key role in Network Management, *Computer Technology Review*, Winter 1990, pp. 29 – 33.

Cooper, J.A. The Network Security Management. *Datapro Research Corporation*, NM20-200, Delran, N.J. 1990.

Cisco Systems. NetCentral Product Guide, Santa Clara, California, USA, 1991.

Collins, W. The reality of OSI management, *Network World*, October 9, 1989.

Comdisco Systems, Inc. BoNes Product Guide, Foster City, California, USA, 1991.

Concord Communications, Inc. Trakker LAN Monitor Product Guide, Marlborough, USA, 1991.

CrossComm Corporation. Understanding LAN Bridge and Router Performance, Technical Note, 1990, USA.

CrossComm Corporation. IMS Reference Guide, 1990, USA.

Datapro Research Corp. An Overview of Simple Network Management Protocol, NM40-300, pp. 201 – 207, Delran, USA, 1990.

_____. A look at Selected LAN Management Tools, NM50-300, pp. 701 – 708, Delran, USA, 1989.

_____. AT&T's Unified Network Management Architecture, NM40-313, pp. 101 – 114, Delran, USA, 1989.

_____. Cable Management Systems: Overview, NS60-020, pp. 101 – 107, Delran, USA, 1992.

_____. DEC Enterprise Management Architecture' Datapro Research Corp. OpenView's Architectural Model, NM40-325, pp. 101 – 107, Delran, USA, 1989.

_____. IBM AIX NetView/6000, NS30-604, pp. 201 – 203, Delran, USA, 1992.

_____. IBM LAN Network Manager. NS30-504, p. 101, Delran, USA, 1990.

_____. IBM SNA and NetView, NM40-491, pp. 101 – 108, Delran, USA, 1989.

_____. LAN Design Tools. NS30-202, pp. 301, Delran, USA, 1990.

_____. Managing local area networks. Accounting, Performance and Security Management, NM50-300, pp. 501 – 509, Delran, USA, 1989.

_____. Managing local area networks. Fault and configuration management, NM50-300, pp. 410 – 412, Delran, USA, 1989.

_____. Network Management of TCP/IP Networks: Present and Future. NM40-300, pp. 101 – 108, Delran, USA, 1991.

_____. SNMP Product Guide, NM40-300, pp. 301 – 316, Delran, USA, 1990.

_____. SNMP Query Language, NM40-300, pp. 401 – 404, Delran, USA, 1991.

_____. Synernetics Viewplex LAN Management Tools. NS05-864, p. 101, Delran, USA, 1991.

_____. The LAN troubleshooting Sequence, NM50-300, pp. 101 – 106, Delran, USA, 1989.

Dem, D.P., Till, J. Monitoring LANs from a distance, *Data Communications*, McGraw-Hill, November 1989, pp. 17–20.

Digital Equipment Corp. LAN Traffic Monitor, Product Guide, Cambridge, USA, 1989.

Digilog, Inc. LANVista Product Guide, Montgomeryville, USA, 1990.

Fabbio, R. WizardWare: An Overview, Network & Distributed Systems Management '91, Washington, D.C., September 1991.

Feldkhum, L. *Integrated Network Management Systems*, Elsevier Publisher, 1989, IFIP Congress, pp. 279–300.

Feldkhum, L., Ericson, J. *Event management as a common functional area of Open Systems Management*, Elsevier Publisher, 1989, IFIP Congress, pp. 365–376.

Ferguson, R. The Business Case for Network Management, Distributed Systems & Network Management Conference, Washington, D.C., 1991.

FiberCom. ViewMaster Product Specification, Roanoke, USA, 1991.

Fisher, S. Dueling Protocols, *BYTE*, March 1991, pp. 182–190, San Francisco, 1991.

Fischer International Systems Corp. Watchdog PC Data Security Product Guide, Naples, USA, 1991.

Fortier, P, J. *Handbook of LAN Technology*, Intertext Publications, McGraw-Hill, Inc., New York, 1989.

Frederick Engineering. FECOS Users Guide, Columbia, Maryland, USA, 1991.

Galvin, J.M., McClogbrie, K., Davis, J.R. Secure Management of SNMP networks, Integrated Network Management II, Washington, D.C., 1991.

Gambit Inc. GamOptics System 9000 Product Guide, Yokneam, Israel, 1991.

Gilbert, E.E. Unified Network Management Architecture Putting it All Together, *AT&T Technology*, Vol. 3, Number 2, 1988.

Gilliam, P. A Practical Perspective on LAN Performance, *Business Communications Review*, October 1990, pp. 56–58.

Goehring, G., Jasper, E. Network Management in Token Rings, *Datacom*, Special Edition, October 1990, pp. 44–52.

Herman, J., Weber, R. The LAN Management Market, Northeast Consulting Resources, Boston, USA, 1989.

Herman, J. Enterprise Management Vendors Shoot It Out, *Data Communications*, McGraw-Hill, November 1990, pp. 92–110.

Herman, J. A New View of OpenView, *Network Monitor*, Vol. 5, No. 3, March 1990, Boston, USA.

Herman, J., Lippis, N. The Internetwork Decade, *Supplement to Data Communications*, McGraw-Hill, January 1991, pp. 2–32.

Herman, J. Net Management Directions—Architectures and standards for multivendor net management, *Business Communication Review*, June 1991, pp. 79–83.

———. Net Management Directions—Renovating how networks are managed, *Business Communication Review*, August 1991, pp. 71–73.

Hewlett-Packard Company. HP OpenView Network Manager Server, Palo Alto, California, 1989.

Hewlett-Packard Company. HP ProbeView Product Guide, Palo Alto, California, 1989.

Hewlett-Packard Company. HP OpenView, NM Server Technical Evaluation Guide, Palo Alto, California, 1989.

Howard, M. LAN Management Assessment, IDG Network Management Solutions, April 1990, Anaheim, California.

Huntington, J.A. OSI-based net management, *Data Communications*, March 1989, pp. 111–129.

Huntington, J.A. SNMP/CMIP market penetration and user perception, Interop 1990, San Jose, October 1990.

Huntington, Lee, J. Inventory and Configuration Management, *Datapro Network Management*, NM20-300-101, Delran, USA, October 1991.

Infonetics, Inc. The Cost of LAN Downtime, 1989.

Infotel Systems Corp. LAN interconnecting technologies, Course Material, 1990.

International Business Machines, Inc. IBM Token Ring Problems Determination Guide, Document SY27-0280-1, 1988.

Internetics. Product Guides for Softbench, LANSIM and LANAI, Upper Marlboro, Maryland, USA, 1991.

Intratec Systems, Inc. Telecommunications Facilities Management System, Product Guide, Dallas, USA, 1991.

Isicad, Inc. Command Implementation Guide, Anaheim, USA, 1991.

Industrial Technology Institute. Metasan Product Implementation Guide, USA, 1991.

Krall, G. SNMP opens new lines of sight, *Data Communication—LAN Strategies*, McGraw-Hill, March 1990, pp. 45–54.

LAN Magazine. The Local Area Network Glossary, New York, USA, 1989.

Lannet, Inc. MultiMan Product Guide, Huntington Beach, California, USA, 1991.

Lerner, S., Bion, J. The Well-Managed LAN, *LAN Magazine*, June 1989, p. 78–89.

Lo, T, L. Local Area Networks for Managers, CMG Transactions, Summer 1990, Chicago, USA, pp. 31–40.

Martin, J. *Local Area Networks*, Prentice Hall, Englewood Cliffs, New Jersey, USA, 1991.

Micro Technology. LANCE Product Guide, Anaheim, California, USA, 1991.

Mier, E. Testing SNMP in Routers, *Network World*, July 1991, USA.

Mil 3, Inc. OpNet Product Implementation Guide, Boston, USA 1991.

Miller, H. *LAN Troubleshooting Handbook*, M&T Books, Redwood City, CA, USA, 1989.

Morrison, W. *Ethernet LAN Management: NMCC/VAX ETHERnim*, Integrated Network Management, Elsevier Science Publisher, IFIP 1989.

Mouttham, A., Frontini, M., Griffin, J., Lewin, S. *LAN Management using expert systems*, Integrated Network Management, Elsevier Science Publisher, IFIP 1989.

Nance, B. Managing Big Blue, *BYTE*, March 1991, pp. 197–204.

Nance, B. LAN Tune Up, *BYTE*, August 1991, pp. 287–299.

Network Management, Inc. LANfolio Product Guide, New York, 1990.

NetLabs, Inc. DualManager Product Implementation Guide, Los Angeles, USA, 1991.

Network Managers Limited. NMC 3000 Product Specification and Implementation Guideline, Guildford, United Kingdom, 1991.

Network General Corp. Sniffer Network Analyzer Product Family User's Guide, Menlo Park, USA, 1991.

Novell, Inc. NetWare Management Functions, San Jose, California, USA, 1990.

Novell, Inc. LANAnalyzer and LANtern Product Guide, San Jose, California, USA, 1991.

Nuciforo, T. What a computerized cable management system should do, *Business Communications Review*, July 1989, pp. 22–26.

The OSF Distributed Management Environment, White Paper, Cambridge, USA, 1991.

Objective Systems Integrators. NetExpert-Product Description, Folsum, USA, February 1992.

OSI/Network Management Forum. Forum 002—Application Services, Bernandsville, N.J. OSI/Network Management Forum.

Forum 003—Objects Specification Framework, Bernandsville, N.J. OSI/Network Management Forum.

Forum 006—Forum Library of Managed Object Classes, Name Bindings and Attributes, Bernandsville, N.J.

Patterson, T. Evaluating LAN Security, Network World, October 21, 1991, pp. 47–52.

Presuhn, R. Considering CMIP, *Data Communication—LAN strategies*, McGraw-Hill, March 1990, pp. 55–66.

Remedy Inc. Action Request System—Product Description, Sunnyvale, USA, September 1991.

Quintrel Corp. CableTrak Communication Facilities Management Software, Cedar Rapids, Iowa, USA, 1991.

Rhodes, P.D. *LAN Operations*—A Guide to Daily Management, Addison-Wesley Publishing Company, Inc., Reading, Massachusetts, USA, 1991.

Robertson, B. Name Services—The Key to Large Network Management, *LAN Technology*, October 1990, pp. 42–50.

Rose, M.T. Network Management is Simple: you just need the "right" framework, Integrated Network Management II, Washington, D.C., 1991.

Rothberg, M.L. Cable Management Systems, *Datapro Reports on Network Management Systems*, NS60-020-101. Delran, N.J. March 1991.

Saal, H. The Protocol Analyzer—A Multipurpose Tool for LAN Managers, *LAN Technology*, M&T Publishing, Inc., June 1989.

Saal, H. LAN downtime: Clear and present danger, *Data Communication—LAN Strategies*, McGraw-Hill, March 1990, pp. 67 – 72.

Saen, H. LAN Network Planning and Design, IBM-IEC, La Hulpe, Belgium, 1991.

Sanghi, S., Chandna, A., Wetzel, G., Sengupta, S. How well do SNMP and CMOT meet IP router management needs?, Integrated Network Management II, Washington, D.C., 1991.

Scott, K. SNMP brings order to chaos, *Data Communication—LAN Strategies*, McGraw-Hill, March 1990, pp. 24 – 30.

Scott, K. Taking care of Business with SNMP, *Data Communication—LAN Strategies*, McGraw-Hill, March 1990, pp. 31 – 44.

Security Dynamics. Access Control and Encryption Product Family Guide, Cambridge, USA, 1991.

Spider Systems, Inc. Spider Multi-Segment LAN Monitoring and Analysis Products, Burlington, USA, 1990.

Sun Microsystems. SunNet Manager Product Guide, Mountain View, California, 1990.

SynOptics Communications, Inc. Lattisnet Product Guide, Santa Clara, California, USA, 1990.

SynOptics Communications, Inc. Network Control Engine Product Guide, Santa Clara, California, USA, 1990.

Swanson, R.H. Emerging technologies for network management, *Business Communication Review*, August 1991, pp. 53 – 58.

Teknekron Communication Systems. NMS/Core Product Guide, Berkeley, California, 1991.

Terplan, K. Effective LAN Management, Technology Transfer Institute, Seminar Documentation, Santa Monica, CA, 1991.

_____. *Communication Networks Management*, Prentice Hall, Inc., Englewood Cliffs N.Y., 1991.

Theakston, A. LAN resilience and security, *Insight IBM*, Xephon Publication, August 1991, United Kingdom, pp.15 – 21.

Tjaden, G.S. The Allink Approach to Management Systems Integration, Network & Distributed Systems Management '91, Washington, D.C., September 1991.

Tschammer, V., Klessman. Local Area Network Management Issues, *Datapro Research Corporation*, NM50-300, Delran, NJ, 1989, pp. 100 – 108.

VandenBerg, Chr. MIB II extends SNMP Interoperability, *Data Communications*, McGraw-Hill, October 1990, pp. 119 – 124.

Weil, J. What You Can Do with a Network Analyzer?—Network Management Solutions, Anaheim, USA, 1990.

Weissmann, P.T. Automated Problem Management, *Technical Support*, Vol. 5, Number 10, August 1991, Technical Enterprises Inc., Milwaukee, USA.

Index

M

MAC bridges, 56
MAC layer, FDDI, 49
managed objects (MOs), 6, 13, 14
  CMIP, 166, 167
  SNMP, 166, 167
management information base (MIB and
  MIB II), 66, 69-71
  CMIP, 166
  RMON MIB, 70-71, 349
  SNMP, 155, 157-160, 166
managing LANs, 1-19
  access-control methods, percent-usage of
    various types, 7
  accounting management, lags implemen-
    tation of LAN, 7, 11
  active vs. passive infrastructure compo-
    nents, 14
  centralized vs. decentralized management
    trends, 9
  change management flexibility, 17
  choosing a management strategy for the
    LAN, 3-6
  components of LAN management
    scheme, 6-9
  configuration management, 10
  cost analysis in LAN development:
    money, time and profits, 4-6, 9-10
  current LAN management techniques, 10
  data transmission schemes, Mbps, per-
    cent-usage, 7
  design and planning, lags implementation
    of LAN, 7, 11
  fault management, lags implementation
    of LAN, 7, 10-11
  fragmentation of management structure,
    12
  future development of LANs, 2-3, 346
  human-resource management, 16-17
  instrumentation used in LAN manage-
    ment, 11-16
  integration, hierarchical vs. platform-
    based, 211-213
  integration, horizontal and vertical, 210-
    211
  MAN management vs. LAN manage-
    ment, 3-4
  managed objects (MOs) as component of
    LAN management scheme, 6, 13, 14
  media for the LAN: coax, twisted pair,
    fiber, percent-usage, 7
  monitoring LAN performance, lack of
    polling standards, 8
  open architecture development in LANs
    and WANs, 9
  PBX, 9, 43-45
  PC LAN management products, 233-236
  performance management, lags imple-
    mentation of LAN, 7, 11
  platform requirements, 18
  productivity-enhancement requirements,
    17
  requirements, services and support
    required of LANs, 1, 17-18
  scope of management control in typical
    LAN, 3
  security lags implementation of LAN, 7, 11
  standardization of LAN management, 8-
    9, 18
  technological component of LAN man-
    agement scheme, 7
  topology, percent-usage of various types,
    7
  user administration functions, 11
  WAN management vs. LAN manage-
    ment, 3-4
  worldwide use of LANs, 6
MAP/TOP, 38, 147
media access control (MAC), 36-37
media for the LAN, 7, 25-31
  balanced vs. unbalanced transmission, 28
  bandwidth allocations, 29
  cable management (CMS) and configura-
    tion management, 74-78
  cabling selection criteria, 315
  cabling systems, complete systems, 29-30
  coax, 25, 26
  coax, percent-usage, current-day LAN, 7
  emission problems, 29
  fault management, 96-97
  fiberoptic, 25, 26-27
  fiberoptic, percent-usage, current-day
    LAN, 7
  infrared transmission, 27
  microwave transmission, 27
  radio transmission, 27
  satellite transmission, 27
  twisted pair, 25, 26
  twisted pair, percent-usage, current-day
    LAN, 7
  wireless transmission, 27-28
memory
  cache memory, 117
  expanded memory, 116
  extended memory, 116
Metasan (Industrial Technology Institute),
  321
metrics, performance management
  fixed metrics, 106-107
  performance-measurement metrics, 108-
    109
  variable metrics, 107-109
metropolitan area networks (MANs), LAN
  management strategies vs. MAN management strategies, 3-4
Microsoft WinSNMP, 217
microwave transmission, 27
  interconnected LANs, 53

T